HE GARDEN OF LIFE IS abundant, prosperous and magical. ❧ In this garden, there is enough for everyone. ❧ Share the fruit and the knowledge ❧ Our brothers and we are in this lush, exciting place together. ❧ Let's show others the way. ❧ Kindness. Generosity. ❧ Hard work. ❧ God's care.

# Job-Search

# SECRETS

## That Have Helped
## Thousands of Members

## Kate Wendleton
**author of *Through the Brick Wall:
How to Job-Hunt in a Tight Market***

with Barbara Bruno, Ronna Archbold, Ellis Chase,
Stacy Feldman, John Leonard, Terri Lowe, Patricia Raufer,
and Wendy Alfus Rothman

Five O'Clock Books / New York / 1996

The
Five
O'Clock
Club®

For the thousands of members of The Five O'Clock Club—
These stories are theirs.

Library of Congress Cataloging-in-Publication Data

Wendleton, Kate.
   Job-search secrets that have helped thousands of members/Kate Wendleton.
     p. cm.
   Includes bibliographical references and index.
   ISBN 0-944054-10-2
   1. Job hunting     I. Title

HF5382.7.W464 1996     650.14
                QBI95-20787

For information, address The Five O'Clock Club,
300 East 40th Street - Suite 6L - New York, New York 10016

FIRST EDITION
FIRST PRINTING

9 8 7 6 5 4 3 2 1

*Perhaps the truth lies in what most of the world
outside the modern West has always believed,
namely that there are practices of life,
good in themselves, that are inherently fulfilling.*

*Perhaps work that is intrinsically rewarding
is better for human beings than work
that is only extrinsically rewarded.*

*Perhaps enduring commitment to those we love
and civic friendship toward our fellow citizens
are preferable to restless competition
and anxious self-defense.*

*Perhaps common worship,
in which we express our gratitude and wonder
in the face of the mystery of being itself,
is the most important thing of all.*

*If so, we will have to change our lives
and begin to remember
what we have been happier to forget.*

Robert N. Bellah, Richard Madsen, William Sullivan,
Ann Swindler, and Steven Tipton, *Habits of the Heart*

Dear Member or Prospective Member of The Five O'Clock Club:

I am very happy to bring you this book.

When I started The Five O'Clock Club in Philadelphia in 1978, professionals and managers who were job hunting came to my apartment every Thursday evening. Career consultants from corporations and consulting firms taught us their job-hunting techniques. I will be forever grateful to those experts who helped us get started. We were able to compare their approaches. We experimented. We tried various job-hunting techniques and reported our results back to the group.

At The Five O'Clock Club, it was not enough for us to learn about job hunting—we wanted to learn about the job *hiring* process. What happens when your résumé crosses the desk of a hiring manager? How effective are direct-mail campaigns? Why does one person find a job quickly, while someone else takes longer—even though both work hard and are equally well qualified?

This book answers those questions. We found that there is no one job-hunting technique that works. Job-hunting formulas hold true in the aggregate, but may not for a specific situation. The techniques that work depend, to a large extent, on the industry in which you are interested, the kind of job you want to have within that industry, and on your own style and personality.

This book gives you guidelines, but also gives you flexibility in deciding which job-hunting approach is right for you. When you understand what is happening and why, you can be in a better position to plan your own job-hunting campaign, and not rely so much on chance or on what a specific expert tells you.

Job hunting can be thought of as a project—much like any project you might handle in your regular job. Most of the approaches in this book are businesslike rather than intensely psychological. Thinking of job hunting in a business-type way allows you to use the problem-solving skills you might use at work.

This book is organized for busy people like you. Skip to the part you need. If you already know what you want in your next job, go directly to Part Three to learn the most powerful, up-to-date techniques available today for getting interviews. If you have an interview coming up, go to Part Four to find the latest ideas for getting what you want, including how to assess the interview and turn it into a job offer.

I feel duty-bound to address the issue of career planning. Most people are interested in job-hunting techniques but don't want to give much thought to what they should do with their *lives*. So Part Two touches on the career-planning process just so you will be less likely to skip it completely. If you make the wise decision to spend the time it takes to give your life some direction and a real sense of satisfaction, I urge you to read our book *Targeting the Job You Want*. It is the first in this three-part series for job hunters and career changers.

These books are the result of years of research into how successful job hunters land the best jobs at the best pay. This series replaces the very successful and popular *Through the Brick Wall* series, and with the addition of new material, takes job search to an even higher level of sophistication. Together, these books provide the most detailed explanation of the search process :

*   *Targeting the Job You Want* tells you *where* to look for a job. It is a relatively painless way to think about the career-planning process. In addition, it contains the most comprehensive job-search bibliography around.
*   *Job-Search Secrets* (this book) tells you *how* to look for a job—part-time or full-time, freelance or consulting—and how to negotiate. In addition, it contains worksheets which you may copy for your own use.
*   *Building a Great Résumé* is quite simply the best résumé book on the market. It uses the résumés of real people and tells you their stories.

A few chapters in this book are from the other two. That way, you are not forced to buy all three (although it is best to have all of them), and you won't have to refer to the others when you are in the middle of this one.

Finally, in each book you will find a lot of inspirational writing. I have needed it myself often enough, as have the many unemployed and unhappy working people with whom I have worked. The techniques by themselves are worthless without the right frame of mind. I hope the quotations will inspire you as they have inspired me and my fellow job hunters.

Thank you for supporting The Five O'Clock Club through your purchase of this book. Because of people like you, we can keep the program going and spread to new cities so we'll be there when you need us. Our goal is, and always has been, to provide the best affordable career advice. And—with you as our partners—we will continue to do this.

Cheers, God bless, and good luck!

Kate Wendleton
New York City, 1996

# Acknowledgements

With appreciation to the entire Dobbs Family, of which I am the eldest, for being dependable cheerleaders. To Nancy O'Shea Mercante, my friend and partner at The Main Club. To my key advisors: Kay Shadley, friend and attorney, who has helped me start Affiliates in other cities; Dr. George Barrister, a steady, astute businessman and friend, who is also very funny; and Bob Riscica, Carol Fass, Mario Minoli and James Ahn, who are helping us to take this adventure even further.

I appreciate all of The Five O'Clock Club members, old and new, some of whose stories are contained herein: Members provide feedback on our techniques, which allows our approach to evolve continually with the changing job market. Members also give us information for our database, so we can track trends and know what is going on.

I thank our Affiliates, which have brought this high-quality program to other cities with enthusiasm and dedication to our members. Special mention to the following Affiliate heads: Barbara Bruno (Chicago, IL), Sylvia Gaffney (Rockford, IL), Phil Gittings (Philadelphia, PA), Fred Hopkinson (Toronto, Canada), Robert Maher (Cleveland, OH), Bobbie Rich (Stamford, CT), George Jung and Victoria McLaughlin (Long Island, NY), and Ellis Chase, Jim Borland, and Deborah Brown (NY, NY).

I thank the excellent staff of The Five O'Clock Club, especially Sharon Williams, who keeps our office running smoothly. Our warmest thanks to Norman and Lillian Cohen, who have been devoted and attentive volunteers for years. I am especially grateful to the staff of the Main Club, who have worked with me for so long. The original counselors included: Ellis Chase, Roy Cohen, Barbara Earley, Shelli Kanet, John Leonard, Wendy Rothman, and Gloria Waslyn. Our present counselors include Michael Aronin, Fredi Balzano, Jim Borland, Roy Cohen, Stacy Feldman, Nancy Friedberg, John Leonard, and Ed Witherell. In addition, I would like to acknowledge Patricia Kelly, whose artwork, *Fruytagie*, hangs in our offices and appears in our publications—including this one, and Dorothy Wachtenheim, our cover designer.

We are all especially proud of Workforce America®, which runs The Five O'Clock Club program in Harlem. It was started with the help of the Reverend James Russell, and is headed by Deborah Brown. The initial funding for this program was provided by Deirdre Cavanagh, my friend, and The Brick Church. My deepest appreciation to them both. We also appreciate the help of Tracy Balzano, Tara Stevens, Hank Williams and Deirdre Cavanagh.

Since I came to New York in 1985, I have gotten a number of big breaks from people who believed in me. Edith Wurtzel at The New School for Social Research encouraged me to speak there. Three hundred and fifty people attended, and I later became director of their career center. Abe Fiss at Barnes & Noble agreed to carry my first self-published book in 1986, then my second, and kept reordering them for five years. Many, many others have befriended me, and have helped me to bring you what we have today.

Finally, my deepest appreciation and fondest gratitude go to my trusted editor, Cordelia Jason, for her clarity, creativity, and caring.

K.W.
New York City, 1996

# Table of Contents

**PART THREE—Knowing the Right People:
How to Get Interviews in Your Target Areas**

(IF YOU ALREADY HAVE INTERVIEWS, GO TO PART FOUR.)

## PART FOUR—Getting What You Want:
## The Five O'Clock Club Approach to
## Interviewing and Negotiating

## PART FIVE—Keeping It Going
## After You've Gotten the Job You Want

## Career and Job-Search Bibliography

(See our book *Targeting the Job You Want.*)

## PART SIX—Join The Five O'Clock Club
## "For busy, career-minded people"

# Job-Search

---

# SECRETS

---

## That Have Helped
## Thousands of Members

The Five O'Clock Club®

# Introduction

We've all heard too many painful stories: out of work for over a year . . . networking, mailings, search firms, ads—but can't get a job or even an assignment. Lots and lots of interviews but . . .

At The Five O'Clock Club, we get impressive results. The average professional, manager, or executive who attends on a regular basis gets a job within ten to fifteen weeks. (Many had been looking for a year or more.) That's because they used the principles taught in this book. As you will see, these techniques work at all levels—and for all types of people. They have even been used successfully by actors and actresses, and at least one orchestra conductor. Whatever your field, this book will give you the inside track.

When a job hunter finds a job, he reports to the group. Last week, a man reported that he had been unemployed for three years. His wife had a good job, he spent time with his kids, and he found a few temporary assignments, but he was essentially unemployed, and was trying very hard to get a job. After only four Five O'Clock Club sessions, he found a great one.

The week before, a woman spoke who had been unemployed for a year and a half; she had come to six sessions. Her first session had been a full year earlier, and she had decided to search on her own. After a year, she came back, attended five more sessions, and got a great job.

The week before that, a man who had been unemployed for six months before joining The Five O'Clock Club found a great job. In his four months with the Club, the group had helped him see how he was coming across in interviews (very stiff and preachy) and how to expand his job targets. Some people take longer because they are at the beginning of their search or because they have not searched in many years and need to learn this new skill.

Many job hunters think they have to lower their salary expectations because they are unemployed or have been job searching for a long time. You may have to lower your salary expectations for other reasons, but none of these three people did. Their unemployment did not affect their salary negotia-

tions. In this book you will learn how to negotiate properly and increase your chances of getting what you deserve—whether you are employed or not.

The Five O'Clock Club techniques in this book work whether a job hunter is employed or unemployed. Most job hunters try to get interviews and then try to do well in them. They are skipping two important parts of the process, and are therefore probably not doing the two remaining parts very well. At The Five O'Clock Club, we consider all four parts to be important. They are:

- **Assessment:** Deciding what you want results in better job targets (see our book *Targeting the Job You Want* and Part Two of this book for an introduction to the process). Assessment also results in better résumés (see our book *Building a Great Résumé*).
- **Campaign Preparation:** Planning your campaign results in lots and lots of interviews in each job target. (Part Three)
- **Interviewing:** Interviews result in an assessment of the *company's* needs. (Part Four)
- **Interview Follow-Up:** Follow-up after the interview results in job offers. (Part Four)

As you can see, job hunters who think that interviews lead to offers have skipped a step. Interviews lead to a better understanding of what the company wants. What you do *after* the interview leads to an offer.

Here are a few quick stories to get you started.

## CASE STUDY: PHIL
*Expanded his job hunting targets*
*—and went through the brick wall to get the job.*

Phil had been earning hundreds of thousands of dollars a year as a senior executive in a large publishing company. When I met him, he had been job searching for a year, focusing on twenty-four publishing and health care companies in his geographic area. Given his level, his search was obviously not going to work: his target was too small. He needed to look into other industries and other geographic areas.

In addition, Phil needed a new attitude. He expected people to recognize his credentials and simply hire him—something that had always

*People can be divided into three groups:*
*those who make things happen,*
*those who watch things happen—*
*and those who wonder, What happened?*
Anonymous

happened in the past. Now he needed to go through the brick wall to get a job.

Phil found a job within three weeks after our meeting. He answered an ad in the paper for a job—not in publishing or health care—in another state. (It doesn't matter how you get the interview: through a search firm, an ad, networking, or direct contact.) He was called in for two interviews and then received a rejection letter: the company had decided against him.

But this time Phil wanted to fight for the job. He wrote to the president of the company and said there had obviously been a big mistake. The company reconsidered and hired him.

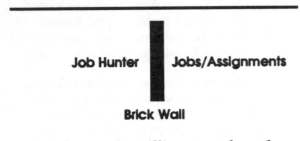

**Job Hunter** | **Jobs/Assignments**

**Brick Wall**

*You have to be willing to go through the brick wall to get the jobs.*

## CASE STUDY: STEELWORKERS
*Who gets hired?*

A colleague of mine, Aaron Nierenberg, tells of a counselor who did a workshop for steelworkers a few years back when many of them were losing jobs. They were not of a mind to do résumés (many of them didn't even speak English), so the counselor concentrated on the most important part of the search process—follow-up.

The counselor asked, "How many of you have already contacted companies about getting a job?" Sixteen hands went up. "Your homework for tomorrow," he said, "is to *recontact* those companies and report back here." The next day, four workers had gotten jobs.

The explanation for this is simple. Look at it from the hiring manager's point of view. The steel industry was laying off thousands of workers, who

went to other steel mills looking for work. Hundreds of workers went to the hiring managers and said, "Have you got any work?" How could a manager easily decide which workers he should hire? But when a worker said, "I was here last week looking for work. Do you have anything now?" the manager then knew whom to select.

Much of the selection process is a self-selection process: the *job hunter* decides which companies he or she wants to work for, and behaves very differently toward those companies than toward others in which he or she is not interested.

Job hunters put most of their effort into getting interviews and doing brilliantly well in those interviews. Then they stop. Five O'Clock Club job hunters keep going and turn more interviews into offers. Don't follow up with a silly thank you note. Instead, *influence* the person. This book will give you a process for analyzing the interview so you can decide what to do next.

### See People Two Levels Higher Than You Are

Norman had been searching for a job for over a year. He did what he had been told: he networked. By now he had met with almost 250 people! Yet he could not find a job. The problem: he was meeting with people at his own level. When he started meeting with higher-level people (through direct contact), he started seeing results. Within two months, he found a great job.

Most job hunters network incorrectly. In this book, we will tell you exactly how to network so you can get the most out of it. We'll also cover the other techniques for getting interviews: through search firms, answering ads, and directly contacting companies.

### Take the Long View

The next job you take will not be your last. Where will you go after that one? When deciding between two or more possibilities, select the one that positions you best for the long term.

Christine is a good example. She had three job offers—which is what we like people to have. Two offers paid $10,000 more than the third one. Which job should she take?

Christine selected the one that positioned her best for the long term—which happened to be the lower-paying job. She is now as happy as a person can be, getting tremendous experience and meeting lots of important people. After a few years, she could easily leave (if she wants) and get much more money than she ever would have gotten had she taken one of the other two positions.

Julio is a portfolio manager with strong connections to South America. He had five job offers and wondered which one he should take. I couldn't help him until I knew his long-term plans. Otherwise, his decision would be based strictly on the money or the kind of people at each company. We spent ten minutes working on his Forty-Year Plan, which is covered in *Targeting the Job You Want*. It turned out that he imagined himself working out of his house five to ten years down the road. Then, the decision-making process became easy. Only two of the companies would eventually allow him to work from home. He selected one of them. Had he selected one of the others, he would have had a problem in a few years.

*Targeting the Job You Want* helps you think about *your* long-term plan. Your next job is simply a step. You can plan that step and the ones after that. Job hunters are not powerless. They can do a lot to influence the hiring process and their own long-term careers.

## A Changing Economy

Today, we know that doing a good job is not enough. Our career prospects can now change for reasons that have nothing to do with our personal job performance, but rather with the performance of our employers. It's a new economy—a world economy—and the changes are not going to slow down. Not only will things not return to the way they were, the amount of change will increase.

Government statistics show the impact of change on job hunters:

**The average American has been in his or her job only four years.**

The average American getting out of college today can expect to have five careers during his or her lifetime—that's not five jobs, but five separate careers! We will probably have twelve to fifteen jobs in the course of those five careers.

**Ten years from now, half the working population will be in jobs that have not yet been invented.** Let's make that more personal: ten years from now, half the people reading this book will be in jobs that do not exist today. That's okay. *Targeting the Job You Want* tells you where some of the new jobs are, but you'll have to do research as well.

**Ten years from now, half the working population will be in non-traditional forms of employment.** This means that half of us will not be working full-time, on payroll, for one employer—a wrenching change in our mindsets. Some of us may work two days a week on payroll for one employer, and three days a week for another. Or three days a week on payroll, with consulting or freelance work on the other days. Or we may be paid by one company that farms us out to another. The variations are endless—and changing.

The situation is unsettling—to say the least. However, we cannot fight it. In this time of dramatic change, few companies really know where they are heading, but some are learning what kind of workers they need: flexible, self-aware ones who continually improve their skills. Gone are the days when it was good enough for employees to simply do their assigned jobs well. America wants and needs a new kind of workforce.

Employees too are learning that they must take care of themselves and remain marketable so they are not dependent on one employer. They are proactively figuring out what they bring to the party, while finding out—and fitting into—the new directions their companies and industries are taking.

## A New Definition of Job Hunting

Job hunting in our changing economy is a *continuous* process and requires a new definition. Job hunting now means continually becoming aware of market conditions both inside and outside of our present companies, and learning what we have to offer—to both markets. This new definition means we must develop new attitudes about our

*It is other people's experience that
makes the older man wiser than the younger man.*
Yoruba Proverb

work lives, and new skills for doing well in a changing economy.

Today's economy requires job hunters to be more proactive, more sophisticated, and more willing to go through brick walls to get what they want. Employers no longer plan your career for you. You must look after yourself, and know what you want and how to get it.

## Understanding How the
## Job-Hunting Market Works

Knowing why things work the way they do will give you flexibility and control over your job hunt. Knowing how the hiring system works will help you understand why things go right and why they go wrong—why certain things work and others don't. Then you can modify the system to fit your own needs, temperament, and the workings of the job market you are interested in.

It is overly simplistic to say that only one job-hunting system works. The job-selection process is more complicated than that. Employers can do what they want. You need to understand the process from their point of view. Then you can plan your own job hunt, in your own industry. You will learn how to compete in this market.

Always remember, the best jobs don't necessarily go to the most qualified people, but to the people who are the best job hunters. You'll increase your chances of finding the job you want by using a methodical job-hunting approach.

## The Five O'Clock Club
## Coaching Approach

Our approach is methodical. Our counselors are the best. Five O'Clock Club counselors are full-time career coaches. Each one has met with hundreds of job hunters. Often we can pinpoint what is wrong with a person's search and turn it around. In this book, you will get that same information. Like our Five O'Clock Club job hunters, you will learn the techniques and hear the stories of other people so you can job hunt more effectively.

Sometimes we call our techniques the *Parachute* for the nineties. The original *Parachute* book (*What*

*Color is Your Parachute?* by Richard Nelson Bolles, Ten Speed Press) was first published more than twenty years ago. It teaches first-time job hunters or career changers how to get jobs. Now we have a nation of skilled workers, managers, executives, and professionals who are out of work or unhappy in their jobs—people who used to be routinely wooed and solicited for their talents. Now these people have to do the selling. They need a very different and specific approach to finding jobs and changing careers.

## How The Five O'Clock Club Works

The groups vary from place to place. Some groups are for professionals, managers, and executives. Others may focus on recent college graduates, for example, or blue-collar workers. Generally, half the people who attend are employed (and perhaps unhappy); half are unemployed. Members are from various industries and professions—usually difficult situations, or they wouldn't need us. The basic format is the same: the group meets every week for two hours. During the first hour, members hear a presentation on an important job hunting technique. These techniques are presented in this book. In between the first and second hours, those who have found jobs report on their searches, and we learn from what they did.

During the second hour, a career counselor leads the group of job hunters in a strategy-planning session for each job hunter: how can this person move his or her search along? How can he get more interviews in his target market or turn those interviews into offers? Job hunters learn from the counselor and from the strategies other job hunters are pursuing. They get feedback on their own searches and critique the searches of others. They aim to get six to ten contacts in the works, and have three job offers.

Those who stick with the process find that it works. That process is presented in this book.

# PART ONE

# FINDING GOOD JOBS

## THE CHANGING JOB-HUNTING PROCESS

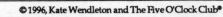

The
Five
O'Clock
Club®

# 11 Hints for Job-Hunting in a Tight Market

*If you haven't the strength*
*to impose your own terms upon life,*
*then you must accept the terms it offers you.*
T. S. Eliot, *The Confidential Clerk*

---

## 1.
### Expand your job-hunting targets.

If you are searching only in Los Angeles or only in Detroit, for example, think of other geographic areas. If you are looking only in large public corporations, consider small or private companies. If you are looking for a certain kind of position, investigate what other kinds of work you also could do.

## 2.
### Expect to be "in search" for the long haul.

The average professional or managerial worker is taking six months to get a job. So though you may find something right away, it is sensible to develop financial backup plans. What kind of side work could you do to earn money in the short run? How could you reduce your expenses? Join a job-hunting group to get support, ideas, and contacts.

When you meet someone who doesn't "have" anything for you right now, that's okay. Plan to get in touch with that person again. In fact, you may meet dozens of people who don't have anything right now. Get to know them and their needs better, and tell them about yourself. Build relationships so you can contact them later.

## 3.
### Keep your spirits up.

An alarming number of job hunters in the U.S.A. are becoming discouraged and dropping out of the job market. Don't you be one of them. Read the next chapter, "When You've Lost the Spirit to Job-Hunt."

Be aware that what you are going through is not easy, and that many of the things you are experiencing are being experienced by just about everybody else. Hang in there, get a fresh start, and eventually you will find something.

## 4.
### Think about developing new skills.

If you suspect your old skills are out-of-date, develop new ones. If you can't get a job because you don't have the experience, *get* the experience. The several months that you will probably be searching is long enough for you to develop new skills. Take a course. Do volunteer work to gain expertise that you can then market. Join an association related to your new skill area.

If you need to earn money immediately, try to do something that will enhance your job search. For example, if you decide to do temporary work, and you want a job in the airline industry, consider doing your temporary work with an airline.

Consider doing something for little or no money simply because it would improve your résumé. A Five O'Clock Clubber got a twelve-week assignment with a Sears consignee during the Christmas rush. The pay was terrible but the job title was Regional Manager. He needed something to do, and the job looked great on his résumé.

## 5.
### Become a skilled job hunter.

Being good at your job does not make you good at *getting* jobs. Good job hunters know what they want, what the market wants, and how to present themselves. Stay competitive. Learn how to job-hunt like an expert. Your future depends on it.

## 6.
### Look for opportunities.

In this economy, opportunities probably will not come knocking on your door. You have to look for them—both inside and outside your present company. Chances are, your present company and even the industry you are in are going to change. So rather than just doing the same old job, think of how you can take on new assignments so that you are at the forefront of the changes. Put out feelers to find out whether you are marketable outside your company. Continually test the waters.

When you are on an interview, try to negotiate a

*You think you understand the situation,*
*but what you don't understand is that the situation just changed.*
Putnam Investments advertisement

job that suits both you and the hiring manager. For example, if the job is for an administrator, and you would like to do some writing, see if they will allow you to do that too.

Don't passively expect to be told where you could fit in. Actively think about your place in their organization. Create a job for yourself.

### 7.
### Target what you want.

As Lily Tomlin said, "I always wanted to be somebody, but I should have been more specific." Be sure you select specific geographic areas, specific industries, and specific positions within those industries.

For example, you may want to be a writer in publishing or advertising in Manhattan or Chicago. Find the names of the people to contact in those cities and industries—or people who know people in those targets. If you target, you have a better chance of finding the job you want.

### 8.
### Learn how to get interviews.

There are a lot of techniques for generating interviews. The basic ones are: answering ads, using search firms, contacting companies directly, and networking. Only 10 percent of all jobs are filled through ads and search firms, so it is wise to learn how to contact companies directly, and how to network properly.

Identify all of the companies you need to contact, and then contact them as quickly as possible. Make sure you consider *every* technique for getting interviews in your target area. Don't focus on getting a job: focus on getting interviews.

### 9.
### See people two levels higher than you are.

When you are in the initial stages of exploring a target area, you will want to do some library research and contact people at your level to find out about that area and see how well your skills match up.

But after you truly have decided to conduct a full campaign in a target area, contact people who are at a higher level than you are. They are the ones who are in a position to hire you or recommend that you be hired.

Make sure you talk to lots of people. It will give you practice and actually relax you. You will find out how much in demand you are, and how much you can charge.

### 10.
### Work at your job hunt
### the same way you would work at a job.

Plan your job-hunting campaign. Work at it 35 hours a week if you are unemployed, and 15 hours a week if you are employed. It's only when you are devoting a certain number of hours a week to your search that you can get some momentum built up. Of course, you also need to be concerned about the *quality* of your campaign. You can have an organized and methodical search by carefully following the process in this book.

### 11.
### Follow-up. Follow-up. Follow-up.

After you have met with someone who had no job for you, keep in touch with that person by letting him or her know how your search is going or by sending a magazine article that would be of interest, for example. After a job interview, consider what they liked about you and what they didn't, and how you could influence their hiring decision. Follow-up is the main opportunity you have to turn a job interview into a job offer.

The
Five
O'Clock
Club

# When You've Lost the Spirit to Job-Hunt

*"I can't explain myself, I'm afraid, Sir," said Alice,*
*"because I'm not myself, you see."*
*"I don't see," said the Caterpillar.*
Lewis Carroll, *Alice in Wonderland*

They're all doing terrific! You're not. You're barely hanging on. You used to be a winner, but now you're not so sure. How can you pull yourself out of this?

I've felt like that. Everyone in New York had a job except me. I would never work again. I was ruining interviews although I knew better—I had run The Five O'Clock Club for years in Philadelphia. Yet I was unable to job-hunt properly. I was relatively new to New York and divorced. Even going to my country house depressed me: a woman wanted me to sell it, join her cult, and have a seventy-one-year-old as my roommate. It seemed to be my fate.

Then I got a call from my father—a hurricane was about to hit New York. When I told him my situation, he directed me to get rid of the cult lady and take the next train out. I got out just as the hurricane blew in, and he and I spent three beautiful days alone at my parents' ocean place. He encouraged me, including playing ten motivational tapes on "being a winner"! One tape taught me:

*The winners in life think constantly in terms*
*of I can, I will and I am. Losers, on the other hand,*
*concentrate their waking thoughts on what they should*
*have or would have done, or what they can't do.*
Dr. Dennis Waitley, *The Psychology of Winning*

My father wined and dined and took care of me. We watched a six-hour tape of my family history— the births and birthdays, Christmases past, marriages and parties. We talked about life and the big picture. I had no strength. He nurtured me and gave me strength.

What can *you* do if you can't get this kind of nurturing? Perhaps I've learned a few lessons that may help you.

---

**There seem to be phases and cycles in a job hunt—there is the initial rush, the long haul, the drought, followed by the first poor job offer and the later better offers.**

## 1. Put things in perspective.

*A depressing and difficult passage has prefaced every new page I have turned in life.*
Charlotte Brontë

You've worked ten or twenty years, and you'll probably work ten or twenty more. In the grand scheme of things, this moment will be a blip: an aberration in the past.

Focusing on the present will make you depressed, and will also make you a poor interviewee. You will find it difficult to brag about your past or see the future. You will provide too much information about what put you in this situation.

*Interviewers don't care.* They want to hear what you can do for *them*. When they ask why you are looking, give a brief, light, logical explanation, and then drop it.

Focus on what you have done in the past, and what you can do in the future. You *do* have a future, you know, though you may feel locked into your present situation. Even some young people say it is too late for them. But a lot can happen in ten years—and *most* of what happens is up to you.

## 2. Get support.

*Woe to him that is alone when he falleth, for he hath not another to help him up.*
The Wisdom of Solomon

The old support systems—extended families and even nuclear families—are disappearing. And we no longer look to our community for support.

Today, we are more alone; we are supposed to be tougher and take care of ourselves. But relying solely on yourself is not the answer. How can you fill yourself up when you are emotionally and spiritually empty?

Job hunters often need some kind of emotional and spiritual support because this is a trying time. Our egos are at stake. We feel vulnerable and uncared for. We need realistic support from people who know what we are going through.

*My life seems like one long obstacle course,*
*with me as the chief obstacle.*
Jack Paar

*There is no such thing as a self-made man.*
*I've had much help and have found*
*that if you are willing to work,*
*many people are willing to help you.*
O.Wayne Rollins

• Join a job-hunting support group to be with others who know what you're going through. Many places of worship have job-hunting groups open to anyone, or you can look in the *The National Business Employment Weekly* for listings of job-hunting clubs. During a later job hunt when I was employed, I reported my progress weekly to The Five O'Clock Club I formed in New York. It kept me going.

Statistics show that job hunters with regular career-counseling support get jobs faster and at higher rates of pay. A job-hunting group gives emotional support, concrete advice, and feedback. Often, however, that is not enough for those who are at their lowest.

*The more lasting a man's ultimate work,*
*the more sure he is to pass through a time,*
*and perhaps a very long one, in which*
*there seems to be very little hope for him.*
Samuel Butler

• If possible, rely on your friends and family. I could count on a call from my former husband most mornings after I returned from breakfast— just so we could both make sure I was really job-hunting. I scheduled lunches with friends and gave them an honest report or practiced my job -hunting lines with them.

• Don't abuse your relationships by relying on one or two people. Find lots of sources of support. Consider joining a church, synagogue or mosque (they're *supposed* to be nice to you).

### 3. Remember that this is part of a bigger picture.

*We, ignorant of ourselves, Beg often our own harms,*
*Which the Wise Power Denies us for our own good;*
*so we find profit by losing of our prayers.*
Shakespeare, *Antony and Cleopatra*
..........

*. . . so are My ways higher than your ways*
*and My thoughts than your thoughts.*
Isaiah 55:9
..........

*You are a child of the universe no less*
*than the trees and the stars; you have a*
*right to be here. And whether or not it is*
*clear to you, no doubt the universe is*
*unfolding as it should.*
Max Ehrmann

Why me? Why now? Shakespeare thought there might be someone bigger than ourselves watching over everything—a Wise Power. My mother (and probably yours too) always said that "everything happens for the best."

*We know that in all things God works*
*for the good of those who love Him.*
Romans 8:28

If you believe that things happen for a purpose, *think about the good in your own situation.* What was the "purpose" of my own unemployment? Because of it:

• I experienced a closeness with my father that still affects me;

• I became a better counselor; and

• I stopped working twelve-hour days.

Though shattered when they lose their jobs, many say in retrospect it was the best thing that could have happened to them. Some say the time of transition was the most rewarding experience of their lives.

*Every adversity has the seed of an*
*equivalent or greater benefit.*
W. Clement Stone

Perhaps you, too, can learn from this experience and also make some sense of it. This is a time when people often:

• decide what they *really* should be doing with their careers—I had resisted full-time career counseling because I liked the prestige of the jobs I had held.

• better their situations, taking off on another upward drive in their careers.

---

• develop their personalities; learn skills that will last their entire lives.

• reexamine their values and decide what is now important to them.

*For what shall it profit a man, if he shall gain the whole world, and lose his own soul?*
Mark 8:36

..........

*The trouble with the rat race is that if you win, you're still a rat.*
Lily Tomlin

### 4. Continue to do your job.

When you were in your old job, there were days you didn't feel like doing it, but you did it anyway because it was your responsibility. *Job hunting is your job right now.* Some days you don't feel like doing it, but you must. Make a phone call. Write a proposal. Research a company. Do your best every day. No matter how you feel. And somehow it will get done, as any job gets done. Some practical suggestions:

• Make your job hunting professional. Organize it. Get a special calendar to use exclusively to record what you are doing. Use The Five O'Clock Club's Interview Record in this book to track more professionally your efforts and results.

• Set goals. Don't think of whether or not you want to make calls and write letters. Of course you don't. Just do them anyway. Spend most of your time interviewing—that's how you get a job.

Depression ➡ Inactivity ➡ Depression.

• If you're at the three-month mark or beyond, you may be at a low point. It's hard to push on. Get a fresh start. Pretend you're starting all over again.

• Finding a job is your responsibility. Don't depend on anyone else (search firms, friends) to find it for you.

• Watch your drinking, eating, smoking. They can get out of hand. Take care of yourself physically. Get dressed. Look good. Get some exercise.

Eat healthful foods. You may need a few days off to recharge.

• Don't postpone having fun until you get a job. If you are unemployed, schedule at least three hours of fun a week. Do something you normally are unable to do when you are working. I went out to breakfast every morning, indulged in reading the *Times,* and then went back to my apartment to job-hunt. I also went to the auction houses, and bought a beautiful desk at Sotheby's when I sold my country house.

• Assess your financial situation. What is your backup plan if your unemployment goes on for a certain number of months? If need be, I had planned to get a roommate, sell furniture, and take out a loan. It turned out not to be necessary, but by planning ahead, I knew I would not wind up on the street.

• Remember: you are distracted. Job hunters get mugged, walk into walls, lose things. This is not an ordinary situation, and extraordinary things happen. Be on your guard.

• Observe the results of what you do in a job hunt. Results are indicators of the correctness of your actions and can help refine your techniques.

• Become a good job hunter so you can compete in this market. It takes practice, but the better you are, the less anxious you will be.

*In nature there are neither rewards nor punishments—there are consequences.*
Robert Green Ingersoll

Finally, two sayings especially helped me when I was unemployed:

*You don't get what you want. You get what you need.*

*and*

*When God closes a door, He opens a window.*

Good luck. —Kate

---

*In the depths of winter*
*I discovered that there was in me an invincible summer.*
Albert Camus

*If you only care enough for a result you will almost certainly obtain it. If you wish to be rich, you will be rich; if you wish to be learned, you will be learned; if you wish to be good, you will be good.*
William James

---

*The circumstances that surround a man's life are not important.*
*How that man responds to those circumstances is important.*
*His response is the ultimate determining factor between success and failure.*
Booker T. Washington

---

*Sometimes it's best if a man just spends a moment or two thinking. It is one of the toughest things he will ever do, and that's probably why so few bother to do it.*
Alonzo Herndon
born a slave; died a millionaire;
Founder, Atlanta Life Insurance Company

The following chart outlines each part of the process. It's best to do every part, however quickly you may do it. Experienced job hunters pay attention to the details and do not skip a step.

The first part of the process is **assessment** (or evaluation). You evaluate yourself by doing the exercises in *Targeting the Job You Want*, and you evaluate your prospects by doing some preliminary research in the library or by talking to people.

**Assessment consists of the following exercises**:
- The Seven Stories Exercise
- Interests
- Values
- Satisfiers and Dissatisfiers
- Your Forty-Year Plan

If you are working privately with a career counselor, he or she may ask you to do a few additional exercises, such as a personality test.

**Assessment results in** :

• a listing of all the targets you think are worth exploring; and

• a résumé that makes you look appropriate to your first target (and may work with other targets as well).

Even if you don't do the entire assessment, the Seven Stories Exercise is especially important because it will help you develop an interesting résumé. Therefore, we have included that exercise in this book.

Research will help you figure out which of your targets:

• are a good fit for you; and

• offer some hope in terms of being a good market.

You can't have too many targets—as long as you rank them. Then, for *each one*, conduct a campaign to get interviews in that target area.

**Phase I: Campaign Preparation**

• Conduct research to develop a list of all the companies in your first target. Find out the names

# Phases of the Job Search
## and the results of each phase:

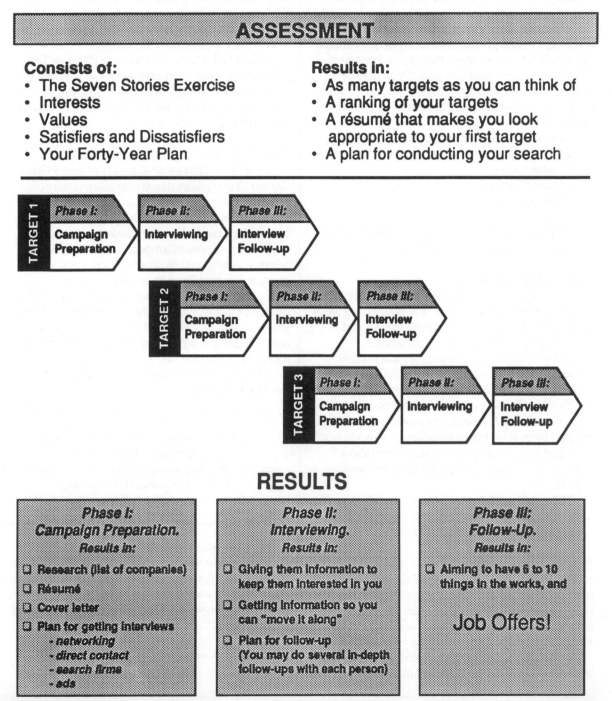

**ASSESSMENT**

**Consists of:**
- The Seven Stories Exercise
- Interests
- Values
- Satisfiers and Dissatisfiers
- Your Forty-Year Plan

**Results in:**
- As many targets as you can think of
- A ranking of your targets
- A résumé that makes you look appropriate to your first target
- A plan for conducting your search

**TARGET 1**
- *Phase I:* Campaign Preparation
- *Phase II:* Interviewing
- *Phase III:* Interview Follow-up

**TARGET 2**
- *Phase I:* Campaign Preparation
- *Phase II:* Interviewing
- *Phase III:* Interview Follow-up

**TARGET 3**
- *Phase I:* Campaign Preparation
- *Phase II:* Interviewing
- *Phase III:* Interview Follow-up

## RESULTS

*Phase I:*
*Campaign Preparation.*
*Results in:*
- ❏ Research (list of companies)
- ❏ Résumé
- ❏ Cover letter
- ❏ Plan for getting interviews
  - *- networking*
  - *- direct contact*
  - *- search firms*
  - *- ads*

*Phase II:*
*Interviewing.*
*Results in:*
- ❏ Giving them information to keep them interested in you
- ❏ Getting information so you can "move it along"
- ❏ Plan for follow-up (You may do several in-depth follow-ups with each person)

*Phase III:*
*Follow-Up.*
*Results in:*
- ❏ Aiming to have 6 to 10 things in the works, and

Job Offers!

*You ain't goin' nowhere . . . son.*
*You ought to go back to driving a truck.*
Jim Denny, Grand Ole Opry manager, firing Elvis Presley
after one performance. An interview on October 2, 1954.

of people you should contact in the appropriate departments in each of those companies.

• Develop your cover letter (Paragraph 1 is the opening; Paragraph 2 is a summary about yourself appropriate for this target; Paragraph 3 contains your bulleted accomplishments ("You may be interested in some of the things I've done"); Paragraph 4 is the close. (Lots of sample letters are in this book.)

• Develop your plan for getting **lots of interviews in this target**. You have four basic choices:

• Networking,
• Direct Contact,
• Search Firms,
• Ads.

You will read lots about each of these methods for getting interviews in this book.

## Phase II : Interviewing

Most people think interviews result in job offers. But there are usually a few intervening steps before a final offer is made. Interviews should result in getting and giving information.

Did you learn the issues important to each person with whom you met? What did they think were your strongest positives? Where are they in the hiring process? How many other people are they considering? How do you compare with those people? Why might they be reluctant to bring you on board, compared with the other candidates? How can you overcome the decision-makers' objections?

This is one of the most important and yet most overlooked parts of the job-search process. It is covered in extensive detail in this book.

## Phase III: Follow-Up

Now that you have analyzed the interview, you can figure out how to follow up with each person with whom you interviewed. Aim to be following up with six to ten companies. Five job possibilities will fall away through no fault of your own.

What's more, with six to ten things going, you increase your chances of having three good offers to choose from. You would be surprised: even in a tight market, job hunters are able to develop multiple offers.

When you are in the Interview Phase of Target 1, it's time to start Phase I of Target 2. This will give you more momentum and insure that you do not let things dry up. Keep both targets going, and then start Target 3.

## Develop Your Unique Résumé

Read all of the case studies in *Building a Great Résumé*. You will learn a powerful new way of thinking about how to position yourself for the kinds of jobs you want. Each of the résumés in that book is for a unique person aiming at a specific target. Seeing how other people position themselves will help you think about what you want a prospective employer to know about you.

Now, it is best to go back to the first part of the process, assessment. In *Targeting the Job You Want*, you will read actual case studies that will show you how real people benefitted from doing the assessment, including the Forty-Year Plan.

However, if your targets are already defined, just keep reading.

---

*Everyone should learn to do one thing*
*supremely well because he likes it,*
*and one thing supremely well because he detests it.*
B. W. M. Young, Headmaster,
Charterhouse School

---

*Life never leaves you stranded. If life hands you a*
*problem, it also hands you the ability to overcome that*
*problem. Are you ever tempted to blame the world for*
*your failures and shortcomings? If so, I suggest you*
*pause and reconsider. Does the problem lie with the*
*world, or with you? Dare to dream.*
Dennis Kimbro,
*Think and Grow Rich: A Black Choice*

# How to Change Careers

*If an idea, I realized, were really
a valuable one, there must be
some way of realizing it.*
Elizabeth Blackwell
(the first woman to earn a medical degree)

---

*... civility is not a sign of weakness, and sincerity is
always subject to proof.*
John F. Kennedy
Inaugural Address, January 20, 1961

---

T ed had spent ten years in marketing and finance with a large cosmetics company. His dream was to work in the casino industry. He selected two job targets: one aimed at the cosmetics industry, and one aimed at his dream.

All things being equal, finding a job similar to your old one is quicker. A career change will probably take more time. What's more, the job hunting techniques are different for both.

Let's take Ted's case. The casino industry was small, focused in Atlantic City and Las Vegas. Everyone knew everyone else. The industry had its special jargon and personality. What chance did Ted have of breaking in?

Ted had another obstacle. His marketing and finance background made him difficult to categorize. His hard-won business skills became a problem.

### It's Not Easy to Categorize Career Changers

The easier it is to categorize you, the easier it is for others to see where you fit in their organizations, and for you to find a job. Search firms, for example, generally will not handle career changers. They can more easily market those who want to stay in the same function in the same industry. Search firms that handled the casino industry would not handle Ted.

### You Must Offer Proof of Your Interest and Competence

Many job changers essentially say to a prospective employer, "Give me a chance. You won't be sorry." They expect the employer to hire them on faith, and that's unrealistic. The employer has a lot to lose. First, you may lose interest in the new area after you are hired. Second, you may know so little about the new area that it turns out not to be what you had imagined. Third, you may not bring enough knowledge and skill to the job and fail—even though your desire may be sincere.

The hiring manager should not have to take those risks. It is the job hunter's obligation to prove that he or she is truly interested and capable.

### HOW YOU AS A CAREER CHANGER CAN PROVE YOUR INTEREST AND CAPABILITY

- Read the industry's trade journals.
- Get to know the people in that industry or field.
- Join its organizations; attend the meetings.
- Be persistent.
- Show how your skills can be transferred.
- Write proposals.
- Be persistent.
- Take relevant courses, part-time jobs, or do volunteer work related to the new industry or skill area.
- Be persistent.

Ted, as a career changer, had to offer proof to make up for his lack of experience. One proof was that he had read the industry's trade newspapers for more than ten years. When he met people in his search, he could truthfully tell them that he had followed their careers. He could also say he had hope for himself because he knew that so many of them had come from outside the industry.

Another proof of his interest was that he had sought out so many casino management people in Atlantic City and Las Vegas. After a while, he ran into people he had met on previous occasions. Employers want people who are sincerely interested in their industry, their company, and the function the new hire will fill. Sincerity and persistence count, but they are usually not enough.

Another proof Ted offered was that he figured out how to apply his experience to the casino industry and its problems. Writing proposals to show how you would handle the job is one way to prove you are knowledgeable and interested in an area new to you. Some people prove their interest by taking courses, finding part-time jobs, or doing volunteer work to learn the new area and build marketable skills.

Ted initially decided to "wing it," and took trips to Atlantic City and Las Vegas hoping someone would hire him on the spot. That didn't work and took two months and some money. Then he began a serious job hunt—following the system which will be explained in the pages that follow. He felt he was doing fine, but the hunt was taking many months and he was not sure it would result in an offer.

After searching in the casino industry for six months, Ted began a campaign in his old field—the cosmetics industry. Predictably, he landed a job there quickly. Ted took this as a sign that he didn't have a chance in the new field. He lost sight of the fact that a career change is more difficult and takes longer.

Ted accepted the cosmetics position, but his friends encouraged him to continue his pursuit of a career in the casino industry—a small industry with relatively few openings compared with the larger cosmetics industry.

Shortly after he accepted the new position, someone from Las Vegas called him for an interview, and he got the job of his dreams. His efforts paid off because he had done a thorough campaign in the casino industry. It just took time.

Ted was not unusual in giving up on a career change. It can take a long time, and sometimes the pressure to get a paycheck will force people to take inappropriate jobs. That's life. Sometimes we have to do things we don't want. There's nothing wrong with that.

What *is* wrong is forgetting that you had a dream. What *is* wrong is expecting people to hire you on faith and hope, when what they deserve is proof that you're sincere and that hiring you has a good chance

of working. *What is wrong is underestimating the effort it takes to make a career change.*

In the future, most people will have to change careers. Your future may hold an involuntary career change, as new technologies make old skills obsolete. Those same new technologies open up new career fields for those who are prepared and ready to change. Know what you're up against. Don't take shortcuts. And don't give up too early. Major career changes are normal today and may prove desirable or essential tomorrow.

## For Other Techniques to Help You Change Careers, take at look at . . .

The following chapters in this book:
- Positioning Power for a Job Change
- How to Improve Your Position Where You Are (see especially "Negotiating the Job")
- Salary Negotiation: Power and Positioning (see especially "Case Study: Charlie—Negotiating a Career Change")

The following chapters in our book *Targeting the Job You Want*:
- Targeting the Jobs of the Future
- Case Studies: Targeting the Future
- Career Makeovers: Five Who Did It (case studies of ordinary people who followed the system and changed careers)

*Stick with the optimists, Niftie.*
*It's going to be tough enough even if they're right.*
James Reston

*I knew that sweat was a lot of it.*
*I had a cot put in my cutting room. I would recut something maybe five times in a night and run it again and again and again. I just knew it was sweat.*
*I had no special touch or anything like that.*
Robert Parrish,
Award-winning film editor-director
Quoted in *The New York Times*

The Five O'Clock Club®

# A Systematic Job Hunt

## Successful Job Hunting is a System

Working the system increases your chances of getting the job you want—faster. Working the system also helps relieve your natural anxiety about what you should be doing next.

The system is the same whether you are employed or unemployed, and even if you are not interested in changing jobs now. The system is the same whether you are looking for full- or part-time employment, consulting, or freelance work.

That's because job hunting in a changing economy means: *continuously becoming aware of market conditions inside as well as outside your present company. And learning what you have to offer—both inside and outside your company.*

The time to become aware of your opportunities is *not* when the pressure is on to find a new job, but *now.*

## The Job-Hunting Process

You select or target a job market by selecting a geographic area you'd be willing to work in, an industry or company size (small, medium or large company), and a job or function within that industry. For example, you may want to be a pressman in the publishing industry in New Hampshire. That's your target market.

Then conduct a campaign for the sole purpose of getting interviews in your target area. A number of those interviews might eventually lead to acceptable job offers.

Job hunting seems to have dozens of equally important steps. There are résumés and cover letters to write, personal contacts to make, search firms to contact, ads to answer, notes to write, and so on. You can lose sight of what is most important.

There are only four main parts in a job-hunting campaign: targeting, getting interviews in each target, interviewing, and following up. Do your best and put your effort into those areas. Everything you do in a job hunt grows out of your targets, which lead to interviews and then to offers. If you have targeted well, can get interviews, are well prepared for them, and know how to turn inter-

*Make it a rule of life never to regret and never to look back.*
*Regret is an appalling waste of energy; you can't build on it;*
*it's only good for wallowing in.*
Katherine Mansfield

views into offers, you will be focused and less affected by mistakes in other areas of your search.

## How Long Will a Job Search Take?

The length of each step in your search can vary considerably. For example, selecting the area in which you want to work (see *Targeting the Job You Want* or Part Two of this book) can be as simple as saying, "I want to be a controller in a small firm." Or it can be as complex as saying, "I want a position of leadership in a growing computer services business in any major U.S. city, where I can run my part of the operation—working with fast-paced but ethical people who are imaginative and leaders in their field. The job should lead to the position of partner."

The entire campaign can be very short. Let's say, for example, that:

• You have focused on a specific, realizable target.
• There are openings in the area that interests you.
• You know of someone in a position to hire you.
• You and the hiring manager "strike sparks" during the interview and it progresses naturally.

## Start to finish could take a month or two.

The average job hunt does take longer. Statistics show that for professionals and middle managers, it takes an average of six months or more to find the job they want. As the previous chapter establishes, *career changers take longer*. And people currently employed usually take longer to find a new job because they often don't work as hard at the hunt.

It can take you longer than a month or two because, among other things:

• You may not be that clear about what you want.
• What you want may not be realistic.
• Maybe it *is* realistic, but there are no immediate openings.
• There may be openings, but you may not know where they are.
• You may hear of some openings, but may not know someone in a position to hire you.
• You may meet someone in a position to hire you, but the two of you don't hit it off.

Devote a large amount of time and energy to your search if you seriously intend to find a suitable job. A thorough search is so much work that the job you finally land will seem easy by comparison.

On the other hand, job hunting is like any other skill: you'll get better at it with practice. You'll learn the techniques, and you'll learn more about what's right for you. You'll become aware of what's happening in your chosen field, so that when you start a formal search it won't take so long.

## The New Approach to Job Hunting

Keep up with changes in your company and your target area. To compete in today's competitive market, you must know:

• yourself
• the market—both inside and outside your company
• how to compete against "trained" job hunters.

## Job Hunting—An Everyday Affair

Job hunting is no longer something that happens only when you want to change jobs. Do it informally *all the time* to stay sharp in your present position.

You should always be aware of what may adversely affect your present security. Don't expect your employer to tell you that the company or your department is heading in a different direction. Be ready when the time for change comes. Take advantage of changes so you can move your career in the direction *you* want it to go. Take control and "impose your own terms upon life."

In today's world, many people job-hunt virtually all the time. Twelve years ago, at a time when U.S. corporations were more stable, I met an executive at a major pharmaceuticals company. He had been with that company thirty years, and planned to stay there until retirement.

Yet, while I was talking to him, he reached into his bottom drawer and pulled out an up-to-date résumé. He was not starting a new job hunt; he believed he should always have an up-to-date résumé and keep on looking—even though he had been working at the same company for thirty years! A good number of his job hunts were "successful" in that his outside exploration got him to his high

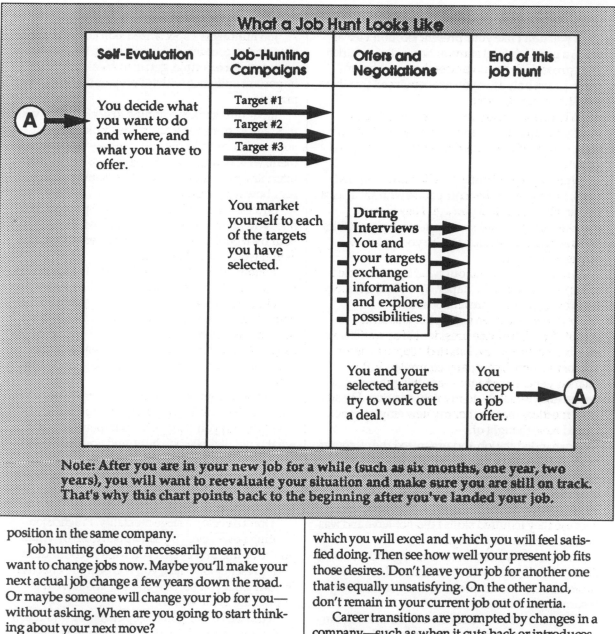

## What a Job Hunt Looks Like

| Self-Evaluation | Job-Hunting Campaigns | Offers and Negotiations | End of this job hunt |
|---|---|---|---|
| You decide what you want to do and where, and what you have to offer. | Target #1<br>Target #2<br>Target #3 | | |
| | You market yourself to each of the targets you have selected. | **During Interviews** You and your targets exchange information and explore possibilities. | |
| | | You and your selected targets try to work out a deal. | You accept a job offer. |

**Note: After you are in your new job for a while (such as six months, one year, two years), you will want to reevaluate your situation and make sure you are still on track. That's why this chart points back to the beginning after you've landed your job.**

position in the same company.

Job hunting does not necessarily mean you want to change jobs now. Maybe you'll make your next actual job change a few years down the road. Or maybe someone will change your job for you—without asking. When are you going to start thinking about your next move?

### Plan Your Next Move

*Plan* your career transitions—your moves from one job to the next—don't have them thrust upon you. First, know which job is right for you: a job in which you will excel and which you will feel satisfied doing. Then see how well your present job fits those desires. Don't leave your job for another one that is equally unsatisfying. On the other hand, don't remain in your current job out of inertia.

Career transitions are prompted by changes in a company—such as when it cuts back or introduces major technological or strategic changes—or by a change in you and your goals for your life. Be alert for a coming transition.

*Our rate of progress is such that an individual human being, of ordinary length of life, will be called on to face novel situations which find no parallel in his past. The fixed person, for the fixed duties, who, in older societies was such a godsend, in the future will be a public danger.*
Alfred North Whitehead

## If You're Thinking About Changing Jobs

If you don't like your present job, don't leave yet. . . . a good job hunt starts at home. Try to enrich your present job or move elsewhere in the company. Leave only after you are convinced that there is nothing there for you.

Whether you want to stay or leave, find out what your options are and what marketable skills you possess. Figure out what would make a good growth move for you.

One way to find out is to talk, on an informal basis, to people in other companies who are at least two levels higher than you are. They have an overview of the broad spectrum of job possibilities and are also in a position to hire you, or know others who might.

Another way to find out what is marketable is to look at the ads in the paper. You could get ideas for growing in your present position.

Let me give you an example. As soon as I accepted the job of vice president of operations for an advertising agency, I started clipping ads for V.P. of personnel, company controller, V.P. of finance, general manager —anything that would apply, even remotely, to my new position. The ads gave me ideas that neither my new employer nor I would have thought of.

I expanded the job and organized the categories of work I should be concentrating on.

These ads also told me the likelihood of being able to get one of those jobs. Even though I clipped lots of ads for V.P. of finance, I would never qualify because they required skills I did not have and was not interested in acquiring.

Ads also let you see who is hiring and what is in demand. Ads teach you the buzzwords of certain professions, and indicate how to tailor your résumé—just in case.

The fact that you're constantly job hunting can only be *good* for your present employer. It motivates you to do better, keeping your company more competitive than if you were not aware of what was happening outside.

## The Practice of Job-Hunting Techniques

Job hunting is a specialized skill just as is public speaking or cooking a gourmet meal. You probably wouldn't, for example, get up to speak before an important audience without preparation and practice.

Job hunting takes planning to decide what your message is; some research; some thinking about your audience and how your message will sound to them; writing and rewriting résumés, letters, and interview presentations; and then some practice to hear how it all sounds.

Successful job hunting is a formal process. But once you know the basics, you can and should put your own personality into your presentations, just as you would in public speaking.

Follow the "rules" for job hunting the same way you would follow the "rules" for public speaking or cooking. As a wise beginner, do everything by the book. After you become skilled, you can deviate a bit—for the better—because you have mastered the basics. You will do what is right for you and the situation you are in. You can exercise sound judgment.

You will then be at the point where it flows. You will find that you are operating from an inner strength, and you'll feel what is important and what is not. It is *your* job hunt, and you are the one calling the shots. You will feel sure enough to do what is appropriate regardless of what some expert says. You will know when it is to your advantage to break the rules.

Don't develop a siege mentality. Practice job hunting now—even if you happen to enjoy what you're doing, and even if you want to continue in your present job. In fact, you will be more effective in your job if you become sharper about what is happening in the world.

The rules of the game keep changing and that's part of the game. Only those who change along with them will be allowed to continue to play.

# What To Do If You Are About to Be Fired

*I don't deserve this, but I have arthritis and
I don't deserve that either.*
Jack Benny

When people are being fired, many say to themselves, "I'm good at what I do. I won't have trouble finding a job." Unfortunately, job hunting calls for special skills. If you are being fired, ask for outplacement help as part of your separation agreement. In full outplacement, counselors guide you in your search, and you are given office space and administrative help. It makes all the difference in finding new employment quickly and confidently. Partial outplacement may consist of a one- or two-day workshop on résumé-writing, interviewing, and general job-hunting techniques, and may also include a few hours with a counselor. You are then left to fend for yourself.

You cannot purchase the services of an outplacement firm yourself. Your old company pays the fee, which usually amounts to 10 to 20 percent of your previous compensation. Full outplacement help will be worth more to you than an extra month's pay. You can get the *Directory of Outplacement Firms* from Kennedy Publications, Templeton Road, Fitzwilliam, NH 03447; 603-585-6544.

If you are currently employed, or outplacement is not available to you, consider your options. A seminar is fine but will not see you through the job-hunting process. Job-counseling firms often charge from four to six thousand dollars up front, and some have been known to lose interest once the fee is paid.

You need advice and support. Job-hunting is stressful and lonely. You may feel that you are the only one going through what you are going through. You may even feel as though you will never work again.

Join The Five O'Clock Club. We offer job-search training and coaching from professional career counselors. You can also meet with a counselor privately to help you figure out your job targets, prepare your résumé, or get individualized help on a specific part of your campaign. You will be with others who are trying to accomplish the same

things you are. See *The Wall Street Journal's* "National Business and Employment Weekly" for listings of ours and other programs in your area. For a listing of current, authorized Affiliates of The Five O'Clock Club, see the information in the back of this book.

Unemployed people sometimes become embarrassed by their situation and pretend they are not looking—which is the worst thing they can do. *When you are unemployed and looking for a job, the more people who know what you are looking for, the better.* Spend time regularly with other job hunters, and also with a professional counselor who can give you solid advice.

## How to Negotiate Your Severance Package

You may want to have a career counselor coach you during this difficult and sensitive time. However, here are some things to consider:

- **Explore your options.**

  During the negotiation, be "pleasantly persistent" as you explore the options that are available to you. The situation may be more flexible than it originally appears.

- **Deal with each compensation issue separately.**

  A severance package is made up of many items. These may include an actual cash settlement, outplacement help, benefits, office space, and other items, depending on the industry and company. You need to look at each component individually. A large cash settlement, for example will quickly be eaten up if you end up paying for outplacement help and benefits.

- **Push to continue your benefits.**

  It costs a company very little to carry employees on its medical plan. But if you tried to duplicate that coverage on your own, it would cost a small fortune.

- **Develop a mantra.**

  Find one that succinctly describes your feelings. The phrase will keep you focused and give

*It is work, work that one delights in,
that is the surest guarantor of happiness.*
Ashley Montagu, *The American Way of Life*

your overall campaign consistency. Use a phrase such as, "I simply want what is fair."

- **Ask for full outplacement.**
You should never underestimate the amount of time it will take you—or the help you will need—to find another comparable position. Depending on the complexity of your situation and your own psychological makeup, your search may last more than a year. If your company only grants you six months' outplacement assistance, you will find yourself cut off in the middle of your job search.

- **Don't take money over outplacement.**
A cash settlement of $5,000—or even $50,000—sounds like a lot, but on your own you will not be able to replicate what you would get with a top-of-the-line outplacement firm. Such firms only work with corporations, who pay the bill. The outplacement firms want to do good work for you so they will get more business from your former employer.

---

**The fact is that people who get ongoing career counseling throughout their search get better jobs faster, and at higher rates of pay.**

---

- **Select the outplacement firm yourself.**
Although your firm may have a relationship with an outplacement firm, many companies will allow you to select the company with which you want to work. If you don't know which firm to select, call The Five O'Clock Club for guidance. You will pay only an hourly fee for this advice.

- **Use outplacement help to launch your own business.**
You may dream of going out on your own, and be tempted to take a cash settlement, believing that the money is the most important ingredient you need to form your new company from scratch. However, a good outplacement firm can help you write a business plan, talk with venture capitalists and merchant bankers, and serve as valued advisors until you are on your feet. This is advice you could never afford on your own. In fact, it costs an outplacement firm more to help someone launch a business than to do a traditional job search. The time involved is longer, and the services required are more complex.

- **Ask to extend your outplacement.**
If your company only offers six months outplacement and refuses to budge, take it—but ask if you could come back and ask for a monthly extension if you are conducting a full and active search and have not landed by that time. Then, right before the six months are up, go in and push for an extra month at a time.

- **You can start outplacement counseling even though you have not completely come to terms with your employer.**
You can be looking for another job at the same time you are asking your company for a better settlement. But bear in mind that the outplacement firm cannot help you with your negotiations with your employer.

- **Find out what other employees have walked away with.**
Use this information to further your own case.

Remember: Every situation is unique. Get help while you are negotiating your severance package. The amount you will spend on a little bit of counseling will satisfy you that you did your very best to get what you deserve and need.

The
Five
O'Clock
Club®

# How Long Will It Take to Find a Job?

*Nothing in the world can take the place of persistence.*
*Talent will not; nothing is more common*
*than unsuccessful men with talent.*
*Genius will not; the world is full of educated derelicts.*
*Persistence and determination alone are omnipotent.*
*The slogan "press on" has solved and always will solve*
*the problems of the human race.*
Calvin Coolidge

Most of the factors that influence the length of a job hunt are under your control. Scan the following topics and read the ones that interest you now. Read the others later.

### Factor #1: Career continuation vs. career change

All things being equal, changing careers takes two to three months longer than looking for a job in the field you are in now. If you want to head your career in a new direction, do it—but realize that it will take longer. (See the chapter: "How to Change Careers.")

### Factor #2: A clear target

You dramatically reduce your chances of finding the job you want if you don't have clearly defined targets.

A job target is a clearly selected geographic area, industry or company size (small, medium or large company), and function within that industry. For example, a job hunter may target the advertising industry in New York or Chicago, and aim at positions in the account management area. That's one target. That same job hunter may target media sales positions in the publishing industry, also in New York or Chicago. That's a second target. They are related, but require quite different campaigns.

You may feel you are willing to take any job that comes along, but attaining results with that approach takes longer than with a targeted approach. When you target, your campaign is focused and more convincing to hiring managers. Your pitch is more polished, and you'll find it is easier to network. Serendipitous leads can certainly be worthwhile, but the core of your campaign should be targeted.

### Factor #3: A clear positioning statement or pitch within that target

You are selling an expensive product—yourself—and you cost many thousands of dollars. To sell this product, know what the "customer "(your prospective employer) wants, what you have to offer, and why the customer would want to buy this product. As you position yourself, figure out what to say about yourself in light of what your customer needs. Know how you fit in.

### Factor #4: Favorable conditions within your target market

If your target area is growing or desperately needs what you are offering, or if there are plenty of jobs for which you would qualify, your job hunt will not take as long.

On the other hand, if you decide to go for a tough target, expect to work hard to overcome the difficulties. Find out how to get in, and then do it.

### Factor #5: True desire to find a job

The people most likely to succeed are the ones who sincerely want to find a job, and work hard at getting it.

Job hunting is a job in itself. If you are unemployed, work at it full-time (with time off for a little fun). If you are employed, treat job hunting as a serious part-time job and work at it.

Many job hunters do not treat finding a job as their top priority. Some may spend time suing their former employer. Others work hard at a job hunt doing the wrong things: when choosing between doing two things, they seem to choose the one less likely to result in job-hunting progress. Some people may spend months in the library getting ready, for example, when they know they should be out meeting people. They may consciously or unconsciously sabotage their own efforts because they were recently fired and are afraid of getting fired again. If you find everything is going wrong all the time, ask yourself if you may be afraid of the future.

### Factor #6: Attitude. Attitude. Attitude.

You may have the right target, the perfect market, and be the perfect match for a company, but if your attitude is wrong, you'll have a hard time. The worst attitude is to expect someone else to find a job for you. Successful job hunters are those who take responsibility for their own success or failure rather than blaming the counselor or the system when things go wrong.

"Attitude" includes:

- taking responsibility for your own job hunt
- the self-confidence you portray
- being able to think and act like a winner even if you don't feel like it (who wants to hire a loser?)
- your drive, your energy level.

Your attitude is as important as the actual job-hunting techniques you use. Flawless technique is worthless with a bad attitude.

### Factor #7:
### Working The Five O'Clock Club system
In addition to being willing to work hard, you must be willing to work the system. Those most likely to find a job quickly are those who go through every step—even if they go through certain steps quickly or find other steps distasteful.

A job hunt is going to take time. The time you think you're saving by skipping a phase will haunt you later. Do not bypass the system. *There are no shortcuts.*

### Factor #8: Good interviewing and follow-up skills
Some people get lots of interviews but no job offers.

You cannot get a job without an interview, in which you'll have to do well. Interviewing is a skill that requires preparation, practice, and an ability to notice what is important to the interviewer so you can take whatever next steps are required.

### Factor #9: Support and encouragement from friends and family/absence of personal disruptions
Recently divorced people, for example, tend to do less well in their jobs and less well in their job-hunting efforts. If you have other things on your mind, they may adversely affect your job hunt. Try to be effective despite these problems.

Job hunters usually need emotional support because this can be a trying experience. Our egos are at stake. Job hunting is not an easy thing to do.

Sometimes the support of family and friends is not enough because they are not going through what you are going through. That's why people join job-hunting groups or get outplacement counseling. You need realistic, honest support from people who know what you are going through. Studies have proved that *those who get ongoing counseling during their searches get jobs faster and at higher rates of pay* than those who simply take a course or decide to search on their own.

### Factor #10: Previous job-hunting experience
If you haven't job hunted in a while, you're probably rusty. People will ask questions you're not used to answering and you may not sound polished. The process requires skills we don't use in our everyday work lives. Inexperienced job hunters usually take longer than those who are used to marketing themselves. You need to develop the skills you'll need to land the job that is right for you.

---

# PART TWO

# DECIDING WHAT YOU WANT

## HOW TO SELECT YOUR JOB TARGETS

# Targeting the Job You Want:
## A Case Study of Newspaper Journalists
### An Introduction to the Assessment Process

*There will be many turnings along the way.*
*It will be easy to get lost in attractive bypaths*
*that lead nowhere. Resist deflections.*
Mahatma Gandhi

In 1995, an esteemed major metropolitan newspaper closed its doors. Some employees could work in another division, but hundreds would have to leave. The firm asked The Five O'Clock Club to help their people, and we did so in partnership with Jim Borland, a counselor at The Five O'Clock Club and senior vice president of a local outplacement firm.

I delivered presentations to the newspaper employees to tell them about The Five O'Clock Club (You can read about The Five O'Clock Club in the back of this book), and to help them start thinking about their career options.

This chapter contains part of a presentation to print journalists. It will give you a feel for the assessment part of the process—at least in an abbreviated form—regardless of the field you are in. For a full version, read our book, *Targeting the Job You Want*.

Before the presentation, many journalists could not see what their options might be if they lost their jobs. After the presentation, they had a much better idea of how the process works and what their options might be going forward.

> I feel a lot of kinship with your newspaper and respect the quality of work done here, having been interviewed by a number of you over the years.

The process I'm going to talk to you about is just one part of a process that can help you decide whether or not to stay here. In this two-hour introductory presentation, I will cover the first steps in managing your own career: the start of self-assessment.

Your company is also providing you with a full-day seminar to take you through the complete Five O'Clock Club assessment and résumé development processes, which are the subjects of our books *Targeting the Job You Want* and *Building a Great Résumé*.

The newspaper has also arranged for you to attend The Five O'Clock Club for up to one full year—whether or not you decide to stay with the company. Finally, you will get a subscription to *The Five O'Clock News*—our publication for busy, career-minded people like you.

Your company is showing a very enlightened approach to career transition. Those who decide to stay with the firm will learn how to better manage their careers. They will start to develop a career plan and investigate what is going on outside the company. Those employees will be smarter and will be able to bring that knowledge back to their jobs. That will make the company more vibrant, and can help it compete in this difficult market.

Those who decide to leave the company will also learn how to develop a career plan, and will get help in finding a new job.

You don't have to make up your mind now about going or staying. Getting involved in the process will help you to think about your options more clearly. In addition, your counselor and your small group at The Five O'Clock Club will help you.

### Regular Folks Have Changed Careers —So Can You

I worked on a project with one of your journalists. She publicized a Career Makeover for readers who wanted to find their dream jobs. She intentionally selected everyday people who did not have the impressive credentials some of you have. I stepped them through the assessment process you will read about in *Targeting the Job You Want*. One vivacious lady, an administrative assistant, wanted to work with animals. A paralegal wanted to work in sports. A homemaker wanted to have her own business. A mechanic wanted to be a teacher in Florida.

After five weeks, they had made astounding progress. The mechanic had investigated being a teacher in Florida. He and his wife have since moved there. The lady who was interested in animals found work doing that. The homemaker

*I've tried relaxing, but—I don't know—I feel more comfortable tense.*
Caption for Hamilton cartoon

---

started her own business doing accounting for the elderly, and so on.

This is a serious program for those who want to work hard at developing a plan and then achieving it. Right now, you probably think of a job search in terms of "Do I have an offer or don't I?" That is not a helpful way to measure the effectiveness of a job search.

At The Five O'Clock Club, we like it when people have six to ten things in the works. It's our magic range. Five of those will fall away through no fault of your own. We like it when people have three offers to choose from, so they can select the job that positions them best for the long term. That's our mantra. We want you to think two jobs out. Your next job will probably not be your last. So take a job that will position you for the job after that.

We have a shorthand way of talking about our methodology. You will find our lexicon in the back of each of our books. When a counselor asks, "How are you doing in your search?" you'll say something like "I have four things in Stage Two and two in Stage Three." That tells us where you stand. I know you don't know what I'm talking about right now, but our lexicon helps us to understand each other clearly without having to go into extreme detail. After all, each person in the group at the Club has only a short time in which to talk about his or her search.

Your company is providing each of you with a set of our books. Study these as if you were in graduate school. Mark them up and take notes and constantly reread them. Most people read a little every morning and a little every night. That way, you'll get the most out of your search, and will reduce the number of mistakes you make.

---

**Study our books as if you were in graduate school. Mark them up, take notes, and constantly reread them. Most people read a little every morning and a little every night.**

---

### Journalists in a Job Search

Most journalists—present company excluded, of course!—are impatient people. They're used to working on deadline. They're used to getting what they want, calling the shots, and asking the questions. They're used to working under stress and motivating themselves. Journalists have guts, brains, moxy and determination—all very marketable traits that will appeal to future employers.

However, the skills needed to conduct a good job search are not necessarily the same as those needed to be a good journalist. Because journalists are used to acting quickly, they may make impulsive job-related decisions rather than getting the information they need to make an informed choice. In a job search, someone *else* asks the questions and calls the shots. Worse than that, the important time frame is *their* time frame, not yours. I'll talk about this more later.

### Follow the Process

The Career Makeover winners followed our process. You will do well if you follow the same process. It works for people at all levels and in all occupations.

I remember a few years ago—on the Monday after Labor Day—a lawyer named Paul came to The Five O'Clock Club. He had been unemployed for a year, and was panicky. He asked me if we had jobs here. I said, "No, we have two-hour sessions. They're broken down into two parts," and I told him how we work. Paul said he needed a job quickly. I told him that the average person who attended regularly had a new position within ten sessions, but he said he didn't have time for that, so he left.

A full year later, he came back—even more panicky because he was still unemployed. He asked if we had jobs, and I told him the same answer. I invited him to stay for at least one session, and this time he did. Within two and a half months, he had the ideal job for him, and has since sent us many people.

The typical journalist has Paul's impatience

and time frame. What they want is this: "Kate, can we sit down for just twenty minutes? I'll tell you about myself, and you tell me what I should do with my life."

The fact is that you do have a lot to offer, and there's good employment out there for you. If you don't panic, you'll be in pretty good shape. Turn potential panic into focus. Turn your free time into a job hunt, and become methodical about it. You can follow our methodology, which has been proven to work.

But let's stop for a minute and brainstorm some of the options open to you. This will broaden your thinking and be helpful when you do your own assessment.

## You Are Not a Stereotype

Saying what the stereotypical journalist should do is like saying, "What should all those Pan Am flight attendants do who lost their jobs?" as if they were all the same. It doesn't work like that.

On TV the other night, I saw a news report on women who were going on tour to play baseball—just like in the movie *A League of Their Own*. Television journalists interviewed some of them: one ball player worked in security for the White House; another was an accountant. They were from different fields, but they all were playing baseball. You can't stereotype people—as I am doing with you just to show you the assessment thought-process. You each have different interests, different dreams, different skills, and even different personalities.

## Positioning Yourself for Your Next Move

None of you is a stereotype. In fact, you need to figure out how to differentiate yourself from other journalists—as well as from journalists at this newspaper—in order to market yourself better.

Part of what you are trying to do is position yourself better and differentiate yourself. While you are used to positioning people—and differentiating them—when you are writing stories,

you probably don't know how to do this on your own behalf. At The Five O'Clock Club, you will develop a pitch about yourself, which we call the Two-Minute Pitch.

Paul, the attorney I mentioned earlier, had been positioning himself incorrectly. He said he was a lawyer and was trying to get a job in human resources. In fact, his most recent position had *been* in human resources. Instead of positioning himself as someone trying to get into a new field, his counselor told him to position himself as a human resources executive with a strong labor-law background. Within two and a half months he accepted a job—in a small to medium-size company—as both head of human resources and senior legal counsel, *and* on the board of the company!

Paul was positioning himself as someone trying to break into a field even though he was already in the field. That may seem extraordinary to you, but you may be doing the same thing yourself. For example, the people who do what you do—but on the Internet—are called "content providers." If you were trying to get a job having to do with the Internet, you might position yourself as someone who wants to become a content provider, when, in fact, you already *are* one. Instead of calling yourself a "journalist," you would use the jargon of the industry you are targeting.

It may sound awful right now to refer to yourself as a content provider—because you may have a lot of pride in calling yourself a journalist. But what about a teacher who wants to work in a corporation? She wouldn't say she was looking for a teaching position. She would say that she was looking for a position as a "trainer," which is what she already is.

Position yourself properly, and use the jargon of the industries you are targeting, or your search will become difficult. As we say at The Five O'Clock Club, you will look like an outsider, and outsiders have more trouble getting good jobs.

*It's not what happens to us, but our response to what happens to us that hurts us.*
Stephen R. Covey, *The Seven Habits of Highly Effective People*

## The Stereotypical Journalist

Let's talk about the stereotypical journalist. What we will do here is similar to the thinking that you will need to do later to figure out what you as an individual bring to the party.

So what are some of the traits and skills that the stereotypical, obviously brilliant journalist at this newspaper brings to the party? I'll write the traits and skills on this flip chart.

[The group calls out skills and traits.]

"Proactive"

Yes. Journalists are known as being proactive. And that is certainly a trait in demand these days. We now have a country of mostly passive workers. We trained our workforce to be passive when we became a manufacturing society, and lots of people worked on assembly lines. Even those in white-collar jobs were managed with the same mentality: Each person was told to do his or her little part and to not think about anything else. Things were relatively stable then, so it worked.

Now companies are in the midst of tremendous change. They need self-reliant self-starters who are independent and get things done. America needs a new kind of worker: someone who is resourceful, proactive, and analytical. Companies need workers who can understand the entire business and how their part fits in. People don't have isolated jobs any more. Instead, they are expected to notice what needs to be done, come up with ideas, do more and think more. America needs workers who are thinking again—workers just like you.

We're off to a good start here. Tell me another trait or skill that the stereotypical journalist has.

"Writing"

This is a skill that truly is lacking today. You would be surprised at the number of senior executives who do not know how to write. They need you.

It was only a few years ago that experts predicted the demise of reading and writing, because television and video were expected to take the place of books. Yet the opposite has happened. Barnes & Noble and other superstores are opening up everywhere and book sales have increased. Even with the advent of the Internet, people have discovered that the content—that is, the writing—is still sorely lacking. The good news is that writing skills are more valued than ever.

Tell me some other words to describe journalists.

"An ability to articulate"

Communication in general is desperately needed—and it's the kind of communication that you are good at: analytical, cut-through-the-fluff, clear communication in this age of too-much information. Tell me some other words.

"Analytical thinking"

Let's talk about thinking. Most people today have been trained to think superficially and have an opinion instantaneously—even on very complex matters. But the stereotypical journalist at least tries to dig in, be thoughtful, and stay objective.

"Deadline-orientation"

Ah, yes. The stereotypical journalist is very deadline-oriented. I talk to journalists all the time, and I am very conscious of their deadlines. If I am being called by a daily news journalist—whether it's TV, radio, or print—they are usually "on deadline," and need a response from me immediately. But if it's a monthly, I know I have more time to think. I am conscious of your time frames—and so are you.

Journalists have to set their own time frames without regard to the needs of the people with whom they are speaking. When you call to interview me, you don't want me to explain to you that I have a lot of meetings set up and cannot possibly squeeze you in right this minute. Most journalists are very polite, but they must still focus on their deadlines. Because of the jobs they do, there's a certain impatience about journalists.

Stereotypical journalist have a personality

very similar to stereotypical senior executives—despite how you may feel about them. Both journalists and senior executives are often impatient, set deadlines, and expect the job to happen when they say it should happen.

In a job search, however, the shoe is on the other foot. Neither you—nor a senior executive—can say, "I want this to happen when I want this to happen." You feel as though you are on a deadline and you want to have a new job by a certain date, but your deadline is irrelevant to them, just as my pressing obligations are irrelevant to you as a journalist. You have to get more in sync with the time frames of the people with whom you are meeting and talking. It's their time frames that matter, rarely yours.

---

## Get in sync with the time frames of the people with whom you are meeting and talking.

---

It's very difficult for journalists—and senior executives—to find that they don't have the control they are used to having. Journalists are used to thinking: "If you don't give me the answer, then I'll call someone else." If you do that in your job search, you may not get very far.

The companies with which you are speaking have a very different time consciousness from yours. A company may say, "We're going to decide a week from Friday," but in fact they don't decide for four months. You think, "They *said* a week from Friday. We had a deadline here." Friday comes and goes. They weren't lying. They meant what they said, but they didn't mean it as a *deadline*. They meant, "We'd like to wrap this thing up by Friday because we hate doing it too." But four months later, they still haven't made up their minds.

So you have to learn how to figure out their real time frame, and also learn how you can nurse this contact along, which is something we will teach you at The Five O'Clock Club. As a journalist, you learn to nurture relationships, but you have to nurture them in a different way in your job search.

For right now, recognize this time-frame difference, and realize that you are not in control. Senior executives are not in control in their job searches either. You have to feel out what is happening on the hiring end, be proactive, and figure out what you should do. Then when they say they will call you on Friday, you won't take it so literally.

Tell me some other things that the stereotypical journalist brings to the party.

"Research"

Journalists are great at research when they are doing a story. But when it comes to job search—and doing research on their own behalf—many journalists skip research altogether.

Some of you have been interviewing with other newspapers that have come to headquarters here. Many a time, those hiring companies have said, "I wish just one person would come in here knowing something about our publication."

Why not do a little research before you go in for an interview? Get to know something about what is going on with them.

If you are in demand, you can do everything wrong in your job search, and it probably won't matter. Many of you will get jobs just because there's a lot of publicity about what is happening with this prestigious publication, and you will get grabbed up. But it's better to know the right way to job-search because the next time you may not be so lucky.

So you are right. Journalists are great researchers, but usually not on their own behalf.

Give me a few more words to describe journalists, and then we'll move on.

"Curiosity"
"Determination"
"Perseverance"
"Pushiness"
"Insight"
"Scepticism"
"A questioning mentality"
"Speed"
"Figuring out what needs to be done"
"Accuracy"

"Investigative"
"Integrity"
"Objectivity"
"Egotism"
"Self-confidence"
"Arrogance"
"Resourcefulness"

These are all important words. We'll show you how to use them in your job search—except a few, like "arrogance." Maybe we'll leave that one out.

## Receiving a Little Help

There's one other trait that makes someone a good journalist but not a good job hunter. In journalism, you don't take favors, ask for help, or become beholden to people. It would be considered unethical.

Job search is the opposite. You want people to help you, do favors for you, refer you to others. People will take you under their wing. Get used to saying thank you and appreciate what they do to help you. Feel some gratitude about it.

The world is not so bad. Some people will like you a lot and want to help you through your search—and not expect anything back. Being able to receive help will be a new mindset for you.

One final point that will help you in your search is that journalists are generally well-respected.

I asked the office manager at The Five O'Clock Club, to help me hand out our books at my first session here. I told her it would give her a day out of the office, but she didn't have to come if she didn't want to.

She was so excited that she couldn't sleep. She told all of her friends. They kept asking her, "Is this the day you get to see those journalists?" She couldn't believe she would get to see them in real life.

The overall reputation of journalists is positive, and will help you in your search—whether or not you wind up staying here.

## Jobs the Stereotypical Journalist Could Have

Now let's brainstorm the kind of work that a stereotypical journalist could do, even though these may not apply to you personally. I'll list them on the flip chart.

"Magazines"

Yes. The stereotypical journalist could work for a magazine. There are 5,000 magazines in this country. If you want to target magazines, you would need to break it down more: what kind of magazines, in which part of the country? Clearly describing your job targets is a large part of The Five O'Clock Club process. We'll talk about that shortly.

"Public relations"

A lot of people in public relations used to be journalists. You're used to making contacts, working on the phone, and keeping to deadlines. In addition, consider your values. Some journalists are motivated by a need to tell the truth, or to do good. You could work for a public relations firm or in the public relations office of a company or organization—such as a hospital or university—that has the same values that you do.

Tell me some other fields.

"Politics"
"College teaching"
"Consulting"

These are great. Let's talk about consulting. You could be a freelance writer, but think about for whom. A woman decided to have her own public relations business. She got a two-day-a-week assignment at a PR firm. On the side, she decided to focus on small manufacturing companies, such as companies that make Venetian blinds, or boilers for buildings, or other esoteric products. Even *those* companies need PR.

Every quarter, she did a mailing [a direct mail campaign] to two hundred small manufacturing companies. Every mailing, she picked up four or five assignments or new clients. She built up a nice business. Last year, she made $60,000. Earning $60,000 in your own business is worth more than earning $60,000 working for someone else because a lot of your business expenses are legitimately deductible.

*During the days, though, she was utterly at peace. Her life was like a single, well-spent hour. Its secret was her lack of remorse, of self-pity.*
James Salter, *Light Years*

When you are thinking of consulting or freelance work, be specific about the kinds of organizations for which you would do work: decide if you want to target small businesses, or not-for-profits, or hospitals, for example.

All of these organizations need the same things: brochures, newsletters, speechwriting, contacts, public relations, annual reports, and so on. Pick the market to which you want to pitch your business, and make yourself look appropriate to that market. At The Five O'Clock Club, we'll show you how.

"Start a small newspaper"

—and then have a job on the side to support that interest, right? You can think about having a job and a dream. A job to earn money, and a dream on the side.

"Law school"

Lots of journalists mention law school. Some people go to law school because they are driven by certain values, such as the expectation that they could do some good for the world. Then they graduate from law school, and find out that much of what a lawyer does everyday does not satisfy their values. They did little prior investigation to determine if their impression of the field was actually true.

Values are driving forces—often the key to future career satisfaction. Find out what you value and then investigate the fields in which you are interested to make sure they will actually mesh with your values. Otherwise, you will be disappointed.

"Writing books"

You could decide to write the great American novel, in which case you would need to have a job to support yourself. On the other hand, whatever you have been writing about— such as health, food, or finance—has given you a certain knowledge base. You could do something within that field or industry. You could work for a company, consult for that industry or for not-for-profits having to do with that industry, teach, or start your own business having to do with that industry or field.

For example, it was only ten years ago, at age forty, that I decided to devote myself to the field of career counseling. My writing gives me credibility in my field, but also allows me to say what I want to say. I think that job search is much more complicated than many people say it is, so in my writing I can show people how it really works. When I write, I also save people money— and time: They already know a lot when they come to The Five O'Clock Club or see a counselor privately.

You too could pick a field and use your ability to write to give you credibility in that field. Let me give you another example.

The story is that many years ago, Max Ansbacher was a regular old lawyer. In fact, I think he used to work for Campbell Soup. At that time, he did research on a new area—the options field—and wrote a book about it. It sold well within that niche of the financial-services community. Then he did more research and wrote another book. Although it was an obscure field at the time, it too sold well in that community. Then Max decided he wanted to work in options. Everyone he met in the options industry had already heard of him and assumed that he was already in the field. He had no trouble getting a job.

There's more to the story. Many people in that field get their business making cold calls over the telephone. Max didn't. In addition to getting leads through his books, he started a newsletter. He got virtually all of his business through his writing. You can do that too.

Many of you will come up with different ideas. Perhaps there is something that you have always wanted to do, or perhaps you will uncover new ideas in your research. I've been told that one of your former journalists opened up a Gymborie, a franchise where children play. Something like that will never be on the list, but that's what happens when you're talking about real people in real life—and not just a stereotype.

**The Internet**

Let's talk a little about the Internet. Right now, few Five O'Clock Clubbers are getting jobs having to do with the Internet, but I feel duty-bound to urge you to start thinking about it because it *may* be the wave of the future.

Those who are getting jobs having to do with the Internet are helping companies figure out how to market on the Internet. Right now, most of the content providers are very low-level. I think that's because financial transactions are not yet possible on the Internet. Companies want to have a presence on the Internet, but they are not really in a competitive mode because there is no money to be made—yet. It may be that senior-level content providers will be needed when companies can start selling things safely on the Internet. On the other hand, maybe nothing will happen. This is just something you should watch.

However, I heard the other day that one of the small Internet-based companies just hired the editor of a prestigious science magazine. He was hired because he was already well-versed in the Internet. Learn about this field now so you will be well-versed if it starts to pick up. This knowledge will be helpful to you even if you stay here. Your company needs people who understand the new technologies—and the Internet is certainly the one to watch right now.

### Growing vs. Retrenching Industries

One thing I can tell you for sure: If you don't target growing industries, you will have to job-hunt more often and will have a more difficult time finding the next position.

At The Five O'Clock Club, we track trends, so I can tell you what is happening in certain industries. For example, the majority of those in banking who lose their jobs leave that industry. The number varies over time, but it is still better if someone in that industry knows the facts at the beginning of his or her search. Otherwise, someone will come into The Five O'Clock Club, say that they've been in banking for twelve years, and everyone they know is in banking, so of course it makes sense for them to target banks. Three months later, they may be still looking for a job.

But if they had known the market situation at the beginning of their search, they might have selected other targets in addition to banking, and would have had a much shorter search.

Tell me your impressions of the newspaper business as a business. What's going on here?

[The audience noted a negative trend in the industry: many major newspapers had shut down.]

Yes, they say it's not so good at the moment. Quite a few papers are folding. They say it's a retrenching industry. You'll have to decide for yourself if this is true. But if it is a retrenching industry, I can tell you the implications of that. Retrenching industries are all alike.

The advertising industry, for example, had been retrenching for thirteen years, and is now finally leveling off. Over the years, many people wanted to stay in that industry no matter what. They loved working in what they still thought of as an exciting, glamorous field. I saw some of the famous top writers—the gurus in the field—who had been making even $300,000 a year, go from that to making $175,000 a year—which was a big blow for them—and then $125,000, and then $75,000 a year.

Many of those who wanted to stay in the business not only had to take pay cuts, they had to leave Madison Avenue and other major metropolitan areas and work in smaller towns—or even Eastern Europe. Some were relieved when they got a long-term assignment in a place that they would have considered undesirable before. At the same time, there were reports about the great advertising that was coming from smaller towns around the country. That's because the ones who stayed in the industry had to leave Madison Avenue.

If the major metropolitan newspaper industry is retrenching, and if you decide you want to stay in it, you are more likely to have to relocate with each job move. In addition, you are more likely to have to search more often—it's like a game of musical chairs: They keep taking the chairs away. What's more, you become less marketable with each move because the industry is becoming smaller. This happens at every level in the hierar-

> *High achievers display a simple, radiating charm. They project a warm glow that emanates from the inside outward. Most importantly, their self-esteem is transmitted with a smile, which is the universal language that opens doors, melts defenses, and saves thousands of words. Their smile is the light in the window that tells all there is a caring, sharing person inside.*
> Dennis Kimbro, *Think and Grow Rich: A Black Choice*

chy—not just the senior levels.

If an industry is retrenching, it is usually not as profitable as the high-growth industries. It becomes less fun because it is attracting less new blood. Those who remain have to do the mundane, core work, which is not as exciting as new developments. There's no money and no movement.

How many more years do you think you will work? If you want to work only a few more years, it's okay if you land a job in a retrenching industry. But if you want to work more than five years or so, you will probably have to search again. Even if you're over fifty, you will probably be working longer than you think. The average American today is living twenty-nine years longer than the average American lived at the turn of the century. And according to Lydia Bronte, author of *The Longevity Factor*, those years are being tacked on to middle age, not old age. Most of us will be working a lot longer than our predecessors did.

The good news is that you are marketable—except for your arrogance, of course. If you think your industry is retrenching—and you would know better than I—then brainstorm as many targets as you can at the beginning of your search. When a specific target does not work out, you will have others to fall back on. If you decide to stay in this field, learn some of the new technologies—such as the Internet—that may affect it in the future.

Right now, I will breeze through some of the exercises in *Targeting the Job You Want*, which you will complete in more detail for the workshop. We'll begin with the Seven Stories Exercise.

## What Successful People Do

When Steven Jobs, the founder of Apple Computers, was fired by John Sculley, the man he had brought in to run the company, he felt as though he had lost everything. Apple had been his life. Now he had lost not only his job, but his company. People no longer felt the need to return his phone calls. He did what a lot of us would do. He got depressed. But then:

> *Confused about what to do next . . . he [Jobs] put himself through an exercise that management psychologists employ with clients unsure about their life goals. It was a little thing, really. It was just a list. A list of all the things that mattered most to Jobs during his ten years at Apple. "Three things jumped off that piece of paper, three things that were really important to me," says Jobs.*
> Michael Meyer, *The Alexander Complex*

The exercise Steven Jobs went through is essentially what you will do in the Seven Stories Exercise. The threads that ran through his stories formed the impetus for his next great drive: the formation of NeXt computers. If the Seven Stories exercise is good enough for Steven Jobs, maybe it's good enough for you.

"Successful managers," says Charles Garfield, head of Performance Services, Inc., in Berkeley, California, "go with their preferences." They search for work that is important to them, and when they find it, they pursue it with a passion.

Lester Korn, Chairman of Korn, Ferry, notes in his book *The Success Profile:* "Few executives know, or can know, exactly what they aspire to until they have been in the work force for a couple of years. It takes that long to learn enough about yourself to know what you can do well and what will make you happy. The trick is to merge the two into a goal, then set off in pursuit of it."

## The Results of Assessment:
## Job Targets—*then* a Résumé

A job target contains three elements:
- industry or company size (small, medium or large company)
- position or function
- geographic location.

If a change is required, a change in any one of these may be enough.

## Looking Ahead—A Career Instead of a Job

Assessment will help you decide what you want to do in your next job as well as in the long run. You will select job targets.

Through your Forty-Year Plan (also found in

*Targeting the Job You Want)*, you will have the opportunity to look ahead to see whether there is some hidden dream that may dramatically influence what you will want to do in both the short and long run. I did my own Forty-Year Plan about fifteen years ago, and the vision I had of my future still drives me today, even though that vision was actually rather vague at the time. Knowing where you would like to wind up in ten, twenty, thirty, or forty years can broaden your ideas about the kinds of jobs you would be interested in today.

The Forty-Year Plan is a powerful exercise. It will help you think long-term and put things into perspective.

The Seven Stories exercise is equally powerful. Without it, many job hunters develop stilted descriptions of what they have accomplished. But the exercise frees you up to brag a little and express things very differently. The results will add life to your résumé and your interviews, and also dramatically increase your self-confidence.

### Here's Looking at You—Individually

In today's seminar, we looked at you as a stereotype. We saw what you had to offer, as well as the job possibilities for you. Now we have to look at each of you as a unique person—at the unique things you bring to the party as well as the job possibilities for you individually. We will do that in The Five O'Clock Club assessment program. You will do the basic assessment exercises that appear in Part Two of *Targeting the Job You Want*. If you are staying with the company, you will use that career plan to help you here. If you decide to leave, the targets and plan will get your search off to a running—and organized—start.

When preparing for the assessment program, *do not skip the Seven Stories Exercise*. After you do the assessment exercises, you will brainstorm a number of possible job targets and a career plan for yourself using the worksheets in the book. Using *Building a Great Résumé*, you will prepare a résumé that makes you look appropriate to those targets. You will do all of this with the help of a Five O'Clock Club career counselor.

Let's go through the Seven Stories Exercise

now. Then we'll register you for assessment and résumé preparation The Five O'Clock Club way, and for the weekly Five O'Clock Club job-search strategy program. Whether you simply need to become more knowledgeable to improve your career here, or whether you want to leave, our weekly program will keep you energized and on track.

### People Who See Themselves as Successful

A follow-up study of the newspaper journalists was conducted for The Five O'Clock Club by researcher Terri Lowe. We think the findings may apply to most employees. For example:

People who saw themselves as successful told us that they:

- are knowledgeable about trends in their present industry
- are satisfied with the steps they have taken in managing their careers
- are able to clearly articulate their strengths
- are able to respond to change effectively
- feel confident that they can market themselves effectively
- have an extensive network of contacts in their present industry.

The study suggests that when people make improvements in the above areas, they are likely to also see improvements in their own career success.

# The Seven Stories
# Exercise Worksheet

This exercise is an opportunity to examine the most satisfying experiences of your life and to discover those skills you will want to use as you go forward. You will be looking at the times when you feel you did something particularly well that you also enjoyed doing. It doesn't matter what other people thought, whether or not you were paid, or when in your life the experiences took place. **All that matters is that you felt happy about doing whatever it was, thought you did it well, and experienced a sense of accomplishment.** You can even go back to childhood. When I did my own Seven Stories Exercise, I remembered the time when I was ten years old and led a group of kids in the neighborhood, enjoyed it, and did it well.

This exercise usually takes a few days to complete. Many people review different life phases in order to capture the full scope of these experiences. Most carry around a piece of paper to jot down ideas as they think of them.

## SECTION I:

Briefly outline below *all* the work/personal/life experiences which meet the above definition. Come up with at least twenty. We ask for twenty stories so you won't be too selective. Just write down anything that occurs to you, no matter how trivial it may seem. Try to **think of concrete examples, situations and tasks, not generalized skills or abilities**. It may be helpful if you say to yourself, "There was the time when I . . . "

| RIGHT | WRONG |
|---|---|
| • Got extensive media coverage for a new product launch. | • Writing press releases. |
| • Delivered speech to get German business. | • Delivering speeches. |
| • Coordinated blood drive for division. | • Coordinating. |
| • Came in third in the Nassau Bike Race. | • Cycling. |
| • Made a basket in second grade. | • Working on projects alone. |

1. _____

2. _____

3. _____

4. _____

5. _____

6. _____

7. _____

8. _____

9. _____

10. _____

11. _____

12. _____

13. _____

14. _____

15. _____

16. _____

17. _____

18. _____

19. _____

20. _____

21. _____

22. _____

23. _____

24. _____

25. _____

## SECTION II:

**Choose the seven experiences from the above** which you enjoyed the most and felt the most sense of accomplishment about. (Be sure to include non-job-related experiences also.) Then **rank them**. Then, for each accomplishment, describe what *you* did. Be specific, listing each step in detail. Notice the role you played and your relationship with others, the subject matter, the skills you used, and so on. Use a separate sheet of paper for each.

If your highest-ranking accomplishments also happen to be work-related, you may want them to appear prominently on your résumé. After all, those were the things that you enjoyed and did well. And those are probably the experiences you will want to repeat again in your new job.

Here's how you might begin:

Experience #1: Planned product launch that resulted in 450 letters of intent from 1500 participants.

    a. Worked with president and product managers to discuss product potential and details.

    b. Developed promotional plan.

    c. Conducted five-week direct-mail campaign prior to the conference to create an aura of excitement about the product.

    d. Trained all product demonstrators to make sure they each presented our product in the same way.

    e. Had a great product booth built; rented the best suite to entertain prospects; conducted campaign at the conference by having teasers put under everyone's door every day of the conference. Most people wanted to come to our booth.

—and so on—

Now it is time to analyze your stories. You are trying to look for the threads that run through them so that you will know the things you do well that also give you satisfaction. Some of the questions below sound similar. That's okay. They are a catalyst to make you think more deeply about the experience. The questions don't have any hidden psychological significance.

If your accomplishments happen to be mostly work-related, this exercise will form the basis for your "positioning" or summary statement in your résumé, and also for your two-minute pitch.

If these accomplishments are mostly not work-related, they will still give you some idea of how you may want to slant your résumé, and they may give you an idea of how you will want your career to go in the long run.

For now, simply go through each story without trying to force it to come out any particular way. Just think hard about yourself. And be as honest as you can. When you have completed this analysis, the stories may help you better express yourself in interviews, and also on your résumé.

---

**Story #1.**

What was the *main accomplishment* for you? _____

_____

What about it did you *enjoy most*? _____

_____

What did you *do best*? _____

_____

What was your *key motivator*? _____

_____

What *led up to your getting involved*? (e.g., assigned to do it, thought it up myself, etc.) _____

_____

What was your *relationship with others*? (e.g., leader, worked alone, inspired others, team member, etc.) _

_____

Describe the *environment* in which you performed. _____

_____

What was the *subject matter*? (e.g., music, mechanics, trees, budgets, etc.) _____

_____

**Story #2.**

Main accomplishment? _____

Enjoyed most? _____

Did best? _____

Key motivator? _____

What led up to it? _____

Your role? _____

The environment? _____

The subject matter? _____

*We are here to be excited from youth to old age, to have an insatiable curiosity about the world .... We are also here to help others by practicing a friendly attitude. And every person is born for a purpose. Everyone has a God-given potential, in essence, built into them. And if we are to live life to its fullest, we must realize that potential.*
Norman Vincent Peale

## Story #3.
Main accomplishment? _____
Enjoyed most? _____
Did best? _____
Key motivator? _____
What led up to it? _____
Your role? _____
The environment? _____
The subject matter? _____

## Story #4.
Main accomplishment? _____
Enjoyed most? _____
Did best? _____
Key motivator? _____
What led up to it? _____
Your role? _____
The environment? _____
The subject matter? _____

## Story #5.
Main accomplishment? _____
Enjoyed most? _____
Did best? _____
Key motivator? _____
What led up to it? _____
Your role? _____
The environment? _____
The subject matter? _____

## Story #6.
Main accomplishment? _____
Enjoyed most? _____
Did best? _____
Key motivator? _____
What led up to it? _____
Your role? _____
The environment? _____
The subject matter? _____

## Story #7.
Main accomplishment? _____
Enjoyed most? _____
Did best? _____
Key motivator? _____
What led up to it? _____
Your role? _____
The environment? _____
The subject matter? _____

# Preliminary Target Investigation: Jobs/Industries Worth Exploring

*Until you know that life is interesting—and find it
so—you haven't found your soul.*
Geoffrey Fisher, Archbishop of Canterbury

---

*Life is God's novel. Let him write it.*
Isaac Bashevis Singer

---

**A study was made of alumni ten years out of
Harvard to find out how many were achieving
their goals. An astounding 83 percent had no
goals at all. Fourteen percent had specific goals,
but they were not written down. Their average
earnings were three times what those in the 83
percent group were earning. However, the 3
percent who had written goals were earning ten
times that of the 83 percent group.**

Forrest H. Patton, *Force of Persuasion,*as quoted by
Ronald W. Miller, *Planning for Success*

---

*Counterbalance sources of stress in your life with
sources of harmony. Develop closer ties to the people
you love. Set up dependable routines in your schedule
to which you can look forward during times of stress:
a few moments each evening in a hot bath, regular
nights to eat out, one day per month in bed, seasonal
vacations. Create environments around you that are
physically and emotionally restorative: a peaceful
workspace, a blossom-filled window box you can see
from where you eat, a permanent exercise nook.
Regularly perform simple tasks that you can be certain
will give you a sense of accomplishment.*
Jack Maguire, *Care and Feeding of the Brain*

A lthough it takes up only a few paragraphs
in this book, Preliminary Target Investigation is essential.

Agnes' Preliminary Target Investigation will
probably take only a few weeks because she is high
in energy and can devote full time to it. She has to
test her ideas for targets in the marketplace to see
which ones are worth pursuing. As she researches
at the library, and by meeting with people in her
fields of choice, she will refine those targets and
perhaps develop other ones. Then she will know
where to focus her job search, and the search will be
completed much more quickly than if she had
skipped this important step.

People who conduct a Preliminary Target
Investigation while employed sometimes take a
year to explore various fields while they continue in
their old jobs. If you are not at all familiar with some
of the job targets you have selected, do some Preliminary Target Investigation *now* through library
research (be sure to read this section) and networking. You will find that some targets are not right for
you. Eliminate them and conduct a full campaign in
those areas that seem right for you and which offer
some reasonable hope of success.

Whether you are employed or between jobs,
Preliminary Target Investigation is well worth your
time and a lot of fun. It is the difference between
blindly continuing in your old career path because
it is the only thing you know, and finding out what
is really happening in the world so you can latch on
to a field that may carry you forward for many,
many years. This is a wonderful time to explore—to
find out what the world offers. Most job hunters
narrow their targets down too quickly, and wind
up later with not much to go after. It is better for
you emotionally as well as practically to develop
*now* more targets than you need so you will have
them when you are actively campaigning. If, on the
other hand, you do not have the inclination or time
to explore, you can move on. *Just remember, you can
come back to this point if your search dries up and you
need more targets.*

Most job hunters target only one job type or
industry, take a very long time to find out that this

---

*Dream. Dream __big__ dreams! Others may deprive you of your material wealth
and cheat you in a thousand ways, but no man can deprive you of the control and use of your imagination.
Men may deal with you unfairly, as men often do; they may deprive you of your liberty; but they cannot take
from you the privelege of using your imagination. In your imagination, you always win!*
Jesse Jackson

target is not working, get depressed, try to think of other things they can do with their lives, pick themselves up, and start on one more target.

Instead, __brainstorm as many targets as possible *before* you begin your real job search__. Then you can overlap your campaigns, going after a number of targets at once. If some targets do not seem to be working as well for you as others, you can drop the targets in which you are no longer interested. And when things don't seem to be going well, you will have other targets to fall back on.

1) __List below all of the jobs/industries that interest you at this point.__

2) If you are not at all familiar with some of the targets you have selected, do some Preliminary Target Investigation *now* through library research or networking. You will find that some targets are not right for you. Eliminate them and conduct a full campaign in those areas which do seem right for you and seem to offer you some reasonable hope of success.

As you find out what is happening in the world, new fields will open up for you. Things are changing so fast that if you conduct a serious search without some exploration, you are probably missing the most exciting developments in an area.

Spend some time exploring. Don't narrow your targets down too quickly; you will wind up later with not much to go after. It is better for you emotionally, as well as practically, to develop *now* more targets than you need so you will have them when you are actively campaigning. If, on the other hand, you do not have the time or inclination to explore, you can move on to the next step. __Just remember: you can come back to this point if your search dries up and you need more targets.__

### JOBS/INDUSTRIES THAT INTEREST ME AT THIS POINT:
(May do some Preliminary Target Investigation to determine what is really going on in each of them.)

_____

_____

_____

_____

_____

_____

_____

_____

_____

_____

_____

_____

_____

_____

_____

_____

_____

_____

_____

# Targeting: The Start of an Organized Search

To organize your search:

1) Brainstorm as many job targets as possible. You will not conduct a campaign aimed at all of them, but will have backup targets in case certain ones do not work out.

2) Identify three or four targets worthy of preliminary research.

3) Research each one enough to determine whether it is worth a full campaign. You can find this out through basic library research and a few networking interviews. This is your Preliminary Target Investigation.

4) If your research shows that a target now seems inappropriate, cross it off your list, and concentrate on the remaining targets. **As you continue to network and research, keep open to other possibilities that may be targets for you. Add those to your list of targets to research**.

As you add new targets, reprioritize your list so you are concentrating first on the targets that should be explored first. Do *not* haphazardly go after everything that comes your way.

5) If you decide the target is worth pursuing, conduct a full campaign to get interviews in that area:

- Develop your pitch.
- Develop your résumé.
- Develop a list of all the companies in the target area and the name of the person you want to contact in each company.

6) Then contact each company through networking, direct contact, ads, or search firms.

**Serendipitous Leads**

Make a methodical approach the basis of your search, but also keep yourself open to those serendipitous "lucky leads" outside of your target areas that may come your way. In general, it is a waste of your energy to go after single serendipitous leads. It is better to ask yourself if this lead warrants a new target. If it does, then decide where it should be ranked in your list of targets, and research it as you would any serious target.

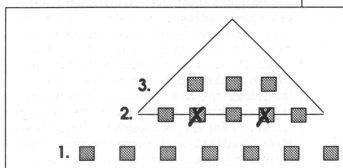

*The boxes above represent different job targets. The triangle represents your job search. As you investigate targets, you will eliminate certain ones and spend more time on the remaining targets. You may research your targets by reading or by talking to people. The more you find out, the clearer your direction will become.*

*__During Phase 1__ of your search, you brainstormed lots of possible job targets, not caring whether or not they made sense.*

*__During Phase 2__, you conducted preliminary research to determine whether or not you should mount a full campaign aimed at these targets.*

*__During Phase 3__, you will focus on the targets that warrant a full campaign. This means you will do full research on each target, and consider using all of the techniques for getting interviews: networking, direct contact, search firms, and ads.*

# How To Target
# the Job You Want

*I always wanted to be somebody,*
*but I should have been more specific.*
Lily Tomlin

You are on your way to finding your place in
the world. Using the Seven Stories and
other exercises, you made a list of your
motivated skills and what you want in a job, and
then you brainstormed a number of possible job
targets that might fit in with your enjoyable accomplishments and/or fit into your vision of your
future. Some of these targets may be very long-
term. Then you thought about what you would be
willing to offer.

Now we will work on firming up your job
targets. You will do some preliminary research on
each target through the library and by talking to
people to see if these areas still interest you and are
practical. Then you will *focus* by selecting two,
three, or four areas to concentrate on, based on
what appeals to you and what you think you have
that is marketable. Then you will conduct a thorough campaign aimed at each area. Because each
campaign takes a lot of work, it is best if we spend
some time refining your targets.

## Selecting Job Targets:
## If Your Targets Are Wrong,
## Everything is Wrong

As we have seen, selecting a job target means
selecting a specific geographic area, a specific
industry or company size (small, medium or large
companies), and a specific position within that
industry. A job target must have all three.

Select your targets. Using this book, conduct a
campaign aimed at each. Concentrate your energies
and you increase your chances for success.

Approach each target with an open mind.
Commit to a target, but only as long as it makes
sense. You can change your mind after you find out
more about it. It makes no sense to strive to be a
ballerina after you find you have absolutely no
ability as a dancer. Commitment to a target lets you
discover your real possibilities and increases your

chances of landing a job of your choice. The unsuccessful ballet student may have something else of
great value to offer the world of dance—such as the
ability to raise funds or run a ballet company.

## The Results of Commitment

Commitment increases the chance that you will
come across clearly and enthusiastically about the
industry and the position you seek; it will help you
do a thorough job of networking the chosen area, of
investigating and being knowledgeable about it, of
conducting a thorough search, and of being successful in that search.

If the result of your initial commitment is that you
realize a job target is not what you thought it would
be, you have resolved the issue and can move on.

Jim, a marketing manager, had targeted four
industries: environmental, noise abatement, shipping, and corporate America, a backup target in
case the other three did not work. He conducted an
excellent search aimed at the environmental target,
an area he had always wanted to explore. It was
only after a brief but committed job search that he
found the environmental area was not for him: the
people in it were different from what he had expected. He would not be able to do the things he
had imagined he would do there. That target no
longer interested him. The noise abatement and
shipping industries, however, were very exciting to
him and he found a good match for himself. Later,
his exploration of the environmental area paid off.
He was employed by a shipping company in the
containment of oil spills.

Commitment to a target means you'll give that
target your best shot. The result is a better job hunt
than if you had no target at all.

## Target a Geographic Area

Targeting a geographic area is usually the
easiest part of the targeting process. Some people
decide that they want to work near their present
homes, while others decide that they would be
willing to move where the jobs are. Are you willing
to move anywhere? Are a small town and a big city
the same to you? Would you move to the Coast? To

*The will to persevere is often the difference between failure and success.*
David Sarnoff

Arizona? Would you rather be near your family? If you want to stay where you are now, target that area as your first selection—and you'll have a better chance of getting offers there. If you really care about where you live, *target it*.

Think about where you stand on this. You will be assigning yourself an impossible task if, for example, you want to be an export manager but want to work only in a geographic area where there are no export management positions. If you must live in a particular area, be realistic about the kinds of jobs open to you there.

Resolve this issue. Then you will know if you'd be willing to change your target industry so you can live where you want, or change your geographic area so you can work in the industry or function that interests you.

### Target an Industry and a Function in That Industry

Many people say they don't care what industry they work in. When pressed, they usually have stronger opinions than they thought.

If you think *any* industry would be okay for you, let's find out. Would you work in the not-for-profit sector? If so, where? In education? A hospital? How about government? A community organization? Does it matter to you?

Would you work for a magazine? A chemical company? The garment industry? How about a company that makes cardboard boxes? Or cheese? Does it matter to you?

Does it matter if the company has forty employees? What about forty thousand? Four hundred thousand? Does it matter to you?

### You've Selected a Target If . . .

. . . you can clearly state the industry or company size you'd be interested in, your position within each industry, and some guidelines regarding geographic location.

For example, if you're a junior accountant, you may already know that you want to advance in the accounting field. You may know that you want to

work for a small service company as an assistant controller in the geographic area where you are now living.

If you have clearly selected your targets, then you can get on with finding interviews in your target area. To do that, you would conduct a campaign your target area.

Here is one person's target list:
By geographic area:

- Washington, D.C.
- New York City

By industry:

- Book publishing
- Magazine publishing
- Advertising
- College administration (weak interest)
- Administration of professional firms (weak interest)
- Nonprofit associations
- Direct-marketing companies.

By function:

- Business manager/General manager-publishing
- International controller
- Corporate-level financial planning analysis
- General V.P. finance/General manager-nonprofit organizations.

### Other Issues You May Want to Consider Even If You Have a Target

Does the style of the company matter to you? Would you rather be in a fast-paced, dynamic company with lots of headaches or one that's more stable, slow paced, with routine work as the norm? Which would you prefer?

What kind of people do you want to work with? Friendly people? Sharp, challenging people? People interested in making a fast buck? People who want to make the world a better place? Think about it. You may have said before that you just want a job—any job—but is anything still okay with you?

*How many things have been looked upon as quite impossible
until they have been actually effected?*
Pliny the Elder

If you want to be in sales, for example, would it matter if you were selling lingerie or used cars or computers or large office building space? What if you were selling cats? Rugs? Butter? Saying you want to be in "sales" is not enough.

Let's take it a step further. If what appeals to you about being a salesman is that you like to convince people, why not be a politician? Or a clergyman? Or a doctor? Or if what appeals to you is money, why not become a trader? Or a partner in a law firm? Remind yourself where your heart lies.

## CASE STUDY: WILLIAM
### *Finally—An Organized Search*
William wanted a job—just about any job he saw in the want ads. He spent months answering those ads. He thought he was job hunting, but he wasn't. He was simply answering ads for positions for which he was unqualified. William didn't stand a chance.

After a long time, William gave up and agreed to follow The Five O'Clock Club system. At first he resisted because, like so many job hunters, he did not want to "restrict" himself. William thought that focusing on only two or three job targets would limit his opportunities and lengthen his search. He wanted to be open to whatever job came his way.

Many job hunters, like William, simply want a job. But William needed to put himself in the position of the hiring manager: Why would he want to hire William? In his cover letters, William took the "trust me" approach. He did nothing to prove his interest in the industry, the company, or even the position he was applying for. His credentials matched the ad requirements only with the greatest stretch of the imagination.

A shotgun approach like William's may lead to a job offer, but it may also lead your career in a direction that is not what you would have preferred. Later, you may find yourself back in the same boat again—wondering what to do with your life, wanting to do almost anything but what you are doing, hoping your next job will miraculously be in a field that will satisfy you.

William's basic problem was not that he wanted to change careers, but that he didn't know what he wanted to do. He was willing to do anything—anything except focus on a specific area and go after it.

William eventually narrowed himself to two targets in which he was truly interested. Then he worked to find out his chances for getting jobs in those fields. William did the exercises in this book, and came up with this list to focus his search:

What I want in a job:

- a challenge in meeting new situations/variety
- a complex situation I can structure
- something I believe in
- a chance to express my creativity through my communication skills
- a highly visible position
- an opportunity to develop my leadership and motivational skills
- sole responsibility for something.

What I have to offer (that I also want to offer):

- enthusiasm for the company's basic mission/purpose
- penetrating analysis that finds the "answer"
- the ability to synthesize diverse parts into a unified whole
- an ability and desire to be in new/untested situations
- effective in dealing with many kinds of people
- strong oral and written communication skills.

Goal: A small or medium-size organization where I can feel my impact:

- service
- health care
- human care
- science
- academia and learning
- human understanding

---

48

*Never has humanity combined so much power with so much disorder, so much anxiety
with so many playthings, so much knowledge with so much uncertainty.*
Paul Valéry, "Historical Fact" (1932)

Description of targeted areas:

- Targeted geographic areas:
  - Major East Coast cities or locales:
    - New York
    - Philadelphia
    - Boston
    - Baltimore
    - Washington

- Targeted industries:
  - First priority is health care:
    - pharmaceuticals companies
    - biotechnology companies
    - hospitals
    - maybe research labs
  - Second priority is not-for-profit community organizations

- Targeted positions:
  - marketing/competitive analysis
  - organizational positioning
  - operations planning

William's first campaign was aimed at pharmaceuticals companies. He discovered what they looked for in new hires, and how he could get a position. In addition, he pursued his second objective: not-for-profit community organizations.

The result: As usual, a career transition takes time. William discovered he could make a transition into the pharmaceuticals industry, but decided not to take the backward step that would require. He learned of a job being created in a not-for-profit organization. Although he was not qualified for this position, he knew he could handle it, and it matched the list of what he wanted.

William went through the steps described in the chapter "How to Change Careers," to convince his prospective employer he could indeed handle the job and was eager to have the chance to do it. This was difficult because the other candidates were better qualified than William—they had been in this kind of job before. For William, it was a career change.

William decided to write a number of proposals. To write them, he first needed to do research, which would not be easy. After some library research, he called the heads of development at six major not-for-profits. He told them he was hoping to get a position at a certain organization, and wanted some ideas of how he could write a proposal of what he would do if he were hired.

Amazingly, his sincerity won the day. All six gave him information over the phone. Because he had done library research, William was able to ask intelligent questions. He wrote a proposal, stating in his cover letter that he had spoken with the heads of development at major not-for-profits, and asked for another interview. It would be nice if that were all it took: William got another interview, but was rejected a *number* of times. Yet he continued to do research, and eventually showed enough fortitude and learned enough that he was hired.

The position was just what he wanted: a brand-new marketing research position at a major not-for-profit organization. He would head his career in a different direction and satisfy his motivated skills. His career was back on track, under his own control. And he's still with the organization today.

### Select *Your* Targets

*The only difference between caprice and a lifelong
passion is that the caprice lasts a little longer.*
Oscar Wilde

List your targets in the order in which you will conduct your search. List first the one you will focus on in your first campaign. If you are currently employed and have time to explore, you may want to select as your first target the most unlikely one. (Job hunters sometimes want to target areas they had only dreamed about before.) Concentrate on it and find out for sure if you are truly interested and what your prospects are. If it doesn't work, you can become more realistic.

On the other hand, if you must find a job quickly, concentrate first on the area where you stand the best chance of getting a job—perhaps the

*For each of us, decisions loom in the near or immediate future. Your responses to them will shape your life and business, possibly for years to come. Consider for a moment: what decisions await you about jobs. relationships, business, markets, R&D strategy, or simply living? And then—what hidden questions should you be asking to help you make those decisions?*
Peter Schwartz, *The Art of the Long View*

field you are now in. After you are settled in your new job, you can develop yourself in the area that interests you in the long run. Remember, it's okay to take something less than your ideal job; just keep working toward your dreams.

Someone who made this work is Nat, who wanted to work for a Japanese company. He thought the Japanese culture suited his temperament. Yet Nat was forced to take a job at another company because the Japanese process was slow (approval had to come from Tokyo). Still, Nat kept pursuing the position with the Japanese firm.

Eventually, his dream job came through—at much more money than he had been making. The Japanese company realized that Nat's personal style, uncommon in America, meshed with Japanese management methods. His maturity—he was fifty-five years old—was also a plus. Nat, his new job, and his new employer were a good fit. Despite many obstacles, Nat pursued his dream and got it. And it was worth it in job satisfaction and in having some say over what happened in his own life.

If you are targeting a geographic area different from where you are now, be sure to conduct a serious, complete campaign aimed at that target. For example, you will want to contact search firms in that area, do library research, perhaps conduct a direct-mail campaign, and network. Use the worksheets on the following pages to plan your targets.

## Measuring Your Targets

You've selected three to five targets on which to focus. Will they be enough to get you an appropriate job?

Let's say, for example, that your first target aims at a small industry (ten companies) having only a few positions that would be appropriate for you. Chances are, those jobs are filled right now. In fact, chances are there may be no opening for a year or two. The numbers are working against you. But if you have targeted *twenty* small industries, each of which has ten companies with a few positions appropriate for you, the numbers are more in your favor. On the other hand, if one of your targets is

large and has a lot of positions that may be right for you, the numbers are again on your side.

## A Rule of Thumb

A target list of two hundred positions results in seven interviews, which result in one job offer. Therefore, if there are less than two hundred potential positions in your targets, develop additional targets or expand the ones you already have. Remember that when aiming at a target of less than two hundred, concentrated effort will be required.

Sometimes, however, one company by itself may be enough. What if a very qualified secretary wanted to work for a regional telephone company? What are the chances she would find a job there? A regional telephone company may have *thousands* of secretaries, and a qualified person would certainly be able to find a job there within a reasonable time frame. Sometimes a *company* can be a target.

In a tight job market, however, you will probably need to *expand your job hunting targets*. If you are searching only in Chicago, or only in the immediate area where you live, think of other geographic areas. If you are looking only in large public corporations, consider small or private companies, or the not-for-profit area. If you are looking for a certain kind of position, what other kinds of work can you do? Think of additional targets for your search, and focus on each target in depth.

In this book, you will learn how to position yourself for each of these targets. That way, when you go after a target, you will have a better chance of looking appropriate to the people in each target area.

*I just want to say one word to you.*
*Just one word.*
*Are you listening?*
*Plastics.*
Buck Henry and Calder Willingham, *The Graduate*

The
Five
O'Clock
Club®

# Target Selection

After you have done some preliminary research, select the targets that you think deserve a full campaign. List first the one you will focus on in your first campaign. If you are currently employed and have time to explore, you may want to select as your first target the most unlikely one, but the one that is the job of your dreams. Then you can concentrate on it and find out for sure whether you are still interested and what your prospects are.

On the other hand, if you must find a job quickly, you will first want to concentrate on the area where you stand the best chance of getting a job—probably the area where you are now working. After you get that job, you can explore your other targets. (To expand your targets quickly, consider broadening your search geographically.)

If you are targeting a geographic area different from where you are now, be sure to conduct a serious, complete campaign aimed at that target. For example, you will want to contact search firms in that area, do library research, perhaps conduct a direct-mail campaign, and network.

**Target 1:**

        Industry or company size: _____

        Position/Function: _____

        Geographic area: _____

**Target 2:**

        Industry or company size: _____

        Position/Function: _____

        Geographic area: _____

**Target 3:**

        Industry or company size: _____

        Position/Function: _____

        Geographic area: _____

**Target 4:**

        Industry or company size: _____

        Position/Function: _____

        Geographic area: _____

**Target 5:**

        Industry or company size: _____

        Position/Function: _____

        Geographic area: _____

The Five O'Clock Club

# Measuring Your Targets

You've selected three to five (or more) targets on which to focus. Will this be enough to get you an appropriate job?

Let's say, for example, that your first target aims at a small industry (ten companies) having only a few positions that would be appropriate for you.

Chances are, those jobs are filled right now. In fact, chances are there may be no opening for a year or two. The numbers are working against you. Now, if you have targeted twenty small industries, each of which has ten companies with a few positions appropriate for you, the numbers are more in your favor.

On the other hand, if one of your targets is large and has a lot of positions that may be right for you, the numbers are again on your side.

Let's analyze your search and see whether the numbers are working for you or against you.

Fill out the following on your own target markets. You will probably have to make an educated guess about the number. A ball-park figure is all you need to get a feel for where you stand.

## For Target 1:

Industry or company size: _____

Position/Function: _____

Geographic area: _____

How big is the market for your "product" in this target?

  A. Number of companies in this target market: _____

  B. Number of probable positions suitable for me in the average company in this target: _____

  A x B = Total number of probable positions appropriate for me in this target market: _____

## For Target 2:

Industry or company size: _____

Position/Function: _____

Geographic area: _____

How big is the market for your "product" in this target?

  A. Number of companies in this target market: _____

  B. Number of probable positions suitable for me in the average company in this target: _____

  A x B = Total number of probable positions appropriate for me in this target market: _____

## For Target 3:

Industry or company size: _____

Position/Function: _____

Geographic area: _____

How big is the market for your "product" in this target?

  A. Number of companies in this target market: _____

  B. Number of probable positions suitable for me in the average company in this target: _____

  A x B = Total number of probable positions appropriate for me in this target market: _____

## Rule of thumb:

A target list of 200 positions in a healthy market results in seven interviews that result in one job offer. Therefore, if there are fewer than 200 potential positions in your targets, develop additional targets or expand the ones you already have. Remember that when aiming at a target of less than 200, a more concentrated effort will be required.

*I believe in prayer.*
*It gives us strength in times of need;*
*it gives us hope in times of despair;*
*it gives us optimism in times of opportunity.*
President George Bush, August 1989,
as reported by IMS News on Family Radio

---

*If you try to ignore the situation, change will slam*
*into you and knock you off balance.*
*Getting angry won't make it go away*
*—in fact, temper typically makes things worse.*
*Wishful thinking is a waste of time too,*
*so don't sit around thinking and talking about*
*"the good old days" with the hope they'll return.*
*You can't even run away from it, because there's no*
*place you can run that's beyond the range of change.*
*Might as well face the problems*
*and find the opportunities.*
Price Pritchett and Ron Pound,
*The Employee Handbook of Organizational Change*

By selecting and ranking your targets, you have completed a very important task. If your targets are wrong, the campaigns you aim at those targets are wrong. Maintain an exploratory mindset—assessing the targets you are pursuing, and being open to others.

Make an organized search the basis for your campaign. Some lucky job hunters know lots of important people and just happen onto their next jobs. Sometimes those jobs are even satisfying. If that has happened to you in the past, count your blessings, but do not rely on that approach to work for you in the future. The world has changed, and organizations are more serious about whom they hire.

Read the next few chapters—about developing a résumé and conducting research—and then use *Building a Great Résumé* to build an even greater résumé for yourself. Then you will be ready to begin an intensive campaign to get lots of interviews in each of the targets you have selected. The campaigns will overlap so you will be able to compare the performance of each and gain perspective.

# Résumé Development:
# How to State Your Accomplishments

*Start where you are with what you have, knowing that
what you have is plenty enough.*
Booker T. Washington

Your accomplishments form the backbone of your résumé. Accomplishment statements are short, measurable, and results-oriented.

You may want to start with your most important story from the Seven Stories Exercise—if it was work-related. Polish up that accomplishment, and a few more. If you want your reader to know about these accomplishments, work hard to state them correctly. When you have finished refining three or four major accomplishments, you'll be surprised by how much of your résumé is already done.

Alternatively, start with your most recent position. State your title, company name, and list your accomplishments. Rather than ranking them chronologically (First I did this, and then I did

that . . . ), rank them in the order of interest to the reader.

After refining the accomplishment statements for your present or most recent position, examine the job before that one. State your title, your company name, and list your accomplishments.

You will feel more hopeful about your job search after you have completed this exercise. Your accomplishments will be stated in a way that will make you proud.

Also consider your accomplishments outside work. These too should be short, measurable, and results-oriented. By doing volunteer work after-hours, many have gained experiences that helped them move from their current fields into new ones.

Here are a few accomplishment statements. They are written in the context of a complete job so you can see how to bullet and sub-bullet. This technique of bulleting and sub-bulleting can be used on any person's résumé.

---

**VICE PRESIDENT OF MARKETING SERVICES**                                        1985-1987

- Contributed to 3 consecutive years of record 9.7% growth.

- Developed marketing and sales <u>**training programs for 5,000 employees**</u>.

  - Program changed "hard sell"/reactive selling to consultative and entrepreneurial approach.

  - Program shifted selling culture and positioned company for growth in the 80's.

- <u>**Repositioned subsidiary**</u> by redesigning logo, signage, brochures, direct- mail solicitations, and collateral materials.

- Introduced customer-satisfaction measurement program that provided feedback to 1,100 branch operations and produced changes in operational procedures.

This example is written the way it would appear on a résumé. Note that certain parts are underlined so the reader cannot miss them. It makes the résumé more scannable.

---

If you want the reader to know that you have developed training programs, does it hit the reader's eye? If you are proud of having repositioned a subsidiary and think it may be important to your next employer, can he find it on your résumé? You will not have to think about highlighting your résumé until it is completely put together. For now, just know that it will be an

option later. *Building a Great Résumé* contains many examples of accomplishment statements for people of all levels.

**Polish up your accomplishment statements.**
Rework the wording of your accomplishments. Think how they will sound to the reader. Do not "tell all." Make the reader want to meet

you to find out more.

In addition, rephrase your accomplishments to make them as independent as possible of the particular environment you were working in. Make your accomplishments seem useful in other companies or even other industries.

Here is an accomplishment statement as originally written:

Compared the changes in various categories of revenue to the changes in various categories of labor. Plotted results on a scatter diagram to show the relationships.

That is so boring. What were you really doing and why? Look at what you did as if you were an observer rather than the grunt working on something day in and day out. What were the results of your efforts?

Here is that same accomplishment statement reworked:

Defined the factors that influence profitability in professional service firms. Resulted in launch of major reorganization of company's largest division.

Sounds better, doesn't it? The first example sounds like a person who is technical and adds up numbers all day—which is what this project was. The rewrite sounds like a person who knew what he or she was doing, had some say in how it was done, and was aware of the impact on the organization—perhaps even pushed for the changes that took place in the company. The new wording makes the reader want to meet this person to learn new insights.

When writing your accomplishments:

• *Focus on results,* as opposed to the process you went through. Focus on the effect your actions had.

• *Use quantitative measures* when possible. If the quantity doesn't sound important, don't use it.

• *Show the part you played* in whatever hap-

pened to your company. If the company grew from $50 million to $200 million, were you an observer or did you have something to do with it? What was your key accomplishment?

• Don't say what you did. *State the magnitude and the effect* it had. For example, if you say you "started up a new computer system," that statement could apply to anyone at any level. What effect did that computer system have on the company? Rework your accomplishment to say:

Developed spreadsheet program to highlight salary inconsistencies within range. Resulted in a more equitable personnel system and savings of $100,000 a year.
or:
Solely responsible for the development of a computerized system that resulted in a new way to analyze accounts. Resulted in $2-million profit improvement and the renegotiation of key accounts.

---

**Now go back and rework *your* accomplishment statements.**

---

**Other areas to list:**

*Skills and equipment.* If you are in a technical job, you may want to list the equipment you are familiar with, such as computers or computer languages or software, and perhaps foreign languages you know.

*Books or articles written; speeches delivered.* One important example implies you have done more. If you have addressed the United Nations, do not mention the speech you gave at a neighborhood meeting.

*Organizations.* List organizations related to the work you are seeking. If you list too many, the reader may wonder how you will have time for work.

## How you will use your accomplishments list

Your list of key accomplishments will help you interview, write cover letters, and prepare your résumé. It is the raw material for the rest of your job hunt.

These are the key selling points about you—the things that will make you different from your competition. They will also whet the appetite of the reader, so he or she will want to meet you. The purpose of a résumé or cover letter is not to tell what you did, but to get interviews. During the interview, you can elaborate on what you did.

Figuring out what you really did is much more difficult than simply reciting your job description. That's the importance of doing the Seven Stories Exercise. It helps you step back from a résumé frame-of-mind so you can concentrate on the most important accomplishments of your life (in terms of what you really enjoyed doing and know you also did well). Then the exercise helps you to think about each accomplishment in terms of what led up to it, what your role was, what gave you satisfaction, what your motivation was, and so on.

When you write your accomplishments, think about your future and those parts of your accomplishments you may want to emphasize, and think about what you *really* did.

## If you think you haven't done a thing with your life

Many people are intimidated when they see other people's accomplishments. They think they have none of their own. Chances are, you aren't thinking hard enough about what you have done. Even obviously accomplished people struggle to express what they have done.

If you think you haven't done much, think again. Even the lowest-level clerks have accomplishments they are proud of. At all levels in an organization, people can be presented with problems and figure out how to handle them.

Don't compare yourself with others, and don't worry about what your boss or peers thought of what you did. Maybe they did not appreciate your talents. Brag about what you have done anyway—even though your boss may have taken credit for the work you did, and even though you may have done it with others. Think of problems you have faced in your company. What did you do to handle them? What was the result for your company? Think of an accomplishment. **Write it down.** Then pare it down until you can show the reader what you handled and the impact it made.

Finally, don't say anything negative about yourself. Don't lie, but don't hurt yourself either. For example, never lie about where you got a degree or whether you got a degree. If you are found out, you will be fired. If you have been unemployed for a very long time, see my specific hints on how to discuss this awkward timeframe in "How to Handle Difficult Interview Questions."

In the next chapter, we will prepare the summary for your résumé, and then help you to put it all together.

---

*I made a commitment to completely cut out drinking and anything else that might hamper me from getting my mind and my body together. And the floodgates of goodness have opened upon me—*
*spiritually and financially.*
Denzel Washington, in "Spotlight: Denzel,"
*Essence*, November 1986

The
Five
O'Clock
Club®

# Positioning Power for a Job Change

Feel stuck in your present position? Peel off your old label, slap on a new one, and position yourself for something different.

Whether you're a branch manager who wants to go into commercial lending, or an operations person who dreams of being a trainer, the challenge you face is the same: you have to convince people that, even though you don't have experience, you can handle the new position.

It's a little like show biz: you play the same role for years and then you get typecast. It can be difficult for people to believe that you can play a different role. To move on to new challenges, you have to negotiate into the new job by offering seemingly unrelated skills as an added benefit to the employer. The key to these negotiations is "positioning" yourself.

## Positioning

Simply put, positioning yourself means stating your skills and qualities in a way that makes it easy for the prospective employer to see you in the position that is open or in other positions down the road.

You may want to stay in your present company. In that case, you are positioning yourself to the person in charge of hiring for the particular department you want to enter. Or, you may want to go to a new company or even a new industry. In this case, you are positioning yourself to a new employer. Either way, the steps are the same:

1) Decide what skills and qualities your prospective employer wants.

2) Search your background to see where you have demonstrated skills that would apply.

3) Write a "position statement" and use it as the basis for your résumé.

4) Use the position statement to sell yourself in an interview.

Your position statement says it all. It should sell your ability, experience, and personality. It brings together all your accomplishments.

The rest of your résumé should support the position statement. For example, if the statement says that you're a financial wizard, the résumé had better support that. It's completely within your control to tell whatever story you want to tell. You can emphasize certain parts of your background and deemphasize others.

---

**You can get typecast.
To move on, you have to negotiate
into the new job . . . by "positioning" yourself.**

---

Thinking through your position statement is not easy, but it focuses your entire job hunt. It forces you to clarify the sales pitch you will use in interviews.

However, a position statement is *not* what many people put on their résumés. They say they want "a challenging job in a progressive and growth-oriented company that uses all my strengths and abilities." That doesn't say anything at all, and it doesn't do you any good.

Let's consider a few examples of statements that *will* work for you:

## Pursuing the Dream Job

Jane, a client-relationship manager at a major bank, has handled high-net-worth clients for more than twenty years. She is taking early retirement and thinking about a second career. Two directions interest her: one, a job similar to what she has done but in a smaller bank; or, the job of her dreams—working as one of the top administrative people for a high-net-worth family (such as the Rockefellers), handling their business office and perhaps doing some of the things that involve her hobbies over the years: staffing and decorating.

If Jane were to continue on her current career path and go for a position as a relationship manager at a smaller bank, she would highlight the years she has worked at the bank. Her position statement, if used in her résumé, would look like this:

*Everything comes if a man will only wait. I've brought myself by long meditation to the conviction that a human being with a settled purpose must accomplish it, and that nothing can resist a will that will stake even existence for its fulfillment.*
Benjamin Disraeli

Over 20 years handling all aspects of fiduciary relationships for Premier-Bank's private banking clients. Successfully increased revenue through new business efforts, client cultivation, and account assessment. Consistently achieved fee increases. Received regular bonus awards.

However, to pursue her "dream" job, Jane's regular résumé won't do. She has to "reposition" herself to show that her experience fits what her prospective employer needs. Her position statement would read like this:

Administrative manager with broad experience in running operations. In-depth work with accountants, lawyers, agents, and so on. Over 20 years' experience handling all aspects of fiduciary relationships for PremierBank's private banking clients (overall net worth of $800 million). Expert in all financial arrangements (trust and estate accounts, asset management, non-profit, and tenant shareholder negotiations).

Her résumé would focus on her work *outside* of PremierBank because these activities would interest her prospective employer: first, her work with the high-class apartment building of which she was president for fourteen years, and then the post she held for ten years as treasurer of a nonprofit organization. Finally, Jane would highlight the work she had done at PremierBank that would be of interest to her prospective employer, such as the account on which she saved a client $300,000 in taxes.

### Ready to Take Charge

Robert had worked in every area of benefits administration. Now he would like to head up the entire benefits administration area—a move to management. His positioning statement:

14 years' experience in design and administration of all areas of employee benefit plans, including five years with Borgash Benefits Consultants. Advised some of the largest and most prestigious companies in the country. Excellent training and communications skills. MBA in Finance. An effective manager who delivers consistent results.

### From Supporting to Selling

Jack wants to move into sales after being in marketing support. He has been an executive in the sales promotion area, so his position statement stresses his marketing as well as his management experience:

10 years' progressive marketing and managerial experience. Devise superior marketing strategies through qualitative analysis and product repositioning. Skillful at completing the difficult internal sale, coupled with the ability to attract business and retain clients. Built strong relationships with the top consulting firms. A team player with an enthusiastic approach to top-level challenges.

Notice how he packages his experience running a marketing department as sales. His pitch will be, "It's even more difficult to sell inside because, in order to keep my job, I have to get other people in my company to use my marketing services. I have to do a good job, or they won't use me again."

Jack lacked a position statement on former résumés. If you do not have a position statement, then your position, by default, is the last position you held. With this statement, however, the employer would receive the résumé and say, "Ah-ha! Just what we need—a salesperson!"

### Making a Career Change

Elliott had been in sports marketing years ago, and had enjoyed it tremendously. However, he had spent the past four years in the mortgage industry, and was having a hard time getting back into sports marketing.

The sports people saw him as a career changer—and they saw him as an mortgage man. Even when he explained that marketing mortgages is the same as marketing sports, people did not believe him. He was being positioned by his most recent experience, which was handicapping him.

When a job hunter wants to change industries—or go back to an old industry—he cannot let his most recent position act as a handicap.

For example, if a person has always been in pharmaceuticals marketing, and now wants to do marketing in another industry, the résumé should be rewritten to make it generic marketing, and most references to pharmaceuticals should be removed.

In Elliott's case, the summary in the new résumé helps a great deal to bring his old work experience right to the top of the résumé. In addition, Elliott has removed the word "mortgage" from the description of his most recent job, his title at the mortgage company now stands out more than the company name, and he has gotten rid of company and industry jargon, such as the job title of segment director, because it is not something easily understood outside of his company.

Notice that the description of what Elliott did for the mortgage business is now written generically—it can apply to the marketing of *any* product. With his new résumé, Elliott had no trouble speaking to people in the sports industry. They no longer saw his most recent experience as a handicap, and he soon had a terrific job as head of marketing for a prestigious sporting-goods company.

If you want to move into a new industry or profession, state what you did generically so people will not see you as tied to the old.

### Bring Something to the Party

When it comes down to negotiating yourself into a new position, seemingly unrelated skills from former positions may actually help you get the job.

For example, some of my background had been in accounting and computers when I decided to go into counseling. My CFO (chief financial officer) experience helped me ease into that career. I applied at a ninety-person career counseling company and agreed to be their CFO for a while—provided I was also assigned clients to counsel. They wanted a cost-accounting system, so my ability to do that for them was what I "brought to the party." I was willing to give the

company something they wanted (my business experience) in exchange for doing something I really wanted to do (counseling executives).

Combining the new with the old, rather than jumping feet first into something completely new, is often the best way to move your career in a different direction. You gain the experience you need in the new field without having to enter at the entry level. Equally important, it is less stressful because you are using some of your old strengths while you build new ones.

Coming from a background different from the field you are targeting can also give you a bargaining chip. If you are looking at an area where you have no experience, you will almost certainly be competing with people who do have experience. You can separate yourself from the competition by saying, "I'm different. I have the skills to do this job, and I can also do other things that these people can't do." It works!

Our book, *Building a Great Résumé,* contains dozens and dozens of additional positioning (summary) statements. In addition, you will see how the positioning statements are used to set the tone for the rest of the résumé.

**Elliott's positioning (summary) statement is on the next page.**

---

("Before" Résumé)

## Elliott Jones

421 Morton Street                                                                 Chase Fortune, KY 23097

**Sears Mortgage Company**                                                               **1987 - present**
**Vice President, Segment Director, Shelter Business**
- Director of $4.6-billion residential-mortgage business for the largest mortgage lender in the nation.
- Organized and established regional marketing division for largest mortgage lender in nation, a business which included first and second mortgages, and mortgage life insurance.

**SportsLife Magazine**                                                                       1985 - 1987
Publisher and Editor
- Published and edited the largest consumer health and fitness magazine and increased circulation 175%.

and so on. . .

---

("After" Résumé)

## Elliott Jones

421 Morton Street                                                                 Chase Fortune, KY 23097

### Summary of Qualifications

Fifteen-plus years of domestic and international senior management experience in the **leisure/sporting goods industry**; multi-brand expertise specializing in marketing, new business development, strategic planning, and market research.

Proven record of identifying customer segments, developing differentiable product platforms, communication strategies, sales management, share growth, and profit generation.

### Business Experience

Sears Mortgage Company                                                                   1987 - present
**VICE PRESIDENT, BUSINESS DIRECTOR**
**Residential Real Estate Business**

- Business Director of a $4.6-billion business. Managed strategic planning, marketing, product development, and compliance.

- Consolidated four regional business entities into one; doubled product offerings. Grew market share 150 basis points and solidified #1 market position.

- Developed and executed nationally recognized consumer and trade advertising, public relations, and direct-response programs.

- Structured a product development process which integrated product introductions into the operations and sales segments of the business.

- Organized and established regional marketing division for largest mortgage lender in nation, a business which included first and second mortgages, and mortgage life insurance.

**SPORTSLIFE MAGAZINE**                                                                       1985 - 1987
**Publisher and Editor**

- Published and edited the largest consumer health and fitness magazine and increased circulation 175%.
and so on. . .

---

© 1996, Kate Wendleton and The Five O'Clock Club®

The Five O'Clock Club®

# Elizabeth Ghaffari: A Résumé Case Study

*Concentrate your strength against your competitor's relative weakness.*
Bruce Henderson,
*Henderson on Corporate Strategy*

Every résumé has a pitch—although it may not be what the job hunter wants it to be. In scanning Elizabeth's "before" résumé, we can easily see that she has had communications and advertising positions in a number of computer companies. That's the total extent of her pitch. When she went on interviews, managers commented: "You sure have worked for a lot of computer companies." Her résumé read like a job description: she wrote press releases, product brochures, employee newsletters, and so on.

Thousands of people can write press releases, so citing those skills will not separate Elizabeth from her competition. But we can get to know her better if she tells us about specific accomplishments.

Elizabeth agreed to do the Seven Stories Exercise. She didn't feel like writing down "the things she enjoyed doing and also did well" because she felt as though she kept doing the same things again and again in every company for which she worked, and she enjoyed them all. Still, I urged her to be specific—details can make a résumé more interesting. And working on the Seven Stories Exercise is a sure way to develop a strong overall message.

She started with an experience on a job early in her career. She had thought of a terrific idea: her company's product could be sold through the same computer systems that were used to sell airline tickets and car and hotel reservations. She convinced the company to let her go ahead with the idea, promoted it to travel agents across the country, and also to the salespeople in her own company. It was so successful, it became the standard way to sell foreign currencies when people were going on a trip.

Most job hunters tend to ignore accomplishments that took place when they were young. But if you had accomplishments early in your career, they may be worth relating because they let the reader know that you have always been a winner.

I said, "That sounds great. Where is it on your résumé?" Elizabeth said: "Well, it's not said exactly that way . . . " Many times job hunters are constricted when they write their résumés, but the Seven Stories Exercise can free them up to express things differently. So we restated that accomplishment.

Elizabeth then worked on another story. She had participated in a conference that had "generated 450 letters of intent."

I said: "It's nice the conference generated 450 letters of intent. But from what you said, I can't tell that you had anything to do with those results, and I don't know if 450 is good or not. Tell me more about it."

Elizabeth said: "There were only 1500 participants in the conference, and 450 letters of intent is a lot because our product is very expensive. I had a lot to do with those results because I developed an aura of excitement about the product by putting teasers under everyone's hotel door every morning.

"And before the conference, I had sent five weekly teasers to everyone who planned to attend. For example, one week, I sent each person a bottle of champagne. This direct-mail campaign had everyone talking about us before the convention started. People were asking one another whether or not they had gotten our mailers. When they got to the convention and found teasers under their doors, they were eager to come to our booth.

"I also trained the teams of employees who were demonstrating the product at the convention. I made sure that each demonstrator delivered the same message."

Now I understood how Elizabeth had played a major part in generating those letters of intent.

Next we needed to think of the message behind this accomplishment. Was her message that she could stick mailers under doors? Or send out bottles of champagne? No, her message was that she knew how to launch a product, and that's what we put on her résumé as the main point for that accomplishment.

In her "before" résumé, Elizabeth said that she wrote press releases and did direct-mail campaigns. Her "after" résumé gives us some examples of what she accomplished with those efforts, and gives us a feel for her ingenuity and hard work.

### The Summary

After we reviewed all of her accomplishments, we tackled the summary. What was the most important point Elizabeth wanted to get across? It wasn't just that she could write press releases and speeches, or do direct-mail campaigns.

She had to think hard about this. The most important thing was that Elizabeth was a key member of the management team. She sat in on meetings when the company was discussing bringing out a new product, or planning how to handle a possible crisis. Elizabeth would not be happy—or effective—in a job where she simply wrote press releases. She needed to be part of the strategy sessions.

What you put on your résumé can both include you and exclude you. A company that does not want the communications person included in those meetings would not be interested in Elizabeth—but then, she wouldn't be interested in them either.

In her summary, instead of highlighting the companies she had worked for, Elizabeth highlighted the industries represented by those companies. She listed Information Services and High-Tech first, because they represented areas of greater growth than Financial Services did.

Elizabeth was—and wanted to be again—a corporate strategist, a crisis manager, and a spokesperson for the corporation. That's how we positioned her.

In every summary in this book (and in *Building a Great Résumé*), the reader can tell something about the writer's personality. It is not enough that someone knows what you have done, they also need to know your style in doing it. For example, a person who had run a department and doubled productivity could have done it in a nasty, threatening way, or could have motivated people to do more, instituted training programs, and encouraged workers to come up with suggestions for improving productivity. Your style matters.

Look at this case study. Because you have done the Seven Stories Exercise, you should be able to come up with accomplishments that will interest your reader. Let him or her know what to expect from you if you are hired.

In Elizabeth's case, we hope the hiring manager will look at her résumé and say: "That's exactly what I need: a corporate strategist who knows how to handle crises, and can also serve as a spokesperson for us."

This is the response you want the reader to have: "That's exactly the person I need!" Look at your résumé. What words pop out? Is this how you want to be seen? If not, let's get going.

After you have worked hard on your résumé, use your summary to develop your brief verbal pitch to be used in interviews and the summary statement in your cover letters. You will see lots of examples of these in *Building a Great Résumé* .

## ELIZABETH GHAFFARI

207 Dobbs Ferry
Phoenix, AZ 44444

Home:  (609) 555-6666

---

## EXPERIENCE

**ORANGE COMPUTER SYSTEMS**                                    1988 - Present
<u>Director Corporate Communications</u>

Plan and supervise all corporate communications staff and activities for diversified financial information services company on a global basis.

- Develop, direct and implement global media, public relations, and internal-communications programs in support of corporate and sales objectives, working closely with executive management team.

- Direct all media-relations activities related to new product introductions and product enhancements; initiate media contacts; respond to press inquiries; coordinate and conduct interviews; and develop all press materials.

- Develop and direct advertising and promotional literature activities, overseeing all corporate publications, including corporate and product brochures, sales materials, and customer and employee newsletters.

**ELECTRONIC DATA SYSTEMS**                                    1986 - 1988
<u>Manager,</u> Advertising and Promotion

Developed and implemented marketing and promotion strategies for Reuters and its North American subsidiaries.

- Worked with market and product managers to identify opportunities for product and sales promotions and new product development for multiple market segments. Conducted market research, developed marketing strategies and implemented tactical plans (e.g. direct response marketing and sales incentive programs).

- Responsible for planning biannual securities analyst meetings and communication product information to investors and industry analysts.

- Orchestrated six product introductions during three-month period, including public-relations activities, promotional literature and training materials.

- Responsible for forecasting and maintaining $4.0 million budget.

- Managed corporate and product advertising programs, hiring and working with various agencies.

## CREDIT LYONNAIS
### Corporate Investment Officer and Product Manager

1984 - 1986

Planned and directed the sales and promotion efforts for the bank's corporate and correspondent sales staff for a variety of products including foreign exchange and precious metals.

- Developed active and profitable business relationships with correspondent banks for sale of precious metals and foreign exchange products.

- Established and developed new account relationships. Brought in eleven new corporate accounts which produced significant business in precious metals and foreign exchange trading areas.

- Managed market study to identify size, segments and opportunities of various markets. Prepared analysis and recommendations for new product development and trading vehicles.

## WASSERELLA & BECKTON
### Director of Marketing

1979 - 1984

Managed all activities of the Marketing Department, including product development, sales promotion, advertising and public relations activities for diversified financial services company.

- Conceptualized and developed national marketing strategy for foreign exchange services offered to travel industry professionals via automated airline reservation systems.

- Developed and implemented business plans for a variety of products, including responsibility for product positioning, pricing, contracts, advertising and promotional materials.

- Promoted from Foreign Exchange Trader to Marketing Representative to Director of Marketing in three years.

## EDUCATION

B.A., Psychology, University of Phoenix

1979

# ELIZABETH GHAFFARI

207 Dobbs Ferry
Phoenix, AZ 44444

Residence: (609) 555-6666
Work: (493) 345-7777

---

## CORPORATE COMMUNICATIONS EXECUTIVE
### with 14 years' experience in

- **High-Tech**     • **Information Services**     • **Financial Services**

#### Experience includes:

- **Global Media and Investor Relations**
- **Customer Videos and Newsletters**
- **Advertising/Promotional Literature**
- **Employee Newsletters**
- **Employee Roundtables/Awards Programs**
- **Speech-Writing/Papers/Public Speaking**

- <u>**A corporate strategist and key member of the management team**</u> with extensive knowledge of financial markets.

- <u>**A crisis manager**</u>: bringing common sense, organizational skills, and a logical decision-making process to solving sensitive, time-critical problems.

- <u>**A spokesperson for the corporation**</u>: developing and communicating key corporate messages accurately and convincingly, under deadline pressure, to multiple audiences including employees, the media, customers and investors.

**Proven team leader and problem solver with highly developed
analytical, organizational, communications, and strategic planning skills.**

---

### ORANGE COMPUTER SYSTEMS
1988 - Present

#### <u>Director, Corporate Communications</u>

- Gained extensive positive media coverage in conjunction with launch of company's first product for new market segment.
  - Planned and conducted <u>**media events in 8 countries**</u>.
  - Resulted in <u>**positive stories in 30 major publications**</u> and trade press: *The Wall Street Journal, The New York Times, Barron's, The Financial Times, Forbes,* and various foreign publications.
  - A first for the company, <u>**positive TV coverage in the United States**</u>: CNN, CNBC, <u>**and Europe**</u>: Sky Financial Television, Business Daily, The City Programme.

- Successfully <u>**avoided communications crisis**</u>, gained positive press coverage and customer support when company sold a major division. Within a 60-day period:
  - Planned and managed all aspects of a <u>**13-city, interactive teleconference**</u>.
  - Developed all written materials including various employee and customer communications, background materials and press releases.
  - Wrote speeches for six executives including both company presidents (present and acquiring companies).
  - Wrote and produced an extensive question-and-answer document covering <u>**union, compensation and benefits issues and business rational.**</u>
  - Selected and trained staff representatives for each of 13 cities.

---

**ORANGE COMPUTER SYSTEMS**, contd.
<u>**Director, Corporate Communications**</u>, contd.

- Developed and implemented <u>**company's first employee awards program**</u> for service excellence.
  - Honored employees who participated in planning sessions.
  - <u>**Led to changes in key areas**</u> including improvements in software manufacturing efficiencies, shortening of the product development cycle, and improved employee morale.

- <u>**Introduced desk-top publishing**</u> program for in-house production of all promotional materials and various customer and employee newsletters.
  - <u>**Reduced outside services expense by 75%.**</u>
  - Created new <u>**corporate standards manual**</u> and reorganized promotional literature system to replace inconsistent product literature.

- Conducted group and individual <u>**employee meetings**</u> to gain and disseminate critical information in identifying and resolving employee-relations problems.

- Prepared quarterly management reports and written/oral presentations to top management and employees to describe corporate accomplishments compared to goals.

- Managed all customer/media/employee communications for sale of three business units.


**ELECTRONIC DATA SYSTEMS**                                              1986 - 1988
<u>**Manager, Advertising and Promotion**</u>

- Prepared written and oral <u>**presentations to boards of directors**</u> and senior managers on various services, concepts and results.

- Planned <u>**product launch**</u> and company participation in global foreign exchange conference. Successful product launch resulted in <u>**generating 450 letters of intent from 1500 participants**</u>. Assured successful product introduction:
  - Developed 5-week <u>**direct-mail campaign**</u> to stimulate interest and create an aura of excitement around product prior to conference. Campaign continued at conference with daily newsletter and door stuffer.
  - Maximized impact of <u>**product demonstrations**</u> through use of compelling visual presentation and environment.
  - <u>**Trained teams**</u> of product demonstrators to assure that information regarding benefits and features would be delivered in consistent way.

- Strengthened company relationships with <u>**industry analysts and investors**</u> by arranging product demonstrations in conjunction with bi-annual industry analyst meetings. Demonstrations stimulated interest and <u>**gained support for strategic direction from investor community**</u> by communicating important strategic and product information.
  - Selected products to be demonstrated, developed promotional materials, organized display area, selected and trained product demonstrators to assure delivery of consistent corporate message.

**CREDIT LYONNAIS**                                             1984 - 1986
Product Manager

- Established and developed new account relationships.
  - Brought in **11 new corporate accounts during 10-month period** producing significant business in precious metals and foreign exchange trading areas.


**WASSERELLA & BECKTON**                                        1979 - 1984
Director of Marketing

- **Developed breakthrough idea to sell** foreign exchange services (currency and travelers' checks) through travel agents the same way hotel space and airline tickets are sold
  **— via automated airline reservation systems.**

  - Sold concept to senior management and **negotiated contracts with three major airlines**.
  - Developed sales and operational procedures. **Hired and trained 10-person sales and operations staff.**
  - **Promoted concept to travel agents** across the country through industry trade shows and sales program.


**EDUCATION**

B.A., Psychology, University of Phoenix, 1979

*There are going to be no survivors.*
*Only big winners and the dead.*
*No one is going to just squeak by.*
Ronald Compton, CEO,
Aetna Insurance Company

---

*Few executives yet know how to ask:*
*What information do I need to do my job?*
*When do I need it?*
*And from whom should I be getting it?*
Peter F. Drucker,
"Be Data Literate—Know What to Know,"
*The Wall Street Journal*, December 1, 1992

---

*Natural talent, intelligence, a wonderful education—*
*none of these guarantees success. Something else is*
*needed: the sensitivity to understand what other*
*people want and the willingness to give it to them.*
*Worldly success depends on pleasing others.*
*No one is going to win fame, recognition, or*
*advancement just because he or she thinks it's*
*deserved. Someone else has to think so too.*
John Luther

## Why Is Research Important?

Research can help you decide which field to go into and is a solid way to develop a list of your target companies. Then you can decide how to contact them and can measure your progress against this list. Research will improve your networking and interviewing skills, and increase your confidence during interviews. You will create a good impression, and look like an insider rather than like someone who is trying to break in. Research will give you an edge over your competition and help you decide which company to join.

## Library Research

Find a university or big-city library that's conveniently located and has an extensive business collection. You will not be completely on your own: librarians are often expert at helping job hunters, so plan to spend some time with the business reference librarian. Be specific. Tell the librarian what you want to accomplish. I always say, "The librarian is your friend." I personally love libraries. I was a librarian in both high school and college. Get comfortable with the environment. Spend time using the reference books. Photocopy articles you can read at home.

Be prepared for the probability that the library will not look as it used to: many card catalogues have been replaced by computer terminals. If electronic information is a new technology for you, do not be intimidated. Ask for assistance. Computer-aided research will make your work immeasurably faster, easier, and more accurate. Let it work for you.

## How I Research

For most of my job hunts, I have **set aside at least two full days strictly for library research**. If I'm not sure of the industry I want to pursue, I may spend two days just researching industries (or professions). One of my favorite sources is the *Encyclopedia of Business Information Sources*. It lists topics, such as "oil" or "clubs" or "finance" or "real estate." Under each topic, it lists the most important sources of information on that topic: periodicals, books, and associations. Using this tool, I can quickly research any field in depth. I also may read the U.S. Department of Labor's reports on various industries or professions.

Once I have selected tentative industries, I may want to network to find out the buzzwords, and to refine my pitch. In addition, networking at this point may uncover other tentative targets, which I may simply add to my list of targets, or I may research at this time.

While networking, I may find someone who will give me a list of people in that field—perhaps an association membership list. Or perhaps someone will invite me to an association meeting and I can get a list there. Otherwise, I could buy the subscriber list from a trade magazine. Or I may need to spend time in the library to gather the list of companies. I may use an industry directory or the local business publication which provides listings of companies.

I have had a lot of success using directories on CD-ROM databases. It cuts my library time in half. By the way, don't let the term "database" intimidate or confuse you. Any collection of information with an organized arrangement can be called a database. Even your phone book could be considered a database, for that matter.

## Taking Notes

When I am conducting my research using a computer in the library, usually I can select the information I need by zip code, industry, company size, and so on. In addition, I can print the information simply by pressing a button.

Othewise, I use standard letter-size sheets to copy down the company name, address, phone number, size (number of employees and sales), and other relevant information (such as business type if I am not familiar with the company). Then I list the names and titles of all the people I think I may want to contact.

I make note of three to five people in larger organizations who are two levels higher than I am, and perhaps the names of one or two in smaller organizations. *Many* people in one organization may be in a position to hire or recommend you. In larger companies, often the manager of one group has no idea that another manager may consider developing a new position or replacing someone.

If I am uncomfortable writing to all three to five people at once, I write to one or two, wait for rejection letters, and then write to a few more. People listed in general directories have a lot of people writing to them because their names are so readily available. Therefore, I often use a targeted mailing, which takes more research per company but increases the number of meetings I get.

In a smaller organization, such as a company of two hundred people or less, the company head is likely to know of all potential openings. Who is in charge of the job openings? The president? Perhaps the general manager? I note both names so I can write to both at once, or one first and the other later. Although names in smaller companies are tougher to come by, these people don't get as many letters as people in larger companies.

If I feel I am able to work in many industries, I get a sense of those that are growing and also fit my needs. I make a long list of the companies that interest me. I call each one for an annual report or company literature (I can easily call thirty companies in half an hour or so). Then I find articles on each industry or company.

My effort is only as good as my list. (One job hunter had a list of sixty companies. But most were out of state and he had no intention of relocating. Only eight were within his geographic target.)

I make sure my list contains companies I am at least somewhat interested in. Then I'll know I am contacting eight good names—not sixty that aren't worth my time. If I know the real size of my target—and it is small—I may decide to contact them with a different technique, such as a targeted mailing with a follow-up phone call.

## What I Do with My Lists

Armed with my list of companies, I have lots of choices. If my target market is large, I may conduct a direct-mail campaign. Or I may divide up my list, do a direct mailing to sixty companies, and a targeted mailing to twenty companies (with follow-up phone calls), and network into a few companies. Or I could network around and ask for specific advice about the companies on my list: which are the good ones, which ones seem right for me, could they recommend others, do they know the names of the people I should contact at these companies, and may I use their name?

I also get the names of companies through magazine articles that cover certain industries, or through networking interviews with people who know that industry. I've also done "research" by going to meetings where the speaker or the attendees were people who should know people in my targeted area.

However I get the names of the people or companies, I use a computer to access a few CD-ROM databases to obtain some more in-depth information. This makes my letters and/or networking meetings much more compelling. Which databases I use depends on the information I am seeking. In the next chapter you will find information on the most well-known, as well as many obscure, automated, electronic tomes.

## Where Else Can You Find Information?

• Personal observations. When you go for an interview, observe everything around you. What are the people like? What are they wearing? How well do they seem to get along?

Ask people: How do you like it here? How long have you worked here? Get there early. Ask everyone you see—the receptionist, people in the bathroom, the person who gets you coffee. This will give you a real feel for what it's like to work there, and will also let you know what the turnover rate is. If everyone says they've been there three or four months, you can be sure you'll be there only three or four months. Don't depend on the interviewer as your sole source of information about the company.

• Associations. Associations are an important source of information. If you don't know anything at all about an industry or field, associations are often the place to start. They tend to be very helpful, and will assist you in getting the jargon down so you can use the language of the trade. *The Encyclopedia of Associations* lists a group for whatever you are interested in. If you are interested in the rug business, there's a related association.

Call them. If they have lots of local chapters, chances are there's one near you, and it will be a great place to network. Call the headquarters, and ask them to send you information and tell you the name of the person to contact in your area. Then call that person, and say you are interested in the association and would like to attend its next meeting. If there is no local chapter in your area, associations can still send you information.

Associations usually have membership directories, which they will sell you. They often publish trade magazines and newspapers that can update you on the business, for instance by noting the important issues facing the industry and telling who's been hired and who's moving. (Perhaps you should try to talk to the people you read about). They may even have a library or research department, or a PR person you can talk to. Often they sell books related to the field.

An association's annual convention is a very quick way to become educated in a field. These conventions are not cheap (they run from hundreds to thousands), but you will hear speakers on the urgent topics in the field, pick up literature, and meet lots of people.

Join an organization related to the field that interests you. Networking is expected. When you meet someone you think may help you, ask if you can meet on a more formal basis for about half an hour.

You can write to members, or network at meetings. If you want to contact them all, you can either continue to network or conduct a direct-mail campaign.

Associations are such an important source of information—especially about the jobs of the future—that they are covered in even greater detail in the next chapter.

• <u>The press.</u> Read newspapers with your target in mind, and you will see all kinds of things you would not otherwise have seen. Contact the author of an article in a trade magazine. Tell him or her how much you enjoyed the article and what you are trying to do, and ask to get together just to chat. I've made many friends this way.

• <u>Mailing lists</u> are not that expensive. You will pay perhaps $100 for several thousand names—selected by certain criteria, such as job title, level, industry, size of company, and so on. You can rent lists from direct-mail houses or magazines. For example, one job hunter contacted a computer magazine and got the names and addresses by selected zip codes of companies that owned a specific kind of computer. It was then easy for him to contact all of the companies in his geographic area that could possibly use his skills.

• <u>Chambers of Commerce</u>. If you are doing an out-of-town job search, call them for a list of companies in their area.

• <u>Universities</u> have libraries or research centers on fields of interest. A professor may be an expert in a field in which you are interested. Contact him or her.

• <u>Networking</u> is a great research tool. At the beginning of your search, network with peers to find out about a field or industry. When you are really ready to get a job, network with people two levels higher than you are.

• <u>The Yellow Pages</u> is a useful source of companies in your local area.

• <u>Databases</u>. A CD-ROM database is an organized arrangement of data that is contained on a compact disk. This is important because:
1. One disk can hold several volumes worth of printed material. For example, the Encyclopedia of Associations is comprised of thirteen volumes. That would fill a couple of bookshelves. However, all thirteen of these volumes are contained on *one* CD!

2. Information can be updated much more frequently on a CD. Publishers can and do release current information on a quarterly basis that is simply "down-loaded" onto a disk. Contrast this with print volumes that have to be reprinted and republished, which can take years. By the time that happens, the new information is often already out of date.

3. You can access and retrieve desired information in a fraction of a second when using CD technology. You simply type into the computer terminal the "key-word" you want to look up. Any information that contains that key-word is presented to you almost instantly. On the other hand, when you use printed works, the job of searching for specific pieces of related information can be.very time-consuming.

## Get Sophisticated About Using Reference Materials

In the next chapter, Wendy Alfus Rothman, a career counselor with The Five O'Clock Club, provides an in-depth examination of how to use specific research resources in all phases of your job search. Her actual case studies show how creative use of the dazzling array of reference works available today has helped real people make great career moves.

In the chapter after that, Patricia Raufer, a member of The Five O'Clock Club, tells you "How to Use the Internet as a Job-Search Tool."

# List of Companies to Contact

> List companies within this industry and the names of the people you want to contact at each company.

For Target _____:
Geographic area: _____
Industry or company size: _____
Position/Function: _____

| Company Name, Address, Phone | Contacts and Titles | Date & Method | Inter-view Date | Follow-up Dates |
|---|---|---|---|---|
| | | | | |
| | | | | |
| | | | | |
| | | | | |
| | | | | |
| | | | | |
| | | | | |
| | | | | |
| | | | | |
| | | | | |
| | | | | |
| | | | | |
| | | | | |
| | | | | |
| | | | | |
| | | | | |

Contact Method:      N = Networking;      D = Direct Mail;      S = Search firm;      A = Advertisement;
O = Other;      Also show "R" if résumé given.      Make multiple copies of this page for your search.

# Research Resources for an Effective Job Search

by Wendy Alfus Rothman

*Wisdom is the principal thing; therefore get wisdom:
and with all thy getting get understanding. Exalt her,
and she shall promote thee: she shall bring thee to
honour, when thou dost embrace her.*
Proverbs 4: 7-8

*And no grown-up will ever
understand that this is a matter of
so much importance!*
Antoine de Saint-Exupéry,
*The Little Prince*

*Research is to see what everybody
has seen and to think what nobody else has thought.*
Albert Szent-Gyorgyi,
*American biochemist*

I f you are like most job hunters, you may have gotten stuck in one or more parts of your job search. You are probably wishing for some magic potion to get you moving again, and in a more productive way.

Research can be the answer. Try to set aside the common notion that research sounds tedious and boring. This is why most people skip it. But they are missing out. You will be at a great advantage if you learn to use this most valuable tool.

Maybe you need help in targeting the right field or industry: you already know what you do well, but you can't turn that information into targets.

Or maybe you need help setting up informational meetings: you just don't know what to say to people that doesn't sound like "job begging." (You know what job begging is: it's when you call your contacts intending to sound intelligent, low-key, and professional, and you end up saying, "So do you know of *any* job openings that might be good for me?")

Or perhaps you wish you were better prepared for an interview so that you could feel confident in your ability to differentiate yourself and rise above your competition. Perhaps you are not sure how to follow up after an interview in order to keep the process moving along.

Whatever phase of the search cycle you are in (phase 1: defining targets and companies within those targets; phase 2: interviewing; or phase 3: negotiating and closing), it's highly likely that you wish you had fresh questions to ask others, and fresh answers to the same old questions others ask you.

That is exactly what research is all about. It is the fastest way to turn a mediocre job search into a powerful, proactive campaign. It gives you the information that drives your search to its destination. It will magnify the results of each step of the job-search process. It is the way to get unstuck from a stalled or stagnating search. (And research can help you keep your job once you have it!)

There are two kinds of research: primary and secondary. Primary research basically means

*The will to persevere is often the
difference between failure and success.*
David Sarnoff, *Wisdom of Sarnoff and the World of RCA*

talking to people, while secondary research means reading materials in print. You need to do both kinds. It is usually wise to do some secondary research before you start talking to people so that your questions are more intelligent and focused.

If you take the time to do this, you will feel more confident and empowered, and people will usually respond better. If you are a person who prefers book work to people work, be careful that you do not spend all your time reading. The point is to take the information you learn, and use it in your conversations with people who can move you closer to your goal of obtaining the job that is right for you.

The biggest problem in doing secondary research is that there is so much information available. And there are a multitude of ways to access the information—from the traditional to the futuristic.

There are reference books, directories and guides, trade journals and newspapers, CD-ROM databases, online databases and electronic information transfer. The task can seem overwhelming.

But it doesn't have to be. There is a way to systematically move through the process, beginning with obtaining big-picture industry information, then moving on to company information, then on to job and salary information.

Some of the research tools mentioned in this section will be available to you, others will not. But don't worry. There is so much out there that if one channel is not available to you, another one will be.

Start by identifying what you want to know. Each stage of the job-search process has its own set of questions, and therefore its own corresponding research tools. Let's begin at the beginning.

## PHASE 1:
### Identifying Targets

In Phase 1 of a job search, you are trying to identify industry targets. First, you do a skills assessment to analyze what you do well and what you like to do. Then the idea is to turn that

knowledge into something that is useful to your search campaign.

Many people get stuck here for a time. Hoping and praying (a popular technique) won't get you unstuck. What *will* get you unstuck is gathering relevant information to help you make a systematic decision.

Here is the information you should be looking for when selecting industry targets:

1) trends and future prospects in a particular industry;

2) areas of growth and decline in that industry;

3) the kinds of challenges the industry faces that could utilize your skills;

4) the "culture" of the industry;

5) the major- medium- and minor-league companies in the industry.

After you get this information, you can begin to determine whether or not you are in sync with a particular industry and whether or not there is a place for you there. It does not require an enormous amount of time and data to begin to address these questions. You really only need a little bit of information, but it has to be the *right* little bit.

One of the first things I suggest to my clients is that they go to the library (almost any library will do for this), and look through **The Encyclopedia of Associations**, published by Gale Research in Detroit, Michigan. This encyclopedia lists a staggering total of 22,000 associations that represent trade and industry groups.

Every industry and almost every niche within that industry is represented here. Thus it is an incredible way to brainstorm possible industry targets. You really begin to get a sense of what you don't know, and what you could find out.

In addition to stimulating fresh ideas, the encyclopedia also provides names of contacts and chief officers, addresses of headquarters, phone numbers, the number of members and chapters, special committees and departments, a description of membership, the aims and activities of the group.

The people who are listed here are people who normally welcome your inquiries—otherwise they wouldn't have their names in the encyclopedia! They are often more than helpful if you phone and ask them to share some information about their industry.

Also listed in the encyclopedia are publications that are a terrific source of information. They can introduce you to industry jargon, issues of importance, authors of significance in the field, and companies that are making news. They also usually have their own section of classified ads that do not typically appear in newspapers.

Another thing that is valuable from this resource is that most associations publish a four-year convention schedule that you can call and request. These schedules include an explanation of panel-discussion groups and conference workshops. They give a sense of what topics have been important in an industry over the past few years.

You can also take note of who led the discussions and workshops, thereby discovering who plays or played a role in shaping the industry. **This resource should not be overlooked!**

There are many other ways to obtain big-picture information, as well. Let's take a look at some examples of real-life situations.

## CASE STUDY: THOMAS
*Turning an Assessment into a Target*

Many people don't even know what they don't know. After seventeen years as a very successful human-resources executive in government administration, Thomas thought he wanted to target the health-care industry, but he didn't really know much about it. He just knew that it was an important growth industry of the nineties. He figured that hospitals were large bureaucracies, similar to government agencies. Therefore he thought he would at least fit into the culture.

After doing an assessment, he realized that, ironically, one of the reasons he wanted to leave his job in the first place was that he actually didn't like working for a large bureaucracy. Now he really didn't know what to do. Rather than

helping him, he felt that his assessment had limited his options.

He had learned that he was happiest when he was helping and directing people. He had also discovered that he wanted to work for a smaller organization, but he had absolutely no idea what to do with this insight.

He decided to do some research. He went to a reference book called **The Encyclopedia of Medical Organizations and Agencies**. This directory lists more than 12,200 organizations and agencies and has 69 subject chapters.

Glancing through the Table of Contents, Thomas realized that health care didn't mean just big hospitals. It could also mean HMO administration, biotechnology, environmental medicine, reproductive medicine, elder care, substance abuse and corporate employee-assistance programs, sports medicine, or many other areas.

By realizing what he hadn't known, he was able to begin to more clearly define his target. And this was just from reading a Table of Contents!

Next, Thomas discovered CD-ROM (Compact Disk Read-Only-Memory) databases. These disks contain highly topical and specialized information that one can access in a fraction of the time it would take to access the same material in its printed form.

The one Thomas chose was **CD Plus/Health**. It is an index to the nonclinical aspects of health-care delivery. These include administration and planning of health-care facilities, health insurance, personnel, HMO's, and related topics. Data are supplied from the National Library of Medicine, the American Hospital Association, and the printed Hospital Literature Index.

As Thomas learned more about the industry, he realized that Employee Assistance Programs (EAP's) are often set up as a business service to corporations through insurance companies. They operate as small business units, while being part of a larger organization—exactly the environment he had been looking for.

Thomas' human-resources and administrative skills would be transferable to these programs, and EAP's would definitely allow him to make a difference in people's lives.

Thomas had found a viable industry target that had both appeal and promise for his personality and background.

## CASE STUDY: JOAN
### Clarifying Her Career Direction

Joan was six years into her career as an attorney, fulfilling her parents' dream and what she had once thought was her dream as well. However, the twelve-hour days and six- to seven-day work weeks were taking their toll. She decided she wanted a change. Like many people, all Joan knew was what she *didn't* want to do. She did some research to alleviate her confusion.

First she browsed through the **U.S. Industrial Outlook**. This is a U.S. Department of Commerce publication that analyzes recent trends and forecasts for over 350 manufacturing and service industries. It is available in both printed and CD-ROM form.

It offers concise industry overviews, assesses international competitiveness, ranks the ten fastest- and ten slowest-growing manufacturing industries, lists trends in selected service industries, and projects the growth rates for 156 manufacturing industries and groups.

Joan also browsed through **Standard and Poor's Industry Surveys**. This reference book is updated quarterly. It consists of two volumes of up-to-date data for all major domestic industries. Prospects for a particular industry are followed by a historical presentation of trends and problems for that industry. Tables and charts accompany the text. Sales, earnings, and market data for the leading companies in an industry are provided.

As Joan researched, she read more and more about the high-technology industry. She began to see how much she had already known about this industry but had always taken for granted. And she realized how much she liked it. She had used many computer systems throughout her education, and continued to use them for her legal research and preparation of briefs.

She continued her secondary research, using the **ICP Software Directory** on CD-ROM. It is a directory with descriptions of more than 15,000 publicly available business-applications software from over 5,000 vendors for microcomputers, minicomputers, and mainframes. It also includes proprietary software products and vendor-contact information.

It became clear to Joan that the software industry was consolidating, with a great deal of acquisition activity. Her legal experience had been in the area of corporate acquisitions.

Research had helped Joan see a great opportunity to use this legal background as a launching pad to enter the arena of high-technology.

## Expanding Your Targets and Identifying Companies

Once you select an industry, you need to make sure that there are enough companies within that industry to warrant the efforts of an entire campaign. For example, if you find that there are only five small companies in your area, you will know before you begin that the odds are not in favor of your success.

Too many people get frustrated during their job search, thinking that they are doing something wrong, when the simple fact is that they do not have enough companies in their target.

If you see that your target is limited, you can make sure that your expectations are realistic. Instead of being depressed that your campaign isn't producing results, expand your target.

Expanding your target usually means identifying more than just the big companies that everyone else is targeting. It means identifying the mid-size and smaller ones—in fact, they are the ones that usually do most of the hiring.

This does more than expand your search; it also helps you understand each company's competitive position. Often this is actually more than the people working in the companies know. Sometimes they are so busy doing their jobs that they don't have time to stay current in their own industries!

After doing this kind of research, you become a person with valuable information to share, rather than just another person looking for a job (remember job begging?). Here are some questions appropriate at this point in your research with regard to each company on your list:

1) How large is this company?

2) Who owns it?

3) How long has it been in business?

4) What are its major products or services?

5) How many employees work there?

6) What are the revenues of the company?

7) How many branches does it have, and where are they located?

8) How many divisions are there, and which are the most profitable?

9) What are the names of the people that would be in a position to hire me?

Once you can answer these questions, you can prioritize the companies in your target as: most likely, possible, or long shots.

You can begin to strategize how to approach them for interviews: some through networking, some through direct contact and letter campaigns, some through search firms and headhunters, maybe some by answering ads.

You can see that without an extensive list of companies in your target industry, it would be extremely difficult to have six to ten things in the works. With the list, your problem may well be which six to ten things to pick first.

## CASE STUDY: SARAH
*Better Networking Through Research*

Sarah worked for a major cosmetics firm. She loved her job and the industry, but due to some internal politics, she decided she needed to change companies. She knew lots of people to call for networking.

When she called them, she would ask them if they knew of any job openings. They invariably told her no. Sarah grew more and more uncomfortable at the prospect of picking up the phone.

Instead, she went to **Ward's Business Directory of U.S. Private and Public Companies**. It profiles 100,000 companies and details their vital statistics. A special feature of Ward's Directory is that it includes companies with relatively small sales volumes.

The directory has information on private as well as public companies. It offers a ranking of companies, small to large, by sales volume within an industry.

All this gave Sarah a quick way to find a company's competitive place among its peers, and to target even further.

As she researched, Sarah realized how little she knew about other firms in her own industry—especially smaller ones. Using Ward's Directory, she was able to construct a list of ten mid-size cosmetics and health/beauty product firms that she felt were poised for growth.

Now when she called her network contacts, she asked their opinions about the viability of those firms. In addition to being impressed that she had done her homework, her friends knew something about the companies she had identified. They had opinions about which ones would fly and which ones would not. These friends were even able to introduce her to some people in several of the companies she had highlighted.

She learned what she needed to know. She never once had to ask about a specific job opening. Thus she eliminated the embarrassment that she used to feel in her networking.

Research was an empowering experience for Sarah. It enabled her to jump-start a stalled campaign.

---

## PHASE 2:
### Preparing for the Interview

One of the biggest errors job seekers make is not properly preparing for the interview. They read the books that give you "answers to difficult interview questions." But the problem is that everyone else has read those same books—including the people interviewing you!

It's pretty simple—the more you know about a company's issues and objectives prior to interviewing with them, the better prepared you will be and the better able to answer any question.

Most job seekers are busy worrying about their own issues and objectives. Be smart: focus on the problems of this particular company. After all, the reason a manager hires someone is that he or she believes that that person can help the firm in some specific way.

The manager is only interested in your issues if they provide evidence of your ability to solve company problems. This is true whether you are a receptionist or a CEO.

## CASE STUDY: GARY
### Becoming an Insider

Gary was interviewing at a major consumer-products company for a position as an organizational psychologist in the staffing area. This company was embarking on an enormous project to set up assessment centers to identify high-potential employees for succession planning.

Gary knew next to nothing about assessment centers, but he knew he had better change that situation fast. So off he went to the library.

He used a CD-ROM database called **ABI/ Inform**. Updated monthly, it indexes and abstracts 800 business and management journals appearing world-wide. These publications cover a wide variety of topics, including management, accounting, finance, economics, advertising, labor relations, and real estate.

Gary keyed in assessment centers. Up came a synopsis of all the articles that have been written about the subject for the past three years. Within thirty minutes, Gary became something of an expert on the history of assessment centers.

He learned about who first used them, their strengths and weaknesses, the "gurus" of the field, and what directions assessment centers will move in over the next few years. He learned the lingo, the history, and the players.

When Gary went back for his third interview, he ended up interviewing with *seventeen* people in that one day. Someone even followed him into the bathroom to keep the interview going! He

won them all over with his expertise in the matter of assessment centers. The decision to offer him a job was unanimous.

## PHASE 3:
## Negotiating and Closing Deals

## CASE STUDY: JENNIFER
### Finding Out What She's Worth

Jennifer had been a marketing manager for a tobacco company for a few years. When the company restructured, she lost her job. She had spent a lot of personal time doing volunteer work as a lobbyist for an association. This led her to decide that she wanted to become a lobbyist for a corporation as her next career move.

Initially she had no idea how to find out about these positions. She did not even know that corporations call lobbyists "government-relations representatives." She learned it by reading through **The American Lobbyists Directory**. It lists 57,000 lobbyists and 25,000 organizations, complete with contact information and phone numbers.

Through this resource, Jennifer was able to identify companies in her target, and generate interviews with many of them. These interviews went well and her follow-up was great. In fact, she was about to get three offers. However, one major topic had not yet been addressed: salary.

Jennifer had deliberately avoided this issue, waiting until the companies knew they wanted her. Now she was at the point where she couldn't stall them any longer. Her problem was that she had absolutely no idea what market rates were for these positions, and she knew she couldn't negotiate without this critical knowledge.

Immediately Jennifer went to the library and got a copy of the **American Salaries and Wages Survey**. It answers salary questions for more than 4,500 occupational classifications at different experience levels, as well as for different areas of the country. She was able to find out salary ranges for her industry, her position, and her geographic location.

Jennifer wanted still more. She went to the **Encyclopedia of Associations** and got the names of four different associations that deal with government-relations people and lobbyists. She called them and explained what information she was seeking.

The associations were able either to tell her salary standards or put her in touch with people in their local chapters who could.

When Jennifer went in for her salary-negotiation interviews, she knew the market rates,the highs and lows, and what she could reasonably request. With this information, she was able to negotiate the most attractive package.

## Using Research Throughout the Campaign Process

Your research techniques may change as your campaign evolves. It is possible that you will only need to do a little bit of investigative work before you land a new position. On the other hand, you may find yourself returning again and again to resources that enrich all the stages of your job search.

## CASE STUDY: SHELLEY
### Uncovering Options for a Career Change

Shelley had spent eight years as a financial analyst in a major brokerage firm on Wall Street. He liked financial analysis, but didn't really like the options for career growth within the broker-age industry.

After doing an assessment, he decided that he wanted to position himself for growth within a mid-size corporation, with the goal of becoming CFO. Shelley thought he would try to target something within the environmental area. However, he didn't know very much about it and was pretty sure that he wouldn't have enough qualifications to break in. So he stayed where he was, feeling trapped in his career.

After some counseling, Shelley realized that he needed to do research to learn more about his target industry. He consulted two reference books.

The first was **The U.S. Industrial Outlook**, also available in a CD-ROM version. It has reports and prospects for over 350 manufacturing and service industries, and is put out by the U.S. Department of Commerce on an annual basis. It analyzes trends and presents forecasts for hundreds of industries. Data are given in both narrative and tabular form. A list of additional references is included at the end of each chapter.

The second reference book was **The Environmental Industries Marketplace**, also published by Gale Research. It gives detailed information on companies in the industry. Together, these books helped to break down this $100-billion market into its component parts.

Shelley quickly realized that his target was too big. He would have to pick from among the many areas these two books identified. Before, he had thought, "The environment is for me." Now he learned that much of the industry wasn't for him.

For example, he discovered that his skills might not be transferable to areas dealing with controlling abuses, such as air and noise pollution or hazardous waste. He could more clearly see opportunity for himself working with companies that provide services to the environmental industry, such as consulting, research or financial services. They related to his experience in financial research and analysis from his days on Wall Street.

Now Shelley had identified a target and specific companies within that target. He knew what he wanted, but he also knew that he would be perceived as an outsider by those in a position to hire him.

Using **The Encyclopedia of Associations**, he was able to contact two industry groups that sent him their newsletters. Reading through these, he learned the jargon, the hot issues and the major trends.

Shelley began to network. As he did, people referred him to companies that might actually hire him. It was time to prepare for interviews.

He wished he could just wave a magic wand

*The greatest obstacle to discovery is not ignorance
—it is the illusion of knowledge.*
Edward Bond, *Washington Post*, January 29, 1984

and know everything that had been written about the companies he was interested in, over the past few years. He wished he could just browse through their annual reports, but that would take so long, and his first interview was in just two days . . .

Off to the library! Shelley used **ABI/Inform,** mentioned before, and **Business Periodicals On Disc.** BPOD combines the ABI/Inform database of article references and abstracts of more than 800 business and management periodicals with the ability to view or print the complete text from many of the periodicals. It is updated monthly, and covers from 1987 up to the present.

He also used the **National Newspaper Index**. It offers combined in-depth indexing of five major newspapers: *The New York Times, The Wall Street Journal, The Christian Science Monitor, The Washington Post,* and *The Los Angeles Times*. It covers the most recent four years, and is updated monthly.

After only about thirty minutes, he had practically the next-best thing to that magic wand: a powerful synopsis of the past three years' worth of press about the companies he would be interviewing with.

As far as the annual report and financial information were concerned, he just had to plug into **Corporate Text.** It provides copies of annual reports for companies traded on the NYSE, AMEX, NASDAQ, and OTC, and is updated monthly.

He also used **LaserDisclosure**. It is a full text database of exact reproductions of original SEC filings, including graphs and photographs, from more than 6,000 companies traded on the NASDAQ, OTC, AMEX, and NYSE. It is updated weekly.

So throughout the job-search phases, Shelley used research tools to keep moving forward. He armed himself with enough information to be sincere, informed, and competitive in the growth industry of his choice.

## CASE STUDY: JONATHAN
### *Searching for the Small Private Company*

Jonathan was a human-resources manager who specialized in staffing and succession planning at a major bank. After twenty years there, he accepted an early-retirement package, but was not yet ready to leave the workforce.

After analyzing his options, he decided he wanted to be in a much smaller company. He investigated the future of human-resources and staffing issues and concluded that temporary services/interim staffing was a good target.

He knew lots of people in the industry—they had been his vendors at the bank! He thought he wouldn't have any problems networking around to find a great job with a small growth firm.

After five or six calls, he realized that he wasn't getting anywhere talking to the people he knew. Without realizing it, he sounded arrogant and inappropriate. He would ask, "Don't you think I would be a great addition to your industry, with all my connections and knowledge?" Although he didn't know why, he did notice that his contacts were not particularly impressed.

Jonathan needed to do some research. First he went to **The Encyclopedia of Business Information Sources**. It is a bibliographic guide to more than 21,000 citations, covering over 1,000 subjects of interest to business personnel.

This resource includes: abstracting and indexing services, almanacs and yearbooks, bibliographies, biographical sources, directories, encyclopedias and dictionaries, financial ratios, handbooks and manuals, online databases, periodicals and newsletters, price sources, research centers and institutes, statistics sources, trade associations and professional societies. It too is published by Gale Research, Inc.

In it, Jonathan found that a firm called Kennedy Publications in New Hampshire publishes a list of temporary-service companies and their areas of specialization. He sent away for it.

He became knowledgeable about the differences between international, national, regional, and independent firms. He also learned the

*Few executives yet know how to ask: What information do I need to do my job?*
*When do I need it? And from whom should I be getting it?*
Peter F. Drucker, "Be Data Literate—Know What to Know,"
*The Wall Street Journal*, December 1, 1992

---

differences between managed services, outsourcing, payrolling, and employee leasing.

He decided that a regional service would probably be the most likely to need someone at his level. He only found five in that category, and that was not enough.

To see if he could expand his target, he went through **Dun & Bradstreet's Million Dollar Directory**. It has information on some 160,000 U.S. businesses that have indicated net worth of more than $500,000.

Still, he was only able to get another five names. He thought perhaps the companies he was interested in were too small and/or private and therefore not in these reference materials. So he tried the **MacMillan Directory of Leading Private Companies**. It has information on over 12,500 companies and wholly owned subsidiaries with sales of $10,000,000.

He also looked through the **Over the Counter 1,000 Yellow Book**. It has the leading growth companies quoted on NASDAQ. It is a comprehensive directory introducing leading, younger growth companies in the U.S.A. It provides the addresses, phone numbers, and titles of 20,000 executives who manage these smaller companies on the cutting edge of innovation.

He also used the **Small Business Sourcebook**. It is a guide to sources of information furnished by associations, consultants, educational programs, government agencies, franchisers, trade shows and venture-capital firms for 100 types of small businesses.

After all that research, he decided that he should include some national firms as well, in order to expand his target. If he included firms that franchised and firms that were international, but not yet operating on American soil, that brought his total number to 55.

Jonathan next used **Gale Globalaccess: Associations**. It provides information on non-profit membership organizations of international, U.S., regional, state, or local interest.

This resource includes professional societies, labor unions, and cultural and religious organizations. From it, Jonathan got the names of four

associations and five trade journals. He spoke to people who belonged to NATS (National Association of Temporary Services) and he read appropriate literature.

Now that he understood the issues more clearly, he felt confident enough to try networking once again. Instead of bragging about his connections, he was able to talk about industry problems and how he would tackle them.

He impressed his contacts with his preparation and insight. It even appeared that he knew plenty of competitive information and trends that these same people wanted to hear about.

Because of the relationships that he developed at this stage of his job search, he eventually was introduced to the company he would end up working for.

## CASE STUDY: MARRISSA
*Researching the International Market*

Marrissa had just returned from overseas, where she had been living and working as a personal assistant to the U.S. ambassador in an Eastern European country. She came back to the States for personal reasons, and needed to find a job. She was fluent in several languages and knowledgeable about diverse cultures.

She wanted to remain a personal assistant to a high-level executive. However, she didn't know where to start investigating corporate opportunities that would value her cross-cultural background without requiring a tremendous amount of travel.

Marrissa began with the **Directory of Foreign Manufacturers in the United States**, Fourth Edition, published by Georgia State University Business Press, 1990. It lists approximately 6,000 foreign-owned manufacturers with operations in the United States. There is indexing by state location, parent company location, and by product.

Next she went to the **Worldwide Branch Locations of Multinational Companies.** Arranged by country, this volume lists contact and descriptive information for about 500 parent companies and their key branch locations. She also used the **European Consultants Directory**. It contains more than 5,000 European consultants and their fields of endeavor.

She went on to consult a reference book called **Principal International Businesses**, published by Dun's Marketing Services. It provides annual information on approximately 55,000 leading companies in 140 countries throughout the world.

Last she used the **International Directory of Corporate Affiliations**, published by the National Register Publishing Company. It is an annual directory of information for over 1,600 foreign parent companies with listings of their divisions, subsidiaries, and affiliates. Also included are 1,500 U.S. companies with foreign holdings.

Marrissa obtained so much information that she designed an entire direct-contact campaign, demonstrating her ability to create executive correspondence. She was able to interview with several firms, turning down several offers before she secured an appropriate position.

### You Can't Always Get What You Want, But If You Work At It, You'll Get What You Need

You've now read several case studies demonstrating the power of research. Sometimes it's difficult to see how these techniques will help you personally. Often the information you get doesn't look as you had hoped. You need to be creative.

Let me say something about being "creative." People frequently give that advice, without explaining.

Doing research does not mean simply collecting data. What you do with the information is critical to your success. Being creative means recognizing the relevance of seemingly irrelevant information. That is what will differentiate you from others.

For example, two clients of mine sold communications equipment in the high-technology industry. Both clients were interviewing at the same company. Both used the same research tools and both were able to learn the same two

things: that the company in question had recently been denied FCC approval of a new product and that their third-quarter earnings were significantly lower than anticipated.

My first client, Peter, had been hoping to find specific sales figures, information about the company's top customers, and about their primary competitors. He was greatly disappointed in his meager findings.

Alvin was my second client. Like Peter, he had been hoping for similar sales-oriented information. However, instead of being disappointed, he was creative.

During his interview, he referred to the FCC problem to ask pertinent and thoughtful questions. He asked how one product could so greatly affect the firm's profit picture. He asked about the positioning of *other* products, about the R&D cycle, about how government regulations affect the overall marketing strategy of the firm. In other words, he used the same limited research information to demonstrate his awareness of the company's problems and his concern with something bigger than his own job: the viability of the corporation and its longer-term goals.

Alvin was perceived as an experienced salesperson, able to produce quickly, with an understanding of how sales are linked to the company mission. Peter was perceived as a salesman. Period. Who do *you* think got the offer?

There are many stories like this one. If you find yourself doing research and wondering, "How on earth will this help me?" remember Peter and Alvin. Turn your bewilderment into the question: "How does *this* piece of information impact my particular area of expertise?"

If the answers were easy, everyone would have them. Taking the time and effort to go that extra mile is what makes you stand apart from your competition.

The information is out there. An extensive bibliography is at the back of *Targeting the Job You Want* to serve as your guide.

Wendy Alfus Rothman is president of Wenroth Consulting, managing director at Advantage Staffing Services, Inc., and one of the original counselors at The Five O'Clock Club.

The Five O'Clock Club®

# Using the Internet as a Job-Search Tool

by Patricia Raufer

When you consider that the Internet is a global network of networks linking individuals, companies, governments, organizations, and academic institutions, it is not surprising that it is a valuable job-search tool. Although the Internet can be considered simply the electronic version of what already happens in a job search, this format offers the benefits of immediacy, connection, and searchability.

Newsgroups and online forums offer networking contacts, while e-mail serves as the communication mechanism replacing phone, fax, and postal delivery. Electronic classified ads are similar to their print counterparts. However, finding them online is not random, and they're often linked to the website of the hiring company. As an information resource, the Internet offers a multitude of sources with search tools that allow job hunters to choose the way that they look for information. It's an incredible vehicle for researching an industry, for finding out about a specific company, for developing target lists, or for learning the buzzwords that should be emphasized in your résumé or in interviews.

## Job Meta-Lists

The best place to get started is with a job-search Meta-List, which is a comprehensive guide that links Internet resources pertaining to job search so that they're accessible from one place. From that starting point, the job hunter can easily access newsgroups, online classified ads, job listings, career websites, company websites and the directories and indexes (called search engines), which in turn serve as Meta-Lists for other Internet resources. Although each job Meta-List has an extensive listing of resources, with all of the information on the Internet, it is impossible to offer a complete guide of all resources. The job Meta-Lists are linked to each other so the job hunter can easily choose a different Meta-List that offers other Internet career resources.

## Newsgroups

Newsgroups on the Internet and chat rooms in online services offer lively discussion on a variety of topics. Newsgroups serve as bulletin boards in which members interested in a particular topic can post messages that are accessible by other Internet users with similar interests, who may then respond with a reply posting. This area can be a rich resource for networking and for getting answers to specific questions. So as not to ask obvious questions, be sure to read the group's FAQ (frequently asked questions) bulletin before posting. This will help avoid unwanted and often acerbic responses (called "flaming").

The area on the Internet that contains newsgroups is called USENET, which is the notation contained on Internet browsers. To choose a newsgroup, access the USENET area from your browser and select from the indicated areas of interest. There's a useful search engine called DejaNews (www.dejanews.com), which archives newsgroup postings and can be sorted by topic.

In addition to providing a networking forum and a means of finding out about the current thinking on issues pertinent to that group, there are newsgroups aimed specifically at job search in which the postings list specific job openings. CareerMosaic (www.careermosaic.com) has an extensive list of job-specific newsgroups. The list includes newsgroups targeting specific cities (nyc.jobs.offered or la.jobs for New York and Los Angeles), regions (ne.jobs for New England or ba.jobs for the Bay Area) or countries (can.jobs, ukjobs.offered, and us.jobs.offered for Canada, the United Kingdom, and the U.S.A. respectively). There are newsgroups for specific industry postings (bionet.jobs for biotechnology or bizjobs.offered for business positions) and many miscellaneous groups (misc.jobs.offered).

The following are excellent job-search Meta-Lists with their Universal Resource Locators (URL's) and the codes for accessing them:

| | |
|---|---|
| Job Hunt | http://rescomp.stanford.edu/jobs |
| The Catapult | http://www.wm.edu/catapult |
| Yahoo | http://www.yahoo.com/Business/Employment |

*Research is the process of going up alleys
to see if they are blind.*
Marston Bates, *American Zoologist*

## Electronic Classified Ads

The help wanted ads, which appear in newspapers, are also available on the Internet. CareerPath (www.careerpath.com) contains job listings from *The Boston Globe, The Chicago Tribune, The New York Times, San José Mercury News* and *The Washington Post.* Access the website and then register online to use this extensive database. For overseas assignments, access the *International Herald Tribune* (www.hodes.com/iht).

## Job Listings

Job openings can also be found at a number of career sites on the World Wide Web. These postings are accessible using search criteria specified by the job hunter so that all openings that match the request are displayed. The job listings may be sorted by geography (country, region, state, city), company name, industry (e.g., banking), position (e.g., accountant), discipline (e.g., finance), or topic (e.g., bank loans).

Job listings provide information about specific positions and are often linked to the website of the hiring company, where you can get further details about the organization. While a certain job opening may not be appropriate, it may lead to information about other areas of the company, so also check out postings that intrigue you but aren't an exact match. Because new companies are being added to the career websites on a daily basis, it pays to visit frequently. Check the postings regularly, since unlike print, they're not always archived and accessible at a later date once the posting has expired. If there's a posting that's of interest to you, download it to disk or print it out immediately, so you're not disappointed when you go back.

## Career Sites

The career sites are online versions of campus career-placement offices offering services to job

searchers of all ages, income levels, and experience. In addition to job listings, these career sites provide counseling services, résumé posting areas, forums, company profiles, news articles, job fairs and information about associations and professional organizations. The job Meta-List provides access to career sites that cater to specific professions as well as those that take a more general approach.

The following list indicates career sites that are not industry-specific:

| | |
|---|---|
| Career Mosaic | http://www.careermosaic.com |
| Human Resource Center | http://human.resourcecenter.corn |
| Interactive Employment Network | http://www.espan.com |
| Jobcenter | http://www.jobcenter.com |
| Job Trak | http://www.jobtrak.com |
| Jobweb | http://www.jobweb.org |
| Monster Board | http://www.monster.com |
| Online Career Center | http://www.occ.com |
| Online Opportunities | http://www.jobnet.com |
| Professionals Online | http://www.prosonline.com |
| NCS Career Magazine | http://www.careermag.com |

## Company Websites

Company websites contain marketing materials in the form of online brochures, annual reports, descriptions of the corporate culture, and job openings, often including employee testimonials or profiles. For a job search, this information is excellent for preparing for interviews. Most corporate websites contain an extensive library of press releases and white papers. These are extremely helpful in keeping up to date on the company and for finding contacts for target mailings and direct-mail campaigns.

Newswires are also available through the online services and provide press releases about new product introductions, new alliances, and other corporate events. They're often the source for the business press. Since the listings are searchable by topic and remain online for about two weeks, they're a good resource if you haven't had time to keep up with trade periodicals.

*Facts are friendly. Facts that tend to reinforce what you are doing and give you a warm glow are nice, because they help in terms of psychic reward. Facts that raise alarms are equally friendly, because they give you clues about how to respond, how to change, where to spend the resources.*
Irwin Miller

## Directories / Indexes (Search Engines)

Even when you know the company name, it is not always possible to guess the universal resource locator (URL) that identifies the corporate website. To help you find it, there are a number of good search indexes that list the organizations and may include a brief description as well as a link to the website. It's impossible to keep up with the many websites that are added each day, so using these search tools alleviates that worry. The question now is how to keep up with the proliferation of search tools. That is almost impossible too. However, I've found that the special-interest magazines often list indexes that refer to their discipline. *CFO* lists websites dealing with finance, while *Success* has those with an entrepreneurial bent.

Internet may be an excellent tool to do a lot of good research and save quite a bit of networking time by providing great information. However, it does not provide the benefits of personal contact and valuable perspectives that one-on-one information-gathering interviews provide. Consider the Internet as simply another job-search tool to be added to your repertoire of Five O'Clock Club techniques.

**2) *Consider the value of the information you obtain online.***

The Internet contains a vast array of information, some of which is very helpful, some of which is just not worth your time sorting through. For instance, websites containing online brochures and press releases maintained by a company on your target list will be well worth a visit, while reading

---

The following list of search engines is by no means complete, but it does include enough to get started:

### Directories

| | |
|---|---|
| CommerceNET | http://www.commerce.net |
| ElNet Galaxy | http://www.einet.net |
| The Federal Web Locator | http://www.law.vill.edu |
| Federal Information Exchange | http://www.fie.com |
| Global Network Navigator | http://nearnet.gnn.com |
| IOMA Business Page | http://ioma.com/ioma |
| InfoSeek | http://www2.infoseek.com |
| Lycos | http://lycos.cs.cmu.edu |
| Open Market's Commercial Sites Index | http://www.directory.net |
| US Patent and Trademark Office | http://www.uspto.gov |
| The WWW Virtual Library | http://www.w3.org |
| WebCrawler | http://webcrawler.com |
| Yahoo | http://www.yahoo.com |

---

## Some suggestions

**1) *The Internet is a tool to supplement your job search.*** With the vast amount of information available online, it's easy to spend hours and hours of good job-search time scrolling through databases, accessing career centers, looking at job postings, or chatting in newsgroups. Be very careful that you do not spend too much time online. The Internet can be interesting, but it can also be somewhat addictive! It may seem like productive time because a few hours online can generate quite a number of leads and interesting contacts. The

through lots of postings in a newsgroup may be a waste of time. Remember that on the Internet, everyone is a publisher, so be judicious not only about where you search but also about what you read and how seriously you take it.

**3) *Electronic methods are untested. Is job search the best place to be a pioneer?***

Some job hunters have even created their multimedia résumé, with extensive background information; it may include video clips or samples of work—all packaged to be transmitted electronically. This method may be appropriate for creative and technical positions because it demonstrates use and understanding of the technology. Job seekers who respond online to postings often send an electronic version of their print résumé. However, just as New Media has not eliminated print, and e-mail is used differently from "snail mail," the electronic résumé has not replaced the standard résumé and cover letter. Using the electronic medium for communication offers the benefit of enabling you to respond quickly, but it is not necessarily the easiest method for the recipient. As with all the communications techniques in job search, choosing the right one is part of the process.

Many of the Internet career websites provide an area in which job hunters post their résumés for access by potential employers. However, access is not always limited to just employers. Therefore by posting your résumé, you're providing personal information, employment history and credentials to people whom you don't know. Would you tack up your résumé on a public bulletin board or hand it out to strangers simply because they asked for it? And how can you follow up effectively if you don't know who has looked at your credentials?

**The Internet may be an excellent tool to do a lot of good research and save quite a bit of networking time by providing great information. However, it does not provide the benefits of personal contact and valuable perspectives that one-on-one information-gathering interviews provide.**

The amount of information that the Internet offers is staggering. For a novice user, it can be overwhelming and frustrating. Even with great search engines to sort through the masses of material, there may be lots of sites that you'll want to visit. Finding specific information may be difficult, so sometimes other reference guides may offer a better alternative. The Internet provides lots of information for technical and scientific fields, but is not as robust for the arts. It's changing constantly. There are no hard-and-fast rules for making the Internet an effective tool for

your search. These tips are just guidelines for getting started. Use them to enrich and expand your job search. You may even find that these newly developed "cyberskills" add another dimension to your résumé and a whole new target of companies positioned for the future.

Patricia Raufer is a member of The Five O'Clock Club and president of Interactive Solutions.

To everything there is a season,
A time for every purpose under heaven: ❧
A time to be born,
And a time to die;
A time to plant,
And a time to pluck up what is planted;
A time to kill,
And a time to heal;
A time to break down,
And a time to build up;
A time to weep,
And a time to laugh;
A time to mourn,
And a time to dance;
A time to cast away stones,
And a time to gather stones;
A time to embrace,
And a time to refrain from embracing;
A time to gain,
And a time to lose;
A time to keep,
And a time to throw away;
A time to tear,
And a time to sew;
A time to keep silence,
And a time to speak;
A time to love,
And a time to hate;
A time of war,
And a time of peace. ❧

Ecclesiastes 3:1-8, as paraphrased in
Kevin W. McCarthy's,
*The On-Purpose Person: Making Your Life Make Sense*

# PART THREE

# KNOWING
# THE RIGHT PEOPLE

## HOW TO GET INTERVIEWS
## IN YOUR TARGET AREAS

# Pre-Campaign Planning

*It is circumstance and proper timing that give an action its character and make it either good or bad.*
Agesilaus II

You sure have done a lot of work so far! You selected three or four targets after conducting a Preliminary Target Investigation, and ranked them so you know which one you want as your first campaign, your second, third, and fourth. You have also developed a preliminary résumé for the first campaign. Now we will plan your *entire* job hunt, just as you would plan any other project. A planned job search will save you time. You will be able to tell what is working and what is not, and change what you are doing accordingly.

Take a look at the chart on the next page. It is a conceptual view of the job-hunting process. There are no time frames for a phase. For some people, the Evaluation Phase (which is covered in *Targeting the Job You Want*) can be as short as ten minutes. For others, it can take years. The time each step takes depends on you and the situation you face.

Do every step, and spend the length of time required for your situation. That time is not wasted. It will save time later because your effort will be organized.

Your campaigns aimed at each target (T1, T2) will overlap. You will start one campaign, and when it is in full swing, you will start campaign number two. Each campaign will be condensed, and your total job search will be *shorter* if you follow this approach than if you conducted all of the campaigns together.

As you can see in the chart below, each campaign has three phases. The first phase is Preparation; the second is Interviewing; the third is Follow-Up. Each phase should be given equal weight.

During the Preparation Phase, you:
• Research and make a list of the companies you want to contact.
• Develop your Two-Minute Pitch and your cover letters.
• Make sure your résumé makes you look appropriate to your target.
• Plan your strategy for getting interviews (through networking, direct contact, search firms, and ads).

When you are in the Interview Phase of campaign one, you may start campaign two.

## CASE STUDY: JIM
### An Organized Approach

Jim, the marketing manager mentioned earlier, had targeted four industries: environmental, noise abatement, shipping, and corporate America, which was a backup target in case the other three did not work. Jim had selected thirty companies in the environmental area, and began to contact them. When he met with an environmental company, he could mention that he had "just met yesterday with another environmental company, and this is what we discussed. What do you think?" *Focusing* on one target at a time can give you credibility and information. Jim can mention other companies he is speaking with, and let a prospective employer know that he is truly interested in that industry. Focus also saves him time. It takes so much time to develop a good pitch, cover letter, and résumé that

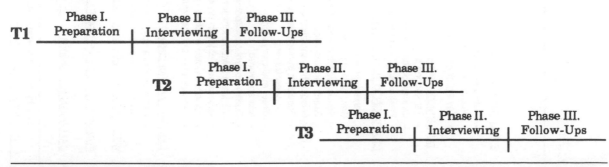

# What a Job Hunt Looks Like Over Time

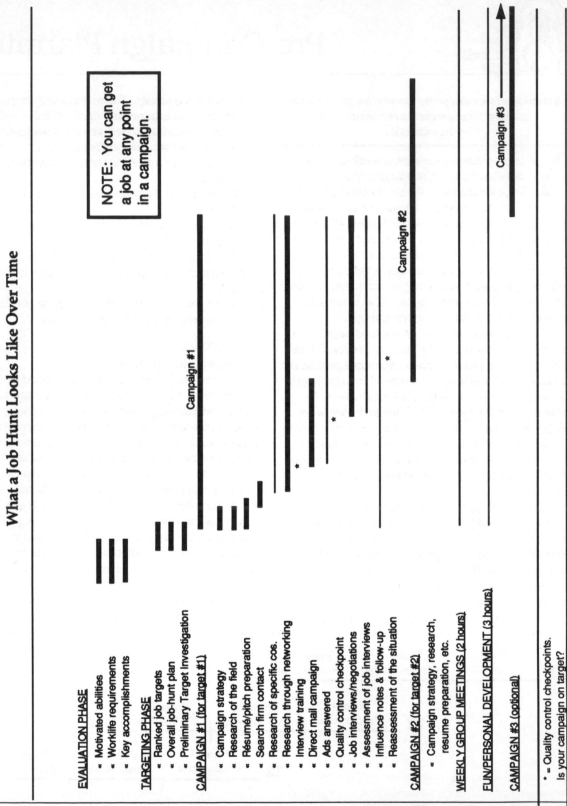

NOTE: You can get a job at any point in a campaign.

Campaign #1

Campaign #2

Campaign #3

EVALUATION PHASE
• Motivated abilities
• Worklife requirements
• Key accomplishments

TARGETING PHASE
• Ranked job targets
• Overall job-hunt plan
• Preliminary Target Investigation

CAMPAIGN #1 (for target #1)
• Campaign strategy
• Research of the field
• Résumé/pitch preparation
• Search firm contact
• Research of specific cos.
• Research through networking
• Interview training
• Direct mail campaign
• Ads answered
• Quality control checkpoint
• Job interviews/negotiations
• Assessment of job interviews
• Influence notes & follow-up
• Reassessment of the situation

CAMPAIGN #2 (for target #2)
• Campaign strategy, research, resume preparation, etc.

WEEKLY GROUP MEETINGS (2 hours)

FUN/PERSONAL DEVELOPMENT (3 hours)

CAMPAIGN #3 (optional)

* = Quality control checkpoints.
Is your campaign on target?

it only makes sense to sell yourself to a *number* of companies. It's too difficult to try one pitch one day and then a completely different pitch the next. It's better to completely test one pitch and have it down pat. That's why you can start your second campaign when you are in the interview phase of the first campaign.

Furthermore, a condensed campaign allows you to test what is wrong and drop what is not working. Job hunters who go after lots of different targets at the same time usually do not develop a great pitch for any one of them, and cannot tell what is working and what is not.

Jim dropped his first target—the environmental industry—except for following up on two possibilities that seemed promising. He also came up with a number of possibilities from his second and third targets. In the end, he got one job offer from each target, and never started his fourth campaign, corporate America, which he was not interested in anyway. In addition, Jim followed up on serendipitous leads, which also could have yielded something. But a focused search was the core of his campaign, with serendipitous leads on the side.

A focused campaign is shorter, even though you're zeroing in on only one target at a time (until you are in the follow-up stage, in which you are following up on *all* of your targets, and generating more leads in each of them). Many executives who follow a targeted approach can cover four good-sized targets in depth in two months. And many executives have that next position within two and a half to four months!

## The Timing of Your Campaigns

In the next chapter, you will plan the strategy for getting interviews in your first campaign. Implement that campaign right away. When you are midway through it, start your second campaign—even if you do not think you will need it.

When you start your first campaign, you will be full of hope. Your résumé will be great, and you will be talking to lots of people. Some will tell you that you should have no problem finding a job. They are being sincere. But job offers dry up. What

once seemed like a sure thing does not materialize.

There seem to be phases and cycles in each campaign—there is the initial rush, the long haul, the drought, followed by the first poor job offer and the later better offers. After a letdown, job hunters can lose momentum. They sometimes think they will *never* find a job.

If, however, you have already started that second campaign, you will know that those cover letters are in the mail working for you. You stand a chance of getting some response from the second campaign. You will do better in the interviews from your first campaign because you will not feel so desperate. Your second campaign backs you up.

Your second campaign could include additional people in the same target market as the first. (Do more research and get more names.) It could be a variation of your first target market (a related field or a related industry) or a new target.

I have had clients start a second campaign even when they were in the final negotiation stages of the first. Those negotiations went better, and helped them land the job because they had the comfort of knowing that the second campaign was in the mail.

If, perchance, your first campaign does *not* work, you will not lose momentum if you are already in the midst of your second—or perhaps even preparing to start your third. It is better not to lose momentum.

## Customize Your Campaign

Think of yourself as a corporation. Given equal economic conditions, certain corporations thrive while others fail. Successful companies adjust their approaches to the changes in the economy. And even when the economy is at its worst, certain companies come up winners.

In many respects, job-hunting management resembles the management of a company. The economy has changed dramatically over the past several years; times are more competitive—for companies and for job hunters. Whether you are managing a company or managing your own career, adjust the techniques you use.

Statistics show that certain techniques work better than others in the aggregate. But consider what might be best for you *and* your situation. The hiring system works differently in different industries and in different companies. Remain flexible: Do what works in the industry and the profession in which you are interested.

In addition, do what works for your personality. For example, certain job hunters phone company executives rather than using the written approach of a direct-mail campaign. What if you are the sort (as I am) who finds it difficult to make calls to people with whom you have had no contact? Or what if you are currently employed and find that heavy use of the phone is out of the question for you? Or it may be that the industry you are approaching considers this technique an arrogant way to do business.

This same rule applies to the techniques you will find in this book. Use what you want. Do what works for *you*.

## A Campaign to Promote Yourself —Just Like Promoting a Product

*In soloing—as in other activities—*
*it is far easier to start something than it is to finish it.*
Amelia Earhart

Airlines run promotional campaigns to get passengers to fly with them. Computer software companies use their promotional efforts to get people to buy their software. You will conduct a promotional campaign to generate interest in your "product."

You and an airline go through the same steps to market your respective products:

• *An airline analyzes the market to determine the kinds of people who are interested in its product, the number of potential customers, and how much need there is for the product.* Analyze your market to determine the kinds of companies that could be interested in you, and the number of companies and positions in your field of interest. Find out how much demand there is for your services in your target market.

• *An airline defines itself by its features,* such as

the kind of seating it has, the cities it flies to, and so on—and it also defines its personality or style. For example, an airline may say it represents the "friendly skies" or is the "only way to fly." Or it may define itself as a bargain or as an exclusive carrier.

Define yourself not only in terms of your skills and experience but also in terms of your style and personality. There are many qualified people for each position, just as there are a number of airlines offering the same kinds of planes going to the same cities. The difference between the airlines is not in their basic product, but in their personality and the way they go about their business.

You and your competition will often be equally well qualified. The difference will lie in your style and in the way you go about your business. For example, a person who had run a department and doubled productivity could have done it in a nasty, threatening way, or could have motivated people to do more, instituted training programs, and encouraged workers to come up with suggestions for improving productivity. Let *your* personality come through.

• *An airline test-markets what it has decided to offer.* If the test results are poor, the airline changes either its basic product (such as its number of seats) or offers the same product in a way that is more attractive to the target market. It could also decide to withdraw from that target market.

Test what you have decided to offer. If it is not of interest to your target market, change what you are offering, the way you are offering it, or the image you are projecting. For example, you can change what you are offering by getting more experience or training in a certain area. You can change your image by looking different or by highlighting a certain aspect of your personality that is of interest to your target market. Or you can change your promotional techniques.

On the other hand, you may decide to withdraw from that market. Perhaps it is inappropriate for you. An example is when you find your target market is in the middle of major layoffs. If you can help turn the company around, you have a chance. If you are comparable to the people it is laying off, consider a different target.

Some people pick a target and stick with it no matter what. But you need flexibility and common sense to figure out what may be going wrong in your campaign. You may need more experience, or you may need to present yourself differently. Or it may be that there is no hope of obtaining an offer in certain markets. No matter how much you may want to work for a foundation, for example, there may not be many positions available. Then, even the best job-hunting techniques will not help you. Change your target.

• *An airline assesses its competition, and so will you.* Who is your competition and how well do you stack up in your basic qualifications? What can you offer that is different?

• *An airline asks itself if the timing is right for a campaign it may be planning.* Consider if the timing is right for what *you* want to offer a particular market. Sometimes there is a great demand for lawyers or engineers, for example, and at other times there is a glut in the market. When the oil business was booming, there was a demand for people in that field. Aerospace engineers could once name their price. You can easily find out the level of demand by testing what you want.

• *An airline asks itself if it is worth it*—if it can afford to do what it would take to offer its product to a certain market. It decides if its return will be adequate, and it makes sure this venture will satisfy other company needs and support company objectives.

Ask yourself if it is worth it. You may find that a field is not what you thought it was: perhaps the pay is too low or the hours too long. Or the field may not fit with your long-term goals. Or it may run contrary to your motivated skills or values, or what you want in a company or a position. You can lower your expectations or you can look elsewhere.

• *There is one major difference between what you and the airline have to after:* The airline has a lot of planes and a lot of seats, but there is only *one* of you. Be particular about whom you sell your services to. Get a couple of potential offers so you can make a comparison and select what is best for you.

## Weekly Group Meetings

*Throughout life our internal lives are enriched by the people we have permitted to touch us.*
George E. Vaillant, *Adaptation to Life*

Not everything can be covered in a book. Meeting every week in The Five O'Clock Club with people like yourself can be a tremendous help. They will become familiar with your job search and can give you feedback on your efforts. The experiences of other people can teach you what to do when the same things happen to you. In the group, you can trade stories and techniques, and network with one another.

Believe it or not, weekly group meetings are *fun* and a respite from the discouraging job of job hunting. They can spark you on: your own situation seems less hopeless. You feel that if they can do it, you can too.

Being in a group with your peers can be more effective than one-on-one counseling with a "pro." A group can take risks that a counselor cannot. For example, even if you have been unemployed for a while, the group may suggest that you not take a position because it is not right for you. You can easily ignore the advice of the group if you want. A counselor has to be more careful about giving advice that can adversely affect a person's financial situation. Your peers have more freedom to discuss your needs and to give a variety of "free" advice.

In one of my groups, there was a dynamic public relations man who had been unemployed for two months. The group came to know him well. He received a job offer to do public relations work for a conservative dental firm. When he told us about the offer, the look on his face clearly showed how unhappy he felt about it. Everyone knew that this would not be the right job for him, and the group discouraged him from taking it.

A few weeks later, he received another job offer—this one from a dynamic company in San Francisco. The company had been searching to fill this position for more than six months, and it was thrilled to find him. So was he: For him, the job was the chance of a lifetime.

## Time for Personal Development

*There is no music in a "rest," Katie, that I know of: but there's the making of music in it. And people are always missing that part of life—melody.*
John Ruskin

If you happen to be unemployed, welcome to the club. Some unemployed people think they don't deserve any fun at all. But it is difficult to job-hunt for a full forty hours a week.

If you have only thirty hours of work to do, you may spread it out to fill forty hours. With too much time on your hands, you may take longer than usual to write a memo or make a phone call or an appointment. You may stretch things out so you will always have "something to look forward to." You will wind up stretching out your search.

Wasting time is itself not the bad part. The bad part is losing your flow of adrenaline. Better to spend thirty-five or thirty-seven hours a week searching for a job and making those hours *intense*—just as you would in a real job—and then rewarding yourself with three hours of fun that week.

During a period of unemployment, I indulged myself by going to auction houses and spending the time it takes to study furniture. Auctions aren't crowded during the day, when everyone else is working. I never regretted the time I spent there. I felt I would never have that luxury again. I worked hard at my job hunt and felt I deserved a break. So do you.

But you don't deserve *too* much of a break. One of the worst things a person can do is start off his or her unemployment with a "well-deserved" vacation. Sometimes the job hunt never gets started. The momentum never builds. Instead, why not look for a job and take two weeks off after you have landed it? If you are unemployed, don't punish yourself, but don't overindulge yourself, either.

Job hunting is a job in itself, hard work that can be discouraging. But since you have to do it, you might as well have fun. You will meet interesting people who may become new friends. And you will learn a lot. That's not so bad.

*We can define "purpose" in several ways. For one, when we know our purpose, we have an anchor—a device of the mind to provide some stability, to keep the surprises of a creative universe from tossing us to and fro, from inflicting constant seasickness on us. Or we can think of our purpose as being a master nautical chart marking shoals and rocks, sandbars, and derelicts, something to guide us and keep us on course. Perhaps the most profound thing we can say about being "on purpose" is that when that is our status, our condition, and our comfort, we find our lives have meaning, and when we are "off purpose," we are confused about meanings and motives.*
Dudley Lynch and Paul L. Kordis,
*Strategy of the Dolphin:*
*Scoring a Win in a Chaotic World*

# Conducting a Campaign to Get Interviews in Your Target Markets

*The codfish lays ten thousand eggs,*
*The homely hen lays one.*
*The codfish never cackles*
*To tell you what she's done.*
*And so we scorn the codfish,*
*While the humble hen we prize,*
*Which only goes to show you*
*That it pays to advertise.*
Anonymous

> **Do not expect to**
> **get a job through:**
> • **Networking**
> • **Direct Contact**
> • **Search Firms**
> • **Ads**
> **These are techniques for**
> **getting *interviews*,**
> **not jobs.**
>
> **After you get the meeting,**
> **you can think about what to do next**
> **to *perhaps* turn it into a job**
> **(See the chapters on Follow-Up).**

## An Overview of the Strategy for Your First Campaign

*If the only tool you have is a hammer, you tend to see*
*every problem as a nail.*
Abraham Maslow

By now, you have developed preliminary job targets, and conducted a Preliminary Target Investigation (through networking and the library) to see which targets are worth pursuing.

Then you selected those that seem to be worth a full campaign, and ranked them in the order in which you want to conduct those campaigns. You are ready to conduct a campaign to contact every company in your first target. When you are busy meeting with people in that target, you will start the campaign preparation for Target 2.

A Personal Marketing Plan, which you may show to your networking contacts, contains your list of targets including the companies in each of those targets. This plan forms the overview of your search.

**For Target 1**, you will now:

1) **Research** to develop a list of all the companies, if you have not already done so. Find out—through networking or research—the names of the people you should contact in the appropriate departments in each of those companies.

2) **Develop your cover letter.** (Paragraph 1 is the opening; Paragraph 2 is a summary about yourself appropriate for this target; Paragraph 3 contains your bulleted accomplishments ("You may be interested in some of the things I've done"); Paragraph 4 is the close. (Many sample letters are in this book.)

3) **Develop your plan for getting a large number of meetings in this target**. There are four basic techniques for meeting people in each of the areas you have targeted for a full campaign. In the following chapters, you will learn more about them. They are:

• networking
• direct contact (direct mail, targeted mail, walk-in, cold call)
• search firms
• ads.

*Opportunities are multiplied
as they are seized.*
Sun Tzu, *The Art of War*

Do not think of these as techniques for getting *jobs*, but as techniques for getting *interviews*. After the interview, think about what to do next to keep the relationship going or perhaps to turn the interview into a job offer.

You organize the names of the people you want to contact, and develop strategies for contacting them:

Only 5 to 10 percent of all job leads are through search firms, and another 5 to 10 percent are through ads. You do not have much control over these leads: you have to *wait* for an ad to appear, and *wait* for a search firm to send you on an interview. Both networking and direct contact are *proactive* techniques you can use to get interviews in your target market. In networking, you contact someone simply by using someone else's name. In direct contact, you contact someone directly— usually after you have done some research and know something about him or her. Networking and direct contact complement each other and gain added effectiveness when used together. You may start your campaign either with direct contact (if you know your target area very well) or with networking (to research an area you don't know well or to find a way to contact people), and introduce the other technique as your campaign progresses.

Consider all four techniques for getting interviews, but spend most of your energy and brainpower on networking and direct contact.

### Selecting the Techniques

*Do not be too timid and squeamish about your actions. All life is an experiment.*
Ralph Waldo Emerson

Select the techniques most appropriate for the industry or profession you are targeting, as well as for your own personality. Each technique can work, but the strength of your campaign lies in your ability to use what is best for your particular situation. Contact as many potential employers as possible and then "campaign" to keep your name in front of them.

Use all of the techniques to:
- Learn more about your target area.
- Test what you are offering.
- Let people know you are looking.
- Contact people in a position to hire you.

### Search Firms

If you are looking for a position that naturally follows your most recent one, you can immediately contact search firms. As I've mentioned, only about 5 to 10 percent of all professional and managerial positions are filled by search firms, so it would seem logical to spend only 5 percent of your effort on them. However, certain professions use search firms more than others do.

Contact reputable search firms that tend to handle positions in your target area. If you don't already have relationships with search firms, find the good ones through networking, by asking managers which search firms they use or recommend. Remember, search firms are rarely able to help career changers.

### Answering Ads

Five to ten percent of all jobs are filled through ads. The odds are against you, so don't spend too much thought or energy on them. And don't sit home hoping for a response. Just answer the ad—so long as it sounds close to what you have to offer—and get on with your search. Maybe you'll hear from them—maybe you won't. (See the chapters on "How to Answer Ads" and "What To Do When You Know There's a Job Opening.")

### Networking

*You must call each thing by its proper name, or that which must get done will not.*
A. Harvey Block, President, Bokenon Systems

Studies show that about 60 to 70 percent of all positions are filled through networking. This is partly because it is an effective technique, and partly because most job hunters mistakenly refer to talking to people as "networking," no matter *how* they wound up talking to them. For example, Pete just found a job. I asked how he got the initial interview. He said, "Through networking." When I asked him to tell me more, he said, "I'm an accountant, originally from Australia. There is an association here of accountants from Australia. I sent for a list of all the members, and wrote to all of them. That's how I got the job."

Pete got the job lead through a direct-mail campaign, *not* through networking. That's why the survey numbers are off, and that's why you should consider using every technique for getting interviews in your target market. You never know where your leads will come from.

*The beginning of wisdom is to call
things by their right names.*
Chinese proverb

Networking simply means getting to see someone by using another person's name. You are using a contact to get in. You want to see the person *whether or not they have a job for you*. This technique is essential if you want to change careers, because you can get in to see people even if you are not qualified in the traditional sense. To stay in the same field, you can network to get information on which companies are hiring, which are the best ones to work for, and so on.

Networking can lead you in directions you had not thought of, and can open up new targets to pursue. You can network to explore even if you are not sure you want to change jobs right now. What's more, it's a technique you can use *after* you land that new job, whenever you get stuck and need advice.

Networking is more popular today than ever before, and it is effective when used properly. But, depending on your target, it is not always the most *efficient* way to get interviews. Furthermore, it is getting a bad name because although people are constantly networking, they are doing it incorrectly. Learn how to network correctly (see the chapters on networking), but combine targeted mailings (a direct-contact technique) with your

networking when you are aiming at small companies or ones that have very few jobs appropriate for you. Networking your way into all of them could take forever. Also, directly contact other people when you would have great trouble getting a networking contact. If the direct contact doesn't work, you can always network in later.

When you combine direct mailing with networking, you can cover the market with a direct-mail campaign and then network certain sections of that market. Or you can network in to see someone, and then perhaps get a list of names you can use for further networking or a direct-mail campaign.

If you do not cover your market, you risk losing out. You may find later that they "just filled a job a few month ago. Too bad we didn't know you were looking." Be thorough. Let *everyone* in your target market know that you are looking.

### Direct-Contact Campaigns

Writing directly to executives is a consistently effective technique for generating interviews. At least 20 percent of all jobs are found this way, and more jobs would result from this technique if more job hunters knew about it. You can write to lots of companies (direct mail) or a few (targeted mail). The techniques are quite different.

Direct contact can save time. You can quickly test your target to see if there are job possibilities for someone like you. If you are familiar with your target area, you can develop your list, compose your letter, send it out, and start on your next target, all within a matter of weeks. Most job hunters contact larger corporations, ignoring smaller firms. Yet new jobs are being created in smaller companies, so don't overlook them.

Direct contact is also the only technique that allows you to quickly contact *every* employer in the area that interests you. You are essentially blanketing the market. Networking, on the other hand, is spotty by nature: you get to see only those companies where your network knows someone. Direct contact is effective for an out-of-town job search. And this technique works whether you are employed or unemployed. It works for all job levels.

*Things which matter most must never be at the mercy*
*of thingswhich matter least.*
Goethe

This technique is an effective one for career changers. You can state all the things that are positive about what you are offering, and leave out anything that does not help your case. Those things can be handled at the interview.

Direct contact can help you get in to see someone you know you cannot network in to see. Shelli, for example, wanted to see someone very senior in an industry in which she had no experience. But she knew the field would be a good fit for her—she researched the industry and figured out how her background could fit in. She targeted six companies, and was able to network into two of them. She knew she would not be able to network into the other four companies within a reasonable time frame: it would take her months to find someone who could only *possibly* help her get in to see the people she'd need to see.

Instead of networking, she researched each of the four companies, wrote to the senior people she was targeting at each company, and followed up with a phone call. Because of her presentation, three of the executives agreed to see her. This saved her many months in her search. Sometimes a targeted mailing can be *more* effective than networking in getting in to see important people. It takes more brainpower than networking, but you already have that.

Direct contact primarily involves targeted and direct mailing, but a junior person can also go from company to company to talk to personnel departments or store managers. So long as job hunters follow up, this technique can work. An executive client of mine used this technique effectively, by walking into a small, privately owned, prestigious store, speaking with the store manager to find out the name of the president, and then calling the president. It led to an executive position with that company. This was "direct contact" because he did not use someone's name to get in to see the store manager or the president. Even when I was very young, I used direct contact to get in to see virtually anyone I wanted.

Sometimes I had trouble getting in, but people eventually saw me because I usually had a good

reason, did my homework, didn't waste their time, was sincere about why I wanted to see them, and was gently persistent. It suits my personality because I am shy about using someone else's name for the core of my effort, I am comfortable about putting my effort into research and writing, and I don't have the time it takes to see a lot of people who may not be right on target for me. As I go along, I network when appropriate.

Direct contact also includes cold calls, which can work for some personalities in some industries.

We will now focus on targeted mail and direct mail:

A **targeted mailing** is similar to networking. You target a relatively small number of people (say, fewer than twenty or thirty) and try to see all of them, *whether or not they have a job for you*. Instead of having a human contact, you *establish* your own contact through the research you do. The meeting is handled exactly the same as a networking interview.

**Direct mail** is used when you have a large number of companies to contact (such as two hundred or more). You would mail a brilliant package to all of them and expect seven or eight interviews from the mailing.

## Using All of the Techniques

A good campaign usually relies on more than one technique to get interviews. Think of how you can divide up your target list. For example, if you have a list of two hundred companies in your target area, you may decide you can network into twenty of them, will do a targeted mailing (with follow-up phone calls) to another twenty or thirty, and do a direct-mail campaign to the rest. That way you have both blanketed your market and used the most appropriate technique to reach each company in your target area. In addition, you could also contact search firms and answer ads.

## Networking vs. Direct Mail

Let's use the banking industry as an example. You could easily network your way into a large bank. You could find someone who knew someone

*Although action is typical of the American style, thought and planning are not; it is considered heresy to state that some problems are not immediately or easily solvable.*
Daniel Bell, sociologist, *Daedalus*, Summer 1967

at a number of them. Each contact you'd make at a large bank could refer you to other people within that same bank—and that increases your chances of getting a job there. Since one person knows others within that organization, networking is efficient. You can meet many potential hiring managers within one company.

On the other hand, it may be difficult to network into smaller banks. Fewer of your friends are likely to know someone there, because each small bank has far fewer employees. Each networking meeting would represent fewer jobs and fewer referrals within each bank. Referrals to other small banks would also generally represent fewer jobs than the larger banks have. It could take forever to network to the same number of potential jobs at hundreds of small banks that could easily be covered by networking at large banks. Networking can be inefficient with smaller organizations, and you may find that you can't put a dent in the market.

You could contact smaller banks directly. They do not expect you to know someone who works there, so they are more open to intelligent mailings. They tend to get fewer contacts from job hunters. You could categorize the smaller banks in a way that makes sense to you—those strong in international banking, for example, or those strong in lending. Or you could categorize banks by nationality—grouping the Japanese banks, European banks, South American banks, and so on. Then you could *target each segment* with a cover letter customized for that market.

Decide which techniques are best for you. Think about how people tend to get hired within your target industry and profession. Also consider your own circumstances, such as whether you are currently employed, how much freedom you have to go on networking interviews, how much use you can make of the phone, and so on. You can always network your way into a few specific companies, but a great number is sometimes not possible.

Remember, networking requires a great deal of time and travel. Direct mail is often appealing to those who are working and must ration their interview and travel time.

*A word of caution to very senior executives:* Because of your extensive networks, you may be tempted to rely exclusively on them to find your next position. As extensive as they are, your contacts are probably spotty. You may be reluctant to do research, because you are used to having others do such things for you. Do your research anyway. Define your targets. List all of the companies in your target areas that are appropriate for you, and the names of the people you need to see in each of these companies. Most very senior executives skip this step, and get their next position serendipitously. That's just fine—if it is a position that is right for you. But many senior executives, in their eagerness to land something quickly, may land something inappropriate, beneath what they deserve, or nothing at all. If you have listed all of the people you should see in your target areas, you increase your chances of having a thorough campaign and you will not miss out on a good possibility for yourself.

If you can network in to see the people you should see in your target market, fine. But if you can think of no way to network in, contact them directly. You will get plenty of serendipitous leads, and meet plenty of people who have business ideas and want to form partnerships with you. These opportunities may be fine, but they are better if you can compare them with those you uncover through an organized search.

### In Summary

Have a list of all the people you should meet in *each* of your target areas or, at the very least, have a list of all the companies in your target areas. Intend to contact all of them. Get meetings with people in your target area through networking, direct contact, search firms, and ads. Do not think of these as techniques for getting *jobs,* but as techniques for getting *interviews*. Plan how you can contact or meet the *right* people in *every* company in each of your target areas—as quickly as possible.
After the meeting, either keep in touch with networking-type contacts (regardless of how you met them) or think about what you can do next to

---

*perhaps* turn the interview into a job offer.

## Getting Polished for a Full Campaign

Before interviewing, be prepared: know exactly what you want and what you have to offer. In the next chapter, you will prepare your pitch to companies. Have your pitch ready even *before* you contact anyone—just so you are prepared. Read the chapters on interviewing, and *practice*. Be a polished interviewer. Remember the cliché: "You don't get a second chance to make a good first impression."

After you have practiced interviewing, contact the people on your "hit list." Start with those who are less important to you, so you can practice and learn more about your target area. You will want to know, for example, your chances in that market and how you should position yourself.

After you have met with someone, follow up. This method works. Read the chapters on following up. Once you have contacted a target area, contact it again a few months later. Keep following up on the people you meet.

Read magazines and newspapers. Attend organizational meetings. Keep abreast of what is happening in the field. Keep on networking.

## A Promotional Campaign to Get Interviews

Sometimes I say to a client who is shy, "So far, you and I are the only ones who know you are looking for a job." Get your name out there. Get on the inside track. You must conduct a promotional campaign to contact as many potential employers as possible. "Campaign" to make sure they remember you.

Make a lot of contacts with people in a position to hire or recommend you. If there are sparks between you, and if you help them remember you, you will be the one they call when a job comes up. Or they can give you the names of others to contact. They may even create a job for you, if it makes sense.

The goal of your promotional campaign is to let the *right* people know what you are looking for. Some discussions will become job interviews, which will lead to offers. Get a lot of interviews so

you will have a number of offers to consider. You want options.

Focus on getting *interviews* in your target area. People who focus on "getting a job" can get uptight when they interview. They do not think of themselves as "looking around" or "finding out what is out there." They act as if they are in a display case, hoping someone will buy them. They may accept the first offer that comes along—even when they know it is inappropriate—because they think they will never get another one.

If you aim to make lots of contacts and get lots of interviews, you are more likely to keep your perspective. If you are an inexperienced job hunter, talk to some people who are not in a position to hire you. Practice your lines and your techniques. Get experience in talking about yourself, and learn more about your target market. Then you will be more relaxed in important interviews and will be able to let your personality come through.

## You Are the Manager of This Campaign

You are in control of this promotional campaign. After reading this book you will know what to say, how to say it, and to whom. You will select the promotional techniques to use and when, and learn how to measure the effectiveness of your campaign.

You will also decide on your image. You can present any picture of yourself that you like. You present your image and credentials in your written communications—résumé, cover letters, and follow-up notes. You have *complete* control over what you put in them and how you present yourself.

How you act and dress also importantly affects your image. Look like you're worth the money you would like. Watch your posture—sit up straight. *Smile!* Decide to feel good and to feel confident. Smile some more. Smile again. Smiling makes you look confident and competent and gives you extra energy. It is difficult to smile and continue being down. Even when you are at home working on your search, smile every once in a while to give yourself energy and the right attitude to help you

*Labor not as one who is wretched, nor yet as one who would be pitied or admired. Direct yourself to one thing only, to put yourself in motion and to check yourself at all times.*

Marcus Aurelius Antonius, *Meditations*

move ahead. This is true no matter what your level. Even executives are better off doing this as they go through their searches. The ones who cannot tend to do less well than those who can.

Whether direct contact or networking, search firms or ads, choose techniques most likely to result in a good response from your target—techniques appropriate to your situation. When you become expert, change a technique to suit yourself.

Modify your approach, or even abandon an effort that is ineffective. You want a good response from your promotional efforts. A "response" is an interview. A polite rejection letter does not count as a response. Some companies have a policy of sending letters, and some have a policy against them. Rejection letters have nothing to do with you. They do not count. Only interviews count.

This is a campaign to generate interviews. Your competition is likely to have polished presentations. Decide on the message you want to get across in the interview, and practice it. There are two kinds of interviews: information-gathering ("networking") interviews, and actual job interviews. Do not try to turn every meeting into a job interview. You will turn people off—and lessen the chances of getting a job. *In the beginning, you are aiming for contact, or networking, interviews.* (See the chapters on networking interviews, as well as information on handling the job interview.)

When things do not work, there is a reason. Be aware and correct the situation. There is no point in continuing an unsuccessful campaign. Remember, when things go wrong—as they will—it is not personal. This is strictly business. It is a project. With experience, you will become better at managing your promotional campaigns to get interviews.

## Why Stagger Your Campaigns?

Why is it unwise to start all of your campaigns at once? Let's pretend your first target is the telephone industry, and your second target is the environmental industry. If one day you talk to a telephone company, and the next day you talk to an environmental company, you will not sound credible. When you meet with the environmental

company, it does you no good to mention that you met with the telephone company.

If, however, you talk to someone in a telephone company, and then another person in that or another telephone company, you can say, "I'm talking to four different divisions of your firm right now, and I'm also talking to other phone companies." Then it sounds as if you really want to work in their industry.

Similarly, when you want to talk to an environmental company, you can mention you are talking to a lot of environmental companies. The information you learn at one company will make you sound smarter with the next.

As you research and meet with people in a target area, the target becomes richer and less superficial. In the beginning of a search, for example, you may be interested in health care—which is too broad a target. Later, however, you may find that the field is more complex than you thought and learn that people have jobs that are not at all what an outsider would expect.

You are an insider when you give back information, such as: "Do you know that Southern Bell has a fulfillment system very similar to yours?"

Or you can say to an environmental company: "I've been talking to a lot of environmental companies, and it seems that a trend in this industry right now is _____. Do you agree?"

This methodical search is the only smart way to do it because you gain momentum. Most job hunters simply "go on interviews," but that's not enough in this economy. Companies expect you to know something about them.

On the following page is one person's Personal Marketing Plan. You may want to use it as a model for your own.

# Sample Personal Marketing Plan

### Personal Marketing Plan
### Joe Doakes

**Target Functions: Vice President/Director/Manager**
- Management Information Services
- Applications Development
- Information Systems
- Information Systems Technology
- Systems Development
- Business Re-Engineering

**Responsibilities:**
- Identification of new information systems technologies and how they could affect the profitability of a company.
- Management of projects for the implementation of information systems or new technologies.
- Providing for and managing a business partner relationship between the information systems department and the internal company departments that utilize their services.
- Implementing and managing a business partner relationship between the company and its primary vendors and its customers utilizing systems technologies, such as EDI (Electronic Data Interchange).

**Target Companies:**

| Attributes | Location |
|---|---|
| • People-oriented | • Primary - North New Jersey or Westchester/ Orange/Rockland Counties in New York |
| • Growth-minded through increased sales, acquisitions, or new products | • Secondary - New York City, Central New Jersey, Southern Connecticut, Eastern Pennsylvania |
| • Committed to quality customer service | • Other - Anywhere along the Eastern Seaboard |
| • Receptive to new ideas on how to do business or utilizing new technologies | |

**Target Industries:**

| Consumer Products: | Pharmaceuticals: | Food/Beverage: | Chemicals: | Other: |
|---|---|---|---|---|
| Unilever | Merck | Pepsico | Castrol | Medco |
| Kimberly Clark | Schering-Plough | T.J. Lipton | Witco | Toys-R-Us |
| Avon | Warner-Lambert | Kraft/General Foods | Allied Chemical | Computer Associates |
| Carter Wallace | American Home Products | Nabisco | Olin Corp. | Becton Dickinson |
| Sony | Bristol-Myers Squibb | Hartz Mountain | Union Carbide | Dialogic |
| Minolta | Pfizer | Continental Baking | Air Products | Siemans |
| Boyle Midway | Jannsen Pharmaceutica | Nestle's | General Chemical | Automatic Data Proc. |
| Revlon | Hoffmann-LaRoche | Haagen-Dazs | Englehard Corp. | Vital Signs |
| L&F Products | Ciba-Geigy | Tuscan Dairies | BASF Corp. | Benjamin Moore |
| Houbigant | Sandoz | Dannon Co. | Degussa Corp. | |
| Mem | A.L. Laboratories | BSN Foods | GAF Corp. | |
| Chanel | Smith Kline Beecham | Campbell Soup | Lonza Inc. | |
| Airwick | American Cyanamid | Cadbury Beverages | Sun Chemical | |
| Church & Dwight | Boeringer Ingelheim | Labatt | | |
| Johnson & Johnson | Roberts Pharmaceuticals | Arnold Foods | | |
| Reckitt & Colman | Winthrop Pharmaceuticals | S. B. Thomas | | |
| Philip Morris | Glaxo | Sunshine Biscuits | | |
| Clairol | Block Drug | | | |
| Estee Lauder | Hoecst Celanese | | | |
| Cosmair | Ethicon | | | |

Aim for a critical mass of activity that will make things happen, help you determine your true place in this market, and give you a strong bargaining position.

I plan to approach this target using the following techniques:

1. Do research (gather information at the library).
2. Network (gather information through people).
3. Conduct a direct-mail or targeted-mail campaign.
4. Contact selected search firms.
5. Join one or two relevant organizations.
6. Regularly read trade magazines and newspapers.
7. Follow up with "influence" notes.
8. Follow up with key contacts on a monthly basis.
9. Answer ads.
10. Aim to give out as much information as I get.

The best techniques for you to use to get interviews depend on your personality and your target market.

For certain targets, search firms may be the most important technique for getting interviews. In other fields, my own for example, people rarely get job leads through search firms. When you are networking in your target market, ask people: "Are there certain search firms that you tend to use? How do you go about hiring people?"

---

*If I insist that my work be rewarding, that it mustn't be tedious or monotonous, I'm in trouble. . . .*
*Time after time it fails to become so. So I get more agitated about it, I fight with people about it, I make more*
*demands about it . . . . It's ridiculous to demand that work always be pleasurable, because work is not necessar-*
*ily pleasing; sometimes it is, sometimes it isn't. If we're detached and simply pick up the job we have to do and*
*go ahead and do it, it's usually fairly satisfying. Even jobs that are repugnant or dull or tedious tend to be quite*
*satisfying, once we get right down to doing them. . . . One of the routine jobs I get every once in a while comes*
*from putting out a little magazine. You have to sort the pages. It's a simple, routine, mechanical sort of job. . . .*
*I never realized that this would be one of the most satisfying parts of the whole thing, just standing there*
*sorting pages. This happens when we just do what we have to do.*
Thomas Merton,
*The Springs of Contemplation*

---

The Five O'Clock Club®

# How to Improve Your Position Where You Are

*A man's work is in danger of deteriorating when he thinks he has found the one best formula for doing it. If he thinks that, he is likely to feel that all he needs is merely to go on repeating himself . . . so long as a person is searching for better ways of doing his work, he is fairly safe.*
Eugene O'Neill

The techniques you use for job hunting inside your company are often the same as those you would use outside. You can look at ads for ideas, network, write proposals, even do some outside interviewing to learn more about how to position yourself and gain a realistic assessment of your value.

## Job Hunters at The Five O'Clock Club Sometimes Stay With Their Present Employers—But in a Stronger Position

Half the people who attend The Five O'Clock Club are employed. Some think they are in danger in their present positions and want to start looking now; others are simply unhappy.

Although employed people come to The Five O'Clock Club because they want jobs elsewhere, a surprising number end up becoming more valued by their present companies. That's because these workers start exploring what is going on outside their companies, pick up new skills that make themselves marketable, and often take that information back to their present employers. Because they no longer feel dependent on one company, they develop greater self-esteem and become more assertive in developing ideas and programs for their present employers. Their employers start to treat them differently.

## CASE STUDY: MARIE
### On Her Way Out: Then Promoted

Marie is the head of the direct-marketing arm of a major not-for-profit. She felt that she was undervalued, and perhaps even being squeezed out. She wanted to get into the for-profit world. To learn more about this target area, her counselor and group at The Five O'Clock Club sug-

gested she read the trade journals, join associations having to do with direct marketing, and get to know people in the field. Marie learned so much in her intensive research that she went a few steps further: she *spoke* at the association meetings, began writing for the trade journals, and even appeared on the cover of one prestigious trade magazine.

This caught the attention of her current employer, who began to value her much more than before. Coincidentally, Marie's boss moved elsewhere in the organization. Marie was surprised that she was asked to take her boss's job. That promotion eased Marie's pressure to find a new job quickly. In addition, her résumé was looking better and better.

If she decides to look for a new job again, she will be helped by her new title and experience, and also by her new visibility as a guru in the direct marketing field. By the way, she continues to stay involved and improve her career—as well as her worth—at her present place of employment. And she continue to attend The Five O'Clock Club to stay sharp in her field.

## Continuous Improvement

This process of staying aware and marketable is what employees of the future will have to do to keep their present jobs longer, or to make career moves within their present companies.

With all of the changes occurring in most corporations, your firm may be one of the important places to look if you want to make a career change—or if you simply want to get ahead.

## Improve Your Present Job

Think of ideas for changing your present job to move it in the direction in which you want to go. If you know where you are heading, you can be open to new assignments or projects that would give you experience in those areas. Assume responsibility for new areas. Move away from old areas that no longer fit in with your long-term career goals. When special projects come up that would give you new skills or update old skills, gradually start working on those projects—feeling them out—and

*. . . the thought of losing my job didn't trouble me as much as it troubled lifers such as, say, Dash Riprock. That is not to say I did not care; I cared immensely. I thrived on praise more than most and thus sought to please. But I was willing to take greater risks than if I had felt deeply proprietary about my career. I was, for instance, willing to disobey my superiors, and that caused them to sit up and take notice far more quickly than if I had been a good soldier.* Michael Lewis, *Liar's Poker*

then taking over the whole thing if it seems right.

Start out working in these areas in an informal way. It will be non-threatening both to you and to the company. You are not asking your company to make a big decision about whether or not you *should* handle these areas—just slip into them. And if things seem not to be working out, be sure to slip out early in the game.

If you slip in by "helping out" on a project, you can get more enmeshed in that project and eventually become an expert in that area. At the same time, be sure not to ignore the work for which you are primarily responsible. If you spend time on the new area and your old job starts to slip, you are in trouble. You've got to do both for a while. When it gets to be too much of a burden for you, you will either have to ask for additional help while you continue to handle both areas, or you will try to unload the area that no longer interests you. Just be sure that the work that interests you is important to your employer.

If you are improving your skills and knowledge—and looking for opportunities—opportunities will present themselves.

### "But I love what I'm doing right now and I want to keep on doing it."

The same thing happened to me. Twice. The first time, I was twenty-one years old and in the computer programming department of a large company. Programmers brought their computer "dumps" to us—the debugging team—and we told them where their programs went wrong. The debugging section was considered an elite group, and I loved my job. But the technology changed, and computers told the programmers where their programs had gone wrong. They didn't need us any more.

The company gave me another job; I don't even remember what it was. I'm sure I didn't like it as much as the debugging job. Technology is often the cause of having our jobs change.

Ten years later, a similar thing happened. I was then a training manager in a large company (by then I had gotten my M.B.A. in Behavioral Science). I was in that job for three years, and one day it

was gone. The company had gone through five downsizings over a number of years, and then decided to cut out the training program altogether. I had loved my job so much that I was oblivious to the larger changes that were taking place. Doing a good job is not enough. Sometimes changes in your company may affect your job.

Technology causes changes; companies change; and sometimes people change. Someday you may decide that your job is not as enjoyable for you as it once was. Maybe the job is the same, but something inside you has changed. Perhaps you now want to move to a more people-oriented job rather than one that is intensely technical. As people get older, their values change. That is fine. But a problem occurs when people who have never given it another thought say that they want a change and they have no idea what kind of change they want.

Deciding where you want to go with your life is not an easy process. And it is not something to be taken too lightly. It is, after all, your life that we're talking about. Start to get ready for your next change—whatever it may be. Even if you love what you are doing right now, figure out what it is about your present position that you find so enjoyable. Then when you want a change, you will have some idea of the kind of change you want.

### A Mindset of Strength

People are used to being dependent on their employers. They say, "My boss won't train me in this new area" or "Only those who went to Ivy League schools get into that program."

Make your own program. Don't let "them" stop you. You operate from greater strength when you do not feel completely dependent on your present employer, and your employer is usually better off as well. If you are well-versed in what is going on in your field or industry, you are more marketable, and your employer benefits from your knowledge and contacts. Take better care of yourself professionally. If you are frustrated that your employer is not doing enough to help you, help yourself.

*I can never be what I ought to be until you are what you ought to be.*
*You can never be what you ought to be until I am what I ought to be.*
Martin Luther King, Jr., *The American Dream*

## Making a Move in a Medium- or Large-Size Company

Many people think that job hunting internally in a large corporation consists of only two steps:

- responding to job postings, and then
- doing well in interviews.

Job postings are one path to a new job, but they are not the way most people move into new jobs within the same companies.

## Ongoing Career Management and Career Exploration

People who are successful in their careers know that "job search" involves ongoing career management and career exploration: building relationships, researching areas inside and outside the company, and developing marketable skills. This approach is more work than simply responding to job postings, but it is a surer and faster way to getting ahead in today's market.

All of this fits in with what we have taught at The Five O'Clock Club since 1978: It is best for both the employee and the employer if "job hunting" is seen as a continual process—and not just something that happens when a person wants to change jobs. Continual job search means continually being aware of market conditions both inside and outside our present companies, and continually learning what we have to offer—to both markets.

With this approach, workers are safer because they are more likely to keep their present jobs longer: they learn to change and grow as the company and industry do. And if they have to go elsewhere, they will be more marketable. Companies are better off because employees who know what is going on outside their insular halls are smarter, more sophisticated and more proactive, and make the company more competitive.

## An Overview of How People Get New Jobs Within Their Present Companies—

Your first move, as already noted, is to gain new skills while staying in your present position. At the same time, you need to learn more about what is going on both inside and outside your company.

You've heard it said that "it's not what you know, but who you know." It's probably a lot of both. You can improve both your skills and your contacts. You can also have an organized internal search at the same time that you have an organized external search. Here's an overview of how to look internally:

- focus on three or more departments, divisions or businesses in which you are interested within the company where you are now employed
- research those departments, divisions or businesses
- build relationships with four to six people in each area
- find out how those functions are performed in other companies
- perhaps take that information back to your present employer, and
- develop the skills you need to make yourself marketable in those departments, divisions or businesses.

Moving internally takes work, but it is less frustrating than simply responding to job postings. Incidentally, an outsider who wanted to work for your company might follow exactly the same approach. Whether you are inside or outside, staying marketable and keeping in touch is how most people get jobs.

## The Details of How to Search for a New Job Within Your Present Company

You are more likely to find a new job within your present company if you use an organized approach, and if you do not "put all of your eggs into one basket." Follow these steps:

1) Find out which departments or businesses within your present company are worth your interest. You can do a preliminary investigation by:

- networking within your company to find out the best areas for you to explore
- doing research through your annual report and other printed materials.

2) Using the worksheet on the following page,

list three departments, divisions or businesses you would like to explore within your present company.

3) Now you need to get to know people in each of those areas. For each one, list the names of four to six people you think you should get to know.

If you don't yet know the names of the appropriate people in those areas, ask others for their advice, or study the organization charts for those businesses. It may even be that people *outside* your company can tell you who to see inside.

4) Now you have to figure out how you will get in to see each of these people. There are three main techniques for getting in to see a person within your present company:

a. **networking directly to that person** through someone you already know (see the chapters on Networking).

b. **building a network** in to that person or in to that general area. Even if the people you know do not work in the areas in which you are interested, they can refer you to people in those areas, who can then refer you on to other people in the department or division.

If you don't know anyone outside your department, you can get to meet more people in your company by:
• serving on committees
• volunteering for internal programs such as United Way or the blood drive
• joining task forces
• meeting fellow employees at association meetings for the field you are targeting, or
• simply meeting people in elevators or the company cafeteria.

You can tell them that you are curious to learn more about their area. Perhaps you could suggest that the two of you have lunch sometime.

c. **contacting the person directly**, such as by writing an internal memo (see the chapters on Targeted Mailings).

On the worksheet, list the methods you are likely to use to meet with each person.

5) Next, figure out what to say to each person. Handle these meetings the same as you would any networking meeting. However, you may also want to ask some of the following:
• what they do there
• the plans for the area
• the kinds of people they tend to look for, even though they may not be hiring at the moment
• how you stack up against the kinds of people they tend to look for. You can ask, "If you had an opening right now, would you consider hiring someone like me? Why or why not?"
• the skills and abilities you would need to move into that area someday
• how they think you might gain the skills and abilities you are now lacking.

As you establish relationships with people in specific businesses, get to know more about each business and understand what skills you need to make yourself more desirable. Just as in Stage 2 of an external job search, your goal is to have people saying, "I sure wish I had an opening right now. I'd love to have someone like you on board." Then when a job opens up, you will be the one most likely to get it.

6) It is usually not enough to find out about an area inside your present company. To be strongly considered for a position, it is a good idea to also learn how that area functions outside of your company. You will be more knowledgeable and more marketable—inside and outside of your company at the same time.

Many functional areas exist across industries: customer service, computers, purchasing, corporate sales, public relations—to name a few.

Still other areas may *seem* to be related strictly to your industry, yet actually are found in many industries. For example, banks are involved in "check transaction processing," which may seem like a function related only to financial institutions. Yet many industries—hospitals, large fund-

The Five O'Clock Club®

I gave a lecture inside a major corporation to encourage employees to manage their own careers. Someone in the audience said, "I've answered six job postings for a certain department. They give the jobs only to people they know." "That's probably true," I said, "and how many people do you think you would have to know in a department to have a chance of getting a job there?" She replied, "Uh, six."

Six is a good estimate of how many people you would have to be in touch with **on an ongoing basis** before you would stand a chance of getting a job in

a certain area—providing you had the skills and personality they were looking for. Make sure you are aiming at a number of departments, and also be sure to build your network and base of support and information *outside* of your present company. That base will make you more marketable inside, and help you to hedge your bets in case things do not work out where you are employed at present.

Beyond that, follow the normal job-search approach used at The Five O'Clock Club.

**For Target _____:**  Dept., div., or business: _____
Position/Function: _____
Geographic area: _____

| People to Contact | Title | Method of Contact | Date of Last Contact | Targeted Date of Next Contact |
|---|---|---|---|---|
| 1. | | | | |
| 2. | | | | |
| 3. | | | | |
| 4. | | | | |
| 5. | | | | |
| 6. | | | | |
| 7. | | | | |

**For Target _____:**  Dept., div., or business: _____
Position/Function: _____
Geographic area: _____

| People to Contact | Title | Method of Contact | Date of Last Contact | Targeted Date of Next Contact |
|---|---|---|---|---|
| 1. | | | | |
| 2. | | | | |
| 3. | | | | |
| 4. | | | | |
| 5. | | | | |
| 6. | | | | |
| 7. | | | | |

*I chose, and my world was shaken—so what?*
*The choice may have been mistaken, the choosing was not . . .*
Stephen Sondheim, "Move On," *Sunday in the Park With George*

raising organizations, direct mail houses—are engaged in heavy transaction processing. Broadly define the field you are in. It may well exist in other industries—but in a very different way. This will open up the industries where you can transfer your skills.

Regardless of where you work inside your company, think of how your function is handled outside—especially in other industries.

You can learn more by:
- joining professional associations
- reading trade journals
- Taking courses
- networking to people outside your company—including those outside your industry.

**The more you know about the areas you are exploring, the more information you can share with people in the departments or businesses you are exploring**. This will put you in a better position to figure out how you can help them.

Using the worksheet on the next page, list the methods you are planning to use to investigate each area outside of your present company.

7) As you investigate, **you may find that you are lacking in certain skills that seem to be in demand**. Acquiring these new skills will make you more marketable, both inside and outside of your present company. Using that same worksheet, list the skills, experiences and knowledge you need to develop, and how you think you may go about acquiring them.

8) Keep in touch (about every two months) with four to six people in each department or business:
- Find out what is happening in the department or business.
- Let them know what is happening to you, such as new projects you are working on and new information or skills you have picked up that would be of interest to them.

9) Continue to research (using the techniques in point 6, above) those areas you have been exploring outside of your present company.

---

### To keep your present job longer . . .

. . . and to help make your company stronger, think of yourself as an investigator on behalf of your organization. Read trade journals about your function and industry. Join associations. Find out what is happening internationally. Investigate the new technologies that are impacting your area.

When you meet people from other companies and industries (and countries) who do what you do, compare what they are doing to the way your company does it. If the way they are doing it is better, take that information back to your company. Keep on investigating and learning. If you decide you need to pick up new skills, find some way to get them.

---

10) Continue to take that information back to those departments or businesses in which you are interested.

11) All the while, respond to job postings for those departments or businesses.

### Do Not Jeopardize Your Present Situation

At first, take the most cautious steps possible. Reading trade journals and joining trade organizations are usually among the safest. You can join simply because you are interested in the subject and because "I thought it would help me do better in my present job if I were more knowledgeable about this area."

### CASE STUDY: JOE
*Making Himself More Marketable*

Two years ago, Joe, a finance professional, found a new job within his present company. It was not easy. Hiring managers saw him as having essentially the same skills as hundreds of other finance professionals. Joe did not want to go through that again. To make himself more marketable, Joe decided to differentiate himself from his

# How to Research Those Areas
# Outside of Your Present Company

It is not enough to keep in touch with people in various departments inside your present company. Chances are, you need to learn more about their work and their issues—and not only from them, but by speaking to people on the outside. In addition, you may need to pick up a few new skills to make yourself desirable.

For each department, division or business you are targeting, list how you plan to learn more about each area, the skills you need to develop, and how you plan to develop them.

Of course, you cannot become expert in every area you are targeting. Just as in an outside search, you will conduct a Preliminary Target Investigation to see which are worth your while, and then you will concentrate on those in which you are sincerely interested, and which you feel are worth it.

You may be able to gain experience in the new field *outside* of your present company (see "How to Change Careers"). If you do not wind up getting such a job inside your present company, you may be able to get a job outside.

For Target _____:  Dept., div., or business: _____
Position/Function: _____
Geographic area: _____

| How to learn about this new area: | Skills, experience, and knowledge needed: | How I plan to develop myself: |
|---|---|---|
| 1. | | |
| 2. | | |
| 3. | | |
| 4. | | |
| 5. | | |
| 6. | | |
| 7. | | |

For Target _____:  Dept., div., or business: _____
Position/Function: _____
Geographic area: _____

| How to learn about this new area: | Skills, experience, and knowledge needed: | How I plan to develop myself: |
|---|---|---|
| 1. | | |
| 2. | | |
| 3. | | |
| 4. | | |
| 5. | | |
| 6. | | |
| 7. | | |

competitors by developing new skills.

Joe started to look—not for a new job—but for information to help him decide which new skills he should develop. He spoke with a number of people both inside and outside of his company, and learned that there would be a strong demand for those who knew Lotus Notes and had his particular background in finance.

When Joe investigated learning Lotus Notes, he found that it would take six months and thousands of dollars. It would be a big investment—even though he already had a computer at home. His department did not use Lotus Notes, so Joe knew he would not be able to convince his boss to pay for his certification. Joe decided to make an investment in himself.

Studying Lotus Notes in the evenings and on weekends, it took Joe a little longer than he had expected. As he got closer to becoming certified, Joe recontacted those people inside and outside his company who had advised him earlier—to let them know of his progress.

Joe's department was downsized just as he was recontacting people. He received a number of offers outside, but one department inside offered Joe the opportunity to work on a Lotus Notes project for three months. Then he would have the hands-on experience he needed. It seemed like a perfect fit because Joe already knew a lot about the company, and that would help him in this project. He jumped at the chance.

In addition, Joe kept up his contacts inside and outside the company. They were glad to hear about his new assignment, and urged him to continue to stay in touch. Joe felt more secure now that a lot of people knew what he was doing. The new project could turn into a long-term assignment or even a permanent position. On the other hand, he knew better than to depend on that, and wanted to have other options in case he needed to line up another assignment.

Joe was starting to feel more in control of his career. He knew that the next move would always be up to him, and he wanted to be ready.

As he continued to develop contacts, he lined up two consulting assignments outside. He could have stayed with his present employer—even full-time—but he decided to become a consultant because it made him feel more secure and more energized.

If you are interested in moving into a different area, you may have to reposition yourself to make yourself more marketable. It is relatively easy to move into the same job in a different department, but more difficult to move into a new job in another department. You may be seen as someone who is trying to break into the new area, who does not have the experience others have in that area. Gain the experience you need to make yourself more marketable.

## Getting Offers Inside:
## Negotiating a New Job

If you have been following the system, you have been talking to people in several areas of your present company. You have also been talking to people outside. Now you are getting offers.

Because you have spent time gathering information both inside and outside of the company:

• You now have insight about your standing in the marketplace.

• You have information that will help you to do better in your new job at your present company.

• You have developed contacts to whom you can turn when you have questions in your new job.

• You understand better what you can do for this new department, division or business within your present company.

Now you have received an offer inside your present company and are in the negotiation stage. The hiring team has told you the work they need to have done. But consider negotiating for additional assignments and experience that you want. Think of other work you can do for the department that would make you even more valuable to them or would give you an opportunity for growth. Define the duties you can undertake immediately so you can provide immediate value-added. This is the time to make sure the job will satisfy their needs as well as your own. Here's an example:

> *Any time we think the problem is "out there," that thought is the problem.*
> *We empower what's out there to control us. The change paradigm is*
> *"outside-in"—what's out there has to change before we can change.*
> Stephen R. Covey, *The Seven Habits of Highly Effective People*

## CASE STUDY: JOAN
### Negotiating the Job

Joan has a strong accounting background, and the real estate area was interested in her because of that. However, Joan was interested in learning more about real estate, and also wanted to have more people contact. She said to the hiring manager, "I know you need my accounting help, and I am very interested in doing that for you. But one of the main reasons I'm interested in your department is because I want to learn about real estate and I also want to have more contact with people. Perhaps I could devote myself to solving your accounting problems, but also sit in on real estate deal meetings so I can learn that area of the business at the same time. After a few years, and if I do well, perhaps I could move into that area completely and train someone new to do the accounting work."

## CASE STUDY: JACOB
### Opportunity for Development

Jacob is interviewing in one division for a controller position having to do with the Middle East and Africa. His strength lies in that area. However, he has always had an interest in Latin America, and thinks this will be a huge growth market in the future. The Latin America market fits in with his long-term plan of being a business head in his company someday for one of those countries. He said to the hiring team: "I know you need my help in the Middle East and Africa, and I love working on those countries. But I am also extremely interested in Latin America. I'm afraid that if I come in here, I'll get to work only on Middle East and Africa. I'd like to also be assigned to one small Latin American country so I can learn more about that area. I happen to be fluent in Spanish and Portuguese so I can get up to speed fast."

## CASE STUDY
### Growing the Job

Instead of just listening to what they need to have done in this job, propose additional respon-sibilities, if you think that is appropriate.

"This job calls for someone to handle customer-service complaints, but I also have excellent writing skills. I could put together an internal newsletter to give other customer-service representatives information on how they could do their jobs better."

## CASE STUDY
### Keeping Up in Your Field

Let the hiring team know the duties you could immediately undertake to make yourself valuable. And think of the additional training you may need, if appropriate, to do even better in this job and to help you be even more valuable in the future.

"I've been working in computers for thirteen years, and certainly understand the systems you have in place and the need you have for upgrading your current systems. I'm afraid, however, that my skills will become obsolete if I spend the two years it will take to completely revamp your current system. I was wondering if I could be involved with the new technologies in a way that would not interfere with getting done what you need to have done. For example, I could sit in on new technology task forces, or be part of a team on a small, new technology project. That way, I would do the work you need to have done, but also feel that I am taking care of my own future."

## Other Areas to Negotiate

In addition to job responsibilities and training, consider negotiating some of the following:
- start date
- date of first review
- additional resources (people, equipment, systems) you would need to do the job well
- work hours, if you have special needs
- travel.

For example,

"I see that this job requires 70 percent field work. I was wondering if there was any way the job could be restructured it so that my field-work time would be limited to 50 percent."

## Salary Increases

In making a move within a company, salary increases are often *not* negotiable. This is because the company is allowing you to grow in your career, and is therefore encouraging you to move to other areas when appropriate. However, the company does not want to be penalized for giving you this relative freedom to change jobs.

## Understand the Political Situation

If you have any questions about company policy, <u>**find people you trust who can advise you**</u>. Observe what others have done. Ask others who have made moves how they did it. Every company is different. An internal search can be very sensitive. Find out the parameters in *your* company before you put yourself at risk.

<u>**Warning**</u>: Most companies still operate under the outmoded model: Employees who try to develop themselves or move elsewhere within the company may be seen as traitors to their immediate bosses and as threats to their employers. Be cautious in planning your internal move.

However, you still must take care of yourself and remain marketable so you are not dependent on one employer. Proactively figure out what you bring to the party, while finding out—and fitting into—the new direction your company and industry are taking.

A few enlightened companies are actually helping their employees to manage their own careers—and become more marketable both inside and outside the company. Those companies hope to have the flexible, high-performing workforces they will need to support the company's ambitious—and changing—plans.

Yes, there is a risk that those highly marketable employees will leave the company. But the alternative is to keep employees strapped into tightly defined jobs, and relatively ignorant about what is going on in the outside world. Smart, competitive companies know that it is better to encourage all employees to be flexible and knowledgeable—at the risk of losing a few— rather than encourage employees to stay stale and dependent on the firm.

The next two chapters, "Predictors of Career Success" and "Six Steps to a Healthy Self-Esteem," will give you important insights before you move on to the next part of the process.

From William Bridges,
*JobShift: How to Prosper in a Workplace Without Jobs*

*The employee-vendor relationship to his or her customers is something like professional/client relationships in the past, but the difference lies in the pace of change. Traditional professional/client relationships were not change-driven. They developed slowly over time, and they settled into mutually satisfying patterns of complementary activity and reward. Today, however, change occurs so quickly and so constantly that customers, both inside and outside the organization, always need something they don't have.*

*All jobs in today's economy are temporary.*

*It is difficult for us today to appreciate how new and different the world of "holding a job" was for village-born people. They could no longer move about among a variety of tasks, in a variety of locations, on a schedule set by the sunlight and the weather and the particular demands of the season.*

The Five O'Clock Club

# Predictors of Career Success:
## A Study Sponsored by The Five O'Clock Club

by Terri Lowe, Ph.D.

### Overview

Given all of the changes taking place in the world of work today, people need to have a new set of skills and resources to ensure their employability (Waterman, 1994). With the changing employer-employee contract, employees are no longer assured of lifetime employment—or even long-term employment—with a single employer. In fact, in some respects the information age is leading the world of work to look more as it did in centuries past. For example, in the agricultural society of the 1800's, individuals took on multiple and varied tasks to ensure their prosperity and survival. Maintaining the farm, planting and harvesting crops, baking the bread and putting a new roof on the family house were all necessary tasks, and everyone in the family pitched in to accomplish them. People had to be "Jacks and Jills of all trades" in order to keep the farm producing and the home fires burning.

It was only in the industrial age that the concept of "a job" was created (Bridges, 1994). Beginning in this era for the first time, a worker reported to work for a given period of time to carry out a relatively structured and unvarying set of tasks, whereupon he or she would return home at the end of the "work day." However, today, workers find themselves, out of necessity, moving back toward the entrepreneurial "Jack or Jill of all trades" scenario. In order to ensure their employability, people need to have a greatly enlarged bag of tricks (e.g., skills and abilities) in order to ensure their prosperity and survival. Consequently, there is a new emphasis on career management. It is up to the individual to manage his or her career effectively—in most cases, with minimal support from the employer.

In order to manage their careers effectively, people need to behave in new ways, develop new skills and new competencies, and approach work with a new mind-set from that of the past fifty to a hundred years. To carry out these new behaviors in a way that ensures their career success, they need to

**Coping Resources ⬌ Coping Behavior ➡ Career Success**

have a new set of coping resources.

*Coping resources* encompass all of the characteristics—psychological, social, intellectual, and behavioral—that an individual brings to the conference table, board room, or design studio. These resources are shaped and developed by the experiences a person has had over the course of his or her lifetime. They enable an individual to get along in the world. Some of the coping *resources* that are especially relevant in the world of work include:

- skills and abilities
- psychological characteristics (e.g., self-esteem, confidence, resilience, etc.)
- self-awareness (knowledge of own skills, strengths, work style, etc.)
- support systems
- knowledge of industry trends
- network of contacts.

*Coping behaviors* are actions an individual carries out, based upon the coping resources at his or her disposal. Some of the coping *behaviors* involved in effective career management include:

- creating a career plan
- development and use of network and knowledge base to market oneself effectively
- acting in anticipation of industry and market trends
- writing an effective résumé
- conducting a job search
- getting the job done well.

The result of successful coping behavior often bolsters an individual's coping resources. For example, by creating a career plan (coping behavior), a person will often begin to feel more confi-

*Faced with the choice between changing one's mind and proving that
there is no need to do so, almost everybody gets busy on the proof.*
John Kenneth Galbraith

dent (coping resource) about the ability to manage his or her career.

Career success is the ultimate result of effective coping behavior and can be measured in a variety of ways. Some key indicators of career success are:

- satisfaction with one's career
- satisfaction with one's compensation
- feeling successful in one's career
- effectively balancing work and personal concerns.

## Study Method

The Five O'Clock Club sponsored a study measuring key predictors of career success for the journalists affected by the newspaper closing.

A 25-item survey measured a variety of issues related to coping resources, coping behaviors, and perceptions of career success among the journalists affected by the paper's closing. Approximately 110 journalists participated in the survey, which was distributed to them at meetings of The Five O'Clock

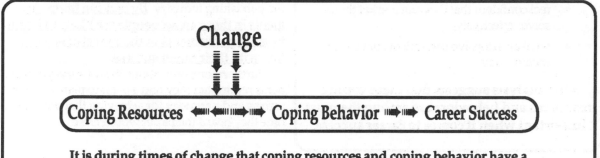

## Change

**Coping Resources ◀━━━▶ Coping Behavior ━▶ Career Success**

**It is during times of change that coping resources and coping behavior have a
heightened importance and relevance to success.**

This model has particular relevance in times of change. It is especially then that coping resources and coping behavior are important to success.

Based on this model, we expect that people:

- who have more coping resources will exhibit more coping behavior
- who have more coping resources will be more successful
- who exhibit more coping behavior will be more successful.

The recent changes at a major metropolitan newspaper illustrate this. Due to increasing competitive pressures in the publishing industry, this paper closed one of their main editions after several years of publication. The shutdown of the edition, although anticipated among industry experts, was a shock to many employees. The Five O'Clock Club was retained by the firm to help employees during this career change.

Club within six weeks of the time the paper announced the closing of the edition.

## Study Results

Key findings provide insight into survey respondents' perceptions of their career success. Results of the survey show that career confidence and confidence in the ability to market oneself effectively are key drivers of perceptions of career success. The survey results confirm the important role of coping resources and coping behavior in achieving career success. However, although all of the items on the charts on the next page are significantly correlated with perceptions of career success, the newspaper survey shows that people rate themselves favorably in only a few of these areas.

### People who see themselves as successful told us that they:

- are knowledgeable about trends in their industry
- are satisfied with the steps they have taken in managing their careers
- are able to articulate their strengths clearly
- are able to respond well to change
- feel confident that they can market themselves effectively
- have an extensive network of contacts in their industry.

**Our analysis suggests that these coping resources and behaviors are among the most important when it comes to career success.**

The majority (about 80%) of respondents feel that they are able to articulate their strengths and respond effectively to change. About half of the respondents (55-56%) also feel confident that they can market themselves, and report being knowledgeable about industry trends.

However, only 36% of respondents indicate that they are satisfied with the steps they've taken in managing their careers, and only 18% report that they are satisfied with their network of contacts in the publishing industry. **By making improvements in these areas, people are likely to begin to see improvements in their level of satisfaction with their career success.**

Furthermore, only about 30% of survey respondents report that they had a backup plan for their careers and a strategy for achieving that plan at the time they heard the paper would close.

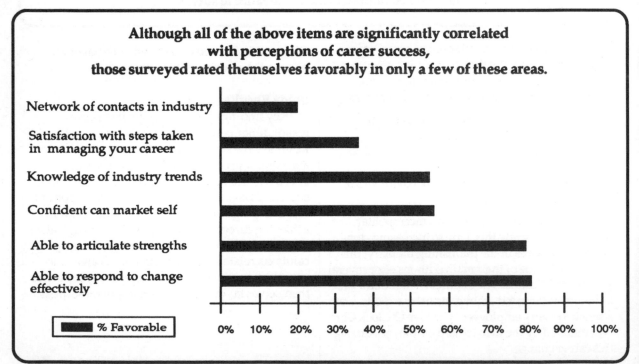

**Although all of the above items are significantly correlated with perceptions of career success, those surveyed rated themselves favorably in only a few of these areas.**

*You must find your own unique pathway in the world; the masses, or majority, never do. Until you set the tone for your own existence, you will follow others, who are, in turn, following you.*
Dennis Kimbro, *Think and Grow Rich: A Black Choice*

---

**When asked to describe their initial reactions when they first heard that the edition would shut down, their comments included:**

| | | |
|---|---|---|
| surprise | shock | annoyance |
| unhappy | disbelief | grief |
| hurt | horror | denial |
| sad | anger | dazed |
| worried | disappointment | panic |
| dread | fear | betrayal |

The respondents may not have been as proactive as they could have been in anticipating change and in managing their careers effectively in light of the changes taking place in their company and industry.

**Career Confidence
is a Self-Fulfilling Prophecy:
If You Have Confidence, You'll Do Better**

Career confidence is a person's sense of having the ability to manage his or her career successfully—no matter what the future holds. Research in a variety of arenas has shown that feelings of confidence with regard to a particular task are significantly correlated with success in doing that task (Bandura, 1986). For example, if I feel confident that I am capable of rewiring the electrical system in my house, I will be more likely to succeed at that task than if I feel less confident. There are a lot of factors that influence career confidence, including skills, abilities, past successes, and the faith that other people express in your abilities.

We measured career confidence in several ways. We asked respondents to indicate the number of industries in which they "were confident they could build a successful and satisfying career." About half of the people (57%) responded by estimating 2 to 3 industries and a large number (34%) indicated 4 to 10 industries.

**People who are confident that they could build a successful and satisfying career in a larger number of industries also report that they:**
- are knowledgeable about trends across industries (not just in their own)
- feel confident that they can market themselves effectively.

Having a high degree of career confidence at one's disposal is a coping resource that is likely to increase one's perceived career success. However, most of the journalists we surveyed do not report having a high degree of career confidence. For example, <u>many survey respondents report that they feel "below average" about the amount of time it will take them to find "a good job."</u> Seventy-eight percent report that it would take the average person one to six months to find a good job. But only 63% feel that they themselves would be able to find a good job within that time frame.

**Self-Marketing Is Key to Career Confidence**

The survey results show that confidence in the ability to market oneself effectively is key to achieving career confidence and feeling successful. However, only about half (56%) of our survey respondents report that they feel they can market themselves effectively .

**Those who feel that they are able to market themselves effectively report that they:**
- have a defined strategy to achieve their plans
- are able to articulate their skills
- are able to articulate areas in which they need to improve themselves
- are able to articulate their strengths.

Being strong in these areas is likely to improve the extent to which one can market oneself effectively. While the majority of respondents feel quite positive about their ability to articulate their skills and strengths, most are less positive about their ability to articulate the areas in which they need to improve themselves and about having a defined strategy to achieve their plans.

By improving their ability to articulate areas needing improvement and defining a strategy to achieve their plans, the journalists surveyed are likely to improve their confidence in their ability to market themselves. <u>Effectively marketing oneself has a strong relationship to career confidence and perceptions of career success.</u>

The situation at this metropolitan newspaper is only one example of events that are becoming much more frequent in today's business environment. Such changes require both new coping resources and coping behaviors. These resources and behaviors play a critical role in determining career success, and will continue to do so in the future. More than ever, as we progress into the

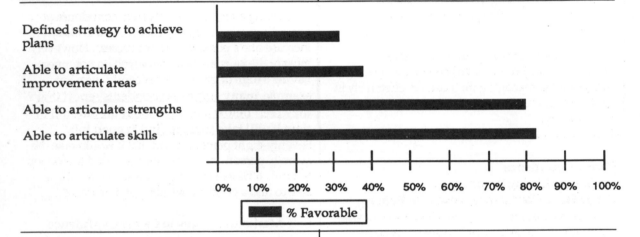

## Conclusions

Although this survey includes only a small number of respondents in a single industry, results suggest some interesting trends noted in the list below.

---

### Some of the key factors in achieving career success

**include career confidence and effectively marketing oneself.**
**Some of the key ingredients include:**

- knowledge of industry trends
- satisfaction with steps taken in managing one's own career
- ability to clearly articulate strengths, skills, areas requiring improvement
- ability to respond well to change
- having a large network of contacts
- defining a strategy to achieve career plans.

information age, people will need to become increasingly entrepreneurial and capable of doing a multiple and varied set of tasks.

### References

Bridges, W. (1994), *Job Shift*, Addison-Wesley

Bandura, A. (1986), *The Social Foundations of Thought and Action: A Social Cognitive Theory*, Prentice-Hall: NJ.

Waterman, R.H., Waterman, J.A., and Collard, B.A., Toward a Career-Resilient Workforce, *Harvard Business Review*, July, August 1994.

Terri Lowe is an industrial/organizational psychologist specializing in climate assessment, team building, and career development. This article originally appeared in *The Five O'Clock News*.

The Five O'Clock Club®

# Six Steps to a Healthy Self-Esteem

by John Leonard

Are you in control of your life and career, or do you feel trapped in some dead-end job that seems to be sucking the energy out of you? Do you believe you have the power to shape your destiny and call the shots, or do you believe you are forever at the mercy of nameless, faceless forces over which you have no control? The answers to these questions can be very different, depending on your level of self-esteem. As Dr. Nathaniel Brandner points out in his book *How to Raise Your Self-Esteem*, "How you feel about yourself crucially affects virtually every aspect of your experience."

Self-esteem is the key component that allows you to confront problems, to improve and promote yourself, to be resilient in the face of apparent failure, and to take charge of your life. When your self-esteem is high, your job means more to you. Problems are not looked upon as roadblocks but as opportunities for success. When your self-esteem is high, you are proactive rather than reactive, you have the confidence to seek out others for their wisdom, and are in turn sought out for your expertise. You have a can-do persona that energizes others and makes them respond to you in very positive ways.

If you already have a high level of self-esteem, great; if you don't, how can you develop it? It is not enough merely to have a "wish list" that will make everything happen as if with an uncorked genie. You need a system, a series of steps to effect the self-improvement that will change your entire approach to life.

A couple of weeks ago I was driving back to the East Coast from a football game in Indiana, late at night, and I picked up a radio talk show from Atlanta. The guest was Jack Canfield, whose *Chicken Soup for the Soul* books (written with Mark Victor Hansen) are models of inspiration for people who don't believe they have the power to change their lives. He told two stories—different people, different situations, different areas of the country, but similar *modi operandi* and similar results. I may have missed some points, but these are the basic stories. First, there was a group of women who wanted out of a ghetto in Chicago. They had no degrees, in fact hadn't even graduated from high school. They traded off baby-sitting responsibilities, took G.E.D. programs, received diplomas, entered community colleges, worked at part-time jobs, earned degrees, went to four-year schools, and ultimately owned houses in the suburbs. Second, there was a chiropractor on the West Coast who desired a practice in Monterey, California. Problem: absolutely no need for another chiropractor in Monterey, which already had one for every eighty-eight people. He surveyed the populace, enclosing a questionnaire with four well-thought-out questions, and analyzed the results. He then opened a practice that responded to the needs expressed, and became hugely successful. In both cases, the people had a plan and the conviction to carry it out, despite the nay-sayers and skeptics who told them it was just a pipe dream.

How do we develop self-esteem? What are some of the steps to take to break what Dr. Brandner calls the "cycle of self-defeating behavior generated by a deficient self-esteem"? I would like to offer six helpful suggestions. Try to follow them rigorously so that they become part of your daily routine. Be warned: This is not some Aladdin's Lamp, which when rubbed, will result in miraculous change; like physical exercise, it will be hard work. The results should make it all worthwhile.

## 1) Know What You Want

Whether it's a new job, new organization, or career change, what do you want? What is your goal? If you could do or be anything in the world regardless of your age, sex, education, what would it be? Why do you want to do or be this thing? What's your motivation? What are the jobs or careers that fit the bill? Do they have a common theme? The Seven Stories Exercise, along with some of the other self-assessment techniques used at The Five O'Clock Club, is valuable in helping you get a handle on what you want to do. Even if you can't pinpoint exactly what this "thing" is, it is still helpful to try to describe it to yourself. Then learn to use your very uncertainty to brainstorm ideas and possibilities with others.

*How few young men realize that their success in life depends more upon what they are than upon what they know. It is self-esteem that has brought the race this far.*
Charles Wesley, black historian

If you are entering a negotiation—or even attending any kind of routine meeting—it is critical to know just what you expect as an outcome. I know people who have gone into negotiations with the attitude of "I'll see what they come up with" or "what they have to offer," believing that such flexibility would provide them with the best negotiating posture. Unfortunately, when the offers were tendered, they lost that "edge," because they didn't have any inner standard with which to measure the appropriateness of the offers.

## 2) Use Self-Talk and Imagineering

Write down a list of adjectives that describe you. Put the negative ones on the left, positives on the right. Then draw a line through the negatives, and replace them with their opposites. When you've finished, prioritize the qualities on this list in terms of their relevance and importance to your goal or objective. This list will be like a bible. Take it with you wherever you go, read it—recite it to yourself—first thing in the morning and last thing at night. In their book *CareerTracking*, authors Jimmy Calano and Jeff Salzman write that you have to reprogram your inner voice with these "affirmations." They can be a powerful device in creating change and promoting self-improvement.

As for what you wrote in the negatives column, in *The Double Win*, Denis Waitley quotes the Old Testament: "As a man thinketh in his heart, so is he." Write down what you have to do in order to realize the positive attributes or descriptives you have substituted on the problem side of the ledger. Do you smoke, but wish to give it up? If you're overweight, what do you want to look like? How are you going to accomplish these objectives? Waitley recommends a technique called "imagineering," while others, including Calano and Salzman term it "visualization." Basically, it involves imagining yourself as if the improvement has already occurred. Sports figures and business leaders are legendary devotees of visualization techniques. Derrick Mayes, the All-American wide receiver for Notre Dame, said he visualizes himself going down the field, eluding the defense, and jumping up in the air to make the catch. Further-

more, he "sees" specific obstacles in his way, and makes the mental adjustment so that when the real-life situation occurs, he can respond within a split-second.

After you visualize the desired outcome, figure out what you have to do to get there. If your objective is a new career, what experience or education is a prerequisite? What must you do to reposition yourself to fit the picture?

## 3) Change Your Perspective

In *The Double Win*, author Waitley writes of a woman in one of his seminars. When asked if she was attending the seminar alone, she replied, "No, I'm divorced." Pursuing it, he asked how long she'd been single. She answered, "I'm divorced two years now." He said, "Then you are single now!" Obviously this woman was in a rut, and needed to change her thinking to reflect her present status in a more positive way. I know job hunters who get stuck by focusing on their failures, not their successes. They only see what experience they lack, not what extraordinary qualifications they present. Negative labels, mistakes, and failures carry forward. It is useful to be able to view the same situation from another vantage point. To accomplish this, many suggest a change in one's routine, from as simple an activity as going to work a different way to developing an appreciation for the arts, or taking up a new sport.

One of the best things you can do is help others. The possibilities here are limitless: work at a soup kitchen for the homeless; deliver meals to the sick or elderly; read to the sensory impaired; work with AIDS patients, or even join a community or religious organization that lends its space to people providing counsel for the out-of-work. In addition to the obvious benefit of helping the needy, you get an entirely new perspective on your own life.

## 4) Get a Mentor

In *The Aladdin Factor*, authors Canfield and Hansen provide numerous examples of people who got ahead simply by going to people who had succeeded in that field. One story cited is that of Bob Richards, the record-setting Olympic pole vaulter of the 1950's. He confessed that before his triumphs, he felt sure he had gone as high as he could go in his quest to beat the world record. He had suffered failure upon failure, without moving one inch higher. Finally, he called the world record-holder, who agreed to see him. After observing Richards, the record-holder made some suggestions to improve his technique. Based on getting that advice, Richards went eight inches higher in his next meet. Canfield and Hansen, among others, strongly advocate that anyone trying to achieve something should "talk to the experts." Those who watch golf tournaments will note that the commentators frequently speak of "going to school on the other person's golf shots." It's the same in any endeavor; an expert usually loves to talk to others about how he or she succeeded. The value of such a mentor is incalculable.

## 5) "Build in" Successes

To elevate your self-esteem, it may be necessary to "stack the deck." A successful job hunter once reported that the last call of the day and week determined the mood of his evenings and weekends, respectively. When I was a kid, playing basketball in the gyms, yards, and playgrounds, I realized that a bad day often carries over to the next one. I decided, therefore, that I needed some measure of success at the end of a day that would allow me to forget the failures. I made it a rule never to "leave the court on a miss." Despite the weather, I forced myself to hit five difficult shots in a row before quitting. Many times I'd hit four, or three, but miss the next, so by the time I eventually finished, I might have had a pretty good "hit" percentage working, and I wasn't shackled so much with the earlier failures. It's obviously different things for everybody, but we all need to "build in" successes—anything that will allow us to forget what didn't work previously.

## 6) Avoid the Nay-Sayers.

In *CareerTracking*, Calano and Salzman urge people to "associate with positive people." For some reason, there are folks who just seem to find the negative in everything. They're down, and they bring everyone around them down too. These people are to be avoided at all costs. I subscribe to a college football publication, and I frequently call the paper to get the "latest scoop." One person there is always negative—"Well, you can't win every year," etc. It drags me down, so I get off the phone as fast as possible. Of course, I know you can't win them all, but I still want to believe at the outset that you can win. Another man sometimes answers my questions about how things are going with my favorite team. He always puts things in a hopeful way, so I'd much rather speak with him. In staying away from the nay-sayers, you keep a positive attitude. This, in turn, will prompt people to seek *you* out.

As I said at the beginning, these steps aren't easy, but they are do-able. The six steps must become habits. I believe we can all develop a vastly improved self-esteem if we incorporate the tips outlined above into our daily lives. It is especially important for job hunters and career changers to have a high level of self-esteem to see them through periods of discouragement. Then you will have the power to shape your own destiny and call the shots.

John Leonard is a career counselor with The Five O'Clock Club and a motivational author and speaker. This article originally appeared in *The Five O'Clock News*.

The
Five
O'Clock
Club®

# Your Two-Minute Pitch: The Keystone of Your Search

Your Two-Minute Pitch is the backbone of your search. You'll use it in job and networking interviews, and in your cover letters. You'll be ready when someone calls and says, "So tell me about yourself."

Your résumé summary statement could serve as the starting point for your pitch. Keep in mind:

- to whom you are pitching
- what they are interested in
- who your likely competitors are
- and what you bring to the party that your competitors do not.

In your pitch, you are *not* trying to tell your life story. Instead:

- Let this person know that you are competent and interested in the area in which he or she is interested.
- Say things that are relevant.
- Come across at the right level.

Think about your target audience and what you want to say to them. Examine your background to find things that fit.

### My Basic Pitch—Target 1

Here's what my pitch was, a number of years ago, to someone interested in my counseling background:

"For over ten years, I've been counseling people who are in the $40,000 to $600,000 range. I run The Five O'Clock Club, which is a career-development group. I also started and am in charge of The New School's career-development program, where we have over fifteen faculty members.

"I spent three years at a major outplacement firm. There I was regularly assigned the most difficult cases—those who had been unemployed a year or more. All of them had jobs within three months.

"I counsel executives in my private practice and also for a major corporation. And I have my M.B.A. in Behavioral Science.

"You can see that counseling is my life, and I'm excited about the situation in your company because..."

### Tailoring the Pitch

This is my basic counseling pitch, but I have to **tailor it to suit the situation**.

For example, for a pitch for a job counseling executives at Citibank, I added that I had worked many years for major corporations (such as...) and understood how corporations worked.

What else would they want to know? That I could work with their kind of employees. So I told them, "I like the kind of employees you have—sharp, aggressive—I like those kinds of people." I wanted to let them know that I knew their reputation.

### My Basic Pitch—Target 2

I'll have more to say about pitching myself to a specific company, but let's first take a look at another way I could pitch myself. Remember, if my pitch is wrong, everything else is wrong.

"I have over twenty years of business-management experience spanning a variety of areas.

"I started out in computers—doing computer programming on very complex projects. Then I was a systems analyst, and finally a trainer of programmers, analysts, and managers.

"Then I went into advertising management, managing a staff of thirteen artists, writers, and others. We developed ad campaigns, did public relations, and so on.

"After that, I went into small-business management, serving as CFO and specializing in turning around small service companies that were in dire financial straits—companies of fifty to a hundred professional employees. In those positions, I managed the accounting and control functions and other administrative areas such as computers, research, public relations, and so on. I also have my M.B.A.

"The reason I wanted to talk to you today is that

I want to get back into business management."

You can see that this is a good pitch if indeed I want to get back into business management, but a terrible pitch if I want to counsel executives.

Both pitches are true about me. But each pitch is tailored to my target market. Notice, for example, that in one pitch I mention I have an M.B.A. in Behavioral Science, and in the other pitch I simply say I have an M.B.A.

You too have to think through what you want to say to the market you are targeting—just as you did when you were developing the summary statement on your résumé.

### What's Wrong with This Pitch?

Take a look at the beginning of my client's pitch, and see if you can tell what's wrong.

"I have eighteen years' experience in education and training: in developing training programs, in running training centers, etc."

What's wrong with this pitch? We can't know until we know to whom he is talking. It turns out that the pitch was wrong because the interviewer was not interested in training, but in personal computers. How much did my client know about PC's? A lot. "Why, I can make PC's dance," he said. "The only problem is that the hiring manager would probably want someone who could network them together, and I've never done that."

"*Can* you do that?" I asked.

"Of course I can do it," he replied.

"Then go *do* it," I said, "so you can tell her you have already done it. Network together the computers you have at home. And join a group that specializes in that. Ask one of the people if you can go along and help him or her network computers together."

Here's the pitch one week later:

"I have eighteen years' experience in computers, specializing in PC's. I have built PC's from scratch, and I've done software and applications programming on PC's. I also understand how important networking is. I've even networked together the PC's I have at home, and I belong to a group of PC

experts, so I always know whom to talk to when tricky things come up. I can do anything that needs to be done with PC's. I can make PC's dance!

"I'm excited about talking to you because I know your shop relies on PC's."

Do you see how a pitch has to be tailored to each specific situation?

### More Tailoring in the Interview

Now, let's get back to my pitch to a specific company. In my two-minute counseling pitch, I laid the groundwork, but that's not enough.

At Citibank, for example, what were the hiring manager's specific needs, and who was my competition? What extra could I bring to the party?

I assumed management would not need someone with my counseling credentials—all they needed was a good counselor. So I toned down my Two-Minute Pitch. Now I needed to find some other competitive advantage.

Here's how the conversation went:

Kate: "Are there other things you would want the new person to do besides counseling? Some special projects?"

Manager: "No, that's all. It's a counseling position, and the person will be counseling executives all day."

Kate: "But what you're really doing is running a small business. Are there things you feel frustrated about that you would like someone to be able to handle?"

Manager: "Well . . . actually there is something. [It didn't matter to me what she said next. I knew it would be my competitive advantage because obviously she had not told anyone else.]

"I don't like the look of the materials we have here. They aren't professional enough. I'd like to have our own logo and our own look."

Kate: "Well, you are talking to the right person. It just so happens that I have an advertising background and I was responsible for corporate literature. I'd like to bring in some of my work to show you."

Her eyes lit up. Finally—someone to take over

this ugly job of redoing the literature.

### Know Something About Them

When you go for an interview, and they immediately say: "Tell me about yourself," how will you know how to position yourself? You don't want to bound into a standard Two-Minute Pitch unless you feel that you know something about them.

If you don't know anything at all about them or the job, you may say: "I'd be happy to tell you about myself, but could you first tell me a little about the kind of job we're talking about?"

### What Point Are You Trying to Make?

Most people write their Two-Minute Pitch and rehearse it in front of a mirror. As you are listening to yourself, think: What *point* am I trying to make? What impression do I hope they'll get about me?

I was listening to a client's pitch, and could not understand the point this executive woman was trying to make. After she had finished:

Kate: "I don't get it. What point are you trying to make?"

Client: "Look, I want them to know that I have twenty years' experience in capital markets, whether it's in aerospace or petroleum, metals and mining, or real estate. *My experience is in capital markets.*"

Kate: "That's a great pitch. Why don't you just tell them exactly that up front?"

### They Won't "Get It" on Their Own. So Just Tell Them

Most job hunters think: I'll just tell them my background, and they'll see how it fits in with their needs. But they probably won't see.

---

**Don't expect the hiring team to figure out something about you. If you have a conclusion you'd like them to reach about you, tell them what it is.**

---

If you want them to see how all of your jobs have somehow been involved in international, say,

"All of my jobs have somehow been involved in international." Isn't that easy?

If you want them to notice that you have always been willing to move wherever the company wanted you to move, then say just that. If you want them to know that you have done things treasury executives rarely do, then tell them that.

If you want them to see that you have developed intensive product knowledge while handling various operations areas, tell them that. Do you want them to know that FORTRAN is your favorite language? Then don't say, "I have five years of FORTRAN experience." That's not your point. Do you want them to know that you can make computers dance? Tell them. Don't make them figure it out for themselves. They won't.

Make your message so clear that if someone stops them and says, "Tell me about John," they will know what to tell the other person about you.

### Communicating Your Pitch

Many job hunters try to cram everything they can into their Two-Minute Pitch, but people can't hear it. Think about those who are considered the great communicators today. We judge communicators very differently from the way we did in the past, when the Winston Churchill type was ideal. Today, our standards are based on the medium of TV. The best communicators speak on a personal level—the way people talk on TV. Whether you are addressing a big audience or are on a job interview, cultivate a TV style—a friendly, one-on-one conversational style—not a "listing of what I've done" style.

The interviewer is assessing what it would be like to work with you. Make your pitch understandable. Before people go on TV, they decide the three major points they want to make—what they want the audience to remember.

What do you want your "audience" to remember about you? Polish both your Two-Minute Pitch and the two or three accomplishments that would interest this person. Prepare your pitch about each accomplishment the same way you prepared your Two-Minute Pitch. For example, don't say,

*You can have anything you want if you want it desperately enough.*
*You must want it with an inner exuberance that erupts through the skin*
*and joins the energy that created the world.*
Sheilah Graham, *The Rest of the Story*

"I started out in this job as a trainer, where I traveled to *x* and *y* and worked on special projects, etc."—if what you really want them to know is "That was a great assignment. My programs accounted for more than two thirds of the company's revenue." Use a conversational tone. Speak the way you would normally speak.

Many job hunters have pitches that are too heavy in content. Let's return to the woman executive we were discussing:

"I have twenty years' experience in capital markets in airlines, real estate and petroleum, metals and mining—assessing customers' and prospects' financial requirements based on the industry's point within the business cycle as well as the specific company's. I assess client credit, etc."

People can't listen to that. It's too dense. It needs some filler around the important words to resemble the way people really talk:

"I have twenty years' experience in capital markets—capital markets has always been my chief interest. I had this experience in three different areas, but the area where I spent the most time was in the airlines. I was also most recently involved in petroleum, metals and mining, and earlier on in my career, I was involved in real estate."

The new pitch is more conversational than a list, or simply getting all the facts out.

## Two Minutes Is a Long Time.
## Show Enthusiasm.

In this TV society, people are used to fifteen-second sound bites on the news. As the communicator, you have to engage the listener. Reinforce your main points. Don't say too many things. Sound enthusiastic.

If you are a boring person, the very least you can do is sit forward in your chair. I once did a magazine article on who got jobs and who got to keep them. I talked to the deans of business and engineering schools.

I learned that the person most likely to get the job was the one who sounded enthusiastic. And the one who got to keep the job was the enthusiastic one—even over people who were more qualified. Employers decided to keep someone who was willing to pitch in and do anything to help the company.

Even more interesting to me is that this same thing is true for senior executives. In my line of work, I sometimes have the opportunity to follow up when someone doesn't get a job. I am amazed by the number of times I am told (about people making from $150,000 to $600,000), that the applicant lacked enthusiasm:

"He was managing 1,300 people, and I don't know how he did it. He just doesn't sound enthusiastic. How could he motivate his troops if he can't motivate me? Anyway, I don't know that he really wants the job. He didn't sound interested."

Display enthusiasm. If you really want this job, act like it. It does not hurt your salary negotiation prospects.

The Five O'Clock Club®

# Summary of What I Have/ Want to Offer—Target 1

**For Target 1:**

Geographic area: _____

Industry or company size: _____

Position/Function: _____

**3-6 personality traits appropriate to this position/industry:**

_____   _____

_____   _____

_____   _____

**3-5 accomplishments that would be of interest to hiring managers in this position/ industry:**

1. _____

2. _____

3. _____

4. _____

5. _____

**Statement of why they should hire me:**

_____

_____

_____

_____

**Other key selling points that may apply even indirectly to this industry or position:**

_____

_____

_____

**Any objection I'm afraid the interviewer may bring up, and how I will handle it:**

_____

The
Five
O'Clock
Club®

# Summary of What I Have/ Want to Offer—Target 2

**For Target 2:**

    Geographic area: _____

    Industry or company size: _____

    Position/Function: _____

3-6 personality traits appropriate to this position/industry:

_____  _____

_____  _____

_____  _____

3-5 accomplishments that would be of interest to hiring managers in this position/ industry:

1. _____

2. _____

3. _____

4. _____

5. _____

Statement of why they should hire me:

_____

_____

_____

_____

Other key selling points that may apply even indirectly to this industry or position:

_____

_____

_____

Any objection I'm afraid the interviewer may bring up, and how I will handle it:

_____

The
Five
O'Clock
Club®

# Summary of What I Have/
# Want to Offer—Target 3

**For Target 3:**

Geographic area: _____

Industry or company size: _____

Position/Function: _____

**3-6 personality traits appropriate to this position/industry:**

_____     _____

_____     _____

_____     _____

**3-5 accomplishments that would be of interest to hiring managers in this position/industry:**

1. _____

2. _____

3. _____

4. _____

5. _____

**Statement of why they should hire me:**

_____

_____

_____

_____

**Other key selling points that may apply even indirectly to this industry or position:**

_____

_____

_____

**Any objection I'm afraid the interviewer may bring up, and how I will handle it:**

_____

The
Five
O'Clock
Club®

# Worksheet to Develop
# My Pitch to Target 1

You must know:
- to whom you are pitching; you have to know something about them.
- what they ideally would want in a candidate.
- what they are interested in.
- who your likely competitors are.
- what you bring to the party that they do not.

## For Target 1:

Geographic area: _____

Industry or company size: _____

Position/Function: _____

1. What is the most important thing I want this target to know about me? (This is where you position yourself. If they know nothing else about you, this is what you want them to know.)

_____

2. What is the second most important thing I want this target to know about me? (This could support and/or broaden your introductory statement.) _____

_____

_____

3. My key selling points: 3 to 5 statements that support/**prove** the first two statements:

1. _____

2. _____

3. _____

4. _____

5. _____

Statement of why they should be interested in me/what separates me from my competition:

_____

_____

_____

_____

Anything else I might want them to know about me:

_____

_____

_____

Any objection I'm afraid the interviewer may bring up, and how I will handle it:

_____

The Five O'Clock Club®

# Worksheet to Develop My Pitch to Target 2

You must know:
- to whom you are pitching; you have to know something about them.
- what they ideally would want in a candidate.
- what they are interested in.
- who your likely competitors are.
- what you bring to the party that they do not.

## For Target 2:

Geographic area: _____

Industry or company size: _____

Position/Function: _____

1. What is the most important thing I want this target to know about me? (This is where you position yourself. If they know nothing else about you, this is what you want them to know.)

_____

2. What is the second most important thing I want this target to know about me? (This could support and/or broaden your introductory statement.) _____

_____

_____

3. My key selling points: 3 to 5 statements that support/**prove** the first two statements:

1. _____
2. _____
3. _____
4. _____
5. _____

Statement of why they should be interested in me/what separates me from my competition:

_____

_____

_____

_____

Anything else I might want them to know about me:

_____

_____

_____

Any objection I'm afraid the interviewer may bring up, and how I will handle it:

_____

# Worksheet to Develop
# My Pitch to Target 3

You must know:
- to whom you are pitching; you have to know something about them.
- what they ideally would want in a candidate.
- what they are interested in.
- who your likely competitors are.
- what you bring to the party that they do not.

## For Target 3:

Geographic area: _____

Industry or company size: _____

Position/Function: _____

1. What is the most important thing I want this target to know about me? (This is where you position yourself. If they know nothing else about you, this is what you want them to know.)

_____

2. What is the second most important thing I want this target to know about me? (This could support and/or broaden your introductory statement.) _____

_____

_____

3. My key selling points: 3 to 5 statements that support/**prove** the first two statements:

1. _____
2. _____
3. _____
4. _____
5. _____

Statement of why they should be interested in me/what separates me from my competition:

_____

_____

_____

_____

Anything else I might want them to know about me:

_____

_____

_____

Any objection I'm afraid the interviewer may bring up, and how I will handle it:

_____

# Getting Interviews and Building Relationships

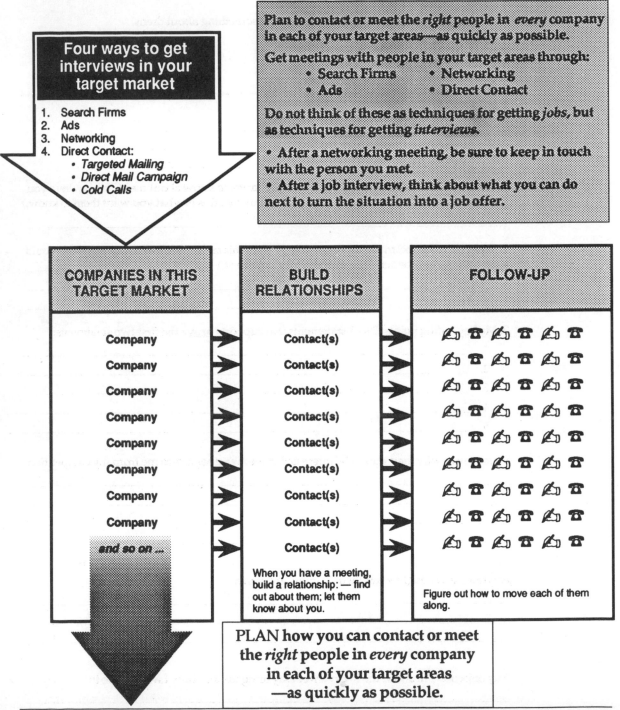

**Four ways to get interviews in your target market**

1. Search Firms
2. Ads
3. Networking
4. Direct Contact:
   - *Targeted Mailing*
   - *Direct Mail Campaign*
   - *Cold Calls*

Plan to contact or meet the *right* people in *every* company in each of your target areas—as quickly as possible.

Get meetings with people in your target areas through:
- Search Firms        • Networking
- Ads                 • Direct Contact

Do not think of these as techniques for getting *jobs*, but as techniques for getting *interviews*.

• After a networking meeting, be sure to keep in touch with the person you met.

• After a job interview, think about what you can do next to turn the situation into a job offer.

| COMPANIES IN THIS TARGET MARKET | BUILD RELATIONSHIPS | FOLLOW-UP |
|---|---|---|
| Company | Contact(s) | |
| Company | Contact(s) | |
| Company | Contact(s) | |
| Company | Contact(s) | |
| Company | Contact(s) | |
| Company | Contact(s) | |
| Company | Contact(s) | |
| Company | Contact(s) | |
| *and so on ...* | Contact(s) | |

When you have a meeting, build a relationship: — find out about them; let them know about you.

Figure out how to move each of them along.

PLAN how you can contact or meet the *right* people in *every* company in each of your target areas —as quickly as possible.

# How to Network Your Way In

*I use not only all the brains I have, but all I can borrow.*
Woodrow Wilson

In the old days, networking was a great technique. We job hunters were appreciative of the help we got, and treated those we met with respect and courtesy. We targeted a field, and then used networking to meet people and form lifelong relationships with them, and to gather information about the area. We called it "information-gathering," but it also often led to jobs.

Today, stressed-out, aggressive, demanding job hunters want a job quickly, and expect their "contacts" to hire them, refer them to someone important (obviously not the person with whom they are speaking), or tell them where the jobs are. The old way worked; this new attitude does not. This chapter tells you how to network correctly.

**Network informally** by talking to acquaintances who may know something about your target area. **Network formally** by contacting people at their jobs to get information about their company or industry. Networking is one way to find out what skills are needed where, what jobs may be opening up, and where you might be able to fit in. Use the networking—or information-gathering—process *to gather information and to build new relationships.*

## Gather information

Networking is one way to find out what skills are needed where, what jobs may be opening up, and where you may be able to fit in. Talking to people because "they might know of something for me" rarely works.

## Build Lifelong Relationships

You are also trying to build lifelong relationships. If a target area interests you, get to know the people in it and let them get to know you. It is unreasonable to expect them to have something for you just because you decided to contact them right now. Some of the most important people in your search may provide you with information and no contacts. Be sincerely grateful for the help you get, form a relationship that will last a lifetime, and plan to **recontact regularly the people you meet**.

Remember, you are not talking to people assuming they have heard of job openings. That approach rarely works. For example, if someone asked you if you happen to know of a position in the purchasing department in your old company, your answer would be no. But if they said, "I'm really interested in your former company. Do you happen to know *anyone* I could talk to there?" you could certainly give them the name of someone.

This is how people find jobs through networking. As time passes, the people you've met hear of things or develop needs themselves. If you keep in touch, they will tell you what's happening. It is a long-term process, but an effective one.

As you talk to more and more people, you will gather more and more information about business situations and careers in which you think you are interested. And the more people you meet and tell about your career search, the more people who are out there to consider you for a job or a referral to a job when they know of one. But, remember, they have to know you first. Networking allows you to meet people without asking them for a job and putting them on the spot. And the fact is, **if they like you and happen to have a job that's appropriate for you, they will *tell* you about it—you will not have to ask**.

People *like* to talk to sincere, bright people, and send on those who impress them. People will not send you on if you are not skilled at presenting yourself or asking good questions.

## CASE STUDY: MONICA
*Networking When You Don't Know Anyone*

Monica moved to Manhattan from a rural area because she wanted to work in publishing. She found a temporary job and then thought of ways to network in a city where she knew no one. She told everyone she had always wanted to work in publishing and would like to meet with people who

To repeat: People will be more willing to help you than you think *if* you are sincere about your interest in getting information from them *and* if you are asking them appropriate questions to which you could not get answers through library research or from lower-level people.

If what you really want from them is a job, you will not do as well. At this point, you don't want a job, you want a meeting. You want to **develop a relationship with them**, ask them for information, tell them about yourself, see if they can recommend others for you to talk to, and build a basis for contacting them later.

Before each meeting, write down the questions you sincerely want to ask *this specific person*. (If you find you are asking each person exactly the same thing, you are not using this technique properly.) Some examples:

### The Industry

- How large is this industry?
- How is the industry changing now? What are the most important trends or problems? Which parts of the industry will probably grow (or decline) at what rates over the next few years?
- What are the industry's most important characteristics?
- What do you see as the future of this industry five or ten years from now?
- What do you think of the companies I have listed on this sheet? Which ones are you familiar with? Who are the major players in this industry? Which are the better companies?

### The Company or Organization

- How old is the organization and what are the most important events in its history? How large is the organization? What goods and services does it produce? How does it produce these goods and services?
- Does the organization have any particular clients, customers, regulators, etc.? If so, what are they like and what is their relationship to the organization?

- Who are your major competitors?
- How is the company organized? What are the growing areas? The problem areas? Which areas do you think would be good for me, given my background?
- What important technologies does this company use?
- What is the company culture like? Who tends to get ahead here?
- What important challenges is the company facing right now or in the near future?

### The Job or Function

- What are the major tasks involved in this job? What skills are needed to perform these tasks?
- How is this department structured? Who reports to whom? Who interacts with whom?
- What is it like to work here? What is the company's reputation?
- What kinds of people are normally hired for this kind of position?
- What kind of salary and other rewards would a new hire usually get for this kind of job?
- What are the advancement opportunities?
- What skills are absolutely essential for a person in this field?

### The Interviewer

- Could you tell me a little about what you do in your job?
- How does your position relate to the bottom line?
- What is the most challenging aspect of your job?
- What is the most frustrating aspect of your job?
- What advice would you give to someone in my position?
- What are some of the intermediate steps necessary for a person to reach your position?
- What do you like or dislike about your job?
- How did you get into this profession or industry?
- What major problems are you facing right now in this department or position?

*Our plans miscarry because they have no aim.*
*When a man does not know what harbor he is making for,*
*no wind is the right wind.*
Seneca the Younger, Roman statesman

worked in that industry. She told people at bus stops, at church, and at restaurants. She read *Publishers Weekly*, the publishing trade magazine, to find out who was doing what in the industry, and contacted some people directly. She also joined an association of people in the publishing industry. At meetings, she asked for people's business cards and said she would contact them later. She then wrote to them and met with them at their offices.

Monica found that one of the best contacts she made during her search was a man close to retirement who was on a special assignment with no staff. There was no possibility of her ever working for him, but he gave her great insights into the industry and told her the best people to work for. He saved her from wasting many hours of her time, and she felt free to call him to ask about specific people she was meeting.

Over time, lots of people got to know Monica, and Monica got to know the publishing industry. She eventually heard of a number of openings, and was able to tell which ones were better than others. Monica is off to a good start in her new profession because she made lifelong friends she can contact *after* she is in her new job.

Using the networking technique correctly takes:

- time (because setting up interviews, going on them, and following up takes time)
- a sincere desire for information and building long-term relationships
- preparation.

### You Are the Interviewer

In an information-gathering interview, *you* are conducting the interview. The worst thing you can do is to sit, expecting to be interviewed. The manager, thinking you honestly wanted information, agreed to see you. Have your questions ready. After all, you called the meeting.

### The Information-Gathering or Networking Process

1. **Determine your purpose.** Decide what information you want or what contacts you want to build. Early on in your job search, networking with

people at your own level helps you research the field you have targeted. At this point in your search, you are not trying to get hired. Later, meet with more senior people. *They* are in a position to hire you someday.

2. **Make a list of people you know.** In the research phase, you made a list of the companies you thought you should contact in each of your target areas. You need lists of important people or companies you want to contact. Then, when you meet someone who tends to know people, you can ask if that person knows anyone on your list.

Now make a list of all the people you already know (relatives, former bosses and coworkers, your dentist, people at your church or synagogue, former classmates, those with whom you play baseball). Don't say you do not know enough appropriate people. If you know one person, that's enough for a start.

Don't discard the names of potential contacts because they are not in a position to hire you. Remember, you are not going to meet people to ask for a job, but to ask for information. These contacts can be helpful, provide information, and most likely have other friends or contacts who will move you closer and closer to your targets.

### People to Contact in Each Target Area

In the chapter "Researching Your Job Targets," you made a list of companies you want to contact in each of your target areas. Then you used the "Sample Personal Marketing Plan" as a model for your own complete list. Now you want to get in to see the people at these and other companies.

For each target, list on the following page the names of people you know, or know of, or even generic names (such as "lawyers who deal with emerging businesses") who can help you in each target. Whether you contact them through networking or a targeted mailing, the meetings will all be networking meetings.

You will not be idly chatting with these people. Instead, you will have your pitch ready (see the chapter on the Two-Minute Pitch), and will tell

# People to Contact in Each Target Area

You made a list of companies to contact in each of your target areas. Now you will show your list to those with whom you network because you want to get in to see those on your list and other companies as well.

For each target, list below the names of people you know, or know of, or even generic names, such as "lawyers who deal with emerging businesses." You will contact them through networking or a targeted mailing. The meetings you set up will be networking meetings. However, you will not be idly chatting with people. Instead, you will have your "pitch" ready (See Two-Minute Pitch), and will tell them the target you have in mind. The target will contain the industry or company size, the kind of position you would like, and the geographic area. For example:

"I'm interested in entrepreneurially driven, medium-sized private companies in the Chicago area. I would do well as a chief financial or chief administrative officer in that kind of company. Can you suggest the names of people who might have contact with those kinds of companies, or do you know anyone who works at that kind of company?"

You will tell *everyone* the target you are going after—including people you meet on the train and at the barber shop or beauty salon. You never know who knows somebody.

| | Target 1 | Target 2 | Target 3 | Target 4 | Other Names |
|---|---|---|---|---|---|
| | | | | | Such as: Dentist Hairdresser Neighbors |

*If you have always done it that way, it is probably wrong.*
Charles Kettering

them the target you have in mind. The target will include the industry or company size, the kind of possible position you would like, and the geographic area. For example:

"I'm interested in entrepreneurially driven, medium-sized private companies in the Chicago area. I would do well as a chief financial or chief administrative officer in that kind of company. Can you suggest the names of people who might have contact with those kinds of companies, or do you know anyone who works at that kind of company or a company on my list?"

Tell *everyone* the target you are going after—including people you meet on the train and at the barber shop or beauty salon. You never know who knows somebody.

3. **Contact the people you want to meet.** Chances are, you will simply call (rather than write to) people you already know—those on your "People to Contact" list. In the beginning of your search, practice on people who know you well. If you say a few things wrong, it won't matter. You can see them again later.

But as you progress in your search, most of the people you meet should not be people you know well. Extend your network beyond those people with whom you are comfortable. (See the graphic on the next page.)

As you build your network of contacts (people you know refer you to people you don't know, and they refer you to others), you will get further away from those people you originally began with. But as you go further out, you are generally getting closer to where the jobs are. Be willing to go to even further networking levels. Many people report that they got their jobs through someone six or seven levels removed from where they started.

You will probably want to contact by letter the people you do not know personally. Force yourself to write that letter and then follow up. People who are busy are more likely to spend time with you if you have put some effort into your attempt to see them. Busy people can read your note when they want rather than having to be dragged away from their jobs to receive your phone call. Often, people

who receive your note will schedule an appointment for you through their secretary, and you will get in to see them without ever having spoken to them. (On the other hand, some job hunters are in fields where people are used to picking up the phone. "Cold calling" can work for them.)

• Identify the link between you and the person you wish to meet; state why you are interested in talking to that person.

• Give your summary and two short examples of achievements that would interest the reader.

• Indicate that you will call in a few days to see when you can meet.

---

### A Sample Note for Information-Gathering

Dear Mr. Brown:

Sandra Lanto suggested I contact you because she thought you could give me the information I need.

I'm interested in heading my career in a different direction. I have been with Acme Corporation for seven years and I could stay here forever, but the growth possibilities in the areas that interest me are extremely limited. I want to make a move during the next year, but I want it to be the right move. Jill thought you could give me some ideas.

I'm interested in Human Resources Management. My seven years' experience includes the development of an Executive Compensation System that measures human resources' complex variables. For the past two years, I have been the main liaison with our unions and am now the head of the Labor Relations section. In this position, I managed the negotiation of six union contracts—and accomplished that feat in only ninety days.

I'd like some solid information from you on the job possibilities for someone like me. I'd greatly appreciate a half-hour of your time and insight. I'll call you in a few days to see when you can spare the time.
Sincerely,

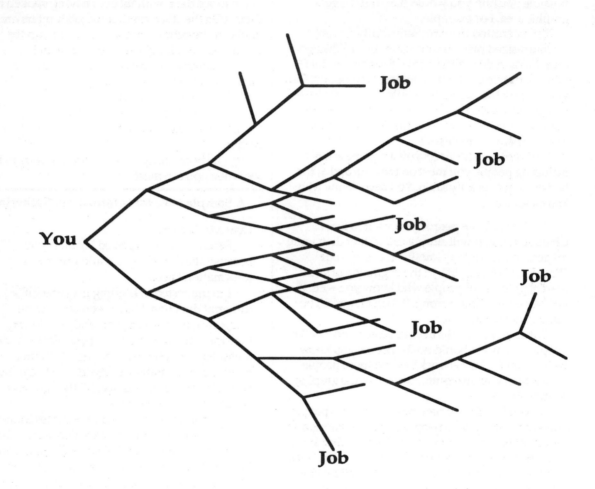

As you build your network of contacts (people you know refer you to people you don't know and they refer you to others), you will get further away from those people you originally knew personally. But as you go further out, you are generally getting closer to where the jobs are.

Be willing to go to further networking levels. Many people report that they got their jobs six or seven levels removed from where they started.

*If there are obstacles, the shortest*
*line between two points may be the crooked line.*
Bertolt Brecht, *Galileo*

*. . . we know that suffering produces perseverance;*
*perseverance character; and character hope.*
Romans 5: 3–4

Enclose your résumé if it supports your case. Do not enclose it if your letter is enough or if your résumé hurts your case.

4. **Call to set up the appointment** (first, build up your courage). When you call, you will probably have to start at the beginning. Do not expect a person to remember anything in your letter. Don't even expect him to remember that you wrote. Say, for example, "I sent you a letter recently. Did you receive it?"

Remind him of the reason you wrote. Have your letter in front of you—to serve as your script—because you may again have to summarize your background and state some of your accomplishments.

If the person says the company has no openings at this time, that is okay with you—you were not necessarily looking for a job; you were looking for information or advice about the job possibilities for someone like yourself, or you wanted to know what is happening in the profession, company, or industry.

If the person says he or she is busy, say, "I'd like to accommodate your schedule. If you like, I could meet you in the early morning or late evening." If he or she is still too busy, say, "Is it okay if we set something up for a month from now? I would call you to confirm so you could reschedule our meeting if it's still not a good time for you. And I assure you I won't take up more than twenty minutes of your time." Do your best to get on his calendar—even if the date is a month away. (Remember that you are trying to form lifelong relationships. Don't force yourself on people, but do get in to see them.)

**Don't let the manager interview you over the phone.** You want to meet in person. You need face-to-face contact to build the relationship and to be remembered by the manager.

**Rather than leave a message, keep calling back to maintain control.** If no one returns your call, you will feel rejected. But be friendly with the secretary; apologize for calling so often. An example: "Hello, Joan. This is Mary Traband again. I'm sorry to bother you, but is Mr. Johnson free now?"

"No, Ms. Traband, he hasn't returned yet. May I have him call you?"

"Thanks, Joan, but that will be difficult. I'll be in and out a lot, so I'll have to call him back. When is a good time to call?"

**Expect to call seven or eight times.** Accept it as normal business. It is not personal.

5. **Prepare for the meeting.** Plan for a networking meeting as thoroughly as you would for any other business meeting. Follow the agenda listed in step 6. **Remember that it is *your* meeting. You are the one running it.** Beforehand:

• Set goals for yourself (information and contacts).

• Jot down the questions you want answered.

• Find out all you can about the person, and the person's responsibilities and areas of operations.

• Rehearse your Two-Minute Pitch and accomplishments.

Develop good questions, tailoring your questions to get the information you need. Make sure what you ask is appropriate for the person with whom you are meeting. You wouldn't, for example, say to a senior vice president of marketing, "So, tell me how marketing works." That question is too general. Instead, do your research—both in the library and by talking with more junior people.

Decide what information you want or what contacts you want to build. Early on in your job search, networking with people at your own level helps you research the field you have targeted. At this point in your search, you are not trying to get hired. Later, meet with more senior people—the ones who are in a position to hire you someday.

Then when you meet the senior vice president, ask questions that are more appropriate for someone of that level. You may want to ask about the rewards of that particular business, the frustrations, the type of people who succeed there, the group values, the long-range plans for the business. Prepare three to five open-ended questions about the business or organization that the person will be able to answer.

If you find you are asking each person the same

questions, think harder about the information you need, or do more library research. The quality of your questions should change over time as you become more knowledgeable, more of an insider—and more desirable as a prospective employee. In addition, you should be giving information back. If you are truly an insider, you must have information to give.

**6. Conduct the interview**. If this is important to you, you will continually do better. Sometimes people network forever. They talk to people, but there is no flame inside of them. Then one day something happens: they get angry or just fed up with all of this talking to people. They interview better because they have grown more serious. Their time seems more important to them. They stop going through the motions and get the information they need. They interview harder. They feel as though their future is at stake. They don't want to chat with people. They are hungrier. They truly want to work in that industry or in that company. And the manager they are talking to can sense their seriousness and react accordingly.

### Format of an Information-Gathering Interview

Prepare for each interview. The questions you want to ask and the way you want to pitch, or position, yourself, will vary from one meeting to another. Think it all through. **Review the Format of a Networking Interview before *every* networking meeting. If you use it, you will have a good meeting.**

• Exchange Pleasantries— to settle down. This is a chance to size up the other person and allow the other person to size you up. It helps the person to make a transtition from whatever he or she was doing before you came in. One or two sentences of small talk: "Your offices are very handsome"; or "Your receptionist was very professional"; or "You must be thrilled about your promotion."

• Why am I here?  The nature of your networking should change over time. In the beginning, you don't know much, and are asking basic

questions. But you can't keep asking the same questions. Presumably, you have learned something in your earlier meetings. As you move along, you should be asking different, higher-level questions—and you should also be in a position to give some information back to people with whom you are meeting. That's what makes you an insider—someone who knows a lot about the field.

This is a basic example of "Why I am here": "Thanks so much for agreeing to meet with me. Allan Methven thought you could give me the advice I need. I'm meeting with CEO's in the Chicago area because I want to relocate here." If the meeting is *in response to a targeted mailing*, you may say something like: "I'm so glad you agreed to meet with me. I've been following your company's growth in the international area, and thought it would be mutually beneficial for us to meet." Remind the person of how you got his or her name and why you are there. He or she may have forgotten the contents of your letter or who referred you.

Here are additional suggestions on "Why I am here" (Notice how there is a progression going from early on to later in the search process):
• I'm trying to decide what my career path should be. I have these qualifications and I'm trying to decide how to use them. For example, I'm good at ____ and ____. I think they add up to____. What do you think?
• I want to get into publishing, and I'm meeting people in the field. Dr. Cowitt, my dentist, knew you worked in this industry and thought you would be a good person for me to talk to.
• I've researched the publishing industry and think the operations area would be a good fit for me. I was especially interested in learning more about your company's operations area, and I was thrilled when Fred Davidson at the Publishing Association suggested I contact you.
• I have met with a number of people in the publishing industry, and I  think some meetings may turn into job offers. I'd like your insight about which companies might be the best fit for

Prepare for each interview. The questions you want to ask, and the way you want to "pitch" or position yourself, will vary from one meeting to another. Think it all through.

Be sure to read this chapter in detail for more information on the networking, or information-gathering, process.

## The Format of the Interview

• **Pleasantries**—this is a chance to size up the other person and allow the other person to size you up. It's a chance to settle down. Just two or three sentences of small talk.

• **Why am I here?** For example: "Thanks so much for agreeing to meet with me. Bonnie Maitlen thought you could give me the advice I need. I'm trying to talk to CEO's in the Chicago area because I want to relocate here." Remind the person of how you got his or her name and why you are there.

• **Establish credibility with your Two-Minute Pitch.** After you tell the person why you are there, they are likely to say something like: "Well, how can I help you?" Then you respond, for example: "I wanted to ask you a few things, but first let me give you an idea of who I am." There are a number of reasons for doing this:
1. The person will be in a better position to help you if he or she knows something about you.
2. It's impolite to ask a lot of questions without telling the person who you are.
3. You are trying to form a relationship with this person—to get to know each other a bit.

• **Ask questions** that are appropriate for this person. Really think through what you want to ask. For example, you wouldn't say to the marketing manager: "So what's it like to be in marketing?" You would ask that of a more junior person. Consider having your list of questions in front of you so you will look serious and keep on track.

• As the person is answering your questions, **tell him or her more about yourself if appropriate.** For example, you might say: "That's interesting. When I was at XYZ Company, we handled that problem in an unusual way. In fact, I headed up the project . . . "

• **Ask for referrals if appropriate.** For example: "I'm trying to get in to see people at the companies on this list. Do you happen to know anyone at these companies? . . . May I use your name?"

• **Gather more information about the referrals.** (Such as: "What is Robert Boyd like?")

• **Formal time of gratitude.** Thank person for the time spent.

• **Offer to stay in touch.** Remember that making a lot of new contacts is not as effective as making not quite so many contacts and then *recontacting* those people later (See Follow-Up).

• **Write a follow-up note, and be sure to follow up again later.**

## Remember:

• You are *not* there simply to get names. It may often happen that you will get excellent information but no names of others to contact. That's fine.

• Be grateful for whatever help people give you and assume they are doing their best.

• Remember too that this is *your* interview and you must try to get all you can out of it.

• This is not a job interview. In a job interview, you are being interviewed. In a networking meeting, *you* are conducting the interview.

*Business is a game, the greatest game in the world if you know how to play it.*
Thomas J. Watson, Jr., former CEO of IBM

me. I wrote to you because I will be in this industry soon and I know you are one of the most important players in it.

• I've worked in the publishing industry for ten years and have also learned sophisticated computer programming at night. I am looking for a situation that would combine both areas because the growth opportunities are limited in my present firm. Anita Lands thought I should speak with you, since your company is so highly computerized.

• <u>Establish credibility with your Two-Minute Pitch</u>. After you say why you are there, they are likely to say something like: "How can I help you?" You respond: "I wanted to ask you a few things, but first let me give you an idea of who I am." There are a number of reasons for doing this:

   1.  The person will be in a better position to help you if he or she knows something about you.

   2.  It's impolite to ask a lot of questions without telling the person who you are.

   3.  You are trying to form a relationship with this person—to get to know each other a bit.

• <u>Ask questions that are appropriate for this person.</u> Really think through what you want to ask. Perhaps have your list of questions in front of you: you will look serious and keep on track.

• <u>As he or she answers your questions, talk more about yourself *if appropriate*</u>. "That's interesting. The fact is that I've had a lot of pubic relations experience in the jobs I've held." By the time you leave the meeting, you should know something about each other.

• <u>Ask for referrals if appropriate</u>.   This is an opportunity to extend your network. "I've made a list of companies I'm interested in. What do you think of them?" "Are there other companies you would suggest?" "Whom do you think I should contact at each of the good companies on this list?" "Could you tell me something about the person you suggested at that company?" "May I use your name?"

As you probe, they may respond that they do not know of any job openings. That's okay with you. You simply need to meet with more people in this industry, whether or not they have positions available: "I'm just trying to get as much information as possible."

Some job hunters get annoyed when they go away without contacts. They are thinking short-term and are not trying to build long-term relationships. But you were not *entitled* to a meeting with the manager. He or she was kind to meet with you at all.

If you get no contacts, be very grateful for what you do get. It may be that he or she has no names to give. On the other hand, so many people network incorrectly (aggressively and abrasively), that managers are often reluctant to give out names until the job hunter has kept in touch for a number of months and proved his or her sincere interest. Many managers feel used by job hunters who simply want names and are not interested in *them*.

• <u>Gather more information about the referrals.</u> (For instance: "What is Dick Knowdell like?")

• <u>Formal time of gratitude</u>. Thank the person for the time spent.

• <u>Offer to stay in touch</u>. Constantly making new contacts is not as effective as keeping in touch with old ones. "May I keep in touch with you to let you know how I'm doing?" You might call later for future contacts, information, etc.

• <u>Write a follow-up note</u>, and be sure to follow up again later. This is most important and a powerful tool. State how the meeting helped you or how you used the information. Be sincere. If appropriate, offer to keep the manager informed of your progress.

• <u>Recontact your network every two to three months.</u> Even after you get a job, these people will be your contacts to help you in your new job—and maybe you can even help them! After all, you are building lifelong relationships, aren't you? See the chapter "Following Up When There Is No Immediate Job."

Remember:

• You are *not* there simply to get names. It may

142

*Many things are lost for want of asking.*
George Herbert, *Jacula Prudentum*

often happen that you will get excellent information but no names of others to contact. That's fine.

• Be grateful for whatever help people give you, and assume they are doing their best.

• Remember, too, that this is *your* interview and you must try to get all you can out of it.

• This is not a job interview. In a job interview, you are being interviewed. In a networking meeting, you are *conducting* the interview.

**Follow precisely the "Format of a Networking Meeting."** If you use it, you will have a good meeting.

## Other Interview Pointers

• The heart of the interview is relating your good points in the best way possible. Be concise and to the point. Don't be embarrassed about appearing competent. Be able to recite your Two-Minute Pitch and key accomplishments without hesitation.

• Keep control of the interview. Don't let the person with whom you're meeting talk too much or too little. If he goes on about something inappropriate, jump in when you can and relate it to something you want to say. Remember, this is *your* interview.

• Find out which of your achievements he's really turned on by. That's his hot button, so keep referring to the achievements he likes.

• Be self-critical as you go along with this process. Don't become so enamored with the process that you become inflexible. Don't become a professional information gatherer or job hunter.

• Interview hard. *Probe.* Be prepared to answer hard questions in return.

• Take notes when you are getting what you want. This lets the manager know that the interview is going well, and encourages more of the same. The person to whom you are talking is just like everyone else who is being interviewed—everyone wants to do well.

• Show enthusiasm and interest. Lean forward in your chair when appropriate. Ask questions that sincerely interest you, and sincerely try to get the answers.

• Don't be soppy and agree with everything. It's better to disagree mildly and then come to some agreement than to agree with everything 100 percent.

• Remember your goals. Don't go away from any interview empty-handed. Get information or the names of other contacts.

• Don't overstay your welcome. Fifteen minutes or half an hour may be all a busy person can give you. Never take more than one and a half to two hours.

• If you are meeting over lunch, go someplace simple so you are not constantly interrupted by waiters.

• If you are looking for a job, don't conceal that fact.

• **If the person you are interviewing suggests passing on your résumé to someone else, that is usually not helpful**—unless you know who the person is and can follow up yourself. Say, "I hate to put you to that trouble. Would you mind if I called her myself and used your name?" If the manager does not agree to this, then you must accept his or her wishes.

• **If the person you are meeting tells you of a job opening**, say, "I'd like to know more about that job possibility, but I also had a few questions I'd like to ask you." Continue to get your questions answered. If you follow up only on the job lead, you will probably wind up with no job and no information.

• It is important to remember that these are only suggestions. You must adopt your own style, your own techniques. You'll find that the more you meet with people, the better you'll get at it. Start out with friends, or in low-risk situations. You do not want to meet with your most promising prospects until you are highly skilled at networking meetings. The more you practice, the better you will become.

## Who Is a Good Contact?

A contact is any connection between you and the person with whom you are hoping to meet. Most often the contact is someone you've met in another information-gathering interview, but think a little, and you will find other, creative ways to establish links with people. (Also see the chapter

*Let your questions focus on the other person. Say, "What do you think?"*
*rather than "Do you agree with me?"*
Barry Farber, radio interviewer, *Making People Talk*

"Targeted Mailings: Just Like Networking." Here are a few real-life examples:

Example one: A man's mother used to clean the office of the president of a good-sized corporation. One day the son wrote to the president, "My mother cleaned your office for twelve years." He was granted an interview with the president and shown a good deal of courtesy. This may seem far-fetched, but it happened.

Example two: Clara wanted to leave a company where she had worked for nine years. She thought about the person who had taught her data processing twelve years earlier. Her teacher had left the company to form his own business. She had never kept track of him, but he had impressed her as worldly, and she thought he would be a good person to give her advice.

She wrote to him on personal stationery:

---

Dear Mr. Jones:

You taught me data processing in 1972. I remember it well, since it was the start of my career, and I thought you would be a good person to give me the advice I need.

I'm interested in making a move during the next year or so, but I want it to be the right move.

I now have ten years of computer experience, specializing in financial and personnel systems. I have used third-generation languages and have designed complicated systems. For example:

• Led a three-person team in developing a human resources system that linked salary administration, performance reviews, and employee benefits packages.

• Developed a sophisticated accounting system that allowed all of the PC's in the company to access certain information on the mainframe. All departments in the company could see the same, updated information.

I'll call you in a few days to set up a mutually convenient time to get together.

---

Of course, the man did not know Clara from Adam. She had been one of twenty-eight students in the class he taught at a large company, and was probably the most shy of the group. In fact, after she wrote to him, she became afraid and did not call for two weeks.

When she finally did call, she was told the business had been acquired by another firm and her former teacher had moved from Philadelphia to Chicago. She felt like a fool calling Chicago, but she finally got up the nerve.

When she identified herself to the secretary, she heard, "Clara Horvath! We've been trying to reach you everywhere. Your note didn't contain a phone number!" The secretary said Clara's former teacher was now a senior vice president in Chicago—and had sent the note to the head of the Philadelphia office.

When she called the Philadelphia office, the secretary said, "Clara Horvath! We were hoping you would call. Your note didn't have your phone number."

The secretary arranged for Clara to see the head of the Philadelphia office, who developed a job description for her. According to company policy, the job would have to be posted internally and the head of the Philadelphia office would have to interview qualified in-house candidates. After developing a job description to suit Clara, however, the chances were good that he would not find someone internally with her same qualifications.

Clara went to work at the company, and it was many months before she finally met the man who was her former teacher. Neither one of them recognized each other, but that was fine!

**Other Sources of Contacts**

Be sure to read the chapters on research for lots of ideas about associations, alumni groups, and so on. In addition, you can consider:

• Contacting acquaintances—even more than friends. Friends may be reluctant to act as contacts for you. You are more of a reflection on them than you would be for an acquaintance. And if things don't work out, they could lose your friendship—but acquaintances don't have as much to lose.

• Network every chance you get—on the bus, at parties. Don't be like those job hunters who don't

*Life is a series of collisions with the future;*
*it is not a sum of what we have been but what we yearn to be.*
José Ortega y Gasset

tell anyone they are looking for a job. You never know who knows someone who can help you. Everyone you meet knows lots of people.

• Don't contact someone on the strength of *Dun and Bradstreet, Poor's,* or other directories. There is no true link between you and that person. Use your imagination to think of a better link.

## Out-of-Town Search

The principles are the same wherever you are. If you have targeted another city, sometimes it is difficult to get face-to-face meetings with some of the people you would like to talk to. But plan ahead. If you are making business trips to, or attending seminars or taking a vacation in that city, think about with whom you would like to make contact there for your network. Telephone or write to him or her well in advance for an appointment. Keep your ears open about who might be coming through your area, and try to get time with him or her if you can.

## Summary

Networking is a powerful job-hunting tool—if it is used properly, which most often it is not. It is also a life skill that you can and should use throughout your career. Become expert at it, and do not abuse people. Give them something back.

*Keep away from people who belittle your ambitions. Small people always do that, but the really great make you feel that you, too, can become great.*
Mark Twain

*Our dignity is not in what we do but what we understand. The whole world is doing things.*
George Santayana, *Winds of Doctrine*

*No matter what accomplishments you make, somebody helps you.*
Althea Gibson, in *Time,* August 26, 1957

*It is better to die on one's feet than to live on one's knees, but some individuals appear actually to believe that it is better to crawl around on one's bare belly.*
Nathan Hare, in *The Black Scholar,* November 1969

*God does not die on the day when we cease to believe in a personal deity, but we die on the day when our lives cease to be illuminated by the steady radiance, renewed daily, of a wonder, the source of which is beyond all reason.*
Dag Hammarskjold

# Are You Conducting a Good Campaign?

*The thing is to never deal yourself out... Opt for the
best possible hand. Play with verve and sometimes
with abandon, but at all times with calculation.*
L. Douglas Wilder, in
"Virginia's Lieutenant Governor:
L. Douglas Wilder is First Black to Win Office,"
*Ebony*, April 1986

## How you know you are in a *campaign*:

You feel as though you know
a critical mass of people within that industry.
When you go on "interviews," you contribute as
much as you take away. You have gained a
certain amount of information about the industry that puts you on par with the interviewer—
and you are willing to share that information.
You are a contributor. An insider.
You know what's going on.
You feel some urgency and are
more serious about this industry.
You are no longer simply "looking around"—
playing it cool. You are more intense. You don't
want anything to stand in your way because
you know that this is what you want. You
become more aware of any little thing that can
help you get in. Your judgment becomes more
finely tuned. Things seem to fall into place.
You are working harder at this than you ever
could have imagined. You read everything there
is to read. You write proposals almost
overnight and hand-deliver them.
Your campaign is taking on a life of its own.
At organizational meetings, you seem to know
everybody. They know you are one of them and
are simply waiting for the right break.
When someone mentions a name, you have
already met that person and are keeping in
touch with him or her. The basic job-hunting
"techniques" no longer apply.
You are in a different realm, and you feel it.
This is a real campaign.

## The Quality of Your Campaign

Getting a job offer is not the way to test the
quality of your campaign. A real test is
when people say they'd want you—but not
right now. When you are networking, do people
say, "Boy, I wish I had an opening. I'd sure like to
have someone like you here"? Then you know you
are interviewing well with the right people. All you
need now are luck and timing to help you contact or
recontact the right people when they also have a
need.

If people are not saying they want you, find out
why. Are you inappropriate for this target? Or
perhaps you seem like an outsider, and outsiders
are rarely given a break.

During the beginning of your search, you are
gathering information to find out how things work.

Why should someone hire a person who does
not already work in the field? There are lots of
competent people who have the experience and can
prove they will do a good job.

There is a test to see if perceived as an insider. If
you think you are in the right target, talking to
people at the right level, and are not early on in
your search, you need feedback. Ask people, "If you
had an opening, would you consider hiring someone like me?"

Become an insider—a competent person who
can prove that he or she has somehow already done
what the interviewer needs. Prove that you can do
the job, and that the interviewer is not taking a
chance by hiring you.

## The Quantity of Your Campaign

You need to find a lot of people who would hire
you if they could. You know by now that you
should **have six to ten things in the works at all
times**. This is the only true measure of the effectiveness of your campaign to get interviews in your
target area. If you have fewer than this, get more.
You will be more attractive to the manager, will
interview better, and will lower the chances of
losing momentum if your best lead falls apart.

Use the worksheet "Current List of My Active
Contacts by Target." At the beginning of your

*There is a tide in the affairs of men,*
*Which, taken at the flood, leads on to fortune; . . . On such a sea we are now afloat;*
*And we must take the current when it serves, Or lose our ventures.*
Shakespeare, *Julius Caesar*

search, these will simply be networking contacts with whom you want to keep in touch. At that stage, your goal is to come up with six to ten contacts you want to recontact later, perhaps every two months. In the middle of your search, the quality of your list will change. The names will be of the right people at the right level in the right companies. Finally, the six to ten names will represent prospective job possibilities that you are trying to move along.

If you have six to ten job possibilities in the works, a good number of them will fall away through no fault of your own (job freezes, or hiring managers changing their minds about the kind of person they want). Then you'll need to get more possibilities in the works. With this critical mass of ongoing possible positions, you stand a chance of getting a number of offers and landing the kind of job you want.

## Developing Momentum in Your Search

A campaign builds to a pitch. The parts begin to help one another. You focus less on making a particular technique work and more on the situation you happen to be in. This chapter gives you a feel for a real campaign.

In your promotional campaign to get interviews, you see people who are in a position to hire you or recommend you. Keep in touch with them so they will . . .

- think of you when a job opens up
- invite you to create a job for yourself
- upgrade an opening to better suit you
- give you information to help you in your search.

When you are in the heat of a real campaign, a critical mass of activity builds, so you start:

- hearing the same names
- seeing the same people

- contributing as much as you are getting
- writing proposals
- getting back to people quickly
- feeling a sense of urgency about this industry
- writing follow-up letters, making follow-up phone calls.

*. . . the secret is to have the courage to live.*
*If you have that,*
*everything will sooner or later change.*
James Salter, *Light Years*

*Eventually, and often after the survival of a long and profound crisis, often after the painful shedding of one skin and the gradual growth of another, comes the realization that the world is essentially neutral.*
*The world doesn't care, and is responsible neither for one's spiritual failures nor for one's successes.*
*This discovery can come as a profound relief, because it is no longer necessary to spend so much energy shoring up the self, and because the world emerges as a broader, more interesting, sweeter place through which to move.*
*The fog lifts, as it were.*
Frank Conroy,
*The New York Times Book Review*, January 1, 1989

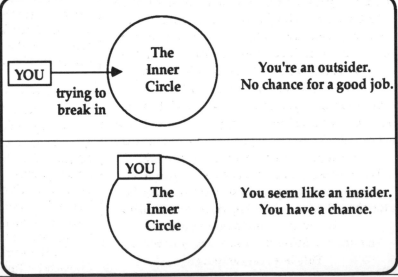

YOU trying to break in → The Inner Circle — You're an outsider. No chance for a good job.

YOU — The Inner Circle — You seem like an insider. You have a chance.

The Five O'Clock Club®

# How to Shake Hands Effectively
## Getting Your Meeting Off to the Right Start

By Ronna Archbold

Note: This chapter and the following two give different and interesting perspectives on getting the most out of your meetings.

Handshaking is an ancient ritual. It is reported as long ago as 2800 B.C. in Egypt. According to historian Charles Panati, folklore places the handshake even earlier and speculates that because the right hand is the weapon hand, presenting it open and without a sword came to be seen as a sign of peace and acceptance. Though archaic in origin, the handshake is still the accepted form of greeting in our society in modern times. In both social and business situations, the handshake is important.

In the work world, it is a great way to network, get acquainted, and get hired. A CEO of a Fortune 500 company told me that once when he had to choose between two candidates with similar qualifications, he gave the position to the candidate with the better handshake.

Body language is a major factor when we make judgments about a person. And there is no gesture so underestimated as the handshake. In the business arena, this first approach to conversation and connection is critical. It is valuable to learn and practice how to extend and receive a good handshake. It should become an indispensable part of our business style.

Let's reminisce about the handshakes we have experienced. I have counted five basic types. Perhaps you can think of others.

First, there is the Knuckle Cruncher. This type of person is earnest but nervous. While meaning to convey warmth through a tight grip of your hand, he or she only succeeds in causing you pain. The impression created is definitely that of a person who lacks sensitivity. (The situation is exacerbated if you're wearing a ring on your right hand.)

Then there is the opposite problem—the Dead Fish Handshaker, who places a limp, lifeless hand in yours. While the Knuckle Cruncher hurts you, at least you feel there is some desire to express a real feeling. But the Dead Fish Hand-shaker is sending only a negative message. He or she gives the impression of having a lackluster personality. This handshake usually doesn't get the second interview, much less the job.

Another type is the Pumper, who is overly eager but also insecure. This person doesn't know when to quit, almost as if stalling because of not being sure of what to do next. So he or she just keeps on vigorously shaking your hand up and down—and, along with it, your entire arm. You may not feel pain but you certainly feel foolish.

How about the Sanitary Handshaker? This person will barely put three or four fingers in your hand—and then withdraw them quickly, almost as if afraid of catching a dread disease. Such people appear timid and sheepish, to put it mildly.

Finally, there is the Condolence Handshaker. This is the person who comes across as too familiar, clasping your right arm or hand with his or her left hand—and perhaps attempting to hug or even kiss you. This behavior may be appreciated at a funeral, but in the world of business, it comes across as condescending and very inappropriate.

---

**The Condolence Handshaker comes across as too familiar, clasping your right arm or hand with his or her left hand.**

---

The protocol for handshaking is simple to learn, but it does require refining. Here is what you should do: Walk up to the person you wish to meet. Look into his or her eyes, smile, and extend your hand. Offer a warm, firm, palm-to-palm handshake. It is that simple. Be sure that your weight is equally distributed on both feet and that your handshake is from the elbow. Do not fall into any of the pitfalls just described.

Women are the newcomers to handshaking in the business arena. They tend to offer weak wrists, twisted bodies, and tilted heads. Hold yourself so that you face straight forward. Be confident, interested, kindly, and sincere.

As you proffer your hand to a stranger or a distant acquaintance, simultaneously say, "My name is . . . " (Usually it is best to use both first and last names.) This way you may do away with that awkward moment of the forgotten name. The person being greeted is often relieved at being reminded, and will usually respond by saying his or her own name, which will in turn relieve you. This way everyone is excused from having to say, "I'm sorry, but I've forgotten your name." It should be added that there is nothing awfully wrong about admitting that we need a refresher course on each other's names. Still, saying your own name right away is often the least awkward way of gaining the information. Even if the forgotten-name admission becomes necessary, it is more easily accomplished in the midst of a warm handclasp.

---

**As you proffer your hand to a stranger or a distant acquaintance, simultaneously say, "My name is . . . "**

---

It used to be considered courteous for men to wait for women to extend their hand, but that is not the case in business today. Either women or men may initiate the handshake. Also, both men and women should rise to shake hands. Regardless of gender, rising to greet someone is a compliment; it shows energy and eagerness to connect.

Does your hand tend to get clammy in social situations? If so, then use a spray-on underarm deodorant on the palm of your hand before attending a stressful event. The clammy hand is usually only a temporary nervous response. In time you will probably get to the point where you don't experience this reaction. When holding a beverage, keep it in your left hand. This way, not only are your freeing your right hand to be ready for handshaking, but if it's an icy drink, you're also avoiding the cold, damp feeling that the glass can give to your hand.

If your right hand or arm is disabled, extend your left hand without hesitation and warmly squeeze the proffered right hand. Do not explain or apologize that you can't shake hands in the traditional manner.

The rewards of learning, practicing, and using this protocol are many. You will most likely notice that people say something like: "Thank you for speaking to me" or "I'm so glad you came over." (It is safe to interpret this to mean that he or she didn't know how to initiate contact and is relieved that you did.)

Once you have mastered the handshake, it will become a normal part of a presentation that will help you gain a lot—a new career or job, new clients, new friends, acquisitions, mergers, and so on. You will be making an incredibly positive impression. You may even find yourself shaking the hand of the great person who is your future spouse!

When you correctly use the protocol for initiating contact, your business opportunities will multiply fast. You will be perceived as a person who is knowledgeable, possesses excellent social skills, and has leadership capabilities. You will make a great first impression. A healthy sense of self-confidence will become your style.

"Any person who has charm and some confidence can move in and through societies ranging from the most privileged to the most needy. Style allows the person to appear neither inferior in one location nor superior in the other."
—Maya Angelou

An excellent handshake shows your charm and self-confidence. Role-play. Practice until it flows naturally like an automatic reflex. When you develop your handshake, it will become incorporated into your body language and become an integral part of *your style*.

---

Ronna Archbold is the electronic publishing sales manager for the East Coast and the federal government for Reed Reference Publishing. Ms. Archbold consults, writes, and trains in the field of protocol and sales.

---

This article originally appeared in *The Five O'Clock News*.

# What's in It for Them?
## A Networker's Guide to Feeling Better About the Approach

By Ellis Chase

Networking. Networking. Networking. And more networking. The word has been so overused that it can now have a negative, exploitative feel to it. It is also one of the most misunderstood terms in contemporary job-search technique, with the culprits often being career/outplacement consultants themselves. The word networking evokes unspoken yet common fears: "Why should anyone—least of all a stranger—want to see me?" or "I hate feeling beholden to people, or asking for favors." Despite all the negative associations, statistics still show overwhelming success with the use of networking techniques.

Instead of backing someone into a corner with an outright demand for help, leads or jobs, Networking should be a courteous, subtle technique leading to the building of long-term relationships.

Job seekers often fail to recognize that there can be as much reward for the network*ee* as there is for the network*er* because they view the process as a one-way proposition rather than seeing that it can benefit both parties. The following is a list of possible reasons why a contact would *want* to see the job seeker:

1) Any person who is attuned to the vagaries of a changing work world is aware of the value of knowing people at all levels, and in related areas. Some people being approached, however, have been insulated in one area for a protracted period. Clearly, the more people they know and the more settings with which they're familiar, the better the options for future moves, knowledge, and even business. Therefore, there is a great deal to be gained by the contact for his or her own career development.

2) Job seekers are always a source of competitive information about other players in their field. While the networker must be discreet, giving out a little bit of news can not only demonstrate sophistication in the field, but corroborate beliefs previously held by the networkee, which is reassuring.

3) Gossip. This is great for entertainment value and relationship-building—who's moved where, who's left where, who got a promotion.

Job seekers are great sources of tidbits, because they have been "getting around" probably far more than the person they've approached.

4) This is the one that most people have trouble believing: There are actually people out there who do enjoy helping—just for the sake of helping. And for them, that is the reward. Perhaps they've been in a similar situation themselves, which makes them empathetic. Or they simply may be altruistic people.

5) People who have landed a new position are, in my estimation, the most willing networking targets. These recent successes are usually eager to demonstrate their accomplishment—and share the wealth. They are definitely feeling good about themselves and may want to indulge in a little boasting. And their contacts are still "warm," which is a help to you.

6) Always implicit in a networking interaction is the idea of returning the favor. Job seekers should do even better than that. In thank you letters, it is good to include a statement like "If I can ever return the favor (or kindness, or assistance, or help), please do not hesitate to call on me." Being thanked makes the networkee feel good and also demonstrates that the campaigner was not merely using the situation to get ahead. Remember, the key to the whole deal is relationship-building.

7) Most people these days are planning their next moves, as they should be. A job seeker can be an observer of current practices as well as future trends. This is one of the most significant ways that the job seeker can be of value to his or her contact.

8) There is an off chance that a position might be available in the networkee's organization, or that he or she might know of an opening elsewhere. Either way, there is something to be gained by the contact. If the opening is in his or her area, then the benefit is obvious. If the opening is elsewhere, the referring person could end up the hero. But this happy outcome should not be depended upon, or the general emphasis of

networking will be lost.

9) In an article for *The National Business Employment Weekly* in 1989, I pointed out that from the point of view of the hiring manager, networking can be a financial windfall. Networking costs prospective employers nothing, especially when compared with recruiters (exorbitantly expensive) and advertising. Networkers should think of themselves as cost-saving for prospective employers, when they find themselves in those situations in which a networking interview changes into a job interview.

10) Don't forget ego. People love being asked for advice; this is one of the cornerstones of networking technique. It is flattering for the networkee to be placed on a pedestal, bestowing the benefits of his or her accumulated wisdom and experience (otherwise known as the "almighty guru" approach).

Someone who is conducting a job search is obviously susceptible to all sorts of mood swings, self-doubt, and disappointments. However, the campaigner does not have to be put in a vulnerable position that most assume is necessary. It is imperative to think of the job-search process as a professional interaction, not a desperate plea for help. Constructive networking should be an *exchange* of ideas—with career-growth potential for everyone involved.

Ellis Chase runs an Affiliate of The Five O'Clock Club and was one of the original counselors at The Five O'Clock Club. He also runs an office for Right Associates, a major outplacement firm.

This article originally appeared in *The Five O'Clock News*.

*Human ... life is a succession of choices, which every conscious human being has to make every moment. At times these choices are of decisive importance; and the very quality of these choices will often reveal that person's character and decide his fate. But that fate is by no means prescribed: for he may go beyond his inclinations, inherited as well as acquired ones. The decision and the responsibility is his: for he is a free moral agent, responsible for his actions.*
John Lukacs, *A History of the Cold War*

*It is work, work that one delights in, that is the surest guarantor of happiness.*
Ashley Montagu, *The American Way of Life*

*Every man is born into the world to do something unique and something distinctive and if he or she does not do it, it will never be done.*
Benjamin E. Mays, "I Knew Carter G. Woodson," *Negro History Bulletin*, January-March 1981

*I have seen the future, and it's a lot like the present, but much longer.*
Dan Quisenberry, professional baseball player

The Five O'Clock Club®

# Working the Weddings
## Make Good Use of Every Chance to Network

By Stacy Feldman

Like many of you, I look at the Sunday newspaper—in my case, *The New York Times*—as a vast source of job information. I scour it every week. Here are some of the hot leads I found in just one Sunday's paper: 1) An opening for an associate at Millsport, a sports marketing company in Stamford, Connecticut; 2) A position at BPB Associates, a hedge fund consulting company; 3) and a fund-raiser slot at the UJA Federation. I also got some good networking names: The president of the Virgin Islands Advertising Partnership, based in St. Thomas, and two coffee-industry experts—a trader for Pacific Fruit Company, and the president of an exporting firm in Guatemala. Now, where did I find these leads? In the classifieds? No. In the business section? No. In the news? No. I found these leads, and more, in what some have called the women's sports pages: the nuptials.

---

**I found these leads, and more, in what some have called the women's sports pages.**

---

Why would you want to read the wedding announcements? Why should you care about the wedding plans of a bunch of well-connected twenty-year-olds? Information, that's why! First of all, they're not all young. The age range is inspirational. In one issue, as a matter of fact, there was a thirty-five-year-old bride, a thirty-eight-year-old, and a forty-nine-year-old! (Go, girl! Damn the statistics—full speed ahead.) This means that you can get information on people in different stages of their careers.

What kind of information? For each wedding announcement, you get the bride's name, school, company, and position. Same for the groom. Or, you may find out that one of the happy couple is leaving a job—marriage does that to people. The magic words are "until recently." Here's an example: ". . . <u>until recently</u> a manager in the affiliate-relations department of MJ Broadcasting, a radio production company." That position may still be

open. And, if the newlyweds are kids, take a look at Mom and Dad, on both sides, plus divorces and remarriages: Names galore! Just try getting this sort of stuff from a cold call. People who guard their privacy as if it's gold are quite willing to tell all to the world on this joyous occasion. So take advantage of it.

And the industries! This week alone: Printing and graphics, public television, lots of law firms, banks, discount brokers, pharmaceuticals, academia, sports, health care, and more. And this information is useful for relocation, too. Remember that the *Times* is a national paper, and the nuptials prove it. This week, I found names from Denver, Cleveland, Washington D.C., and San Diego.

You can also get insights into corporate culture that may not show up in the more usual places. For example, I learned that Van Eyck Securities Corporation, a mutual fund company, has a position called "manager of creative services." I suspect that it's some sort of advertising job, but it might be something else entirely. Maybe it's an open door for a liberal-arts type to walk into the world of finance. I also noticed a wedding where both the bride and groom worked in capital markets at Bankers Trust. (It seems that a job at BT can provide some non-traditional benefits.) Of course, banks have all those stuffy rules about fraud and collusion, so there may be a transfer in someone's future soon.

When you're looking for a job, use the recommended sources—they're all valuable. But don't be afraid to try some unusual sources, too. You never know which happy couple will lead you to your next job.

---

Stacy Feldman is a human resources consultant and a career counselor with The Five O'Clock Club.

---

This article originally appeared in *The Five O'Clock News*.

**Peter Doris**

20 Trinity Place
New York, New York 10000
(222) 555-2231

March 10, 19x6

Mr. James Cantor
Executive Vice President
Young & Rubicam
285 Madison Avenue
New York, New York 10017

Dear Mr. Cantor:

I am following up the suggestion of Kate Wendleton, who refers to herself as a fan of yours, and am writing to ask for your counsel on my current career plans.

I have recently decided to leave my present company, McGraw Hill Publishing, and continue my career elsewhere. I do not expect that you will know of a particular situation for me, but rather, I am seeking your advice.

I have targeted the advertising industry as part of my search strategy because I believe that with my skills in financial planning and problem solving, combined with international experience, I could make an important contribution to good business management. In addition, I believe I would enjoy working in the dynamic and creative environment of most agencies.

Thus, Kate suggested that I particularly ask for your response to my thoughts on how my experience in financial management in the publishing industry can be productively employed in advertising.

Briefly, my experience includes commercial banking (1967-1969) followed by financial analysis at CBS (1969-1971). The largest part of my career has been with Time, Inc. (1971-1983) where I served in a variety of financial and administrative assignments, including tours as International Finance Manager, Financial Director of Time's fully independent Mexico subsidiary, and an assignment in the direct marketing group. Following Time, I became a principal in a small publishing company, and since 1984 have been Vice President, Administration, at McGraw Hill Book Clubs.

I look forward to speaking with you, and will call in a few days to see when we can meet.

Sincerely,

Peter Doris

The
Five
O'Clock
Club

# Networking Cover Letters

---

> This note was handwritten on
> informal off-white stationery.

May 19, 19xx

Dear Mr. Englander,

Bob Snell suggested I contact you because he thought you could give me the information I need.

I'm interested in heading my career in a different direction. I've been with Rohm and Haas for nine years and I could stay here forever, but the growth possibilities in the areas that interest me are extremely limited. I want to make a move during the next year, but I want it to be the right move. Jack thought you could give me some ideas.

I'm interested in human resources. My nine years' experience in data processing included the design and implementation of Rohm and Haas' Salary Administration system as well as 3 years as Training and Development Director for the MIS Division. For the past two years, I have been in our Advertising Department and am now Advertising and Marketing Services Manager. What I'd like from you is some solid information on the job possibilties for someone like me.

I'd greatly appreciate half an hour of your time and insight. I'll call you in a few days to see when you can spare the time.

Sincerely,

Kate Wendleton

---

**Jaye Smith**

February 2, 19xx

Mr. Herbert Anderson
Executive Vice President
Green Card International, Inc.
888 Sixth Avenue
New York, New York 10000

Dear Mr. Anderson:

Sheryl Spanier suggested that I get in touch with you.

I am a seasoned financial services marketer at SanguineBank with a strong package goods background, and extensive experience in product development and merchandising, branch management, electronic banking and innovative distribution planning.

    • I created the SanguineBank Investment Portfolio, the bank's first complete presentation of its retail savings and investment products, and devloped successful ways to sell the SanguineDip account in the retail setting.

    • As an Area Director in the New York retail bank, I doubled branch balances in Mid-Manhattan in only three years.

    • Prior to SanguineBank, I rebuilt the baby shampoo division for Johnson & Johnson, and managed all bar soap marketing at Lever Brothers.

    • Most recently, I have been developing a set of PC-based funds transfer products for SanguineBank's Financial Institutions Group.

A résumé is enclosed for additional background.

I am seeking to move to a new assignment that would take full advantage of my consumer financial services marketing experience, and am extending my search outside of SanguineBank as well as inside. Lucas thought that it would be worthwhile for us to meet briefly. I'll call in a few days to set up an appointment, if appropriate.

I'm looking forward to meeting with you.

Sincerely,

Jaye Smith

# How to Contact Companies Directly

*I don't know anything about luck.*
*I've never banked on it and I'm afraid of people who do.*
*Luck to me is something else: hard work and realizing*
*what is opportunity and what is not.*
Lucille Ball

**B**eth conducted five direct-mail campaigns. She selected five clear targets and developed lists of names for each, ranging in size from fifty to two hundred names. She mailed a cover letter and résumé to her first list. When she started to get calls for interviews, she mailed to her second list. At approximately two-week intervals, Beth would send out another mailing. She received an excellent response (that is, calls for interviews) from three of her five mailings.

To develop her interviewing skills and investigate each target area, Beth first interviewed at firms she did not care about. She treated these interviews as networking meetings. Beth probed, for example, to find out what the manager thought of other companies on her list. If the comments were generally negative, she dropped those companies. If the comments were positive, she asked if the manager might know someone in that company whom she could contact. She got a lot of mileage out of her campaign because she combined direct mail with networking, and worked the system with great energy.

The entire process took only one and a half months. Beth had clear targets, followed the process, and prepared thoroughly for her meetings. She explored career possibilities in which she had been somewhat interested, and refined her career direction. She turned down a number of job offers before she accepted a high-level position that allowed her to combine her strongest skill area with something that was new to her and satisfied her long-range motivated skills. Beth took a two-week vacation before she started that job. She deserved it.

Jack's campaign strategy was very different. Jack is intelligent, articulate, research-oriented— and also very shy. He targeted an industry that would result in a career change for him. He had read a lot on this industry, and wanted to find out the job possibilities within it.

Jack meticulously researched companies and selected twenty in which he was seriously interested. They were huge corporations, and that made it relatively easy to get the names of people to contact. If he had simply mailed to that list, however, he might have gotten no response. As you will see later, twenty names is generally not enough for a direct-mail campaign. The effort would have been even more futile in Jack's case because he had, essentially, no hands-on experience in that field.

Jack did a targeted mailing—that is, he wrote to the twenty people, and *followed up with phone calls* to all of them. His well-written and convincing letter proved his sincere interest in and knowledge of the field. He sent it—without a résumé, because he was making a major career change—and told each of the twenty he would call him or her. He sent all the letters at once, and called every person. It was quite an effort. Jack got in to see just about every person on his list, and—as usually happens—some of them took a personal interest in his case. They gave him the names of others, and told him how to break into the field. Two of his contacts volunteered to sponsor him in their company's training program.

## How It Works

Approximately 20 percent of all jobs are found through direct-mail campaigns. This technique is even more effective when you combine it with networking—as both Beth and Jack did.

You will do better in your direct-mail campaign when you:

- have clearly identified your target market
- are familiar with the problems faced by companies in that market
- know what you have to offer to solve its problems.

Know enough about your target market to compose an appropriate cover letter and to hold your own in an interview. If you don't know enough, learn more through library research or networking. If you feel that you may be caught off-guard in an interview because of a lack of knowledge of your target market, do not use this technique until you have gained at least some knowledge.

These are not job interviews, but exploratory meetings that may lead to:

- more information
- names of other people to contact
- a job interview.

*Conduct the meeting using the same format as that of a networking meeting.*

Don't let the interviewer know you blanketed the market. If a company wants to see you, quickly do a little research on it. Tell the manager you wrote to him as a result of your research, and name something specific about the company that interested you.

It doesn't matter if your meetings come from a direct contact or from networking. What matters is that you get in to see people who are in a position to hire you.

### Benefits of This Technique

Direct mail blankets the market. In one fell swoop, you can find out what the chances are for someone like you in that market. You "market test" what you have to offer, and also get your name out quickly to prospective employers. This technique is fast and as complete as you want it to be, as opposed to networking, which is slower and hits your target in a spotty manner.

### What Is a Targeted Mailing?

A targeted mailing is direct mail followed by a phone call. Use it when you would like to see every person on your small list. Research so you can write customized letters (you may want to call for annual reports, for example, or talk to people to get information about a company). Follow the process for networking, paying special attention to the follow-up call, which requires a great deal of persistence. As with networking, you want to meet with people whether or not they have a job to offer.

### An Easy Way to Contact Lots of People

Typically, job hunters do not contact many people. Either the job hunter is unemployed and has the time to contact lots of people but may be suffering from low self-esteem—or is employed and simply does not have the time to contact people during the day. The direct-mail campaign allows a person to contact lots of potential employers despite reluctance or a lack of time.

Sometimes job hunters hit a slump and find networking overly stressful. Direct mail can help you get unstuck. You can hide away for a short while and grind out a mailing. You can sound more self-confident on paper than you actually feel, and can get your act together before you go out and talk to people. A direct-mail campaign can be a way out of a bind. But eventually you must talk to people. You cannot get a job through the mail. Don't use this technique to avoid people forever. You are writing so you can get in to see them.

### The Numbers You'll Need

In a small industry, your list will be smaller. In a larger industry, your list may be so large that you'll want to hit only a portion of it, as a test, and then hit another portion later.

The "response rate" is measured by the number of interviews you get divided by the number of pieces you mailed. Interviews count as responses; rejection letters do not. Interviews count because there is the possibility of continuing your job search in that direction. Rejection letters, no matter how flattering, have ended your search in that particular direction.

In direct mailing, a 4-percent response rate is considered very good. The basic rule of thumb is this:

A mailing of two hundred good names results in

- seven or eight interviews, which result in
- one job offer.

If your list is smaller, you may still do okay if you are well suited to that target and if there is a need for your services. If, however, your list has only ten names, you must network in, or use a targeted mailing with a follow-up phone call.

Another factor that affects your response rate is the industry to which you are writing. Certain industries are very people-oriented and are more likely to talk to you. Targeting industries that have a great demand for your service should result in a lot of responses.

*The man without purpose is like a ship without a rudder—a waif, a nothing, a no man.*
*Have a purpose in life, and, having it, throw such strength of mind and muscle*
*into your work as God has given you.*
Thomas Carlyle

Assuming that the job you are seeking is reasonable (that is, you have the appropriate qualifications and there are positions of that type available in the geographic area you are targeting), persistent inquiries will eventually turn up some openings.

## Should You Enclose Your Résumé?

If your résumé helps your case, enclose it. Beth enclosed her résumé; Jack did not. Direct-mail experts have proved that the more enclosures, the greater the response rate. You never know what may "grab" the reader, and the reader is likely to glance at each enclosure. Your résumé, if it supports your case and is enticing, is another piece to capture the reader's attention. I have been called for interviews because of what was on page three of my résumé.

If, however, your résumé hurts your case, change it—or leave it out altogether. A résumé may hurt your case when you are attempting a dramatic career change, as Jack was. (Read the chapter "How to Change Careers" to get more ideas on how you can support your case.)

## Cover Letters

The format you follow for your cover letter essentially can be the same whether you enclose your résumé or not. Your cover letter focuses your pitch more precisely than your résumé does and makes the reader see your résumé in that light. You can pitch to a very precise segment of the market by making only minor changes in the letter. The format for your cover letter is:

**Paragraph 1—The grabber.** Start with the point of greatest interest to your target market. This is the equivalent of a headline in an ad.

If your background is enough of a grabber for the target market to which you are writing, use it. For example, if you want a job in sales and have an excellent track record in that area, then open with a terrific sales accomplishment. Or if your expertise is in turnaround management, your cover letter might start like this:

As vice president of a $250-million company, I directed the turnaround of an organization that was in serious financial difficulty. As a result, this year was more profitable than the previous ten profitable years combined.

On the other hand, you can open your letter with a statement that shows you understand the problems faced by the industry to which you are selling your services. A successful letter to advertising agencies started like this:

Many ad agencies are coping with these difficult times by hiring the best creative and sales people available. While this may maintain a competitive edge, many agencies find their bottom line is slipping. The usual response is to send in the accountants. These agencies, and perhaps your own, need more than accounting help. As vice president of operations, I . . .

Here's a variation on the same theme—but aimed at companies that are probably doing well financially:

I know this is a time of rapid growth and high activity for Internet-based firms. I believe this is also a time when Internet-based firms must be as effective as possible to maintain their competitive edge. If you are looking for new developers—either on an ad hoc or a permanent basis—consider a person like me.

If you work for a well-known company in an area that would be of interest to your target market, you could start your letter like this:

I am at present with X Company in a position where I . . .

Perhaps your background itself would be your key selling point:

I started out in computers in 1976 and have been involved with them ever since. I am now at . . .

If you are targeting a small number of companies, mention your specific interest in each company:

I have been interested in [your company] for a number of years because of. . .

*What makes men happy is liking what they have to do.*
*This is a principle on which society is not founded.*
Claude Adrien Helvetius

**Paragraph 2**—A summary of your background aimed at a target—perhaps taken from the summary statement on your résumé.

**Paragraph 3**—Your key accomplishments that would be of interest to this target market. These can be written in a bulleted or paragraph format. Make them lively and interesting.

**Paragraph 4** (optional)—Additional information. This could include references to your education or personality, or other relevant information, such as:

I am high in energy and integrity—persuasive, thorough, and self-confident—a highly motivated self-starter accustomed to working independently within the framework of a company's policies and goals. I thrive on long hours of work, and enjoy an atmosphere where I am measured by my results, where compensation is directly related to my ability to produce, and where the job is what I make it.

**Final paragraph**—**The close.** Such as:

I would prefer working in an environment where my leadership and problem-solving abilities are needed, and would be pleased to meet with you to discuss the contribution I could make to your organization.

Or use a statement like this one—which excludes those who may want to hire someone lower-level:

Hiring me would be an investment in the mid-$70,000 range, but the return will be impressive. I would be pleased to meet with you to discuss the contribution I could make to the performance of your organization.

Or this statement for a direct-mail campaign, where you will not be making follow-up phone calls, especially to a list to which you have some relationship, such as that of an organization of which you are a member:

I can understand how busy you must be, and therefore do not want to bother you with a follow-up phone call. However, I trust that you will give me a call if you come across information that would be helpful to me in my search.

---

*You gain strength, courage and confidence by every experience in which you really stop to look fear in the face. You are able to say to yourself: "I lived through this horror. I can take the next thing that comes along." . . . You must do the thing you think you cannot do.*
Eleanor Roosevelt

---

*We African-American women have always worked outside of our homes, in slavery or in freedom —in the fields, in the kitchen, or in the nursery.*
Frederica J. Balzano, Ph.D., "And Ar'nt I a Woman?"
*The Five O'Clock News*, September 1995

---

*Happiness is not a matter of events; it depends upon the tides of the mind.*
Alice Meynell

---

*Pain: an uncomfortable frame of mind that may have a physical basis in something that is being done to the body, or may be purely mental, caused by the good fortune of others.*
Ambrose Bierce

# Targeted Mailings:
# Just Like Networking

*Life is like playing a violin*
*solo in public and learning*
*the instrument as one goes on.*
Samuel Butler

---

*There's nothing to writing.*
*All you do is sit down at a typewriter and open a vein.*
Walter ("Red") Smith, in *Reader's Digest,*
July 1982

---

*There is no way of writing*
*well and also of writing easily.*
Anthony Trollope, *Barchester Towers*

---

*Who has begun has half done.*
*Have the courage to be wise. Begin!*
Horace, Epistles

---

Networking is not the only way to job-hunt. Consider targeted mailings when:

• You want to see a particular person but have no formal contact. You must think of how you can create some tie-in to that person, and contact him or her directly.

• You have selected twenty to thirty companies in your target market that you really want to get in to see, and there are only a few jobs that would be appropriate for you in each company.

For the twenty or thirty companies you have chosen, research the appropriate person to contact in each one. Ask each for a meeting—whether or not they have a job for you. You want to get in to see them *all* because your target is very small.

## The Letter

• **Paragraph 1:** The opening paragraph for a targeted mailing would follow the format for a networking letter: state the reason you are writing and **establish the contact** you have with the reader.

Congratulations on your new position! I know you are extremely busy (I've heard about it from others). After you are settled in, I would be interested in meeting with you. I think it would be mutually beneficial for us to meet, although I have no fixed idea of what could come of it.

After you have found out something about the person or the company, pretend you are sitting with that person right now. What would you *say* to him or her? Here's what one job hunter wrote to an executive:

I agree. Your position *is* truly enviable.

With the merger of AT&T and United Telecom completed. AT&T is now positioned to become an even greater force in shaping telecommunications for the future, both domestically and internationally. However, with all the challenges come the inevitable need for control, resolution of legal and regulatory issues, competitive threats, pricing issues, and reexamination of both the positioning and global packaging of AT&T. Clear, focused strategic and business plans become essential for success. I believe I can help you in these areas.

See the next chapter, "Targeted Mailing Cover Letter: A Case Study," for the rest of this letter. Here's another letter that reflects a great deal of thought:

As the banks look back on their risky involvement with groups like Campeau, it is clear that a better understanding of the retail business would have saved them from considerable losses. As a result, I'm sure many banks and lending institutions have gone to the opposite extreme. Another solution, however, would be to have an unbiased expert merchant involved in evaluating their retail plans.

Your opening should reflect whatever you know about the company or the person:

Whenever people talk about companies with excellent internal temporary services departments, Schaeffer's name always comes up. In fact, the people who run the Amalgamated Center, where I am now assigned, speak often of the quality of your work. I am interested in becoming a consultant in this field, and I hope to meet with you.

- **Paragraph 2**:
Give a **summary about yourself**.

- **Paragraph 3**:
Note a few **key accomplishments that would be of interest to this target**.

- **Paragraph 4**:
Ask for **half an hour** of their time, and say you will **call them in a few days**, for example:

I am sure a brief meeting will be fruitful for us both. I will call your new secretary in a week or so to see when I can get on your calendar.
Or
I hope you will allow me half an hour of your time and insight to explore this area. I will call you in a few days to set up a mutually agreeable time.

If you plan to follow up with a phone call, say so. (But if you say so, do it—or you may get no response while they wait for your call.)

### Out-of-Town Search

For an *out-of-town search* (perhaps placed next to the last paragraph):

As a result of many years' travel to Seattle, I would prefer to live and work in that area. In fact, I am in Seattle frequently on business and can arrange to meet with you at your office.

### Scannable Letters

As we have seen, other variations include the use of **underlining key points**, which can increase your response rate. This helps the busy reader scan the letter, be drawn in, and want to read the rest. Underlining makes certain key points pop out at the reader—anywhere in your text. Underline parts of sentences in no more than five places. Read the underlined parts to make sure they sound sensible when read together, have a flow, and make your point.

Even when I look at my own letters, I sometimes don't want to read them before I make them scannable. I rephrase my letters, underlining in a way that will make sense to the reader. People will read the salutation, then the first few words of your letter, and then the parts you have underlined. If they find these things compelling, they'll go back and read the rest of your letter.

Underlining should make sense. Don't underline the word "developed," for instance, because that doesn't make sense. Underline the word after, which is *what* you developed—because that's probably the compelling part.

### Do What Is Appropriate

Strange as it may seem, **sometimes it can be very effective to ignore all of this**. Do what works in your target area. Nat, who was interested in Japanese banks, wrote to forty banks with a four-line cover letter that said something like: "Enclosed please find my résumé. I have had twenty years of banking experience, am mature,..."

*The way to get good ideas is to get lots of ideas and throw the bad ones away.*
Linus Pauling, American chemist*

---

Nat knew his market. He thought the Japanese would be put off by the typically aggressive American approach. He got an excellent response rate—and the kind of job he wanted.

Remember, it is sometimes better to follow your instincts rather than listen to the experts. You're smart. You know your market better than we do. Make up your own mind.

### The Follow-Up Call (After a Targeted Mailing)

When you call, you will probably have to <u>start again from the beginning</u>. Do not expect them to remember anything in your letter. Do not even expect them to remember that you wrote to them. For example, when you phone:

- "I sent you a letter recently. Did you receive it?"
- Remind them of the reason you wrote. You may again have to summarize your background, and state some of your accomplishments.
- If they say they have no job openings at this time, that is okay with you—you were not necessarily looking for a job *with them*; you were looking for information or advice about the job possibilities for someone like you, or perhaps you wanted to know what is happening in the profession, company, or industry.

<u>Leave messages that you called, but do not ask to have them call you back.</u> Chances are, they won't, and you will feel rejected. However, be friendly with the secretary, and apologize for calling so often. If she would like to have her boss call you back, tell her thanks, but you will be in and out and her boss will be unable to reach you: you will have to call again. After the first call, try not to leave your name again. <u>Expect to call seven or eight times</u>. Do not become discouraged. It is not personal.

### The Meeting

When you go in for your meeting, <u>handle it as you would a networking interview</u> (unless the manager turns it into a job interview):

- Exchange pleasantries.
- State the reason you are there and why you wanted to see this particular person.
- Give your Two-Minute Pitch.
- Tell the manager how he or she can help you. Get the information you want, as well as a few names of other people you should be talking to.

As we have said, <u>be grateful for whatever help people give you.</u> They are helping you the best they can. If they do not give you the names of others to contact, perhaps they cannot because of a feeling of insecurity in their own jobs. Appreciate whatever they do give you.

For a more detailed description of how to handle the meeting, refer to the chapter "What to Do When Your Networking Isn't Working."

### Form a Relationship

Take notes during your meeting. Your follow-up notes will be more appropriate, and then you will feel free to contact this person later. Keep in touch with people on a regular basis. Those who know you well will be more likely to help you.

A targeted mailing is a very powerful technique for hitting *every* company in a small target area. A direct-mail campaign hits every company in a large target. Both can dramatically move your job hunt along. Try them!

### Follow Up

<u>Follow up with a customized note specifically acknowledging the help you received.</u> These notes follow the same concept as follow-ups to networking interviews.

### Final Thoughts

You will strike sparks with certain people you meet. They will develop a true interest in you and will surprise you with their help. I have had people invite me to luncheons to introduce me to important people, or call me when they heard news that would interest me. I have even made new friends this way.

Of course, I have done my part, too, by keeping

in touch to let them know how my campaign was going. If you are sincere about your search, you will find that the people you meet will also be sincere and will help. It can also be a very heart-warming experience.

## CASE STUDY: AHMED
### Research and Focus

Ahmed had just moved to the United States from Turkey, so he had no contacts here. He had a background in international sales and trading.

He targeted nine major employers, and did extensive research on each one. Then he wrote to the head of international sales at each of the nine companies. In his introductory paragraph, he said things like "I notice that your international sales have declined from 6 percent to 3 percent over the last year. I find that very disturbing. I was wondering why that is happening, given the state of the market now . . . "

Paragraph two was his summary. Paragraph three were his bulleted accomplishments. Paragraph four was the close: "I would really appreciate meeting you . . . "

He called only two of them—because the other seven called him before he had a chance. This targeted mailing resulted in nine meetings and three job offers.

## Direct Contact Requires
## Research and Excellent Writing Skills

Targeted mail works only if you've done your research and if you're a good writer. Furthermore, you must target the right person and have something interesting to say to each person you are contacting. That's why direct contact works best for job hunters who clearly understand their target markets and the issues that are important in them. And that's also why most people do not attempt direct contact until after they have done their research—through preliminary networking or the library.

## Are You Sincere?

It's not enough to write to people and expect to get in to see them. They are probably busy with their own jobs, and may be contacted by quite a few people.

Unless you sincerely want to see a person, you won't develop strategies to figure out how to get in to see him or her. You won't do your research. You won't do the follow-up phone calls that are required to prove your sincerity. You won't prevail when someone doesn't return your phone calls.

If you really want to see this person, you'll persevere. And you won't mind asking for an appointment one month from now if he or she is too busy to see you now. You may even say, "I know you're busy now. How about if we schedule something for a month from now, and I'll call you in advance to confirm."

## To Enclose Your Résumé or Not?

A cover story in *Time* magazine was titled "Junk Mail." People said, "Why do junk-mail companies enclose so many things in these envelopes that we get? They're wasting paper." In the Letters to the Editor, the junk-mail companies said they had no choice because the response rate increased so dramatically with the number of additional enclosures that have the same message. If they have fewer enclosures, their response rate decreases dramatically.

The same is true for the mailings you are sending. Some people say, "If they see my résumé, they'll know I'm job-hunting." But they'll probably know it anyway from your letter. People are very sophisticated today.

My rule of thumb is this: If it supports your case, and it has a message that complements your cover letter, then enclose your résumé. You can say, "I've enclosed my résumé to let you know something more about me." If you have a brilliant résumé, why not enclose it?

On the other hand, if you want to make a career change, you probably do not want to enclose your résumé because you can probably make a stronger case without it.

Do what is appropriate for you. Try it both ways and see which works better for you and your situation.

## Stating Your Accomplishments in Your Cover Letter

Think of which of your accomplishments are of interest to your target market. You may want to list different accomplishments for the different industries to which you are writing.

Rank your bulleted accomplishments generally in order of importance to the reader, as opposed to chronologically or alphabetically. It may be that some other logic would be more appropriate in your case. Then do that.

## CASE STUDY: RICK
### *Out-of-Town Search*

A Five O'Clock Club job hunter was looking for a job in Denver. He conducted research by getting a listing of companies from the Denver Chamber of Commerce. He called each company and asked for the name of the department head for the area in which he was interested. He wrote to each one, and followed up with a phone call.

He was employed at the time. Yet most of his effort did not take time away from his job. He did his research and wrote his letters on the evenings and weekends. Networking would have been an impossible way for him to start his search, especially in another part of the country. But after he had made these initial contacts, and had traveled to Denver, then he could network around.

He wound up with something like eighty companies to contact—too many for follow-up phone calls. Even twenty is a lot. He followed up with twenty companies, and scheduled a three-day trip to Denver. Before he went, he had set up eight meetings—for the first two days of his trip. When he met with those first eight, he networked into four additional companies, and held those meetings on the third day of his trip.

He didn't have a lot of money, so he couldn't stay long in Denver. But this is also the best way to conduct an out-of-town search—a few days at a time.

When job hunters visit a city for two weeks, and hope that something will happen, they usually come home empty-handed. It's better to do your research, contact all of the companies ahead of time, and go there with meetings already set up. The meetings could be with search firms, in answer to ads, or through networking or direct contact.

Go for three days. Tell the people you meet that you are planning to be in town again in a few weeks, and would like to meet with other people in their company, or in other companies. Go back home, do more work, return in another three or four weeks, and stay for another three days. Then you develop momentum in your out-of-town campaign. A one-time visit rarely works.

Rick went back again six weeks later. It took a few more visits to land the job he wanted, but he did it all with direct and targeted mail as the basis for his campaign, supplemented by networking.

The following pages contain case studies of people who have been successful with targeted mailings. Rather than simply copying their letters, think of *one* actual individual on your list to whom you are writing, and think of the compelling things you should say to make that person want to meet with you. Even if you write exactly that same letter to twenty people, it will sound more sincere and have more life.

The
Five
O'Clock
Club®

# Targeted Mailing Cover Letter: A Case Study

*Faint heart never won fair lady.*
Cervantes, *Don Quixote*

Cristina was very interested in AT&T. She researched the company and decided to write to the vice chairman of the board. This was an appropriate person for her to write to because he was head of strategic planning, which was her area of expertise.

She wrote a cover letter using our standard format. The cover letter started out by saying, "I agree with you completely. . ." Then she quoted from an article in which he was mentioned. She was attempting to establish a business relationship with him.

Paragraph two was her summary paragraph. Paragraph three contained her bulleted accomplishments. Paragraph four was her close.

Before sending the letter, she called the company to find out the name of his secretary. It was Kim. Then she called to say that she was writing a letter to Mr. van Hecke, and would Kim please look out for it?

In the last paragraph of her letter, she said, "I would very much appreciate the opportunity to meet with you for half an hour to introduce myself . . . I'll call Kim next week to set up an appointment."

She wound up meeting with the vice chairman, and four other very senior people at that company. But the company had a hiring freeze,

and she ended up working elsewhere.

Was Cristina's targeted mailing successful? The answer is yes! Did you forget? Mailings, networking, search firms, and ads are techniques for getting *interviews*. If she got an interview, the technique was successful. Cristina got the meeting she had wanted, and more.

By the way, she had enclosed her résumé. She was careful not to mention the business she had been in because it was very different from the one at AT&T. But she knew her skills were transferable because she had done so much research on AT&T and could prove it in her letter. She could talk about her background without emphasizing the exact product or service with which she had been involved.

## Why Not Network Instead?

When Cristina wrote to the vice chairman of the board, she really wanted to see him. If she had decided to network in, it would have taken her a very long time to meet someone who would be willing to introduce her to such an important person. Instead, she did her homework: extensive research and intensive follow-up. Be sure to include targeted mailing in *your* bag of tricks.

Note: Do not necessarily aim for a person at the top of the company. See people who are appropriate for your level. As a rule of thumb, you want to see people who are two levels higher than you are.

**Cristina Mejias**
143 West Hill Road
Greenwich, CT 02555
212-555-1212 (day)

August 1, 1991

Mr. John van Hecke, Vice Chairman
AT&T Corporation
Corporate Planning and Development
One Stamford Forum
Stamford, CT 06904

Dear Mr. van Hecke:

I agree. Your position is truly enviable.

With the merger of AT&T and United Telecom completed, AT&T is now in a position to become an even greater force in shaping telecommunications for the future both domestically and internationally. However, with all the challenges comes the inevitable need for control, resolution of legal and regulatory issues, competitive threats, pricing issues, and reexamination of both positioning and global packaging of AT&T. Clear, focused strategic and business plans become essential for success. I believe I can help you in these areas.

I offer twenty years of experience in management and marketing with over half that time focused on the international markets. In addition, having been primarily involved in start-up and turnaround ventures, I was directly responsible for developing both five- and ten-year strategic plans and one-year operating plans.

Other areas where my experience could be of assistance to your Corporate Planning and Development area:

- Established and implemented a global marketing and sales strategy which insured consistency of message and product delivery to customers.

- Developed an "insider" approach in the local markets for the products and services sold while adhering to corporate values.

- Instituted a global program aimed at insuring zero defects for multinational clients. Given AT&T's product mix and its strategy for global expansion, superior quality service is essential for success.

- Developed, installed and managed a centralized core system for the business noted as the best in the industry.

- Hosted quarterly global sales and marketing conferences and training sessions to cement team spirit and ensure product, corporate and local communications were current and correct.

- Developed a global risk management program to control risk with "common" sense" procedures to ensure compliance and support.

- Traveled globally at an 80% level. Focused on visiting/selling/ cheerleading clients, prospects, industry leaders and staff.

- Created and implemented a global promotion and advertising campaign to establish an image of a global yet local player.

I would very much appreciate the opportunity to meet with you for half an hour to introduce myself, discuss the AT&T environment and identify any areas of your organization or the corporation which may have the need for someone with my background and experience. I have the maturity and sophistication to deal with the wide variety of personalities, problems and opportunities presented by the international markets plus the persistence to see things through to meet your goals.

I'll call Kim next week to set up an appointment. I look forward to meeting you.

Sincerely,

Cristina Mejias

# Targeted Mailing:
# My Own Case Study

*Beginnings are always messy.*
John Galsworthy, English novelist

*I take a simple view of living.*
*It is: keep your eyes open and get on with it.*
Laurence Olivier

I enjoy research and writing. I sincerely want to meet with the people to whom I write, and I therefore don't mind doing a lot of work to get in to see them. I use both targeted- and direct-mail campaigns.

A number of years ago, IBM announced a new president of a company that had to do with employment. I thought I should get to know him because I was in the career-counseling field—although I couldn't find out exactly what the new company would be doing. I knew quite a few people who had tried to network in to see him—with no success. The man was inundated with letters from people trying to see him, using the name of somebody important at IBM. He turned them all down.

I wrote him a targeted mailing, and enclosed a résumé. Before I wrote paragraph one, I tried to think about him as a person. That's what you need to do to make your letters more personal. "Gosh," I thought, "he must be so proud to be president of this company! He's probably never been the president of a company before."

When I am working with my clients, I want them to imagine the person to whom they are writing, and write a letter aimed at that specific person—even in a direct-mail campaign, where they may write to sixty or a hundred people. It is still better to write that first letter with someone specific in mind (even if you don't really know that person), rather than writing to a mailing list.

What you want to say to that specific individual becomes the opening to the letter. In this case, I had to hedge my bets because I didn't know exactly what the company did, so I alluded to that fact. In paragraph two, I gave my summary statement. In paragraph three, I had bulleted accomplishments.

Before I sent the letter, I called and found that he had only a temporary secretary. So, in paragraph four, I referred to that.

I mentioned that I thought it would be fruitful for both of us if we got together. And I enclosed my résumé.

As usual, I got cold feet after I sent the letter. What happens is that I start thinking, "Why would this person ever want to see me—especially when I know he has rejected so many?" Sometimes I get so scared that I wait too long to follow up. Then I write again, usually saying that there is some information I left out of my first letter. I send off that second letter, and by that time, I can usually get up my nerve to follow up with a phone call.

In this case, the secretary was expecting my call, and the company president had asked her to reserve forty-five minutes for me.

When I met with him, he told me he had received over eight hundred letters, but met with only four people—including me. He said my letter was one of the most intelligent he had received, and that I sounded sincere. In case you think the credentials that you see in this letter are what got me in, I'd like to point out that I used this technique even early on in my career when I had virutally no credentials. The four-paragraph approach increases anyone's chances of writing an intelligent letter.

A targeted mailing requires clear thinking, clear writing, and making a case for oneself. Most people realize this. On the other hand, when job hunters have a networking contact, they tend to cut short the hard work required to get in to see someone. And sometimes people resent getting networking letters and feeling as though they are being coerced.

Everyone is networking these days, and it certainly is an important technique—but it's not the only one. At least consider the other approaches to getting interviews in your target market.

**Kate Wendleton**
444 East Grenopple Street
New York, New York 10000

February 10, 1992

Mr. Mike Aronin
President, Employment Solutions, Inc.
c/o IBM Corporation
555 Black Horse Pike
Runnemede, NJ 07555

Dear Mr. Aronin:

Congratulations on your new position! I know you are extremely busy (I've heard about it from others). After you are settled in, I would be interested in meeting with you. I think it would be mutually beneficial for us to meet, although I have no fixed idea of what could come of it.

I have started up, managed, and delivered a number of employment/counseling services. I also have a strong business background:

- I am Founder and Director of The Career Center at the New School for Social Research.
- I am Founder and Director of The Five O'Clock Club®, a career counseling group that attracts forty to sixty job hunters a week in Manhattan. We have seven counselors who coach the job hunters through their searches.
- When I served as CFO of a outplacement firm that had a professional staff of 100, that company was very successful and profitable.
- I counsel senior executives at a major financial institution, a good prototype of an internal service, and the only one that has a full-time staff serving clients (others rely on outside consultants).
- One of my books will be published in the Fall by the Villard division of Random House under the title, *Through the Brick Wall: How to Job-Hunt in a Tight Market*.

I know a *lot* of people in the field, and perhaps have knowledge of some important developments in outplacement of which you may not be aware. I am sure our meeting will be fruitful for us both. I will call your new secretary in a week or so to see when I can get on your calendar.

Yours truly,

Kate Wendleton

# Targeted Mailing Cover Letters

---

## James J. Borland, III

140 West 81st Street
New York, New York 10000

July 17, 19xx

Mr. George Jung
Merrill Lynch
Liberty Place
165 Broadway
New York, New York 10000

> This letter was sent after
> a cold call to Mr. Jung
> about the possibility of a
> stockbrokering position.

Dear George:

I appreciate your offer to review and forward on my résumé. I think you'll see how I've used my skills of persuasion throughout the years. For example, while working on the "Friends of Bill Thomas" Mayoral Campaign, I was on the phone all day long convincing politicians across a broad spectrum to either publicly commit to my candidate or, as was the case at the outset when resistance was strong and reactions negative, to cooperate behind the scenes. The continual give and take involved a lot of listening as people wanted to state their case, vent frustrations with personalities, and so on. One had to cajole and "massage" the local political types in an effort to have them deliver us an audience at events that we staged in their communities. These same techniques—reasoning with people, getting my message across, listening, possessing a desire to please—all these would be assets in a job where rejection is the norm.

On the other hand, I find I enjoy analyzing business. For example, in my current job I monitor revenue and other statistics daily to determine trends and affect policy. While also working on systems problems (we are a computer-driven collections operation), the line management position I hold in day-to-day operations is responsible for a net revenue of $2 million plus per year. I supervise 22 city marshals who participate in the street impoundment program and also deal directly with 3 garage towing operations under contract to us. I've also been negotiating with realtors and prospective sub-contractors to expand our operation.

I enjoy working in an atmosphere where there is a lot of activity, where I'm measured by my results, where compensation is directly related to my ability to produce, and where the job is what I make it. I want to be with interesting people, people that matter, people that can have an impact. I feel that the securitites business and the opportunity to train and grow the best at Merrill would be a challenge and an education. In this situation, I feel the most severe limitations and constraints would be my own and I like that.

I would be pleased to meet with someone in your organization to further discuss how my qualifications may lead to a career with Merrill.

Sincerely,

*Philip Gittings*

*10 West Fortieth Street*
*West Beach, New Jersey 08000*
*(222) 555-2231*

April 30, 19xx

Name
Title
Company
Address
City, State, Zip

> **Phil sent this letter to
> 15 pharmaceutical industry executives.
> He did not include a résumé
> —it would not have helped his case
> because his target was dramatically
> different from his background.**

Dear M. Name:

I am writing to you because I am very interested in working for your company.

As biomedical research advances on international fronts, companies with global health care and pharmaceutical interests are facing intensified multinational competition. Dealing effectively with this kind of environment may require the resources of capable international planning analysts:

- to coordinate diverse, market-driven approaches to worldwide competition
- to channel regionally-developed strategic market plans in the direction of common organizational goals
- to establish and communicate that common vision which ensures worldwide leadership

As an international market planning analyst with Exxon, I have dealt with these issues and would add important expertise to your planning and marketing activities. I have seven years experience in market planning, operations and financial analysis, gained through five diverse assignments with Exxon International Company. During this time, I have made some meaningful contributions to the organization's worldwide efficiency, competitiveness, and strength:

- Developed an international market planning approach for a $4 billion product line. It was acknowledged worldwide for substantially improving overall marketing potential and global communications.
- Analyzed the industry environments of several international product lines. Developed corporate outlooks and goals consistent with worldwide perspectives.
- Evaluated the reasonableness of regional market strategies (Europe, Far East, and America, Canada, U.S.A.). Worked with foreign marketing managers to assess competitive strengths and to define appropriate objectives and positioning.

My assignments with Exxon have taught me how to plan, market and manage effectively the international product lines of a highly decentralized organization. The industry environment is one where widely varying economic conditions, regulatory requirements and political practices are standard considerations. I would be immediately beneficial to your organization and in your industry because of this tested experience.

In additon to my market planning responsibilities, I have also performed financial and cost/benefit analyses for efficient use of assets. I have implemented analytical applications on both mainframe and micro computers. I have delivered oral and written presentations to top level executives. My educational background includes an M.S. in Industrial Administration, earned from Columbia in 1978, and a B.S. in Mathematics and English.

Due to the restructuring of the oil industry and my assessment of the opportunities there, I am looking to match my skills with organizations that offer potential. Along with my credentials, I bring an intensely personal motivation to meet the challenges of contemporary health care issues and to participate in the exciting developments that are promised the pharmaceutical industry by emerging technologies.

I am confident that I can contribute importantly and meaningfully to your firm's international marketing and planning efforts. I look forward to an exploratory meeting with you, where we can discuss in more detail my qualifications and how they can be of use to you.

I will call in a few days to see when a personal meeting can be arranged.

Sincerely,

> **Phil got in to see all of the people he wanted to see—because of his persistence in the follow-up phone calls. He was offered a number of options in the pharmaceutical industry, but he turned them down and accepted a position in a completely different field.**

November 10, 19xx

Ms. Harriet Greisser
President
Creative Concepts
155 Fifth Avenue
New York, New York 10000

Dear Ms. Greisser:

Would you like to meet an effective sales professional with a successful track record in your industry? After running my own business for the last couple of years, I am considering a change. Because of the caliber of your company, I think you would be an excellent person to talk with.

I've been in the corporate communications business for twelve years as president of my own company and as a sales executive with a leading producer of industrial shows and meetings.

As head of sales for Petersen and Johnson, Inc., I:

- Increased their business by more than $3 million.

- Initiated proposal bids for an additional $2 million of potential sales.

- Put their name on the map with such companies as Johnson & Johnson, Toshiba, Lever Brothers, CBS Records, and ABC-TV.

I would appreciate half an hour of your time and insight to explore opportunities in this changing industry.

I'll give you a call within a week.

Sincerely,

Sharon Nuskey

**Fred Hopkinson**

November 10, 19xx

Ms. Vera Sullivan
SVP & Controller
Bankers Trust
433 Market Street
San Francisco, CA 94000

Dear Ms. Sullivan:

I am writing to you as I am seeking a senior financial and/or operations position in the San Francisco Bay area. Although I enjoy working for Chase Manhattan Bank, I'm afraid my 12 years in San Francisco has spoiled me forever, certainly relative to living in New York.

I am a senior financial manager with a strong background (Bank of America, Wells Fargo, Chase) in financial control and analysis, budgeting, forecasting and data processing operations. I have strong management and administrative skills, have managed large groups of people and have successfully turned around problem operations. I have an extensive knowledge of personal computers as well as database and spreadsheet
applications.

I would very much appreciate the opportunity to meet with you for half an hour to introduce myself, discuss the current environment at Bankers Trust, and identify any areas of the bank which may, in the future, have a need for someone with my background and experience. I would also appreciate your ideas on other financial institutions in San Francisco which may offer future career opportunities.

I will be in the Bay area in early December (I still maintain my home in San Rafael) and will call you in advance to schedule a mutually convenient time. I appreciate your consideration and look forward to the possibility of meeting you.

Sincerely,

# Direct-Mail Campaigns

*Perfection of means and confusion of goals seem, in
my opinion, to characterize our age.*
Albert Einstein

## Does Direct Mail Work?

A technique "works" if it helps you to get interviews in your target market. When you are mounting a full campaign, your goal is to have the companies in your target market know about you as quickly as possible. You can supplement your networking by using search firms and answering ads, but you will still not have hit most of the companies in your market. Regardless of how you get in, if you find you are being well-received by some companies in your target market, consider direct mail and/ or targeted mail for the rest.

If you use direct mail, consider mounting campaigns to a number of targets. Out of four campaigns, for example, maybe two will be effective and result in meetings, and two won't work at all. Part of it is selecting a target that is likely to be interested in you. Another part is being able to express yourself clearly and compellingly in writing. And a third part is a numbers game. If you get no response when you mail to a very small number, it is not a good test.

Most job hunters expect every letter they write to result in a meeting. That's unreasonable.

They don't expect every search-firm contact or every ad to result in a meeting. The same is true for direct contact.

## CASE STUDY: DIANE
### *Getting More Job Possibilities in the Works*

Last week, Diane accepted a job offer. She had uncovered two job possibilities through networking, but she wanted to have the requisite "six to ten things in the works." So she did a mailing of 250 letters, which resulted in four more job leads. Admittedly, that's a very small response rate from a mailing, but she wound up with four more job interviews than she would have had exclusively through networking.

## Act As If This Company Is Important to You

One time I wrote a direct-mail letter to 200 companies. A manager at one company said to me, "How did you hear of us? No one ever writes to us." I said, "Oh, a number of people have mentioned your company." "Really. Who?" I said, "Pierre Charbonneau and Lillian Bisset-Farrell, to name two [making up the first two names that came to my mind]." The manager said, "I don't know them." "Well," I replied, "they've heard of you!"

If they take your letter personally, you cannot tell them that you sent that same letter to 200 people.

# Bart Lewis: Making It Sound Personal

*Out there things can happen*
*to people as brainy*
*and footsy as you.*

*And when things start to happen*
*don't worry. Don't stew.*
*Just go right along.*
*You'll start happening too.*
Dr. Seuss, *Oh, the Places You'll Go!*

---

*Results! Why, man, I have gotten a lot of results.*
*I know several thousand things that won't work.*
Thomas A. Edison

B art is an organizational-development person. He wrote a letter to sixty fellow members of the Organization Development Network, saying: "As a fellow member of the OD Network, I thought perhaps you might come across information that might help me in my job search. I am interested in making a career move and I sure would appreciate hearing from you." Paragraph two was his summary. In paragraph three, he listed his accomplishments.

Paragraph four was very clever because he had no intention of calling these people, and he didn't want to make it sound like a mass mailing, so he said a variation of "I don't want to bother you with phone calls, but I trust you will give me a call if you come across information that would help me in my search."

He got six calls back about real job openings. He did another mailing to another sixty people in the same organization, got another six meetings, and he eventually wound up with a job offer.

Which technique did he use? It was a direct-mail campaign.

If you have an association list, consider using it for a direct-mail campaign, and be sure to mention your membership in that association in your opening paragraph.

**Bartholomew Lewis**
2421 Maindays Boulevard
Columbus, Ohio 43700
231-555-1212

April 6, 1992

Name
Position
Company
Address
City, State, ZIP

Dear Name:

As a fellow member of the Organization Development Network, I am writing to explore with you potential opportunities in your organization.

Currently with Bell South as an internal Corporate Human Resources consultant, I am seeking an opportunity in organization and management development. Perhaps it would facilitate this process if I share key highlights of my background:

- Management Development specialist with over **6 years of experience** developing and making presentations.

- At **Bell South**, I am responsible for designing and implementing projects to enhance the professionalism of over 2,000 managers worldwide. This involves:

    - **Executive and High Potential Development** - Assessing and identifying top performers to: meet specific business talent needs; attend Executive University programs; facilitate succession planning.

    - **Needs Analysis** - Running focus groups throughout the US and Europe for the purpose of creating and designing training programs.

    - **Organizational Research** - Use of statistical and research design (SPSSX) to conduct surveys, climate studies, turnover studies.

- Experience in Asia as a process consultant to an American-based company. **Fluent Japanese**.

- Hold **2 master's degrees from Columbia University** in Organizational and Counseling Psychology.

What do you think? Are there any possibilities within your purview for someone with my skills and experience base? I realize you are busy and I don't want to be intrusive by phoning; however, if there is an interest or you would just like to discuss some ideas, please contact me at 231-555-1212. Attached is my résumé. I look forward to your input. Thank you.

Sincerely,

The
Five
O'Clock
Club®

# Bruce Faulk: Before and After Direct-Mail Letters

Because of The Five O'Clock Club approach, he became more methodical about everything he did in his search for his next acting job. Bruce's "after" letter is on the next page.

By the way, after appearing on Broadway as the youngest actor in *Hamlet*, Bruce toured the United States, and is currently touring Europe with *Hair*.

Bruce's letter proves that the approach works for anyone—regardless of their profession. At The Five O'Clock Club, we have worked with everyone from orchestra conductors to fine artists.

This just in from Bruce:

> **The "before" version of Bruce's direct-mail letter**

Dear David Rottman:

I am sending you my picture and résumé on the advice of Casey Childs, who has directed a number of <u>A Different World</u> episodes. I hope that you will keep me in mind for any upcoming projects which I might be right for. I will keep you apprised of my situation. Thank you.

Sincerely,

Bruce Faulk

---

Kate -

Europe is all I expected and more—so much so that I've extended my tour here a few more months. So far, most of the tour has been all over—and I do mean *all* over Germany; but there's still a lot of time for Zurich (where I am now) for the rest of Switzerland, for Austria, and a month and a half right outside Amsterdam. Next month, I'm off to Cannes, France, and a week in Sweden.

Not too shabby for a former receptionist?

Hope all is well with you. Please give everyone my love.

Always,
Bruce

---

**Bruce J. Faulk**
286 North 50th Street - Apt. HL
New York, NY 10099
212-555-9809

March 18, 1991

Dear Mr. Rottman:

Casey Childs, who has directed A Different World, suggested I contact you. He thought you and I might be able to work together.

I am a graduate of the High School of Performing Arts and Carnegie-Mellon University. I have performed repeatedly Off-Broadway in New York. You may be interested in some of my specific experiences. For example:

I am particularly proud of my work in The Island, a South African one-act by Athol Fugard. Many people said it was the best thing done that year at Carnegie. In fact, we were asked to repeat the show for Black History Month at the Pittsburgh Civic Center. (In addition, I was interviewed on TV as part of the show's promotion.) It was extremely well received, and many people came up to me on the streets of Pittsburgh and said how much it meant to them; I have a video of the performance if you are interested in seeing it.

Another example of my work is Broadway Cabaret. I played the part of the emcee, warming up the audience for about 10 minutes before opening the show and then singing and dancing throughout. We played to a packed house and a standing ovation every night of the run; it was the most popular show of the season and was asked to be extended. I was glad to develop a serious working relationship with the Director/Choreographer, Billy Wilson.

I am a professional, I know how to put a part together, get a job done, and I work very hard on whatever I take on. In addition, I am easy to work with and have a good sense of humor.

I will keep you apprised of my situation so that you may have a chance to see me in a piece. Casey thought you and I could work together. I hope that we can.

Sincerely,

Bruce J. Faulk

**Kazunori Morishita**

April 20, 19xx

Name
President or CEO
Company
Address
City, State, Zip

Dear Mr. Name:

> If you have a target list of hundreds of companies, divide them into separate markets. Tailor your letters to each target market, such as the "inorganic chemicals industry" in this example. Add the last line for those you plan to call directly, perhaps 20 out of every 100 mailed.

(In many companies) *OR* (In the inorganic chemicals industry), the use of **technology has not kept pace with the expansion of markets** and the need for more sophisticated information to service those sales opportunities. The need for logical, manageable information and its dissemination is paramount in today's world. I can help you with solutions to those issues.

I am a **Senior Information Systems Executive** with experience in **managing the information needs for companies ranging from** $250 million to over $1 billion in annual sales. As a key member of the management team I can direct the implementation of technology to achieve the profit objectives of your organization. My experience has been both domestic and international and I have a unique ability to control major development projects to successful conclusions.

Here are some specific examples of my accomplishments:

* Developed a composite information data base. Resulted in **higher market share** and greater penetration into existing market segments.

* Saved $1 million annually on a $5 million data processing budget.

* Consolidated the technologies and systems of over $1 billion in acquisitions avoiding problems frequently associated with multiple acquisitions.

I am a strong hands-on strategic planner and leader and I would welcome the opportunity to discuss how my skills and experience could contribute to your company's objectives. I will call you in a few days to set up a mutually convenient time for us to meet.

Sincerely,


Kazunori Morishita

Enclosure

## Steven Worth

2 Bigelow Lane
Nashville, Tennessee 37333
(555) 555-2231 (day)

May 10, 19xx

Name
President
Bank Name
Address
City, State, Zip

> Steve sent this letter to 200 banks.
> It resulted in 8 interviews and 2 offers.

Dear Name:

Many companies' banking relationships are being disrupted because of new controls and regulations and the impact of mergers and acquisitions. In addition, frequent changes in account officers and terms of service are causing a loss of understanding between bank and customer.

Smooth-running banking relationships can make all the difference in the effective conduct of business. How can you, as President of XXX Bank, stay abreast of what is happening and even benefit from current developments?

I can help you with these issues. I offer twenty years experience in banking, most recently as Vice President with Mellon Bank's International Department. Furthermore, few have my connections in and knowledge of the industry.

Here are two specific areas where my experience could benefit you:

**Banking Relationships**: I know my way around the industry and know what a bank should be able to do for its customers. My experience would enable you to maximize the services available from your bank and enhance the degree of comfort the banks feel towards you, their customer.

**Assessment of Credit Risk**: Much of my career has been spent in the area of credit assessment and my broad experience could help you avoid many of the pitfalls inherent in doing business.

I have the maturity and sophistication to be able to deal with a wide variety of personalities and problems and the persistence to see things through to a satisfactory conclusion.

I would welcome the opportunity to discuss with you how my skills and background could contribute to your company's goals.

Yours sincerely,

Steven Worth

M. Catherine Wendleton
410 Main Street Lancaster, PA.
(555) 555-2231

May 10, 1983

Dear Name:

> **Sent to 60 presidents of small/medium-sized advertising agencies or the appropriate people in large agencies. Resulted in 5 exploratory interviews that then led to additional interviews and 3 job offers.**

Many agencies are coping with these difficult times by hiring the best creative and sales people available. While this may maintain a competitive edge, many agencies find that their bottom line is slipping. The usual response is to send in the accountants.

These agencies, and perhaps some of your own subsidiaries, need more than accounting help. As Vice President of Operations for a $10 million advertising agency, I directed the turnaround of a company that was in serious financial difficulty. As a result, 1982 was the most profitable year in company history, and 1983 promises to be better yet.

This experience has taught me what can cause an agency to get into trouble. I know the danger signs, and I can teach a company how to run itself with true efficiency and economy—not just with heavy-handed frugality. I have a record of success in making an agency run more smoothly and profitably:

- Trouble-shoot in all areas of agency operations (except Creative output).

- Improved employee productivity by 30%. Reduced the number of unprofitable accounts by 83%.

- Set up a management information system that gets to the core of the problems and encourages managers to act. Cleaned up a flawed computer system.

- Dramatically reduced the number of crisis situations in Creative and the number of over-budget situations.

- Instituted a comprehensive salary and performance review system. Developed hiring procedures to reduce turnover.

- As Chairman of the Executive Committee, instituted tight budgetary controls, improved responsibility accounting, and account margin and cost controls.

I have an M.B.A. as well as 12 years of progressive management responsibility in finance and strategic planning, data processing, personnel, and advertising and marketing.

As a result of many years travel to New York, I would prefer to live and work in the New York area. In fact, I'm in New York frequently.

Hiring me would be an investment in the $xx,xxx range, but the return will be impressive. I would be pleased to meet with you to discuss the contribution I could make to the performance of your organization.

Yours truly,

Kate Wendleton

# Direct-Mail Campaign

This same letter could be used to contact search firms.
Just change the next-to-the-last sentence to read:
"If you have a search which requires these skills,
I would like very much to get together."

**Winifred Downes**

February 2, 19xx

Name
Title
Company
Address
City, State, Zip

Dear Mr. Name:

I am a seasoned financial services marketer with **ten years at Asarco Financial** and heavy package goods experience at Lever Brothers, Johnson & Johnson and Procter & Gamble.

My experience is in **developing and marketing financial products and services**, including electronic banking products, investment packages and basic banking services, to both consumer and corporate markets. I also have a strong track record in **building effective sales teams and turning around troubled businesses**. I am currently exploring opportunities to build a financial services business or to inject new life into an existing one.

A résumé is enclosed for additional background. If you would like to discuss the possibilities, I would like very much to get together.

I look forward to hearing from you.

Sincerely,

Winifred Downes

# How to Answer Ads

*Of all sad words*
*Of tongue and pen*
*The saddest are these:*
*"It Might Have Been."*

*Let's add this thought*
*unto this verse:*
*"It Might Have Been*
*A Good Deal Worse."*
Anonymous

S ome people get excited after they have answered an ad in the paper. They know this is the job for them.

Do not be surprised if you answer thirty or fifty ads and get no interviews. Your résumé is with perhaps thousands of other responses. What's more, your résumé is not being screened by the hiring manager.

Chances are, your cover letter and résumé will be screened by someone like a twenty-year-old I met. She reviewed résumés on behalf of blue-chip companies, screening thousands of professionals and managers in the $40,000 to $100,000 range. She decided who would get interviewed.

This young woman was good at her job, and often took a personal interest in the people whose résumés she saw—but she was only twenty years old. Writing a cover letter to "intrigue" or strike a responsive chord in her wouldn't have worked.

While intrigue, subtlety, and personality may work in direct-mail campaigns and networking, stick to the basics in answering ads. If the ad asks for specific qualifications and experience, highlight those areas from your background. Respond point by point to each item mentioned. Show how you have everything they want. Keep your cover letter crystal clear. Remember, the reader of your letter may be twenty years old. If you don't fit exactly, you will probably be screened out.

If an average ad in *The Wall Street Journal* or *The New York Times* gets a thousand responses, you have 999 competitors. Answer ads—I believe in doing everything to help your job hunt.

If you qualify for the job, make that apparent by following the format of the letter on the following page. If you do *not* qualify, use the paragraph format used in networking cover letters. If you don't get in by responding to the ad, *network* into the company or contact someone there directly (not the person mentioned in the ad). See the chapter "What to Do When You Know There's a Job Opening."

**ROBERT LEE**
38 Cicily Place
West Hamstart, MO 59684

March 23, 19xx

Nancy Friedberg
Employment Manager
National Data Labs
22 Parns Avenue
East Hamstart, MO 59684

> If you meet all the requirements of the job, then make it very clear to the screener that you should **not** be screened out. And read "What to Do When You Know There's a Job Opening" in this section.

Dear Ms. Friedberg:

I believe I am a good fit for the Assistant Controller position that was advertised in the Hamstart Times on March 20, 19xx.

Having been continually challenged and rapidly promoted at Toronto Dominion Bank, I have a proven track record in controllership functions. I've headed up the controllership function in every major area of the company including credit cards, travelers checks, and private banking. As you may be aware, Toronto Dominion has a rigorous budgeting, financial analysis and cost accounting process, similar to National Data Labs, and this has contributed to the success of the organization.

Here is a breakdown of my experience vs. your requirements:

| Your Requirements | My Experience |
|---|---|
| • 12+ years experience in private accounting/management | • 14+ years experience in financial management |
| • A BBA, MBA a plus. | • BBA in Finance MBA in Financial Management |
| • Financial Analysis/ Cost Accounting Skills | • Strong Financial Analysis skills - Controllership functions |
| | • Strong Cost Accounting skills - Designed Cost Accounting/ Unit Cost Methodologies |

I consider myself a sophisticated management professional with a significant number of business accomplishments, coupled with an excellent ability to communicate both orally and in writing.

I would welcome an interview with you to review my experience in financial management.

Sincerely,

Bob Lee

The Five O'Clock Club®

# How to Work With Search Firms

*Once-in-a-lifetime opportunities come along all the time—just about every week or so.*
Garrison Keillor
*A Prairie Home Companion*

I f you understand how search firms work, your expectations will be more reasonable, and you will better understand how to approach them.

Contrary to what some people think, a recruiter in a search firm does not place hundreds of managerial and professional people per year. Their search assignments are very specific and require extensive research, networking, and screening prior to presenting qualified individuals to their client companies. Therefore, the average recruiter places one or two people a month.

The work recruiters do is in some respects similar to the work done by realtors. Recruiters "represent" positions that need to be filled (the equivalent of houses for sale), and they recruit qualified people to fill those positions (house hunters). They match up their job opportunities with their qualified candidates, just as realtors match up house hunters with the houses on their lists. In both fields, possibilities are sometimes presented as "once-in-a-lifetime" opportunities.

There are reputable, professional search firms, just as there are reputable, professional realtors. But recruiting is basically a sales profession, and recruiters are interested in working with individuals who are marketable—just as realtors prefer houses that are marketable. Therefore, the more marketable you are, the more likely a search firm will be interested in handling you. If you are too difficult to categorize, are trying to make a major career change, require an unreasonable compensation, or have other drawbacks, search firms are unlikely to work with you.

Make it easy for search firms to market you. Here are a few suggestions:

- Summarize your marketable characteristics in your cover letter. Recruiters need to categorize you anyway, so make it easy for them.

- Clearly state your target market (geographic area, industry, and position) and your salary range. For example: "I'm interested in a financial position in the direct-marketing industry in the New York or Chicago areas. I'm looking for a salary in the $65,000 to $70,000 range."

- Next, state your key selling points—your summary and accomplishments. Recruiters present your *accomplishments* to client companies—not your job description. Tell them what to say to sell you. It will make their jobs easier and thus make them more likely to want to handle you.

- Be honest. According to Barbara Bruno, president of H&R Consulting in Chicago, "Search firms will check references and verify whatever information you give to them. Their reputations are based on the caliber of individuals they represent. If you misrepresent information, it could cost you the perfect career opportunity."

### Sample Search Firm Cover Letter

Search firms need to know your target: the kind of job you want and where. They also need to know your salary requirements. The letter on the following page uses our formula for cover letters presented earlier.

### A Typical Search Firm Marketing Call

Here is what may happen if you have made it easy for them. They place a few phone calls. "Joe," they say, "I've got someone you may be interested in. He's a highly skilled individual who has the exact profile you have hired through me before." And then they may read from your cover letter. "He's got fifteen years of financial experience in the direct-marketing industry. [Then they will stress your accomplishments, especially those that saved a past employer time or money.] He's an energetic, ambitious person—a real self-starter. When would it be convenient for us to set up an interview? He's available next Tuesday or Wednesday morning. . .

> Search firms need to know your target:
> the kind of job you want and where.
> They also need to know your salary requirements.
> This letter follows our formula format:
> Paragraph 2: Summary.
> Paragraph 3: Bulleted accomplishments.

Dear Ms. Bruno:

In the course of your search assignments, you may have a requirement for a technically knowledgeable IBM AS400—System 38 professional.

I have been both a "planner" and a "doer" of the phases of the System Development Life Cycle at companies such as General Motors and Proctor & Gamble where I have spent most of my career. My accomplishments span the gamut, including the following:

- Evaluation of Application and System Software and Hardware:
- Installation/Setup of a new computer site;
- Conversion of RPG and COBOL programs;
- Requirements for and design of applications;
- Development and programming;
- Quality Assurance and Testing;
- Optimization of performance for Applications and Systems.

At this juncture, after many years of commuting to Manhattan, I'm interested in seeking permanent employment in New Jersey, where I live.

The enclosed résumé briefly outlines my experience over the past 15 years. My base is now in the $70,000 range plus the usual fringes.

If it appears that my qualifications meet the needs of one of your clients, I would be happy to further discuss my background in a meeting with you.

Yours truly,

> Do not send your résumé to search firms unless you know their reputation. A disreputable agency could "blanket" the market with your résumé, and cheapen your value. Make sure the search firm tells you *before* they send your résumé to anyone.

*Life will give you what you ask of her if only
you ask long enough and plainly enough.*
E. Nesbitt

Oh, I know you don't have any positions currently available. After I interviewed him, I just thought of you. I really think he'd be worth your time to interview."

## Should I Follow Up with a Phone Call?

The short answer is no. Recruiters are very aware of the positions they are trying to fill at the moment, and all of their energies are going into finding good matches for their client companies. If they have a position in-house that is appropriate for you, and if they are not already too far along with the search, they may call you in. A follow-up phone call from you will do no good, and just cuts into their busy day. We advise job hunters to send their résumés to search firms, and then get on with other aspects of their searches.

It is better to form long-term relationships with reputable search firms. You can do this by helping them when they have an assignment they are trying to fill—even though it is not right for you. Perhaps you could suggest the names of other people they should call. Then when you are ready to make a move, they are already aware of you and your character, and are more likely to consider you when they have an opening that *is* right for you. Read Barbara Bruno's chapter, which follows this one, to find out how you can establish long-term relationships with search firms that cover your specialty, and perhaps even get the search firms to call *you*.

## Which Companies Use Search Firms?

Search firms are used by small- to mid-sized companies that have limited personnel departments. The search firm acts as an extension of their human resources staff. In addition, smaller companies often must use search firms because applicants don't contact them as often as they do larger companies.

Search firms are also used by major companies that have specific needs. Major corporations expect the search firm to identify the best individual in their industry nationwide—and usually in a very short period of time. Search firms are expected to know—or be able to find out quickly—the impor-

tant players in a specialty.

Search firms are also used to fill jobs where there is a labor shortage. This could be for a specialty that is much in demand at the moment, an executive-level position, a field that is so unusual that the search firm may have to look outside the company's normal geographic area, or even for common positions that the company is having difficulty filling.

To find the names of search firms, use the *Directory of Executive Recruiters*. Despite its title, it lists firms for most job levels and job categories, and also by geographic area. It is carried by many libraries, or you can get your own copy from Kennedy Publications, Templeton Road, Fitzwilliam, NH 03447.

## Retainer vs. Contingency Search Firms

The "search firm" field has become more complex in recent years. See the chapter "The Changing Face of the Personnel Services Industry" to find out the other segments of this market, such as temporary service firms.

Whether retainer or contingency, search firms are hired by companies to fill positions. Companies pay search firms about a third of the new person's salary. Retainer firms receive an exclusive assignment to fill a position, and get paid whether or not they find the person for it. Contingency firms are paid only if they fill the position, and a number of contingency firms could be working on filling the same position. The one that fills it gets the fee.

Do not send your résumé to search firms unless you know their reputation. There may be a disreputable agency that could blanket the market with your résumé, and cheapen your value. Make sure the search firm tells you before it sends your résumé to anyone. If a search firm has sent your résumé to lots of places, it will have gotten to companies before you have had a chance to get in on your own. If a company has a policy of not paying a fee to search firms, it will not consider you for a position because you were "introduced" by a search firm. If it *is* willing to pay a fee, but two search firms have sent in your résumé, the company will not hire you because it does not want to get into an argument about which search firm to pay. Simply have a search firm tell you ahead of time which companies it wants to contact on your behalf. You can find good search firms by asking your networking contacts for the names of the firms they use.

### How Can I Get the Search Firm to Increase the Salary Being Offered?

The answer is: In most cases, you can't. A search firm is hired by a client company to fill a certain position at a certain salary. A search firm needs to know your salary requirements. The salary cap can sometimes be negotiated based on the level or experience of the candidate. However, if the search firm does not put you in for the job because your salary requirements are too high, you should contact the firm directly. Read the chapter "What to Do When You Know There's a Job Opening."

Let's remember the purpose of search firms: They cannot get you a job. Search firms can help you get *interviews* in your target market. You can also get interviews through ads, networking, and direct contact. When a search firm tells you about a specific job at a specific salary, decide if you want the *interview*. Once they get you an interview; you have to do the rest yourself.

Remember our basic principle regarding salary negotiation: Do not negotiate the salary until you have received an offer. After you have gotten the interview, turn it into an offer by following up with the company. Once you have the offer, you may have to get involved in the negotiating process yourself. On the other hand, there are some search firms that are excellent at negotiating on your behalf if the company really wants you. You will have to use your judgment about doing the deal yourself, or putting your compensation negotiation in the hands of the search firm.

### A Final Word About Search Firms

Some search firms give the industry a bad name. If you are belittled or badgered by a search firm, do not take it personally, but do move on. The possible damage to your ego isn't worth it. A recruiter may, for example, hurt your ego so that you will accept a position that is rather low in salary.

Search firms work for the companies that hired them, not for you. A firm may want the best fee and not care about a good placement for you. That firm may want to place you quickly at a low salary level and move on.

If you refuse a job offer, a search firm will still present you to their other client companies. Getting an offer proves you are marketable. If you've gotten one offer, most will conclude you can get another. They will drop you, however, if they feel you are just shopping the market and are not interested in making a move. After all, they are running a business. So don't be frivolous in refusing offers.

But don't be afraid to turn down an offer if it is not appropriate for you. It is important that you not be talked into accepting an offer you don't want by a recruiter who is trying to satisfy the needs of the client company. Recruiters are just trying to do their job: selling the benefits of the client company's position. Contact a number of search firms in your specialty. Depending on your target market, they may be a very important tool for getting interviews.

The Five O'Clock Club®

# Increase Your Visibility: Headhunters Will Call You

by Barbara Bruno

Note: This chapter and the next were written by Barbara Bruno, president of a major search firm in Chicago and also head of an Affiliate of The Five O'Clock Club. Here is her insight into how to deal with search firms.

When you are in an intensive search, you may have no alternative but to contact search firms (sometimes called "headhunters"). But why not set it up so that you are more desirable and search firms call you? There are several reasons you may want to have search firms calling you:

1.  Headhunters have access to many positions that are not advertised.

2.  Headhunters can give you a tremendous amount of insight into the companies they represent, including specific interviewing preparation.

3.  When top companies need to attract the *best individual in their industry*, they turn to search firms, who have built up extensive networks in their specialty.

4.  Having a search firm call you is one of the best passive ways to conduct a job search while you are employed.

5.  The process is extremely confidential.

6.  When a search firm calls you, you can test your marketability without risking your current position.

7.  A lot of job growth is in the small- to mid-size firms, which may use search firms to recruit their top talent.

8.  Headhunters must keep abreast of current and future trends, which they can share with you.

9.  If a headhunter understands your long-term career goals, he or she can help you attain the appropriate position to prepare you for these goals.

10.  You have nothing to lose and everything to gain. There is no obligation on your part to accept any position, unless you feel it is your next appropriate career move.

11.  Companies are frequently faced with a position that must be filled expeditiously, so they use a search firm. It's best if the search firm already knows that you exist.

12.  If a headhunter recognizes your marketability and develops a rapport with you, he or she will contact you with the best opportunities.

These reasons are very positive, but you must be aware that there are headhunters who are not reputable. This profession is no different from any other. You must check out the firm and individual with whom you are dealing before you place your career in their hands.

### How to Position Yourself So You Will Be Called

Visibility is the key to hearing from a headhunter. This includes visibility in your current company, profession, or industry—as well as visibility in organizations. Recruiters monitor promotions announced in newspapers, work from association/organization directories, subscribe to industry-related publications, and use various research directories in reference libraries. Headhunters also use the Internet as a source of information.

#### Become a Referral Source

It is also important to establish a rapport with headhunters who contact you. Their current opportunity may not be appropriate for you, but if they know what you will accept, they will contact you when that opportunity crosses their desk. If you become a referral source—someone who recommends candidates—you will receive calls on a regular basis.

Headhunters present current positions they are representing, but can also market you to their top client. In order for them to make a marketing presentation, your marketability must be clear, your salary demands must be competitive and your availability immediate with appropriate notice. Interviewing availability is also an important factor when weighing your marketability.

When you receive a call from a headhunter, it indicates that they have identified you as someone who is a possible "fit" on one of their search assignments. The chances of being placed by a headhunter who contacts *you* is much higher than if you contact them. In most cases, it also enables you to negotiate a more lucrative compensation and benefits package.

Headhunters are dependent on referrals, so it is in their best interest to treat you in a professional and ethical manner. The next time a headhunter leaves a message on your voice mail— even if you don't know the person—return that call. This recruiter may represent your next career opportunity!

### Which Kind of Firm to Contact

When you decide to use a search firm to assist in your job hunt, you must first do extensive research. Search firms are part of the personnel services industry, which has dramatically changed over the past decade. There are so many different segments of this industry that you must first identify the appropriate type of firm to fit your needs, i.e. retained search, contingency search, temporary services, or contract staffing. Read the next chapter to become familiar with these disctinctions. Most search firms specialize in certain industries or professions. Only contact firms that specialize in placement within your specific area of interest.

### How to Recognize a Good Headhunter

A headhunter is a salesperson. It is his or her responsibility to attract the highest caliber of individual for his or her clients. Here are a few suggestions:
1. Work with headhunters who specialize in your field. Ask questions to test their knowledge of your industry.
2. Ask other pertinent questions:

a. Do they fax résumés only *after* they get permission from the individual?

b. When they have an appropriate position, how are interviews arranged?

c. Are all interviewing expenses paid?

d. How many years have they been in business?

e. Do they place nationwide or locally?

f. Are they members of their state or national professional associations?

g. Are they certified?

h. Do they belong to a nationwide network?

i. Any there any financial or contractual obligations?

j. Do they represent permanent opportunities, contract services, or professional temps?

Companies pay headhunters a percentage of a person's first year's earnings for their efforts in attracting top talent. If your job or salary history is very sporadic, if you have changed professions several times or are contemplating a total career change, headhunters may not be as effective as other techniques for getting interviews in your target markets. What they are paid for is their ability to locate "experienced individuals who can hit the ground running."

---

Feel free to call one of the following associations to find out about a specific firm:

- National Association of Personnel Services
  3133 Mt. Vernon Avenue
  Alexandria, VA 22305
  703-684-0180
- Assoc. of Executive Search Consultants
  230 Park Avenue, Suite 1549
  New York, NY 10169
  212-949-9556
- Natl. Assoc. of Temporary Services
  119 South Saint Asaph Street
  Alexandria, VA 22314-3119
  703-549-6287

The
Five
O'Clock
Club®

# The Changing Face of the
# Personnel Services Industry
## A Reference Guide

by Barbara Bruno

*The personnel services industry had its start in the 1800's when whaling ships were in need of sailors. Companies formed to provide these sailors on a "per voyage" basis, for a percentage of the "take." The first employment agency license was issued in Boston in 1905. One of the requirements for attaining a license was a minimum of three hitching posts in front of each office. When the Second World War broke out, employment agencies were used to find women to fill positions which were traditionally held by men.*

Over the years, the personnel services industry has changed dramatically, and does not even resemble what it was just ten years ago. It's important to understand the services that are offered to make the best use of this industry as part of your job-search process.

You have four basic choices for generating interviews in your target market, as outlined in this book: networking, direct contact, search firms, and ads. The category of "search firms" is actually very broad, and includes the following: contingency search firms, retained search firms, employment agencies, temporary service firms, staffing service firms, contract staffing firms, employee leasing firms, and employment networks. To help you decide which service can best meet your needs, here is a brief glossary of each segment of the industry, which you may want to keep for future reference.

- **Contingency Search Firms.** The primary function of a contingency search firm is to fill job openings for employers. The employer always pays the service charge. Payment is contingent upon an offer of employment from the employer and acceptance by the candidate. The service charge is based on a percentage of the starting salary. Synonymous terms can include personnel recruitment firm, personnel consulting firm, personnel placement firm, personnel service and search firm.

- **Retained Search Firms.** The main func-

tion of retained search firms is to identify candidates to fill openings for employers. The employer pays a retainer to engage the firm's search capabilities. Payment is not contingent upon hiring the candidate. A synonymous name for a retained search firm is an executive search firm.

- **Employment Agencies.** The main function of employment agencies is to find jobs for people. The agency builds a backlog of screened candidates by advertising and through referrals from satisfied candidates and employers. A fee is charged when an offer of employment is extended by the employer and accepted by the candidate. Either the candidate or the employer can be responsible for the fee (which is something that needs to be clarified up front). Other names for employment agencies include personnel placement firm, personnel service, and personnel consulting firm.

- **Temporary Service Firms.** Temporary service firms provide staffing assistance to handle strategic or special workloads for client companies. Temporary workers are employees of the temporary service firm. They are assigned to work at a customer's location, often under the direction of the customer's employees. Temporary employees receive their salary and benefits from the service that employs them. The client company is billed an hourly rate for the services of the temporary employee. One of these companies, Man-power, is the largest employer in the U.S.A. today.

- **Staffing Service Firms.** These firms offer a wide variety of services to their client companies, including search, temporary staffing, facilities management, employee leasing, payrolling, outsourcing, and outplacement.

- **Contract Staffing Firms.** These firms are operated exactly the same as the temporary service firms, with two exceptions: The assignments have long duration and usually involve higher-level professional positions, such as management, technical, and engineering.

- **Employee Leasing Firms.** These firms, often called Professional Employer Organizations, are firms which contract with client companies to employ a substantial number of the client company's work force. In most cases, the employee leasing firm and its client enter into an agreement in which various aspects of the employment relationship—such as recruiting, training, supervision, termination, and payroll administration—are divided between the employee leasing firm and the client company. Employees of the employee leasing firm are often assigned to work for the client company on a full-time basis, with no scheduled termination of their assignment.

- **Employment Networks.** There are many networks which consist of a variety of employment firms throughout the country. They share both their positions and their candidates with one another. These networks give a firm national placement capabilities.

Most personnel service firms also have areas of specialization. When you select a firm, always research their areas of expertise to ensure they have contacts within your job targets. If you are unsure of a firm's specialties, call and ask a member of their recruiting staff.

## Is the Firm Ethical?

In order to verify a firm's adherence to stringent codes of ethics, investigate whether they belong to the appropriate professional organizations. Most states have state employment associations. There are two large national associations: The National Association of Personnel Services and the National Association of Temporary Services.

These national organizations can provide you with their membership directories and specialties offered by each firm. The National Association of Personnel Services also offers the most recognized certifications in the industry: CPC and CTS.

CPC is Certified Personnel Consultant (permanent placement) and CTS is Certified Temporary Staffing Specialist (temporary placement). Individuals with these certifications have been in the industry a minimum of two years and have successfully passed a certification examination. Their membership shows commitment to attaining the highest professional designation in the employment industry.

## How to Get a Recruiter to Call You

If you are well-known in your profession for your accomplishments, often you will be referred to a recruiter. The more "visible" you are, the more likely you are to be recruited by one of the aforementioned firms. Ways to increase your visibility include membership in professional organizations, articles in the business section of the newspaper, and affiliation with philanthropic groups.

Search firms are primarily finding candidates for their clients. It is wise to register with search firms to familiarize them with your credentials. They may not have a current position fitting your skills and experience, but if one is listed, you will be the first person they contact.

Recruiters in the personnel services industry are speaking with decision-makers all day. They have information on current trends, salary ranges, company expansions—and this information can be shared with you. Recruiters have positions which are not advertised, and they know their companies' demands and company culture. They will prepare you prior to your interview, which gives you a competitive edge.

Make sure you research this ever-changing industry, check the firm's credentials, and investigate their areas of specialization. It will pay off by giving you the greatest chance for interviews—and job offers!

Barbara Bruno is president, H&R Career Consulting, Chicago, and head of the Chicago Affiliate of The Five O'Clock Club. This article originally appeared in *The Five O'Clock News*.

# What to Do When You Know There's a Job Opening

*To paraphrase Peter Drucker,*
*effective people are not problem-minded;*
*they're opportunity-minded.*
*They feed opportunities and starve problems.*
Stephen R. Covey,
*The Seven Habits of Highly Effective People*

You've heard about a job opening from someone, or you've seen an ad in the paper. Answer that ad. But to increase your chances of getting an interview, find an additional way in besides the ad (through networking or through directly contacting the company).

When using networking or direct contact, most job hunters aim for the hiring manager. After all, that person is the one with the job, so why would you contact anyone else?

But consider contacting someone other than the hiring manager. He or she is being inundated with requests for meetings by people who have heard about the job. To the hiring manager, those who network in may seem just like those who responded to the ad: another job hunter who knows there is a job opening.

But you are different. You're not a grubby job hunter. You're sincerely interested in this company, aren't you? You want to meet with someone regardless of whether or not he or she has an opening, don't you? In fact, you are so interested in this company that you would be glad to speak with other people there, not just the hiring manager.

If you first meet with others, you will learn a lot about the hiring manager, the company, its needs, and the kinds of people who work there. They can refer you in to the hiring manager—with their recommendations. You will be much better prepared than those who got in through the ad. After the formal job interview, you will have advocates in the company who can coach you and speak to the hiring manager on your behalf.

Some job hunters worry that the job may be filled before they get to the hiring manager. That's possible, but unlikely. Most jobs take a long time to fill. Résumés may sit for weeks before anyone even looks at them. In most cases, you will have time to meet with other people first.

To gather basic information, it's okay to meet with people junior to you or at your level to gather information. But it is sometimes difficult for those lower in the organization to refer you up to the boss. Those at your boss's level, or perhaps higher, are in a better position to refer you up, so make sure you aim to meet with them.

## CASE STUDY: MADGE
### I've Followed Your Company

Jean, a participant at The Five O'Clock Club, met with five people at Conference Associates, and received an offer. It was an interesting place, but she decided the job was too low-level, and took another job.

When Jean announced at The Five O'Clock Club that she had turned down an offer from Conference Associates, Madge became very interested in the position.

Jean and Madge had dinner so Madge could learn more about the organization, the job and the people with whom Jean met. Madge also did library research on the organization. Since she knew exactly who all the players were, she could easily have contacted the hiring manager. In fact, she could have networked in through Jean. But that's not what she did.

In this case, we decided Madge should write directly to the president, who was three-up in the chain of command (the person who would be her boss's boss's boss). In her letter, she said she had long been interested in Conference Associates, and she referred to issues Jean had told her were important. **She did not refer to the fact that she knew there was a job opening.**

The cover letter that Madge wrote (with a résumé enclosed) is on the next page. The president suggested that Madge meet with human resources, the hiring manager, and others. By the way, this is not networking. This is a targeted mailing. Through this technique, Madge got the interview she wanted. Through her follow-up, she got the job.

**Madge Wrigley**

345 East Ball Park Avenue
Scottsdale, AZ 44555
(555) 555-0121

July 3, 199x

Mr. Robert J. Potvin, President
Conference Associates
5637 Columbus Avenue
Phoenix, AZ 44555

Dear Mr. Potvin:

These days, the last thing an executive looking to improve profitability probably wants to hear is, "Go to a conference." But that is precisely what he or she may need to find ideas to solve problems back home. I am writing because Conference Associates's goal of encouraging interaction and furthering the exchange of knowledge is one I would like to promote.

I'm currently a manager at AT&T marketing directly to credit card customers. I manage about $32 million in revenue annually. I've been successful in building a market for expensive products, some, such as life insurance, with negative connotations to overcome.

The key has been twofold: setting clear-cut goals and guiding both the creative and managerial processes to see them realized; and carefully researching and identifying a target market, then developing compelling communications to reach them. Now, though, I would like to put my 10 years of business development and marketing experience to work for Conference Associates, specifically in order to take a broader, and global, view of business.

Several aspects of Conference Associates's activities are particularly aligned with my interests and skills:

- The customer orientation: I would like to make <u>companies</u> my customer, evaluating their needs and delivering the services to meet them.
- The Associates's stated goals for expansion in Europe: I firmly believe my international experience could prove beneficial. I'm fluent in French and Spanish, and have worked in France and Sweden.
- I'm an educator at heart: I enjoy managing and developing staff, and making connections among people and ideas.

In sum, I believe I could offer a trained and critical eye to understand the need, and persuasive marketing programs to communicate the service.

At your convenience, I would be most interested in having a chance to speak with you. I'll call your office shortly to see if that may be possible.

Sincerely,

Madge Wrigley

**Madge Wrigley**

345 East Ball Park Avenue
Scottsdale, AZ 44555

August 17, 199x

Mr. Robert Worley
Director, Personnel
Conference Associates
5637 Columbus Avenue
Phoenix, AZ 44555

Dear Robert:

First of all, it was a pleasure to meet you last Wednesday. I enjoyed hearing your assessment of the potential that exists for C.A., and seeing your commitment and enthusiasm for the organization.

You spoke of the unique position of C.A. as a non-profit service organization that more and more is being run like any business in a competitive environment. The role of a new Marketing Director, then, would be to develop a strategy for the business to position C.A. for the next level of growth. It's fortunate that C.A. has a solid base to grow from, including a reputation for quality and service. The challenge would be to enhance that reputation, while building new markets and customers.

One of the things we spoke about was the need for the Marketing Director to work closely and productively with other departments. Ellis Chase and I spoke about that as well. I feel particularly motivated by that type of challenge, and have been successful in working with diverse groups. For example, recently at AT&T a major new segmentation strategy and methodology for my product line required tying in systems, finance and new products, in addition to marketing. It wasn't easy, but the reward is a successful expansion of our business, and a precedent set for productive cross-departmental projects.

Getting a business built depends a lot on people who don't report to you, and buying them into the goals and the process is the only way of getting the job done well. It requires using a balance of sensitivity and toughness, and relating to colleagues with flexibility and creativity. If C.A.'s marketing department is going to become a vital and integral part of the operation, then it has to establish itself as responsive, knowledgeable and resourceful.

I truly believe this position is a solid match with my experience and interests, both for the specific skill base required and the opportunity to build a comprehensive marketing program. I've developed marketing plans for organizations ranging from small non-profits to AT&T, and achieved positive results with the implementation.

The common thread in that success has been what you called "ownership." In both my professional experience and in community volunteer work, I tend to approach the task at hand with energy and commitment. After all, the most effective marketer is the one who can combine strategic development and proven skills with genuine product enthusiasm. I would be most interested in putting that same experience and enthusiasm to work for C.A..

Looking forward to speaking with you again soon,

Best,
Madge Wrigley

**Madge Wrigley**

345 East Ball Park Avenue
Scottsdale, AZ 44555
August 18, 199x

Mr. Ellis Chase
Senior Vice President, Development
Conference Associates
5637 Columbus Avenue
Phoenix, AZ 44555

Dear Ellis:

It was good meeting with you last Wednesday. I got a clear picture of the requirements of the Marketing Director position, and the kind of challenges that would need to be met.

First and foremost, you expressed a need going forward for someone who can develop a comprehensive, integrated marketing strategy, and can communicate that plan effectively and appropriately in all facets of its implementation.

That requires skills of listener, evaluator and diagnostician, coupled with an ability to generate and harness ideas and turn them into positive results. The goal would be to establish C.A. as a leading source of business intelligence and creativity for corporations and their executives.

I've had a chance to think about some of the ways we talked about to accomplish that goal. It seems that both the stated mission of the Associates and its profitability center on building and enhancing the relationship with members, working to have members' resources and activities become a more familiar and integral part of corporate life. One of the priorities you outlined was devising ways to package existing products and services, maximizing both internal marketing efficiency and external perception of value. That would include targeting different people within the same organization with relevant services, as well as determining the right level of pricing.

You also mentioned C.A.'s global objective, trying to serve both U.S. companies that are competing internationally as well as many of their foreign competitors. Although I understand that the Paris affiliate handles much of the activity in Europe, one of the components of an integrated marketing plan would be defining the optimum balance between a U.S. and global emphasis.

I firmly believe that my experience and personality fit the job at hand, and that the skills required play to my strengths. I have demonstrated success in strategic and creative planning, researching and identifying target markets, then developing compelling and appropriate communications to reach them. At both AT&T and previously at RCA, I have developed new businesses and products, including pricing, positioning, and packaging existing services. Efforts I've directed advertising that increased response from 58% to 93%, and market expansion of 30% with new targeting programs.

I've found ways to run marketing activities more efficiently, saving in both fixed overhead and variable production costs. Finally, as I mentioned, I'm in charge of all writing for the business unit, working closely with each area to communicate to group and corporate monthly results as well as the five-year and annual strategic plans.

From the conversations with you and Robert, the goals for the position, the products of C.A. and its environment seem to represent a strong match with my background and interests. I look forward to speaking with you again soon, and having a chance to discuss the position further.

Sincerely,
Madge Wrigley

**Madge Wrigley**

345 East Ball Park Avenue
Scottsdale, AZ 44555

October 18, 199x

Mr. Robert J. Potvin
President and CEO
Conference Associates
5637 Columbus Avenue
Phoenix, AZ 44555

Dear Bob:

While everything is now official and I'll be starting Thursday, October 24th, I wanted to let you know what a pleasure it was to finally meet with you, and how delighted I am to be joining C.A..

When we met, you spoke of approaching the task of marketing C.A. with an eye to challenges and opportunities, building on a strong foundation to find better ways to position ourselves in an increasingly competitive market. That includes keeping the focus on senior level executives. Your outline of the process you've undertaken to evaluate C.A.'s activities was extremely helpful, as well as your expectations for staff to initiate and persuade, even without direct line responsibility. I particularly appreciated your straightforward review of the financial position.

You also spoke specifically of the need for someone to bring to the position not only marketing expertise, but also an enjoyment of your intellectual, knowledge-based product. I firmly believe that genuine product combination. I'm looking forward to working with that combination, and with colleagues who are clearly committed to the organization.

One of them is certainly Melanie. We had terrific meeting, reviewing everything from general history to specific programs. Particular attention was paid to the strategic plan and development of C.A. over the past few years, and the challenge of communicating that strategy both internally and to our customer base. I'm very much looking forward to working with her on integrating a marketing strategy into the overall planning process and new product development, and incorporating that strategy into marketing the programs. I'll also be able to meet with Aaron before I start.

Over the past few weeks, I've had a chance both to think about my conversations with you and others with whom I've met, and to review some of C.A.'s materials (50th Anniversary history, 1991 Annual Report, etc.). I believe there is enormous potential to spread the word—and the work—of C.A. to a wider audience, and to enhance the value of the organization to its current customers. A major component of the task is communication—defining those characteristics that differentiate us in the marketplace, and translating them into language that sells. Your commitment to testing new approaches is welcome, understanding the need for moving thoughtfully and with careful planning.

I look forward to the 24th, and to a wonderful association at my new home.

Very best,
Madge Wrigley

# Following Up When There Is No Immediate Job

*Contrary to the cliché, genuinely nice guys most often finish first, or very near it.*
Malcolm Forbes

During each meeting, you have taken up the time of someone who sincerely tried to help you. Writing a note is the only polite thing to do. Since the person has gone to some effort for you, go to some effort in return. A phone call to thank a person can be an intrusion, and shows little effort on your part.

In addition to being polite, there are good business reasons for writing notes and otherwise keeping in touch with people who have helped you. For one thing, few people keep in touch, so you will stand out. Second, it gives you a chance to sell yourself again and to overcome any misunderstandings that may have occurred. Third, this is a promotional campaign, and any good promoter knows that a message reinforced soon after a first message results in added recall.

If you meet someone through a networking interview, for example, he or she will almost certainly forget about you the minute you leave, and just go back to business. Sorry, but you were an interruption.

If you write to people almost immediately after your meeting, this will dramatically increase the chance that they will remember you. If you wait two weeks before writing, they may remember meeting someone, but not remember you specifically. If you wait longer than two weeks, they probably won't remember meeting anyone—let alone that it was you.

So promptly follow the interview with a note. It is important to remind those to whom you write who you are and when they talked to you. Give some highlight of the meeting. Contact them again within a month or two. It is just like an advertising campaign. Advertisers will often place their ads at least every four weeks in the same publication. If they advertised less often than that, few people would remember the ad.

## What Michael Did

This is a classic—and it worked on me. I wanted to hire one junior accountant for a very important project, and had the search narrowed down to two people. I asked my boss for his input. We made up a list of what we were looking for and we each rated the candidates on twenty criteria. The final scores came in very close, but I hired Judy instead of Michael.

In response to my rejection, Michael wrote me a note telling me how much he still wanted to work for our company, and how he hoped I would keep him in mind if something else should come up. He turned the rejection into a positive contact. Notes are so unusual, and this one was so personable, that I showed it to my boss.

A few months later, Michael wrote again saying that he had taken a position with another firm. He was still very much interested in us, and he hoped to work for us someday. He promised to keep in touch, which he did. Each time he wrote, I showed the note to my boss. Each time, we were sorry we couldn't hire him.

After about seven months, I needed another helping hand. Whom do you think I called? Do you think I interviewed other people? Do you think I had to sell Michael to my boss? Michael came to work for us, and we never regretted it. Persistence pays off.

## What to Say in Your Follow-Up Note

Depending on the content of your note, you may type or write it. Generally use standard business-size stationery, but sometimes Monarch or other note-size stationery, ivory or white, will do. A *job* interview follow-up should almost always be typed on standard business-size ivory or white stationery.

After an information-gathering interview, play back some of the advice you received, any you intend to follow, and so on. Simply be sincere. What did you appreciate about the time the person spent with you? Did you get good advice that you intend to follow? Say so. Were you inspired? Encouraged? Awakened? Say so.

If you think there were sparks between you and the person with whom you met, be sure to say that you will keep in touch. Then do it. Follow-up letters don't have to be long, but they do have to be personal. Make sure the letters you write could not be sent to someone else on your list.

---

### Sample Follow-Up to a Networking Meeting

#### TONY LEE

To:  Leslie Merlin:

Thanks again for contacting Brendan for me, and for providing all those excellent contact names.

There's such a wealth of good ideas in that list that it will take me a while to follow up on all of them, but I'm getting hard at it and will let you know what develops.

Again, thanks for your extraordinary effort. (By the way, should you ever want to "review your career options," I would be delighted to share a few names, or more than a few, with you.)

Stay tuned!

Tony

---

To keep in touch, simply let interviewers/ network contacts know how you are doing. Tell them whom you are seeing and what your plans are. Some people, seeing your sincerity, will keep sending you leads or other information.

It's never too late to follow up. For example: "I met you a year ago and am still impressed by . . . Since then I have . . . and would be interested in getting together with you again to discuss these new developments." Make new contacts. Recontact old ones by writing a "status report" every two months telling how well you are doing in your search. **Keeping up with old networking contacts is as important as making new ones.**

Some job hunters use this as an opportunity to write a proposal. During the meeting, you may have learned something about the company's problems. Writing a proposal to solve them may create a job for you. Patricia had a networking meeting with a small company where she learned that it wanted to expand the business from $5 million to $50 million. She came up with lots of ideas about how that could be done—with her help, of course—and called to set up a meeting to review her ideas. She went over the proposal with them, and they created a position for her.

However, you are not trying to turn every networking meeting into a job possibility. You *are* trying to form lifelong relationships with people. Experts say that most successful employees form solid relationships with lots of people and keep in touch regularly throughout their careers. These people will keep you up to date in a changing economy, tell you about changes or openings in your field, and generally be your long-term ally. And you will do the same for them.

---

*Has a man gained anything who has received*
*a hundred favors and rendered none?*
*He is great who confers the most benefits.*
Ralph Waldo Emerson, "Essay on Compensation"

---

# Follow-Up After a Networking/ Direct-Contact Meeting

*Opportunities are usually disguised as hard work, so most people don't recognize them.*
Ann Landers, Syndicated advice columnist, Rowes, *The Book of Quotes*

---

*If you know anything that will make a brother's heart glad, run quick and tell it; and if it is something that will only cause a sigh, bottle it up, bottle it up.*
Old Farmer's Almanac, 1854

---

*If (a man) is brusque in his manner, others will not cooperate. If he is agitated in his words, they will awaken no echo in others. If he asks for something without having first established a (proper) relationship, it will not be given to him.*
I Ching: *Book of Changes*
China, c. 600 B.C.

---

*In differentiation, not in uniformity, lies the path of progress.*
Louis Brandeis, U.S. Supreme Court Justice, *Business—A Profession*

The follow-up after a networking meeting— or a meeting resulting from having directly contacted a company (through a direct-mail campaign or a targeted mailing) is very different from the way you follow up after a job interview.

Analyze the meeting. In your letter, thank the interviewer. State the *specific* advice and leads you were given. Be personable. Say you will keep in touch. *Do* keep in touch.

**Follow up every few months** with a "status report" on how your search is going, an article or news of interest to the manager.

**Make sure people are thinking about you**. You may contact the manager just as he or she has heard of something of importance to you.

**Recontact those you met earlier in your search.** Otherwise, you're like a salesman who works to get new leads while ignoring his old relationships. Get new leads but also keep in touch with people you've already met.

**It's never too late to follow up.** For example: "I met you three years ago and am still impressed by____. Since then I have_____and would be interested in getting together with you again to discuss these new developments." Make new contacts. Recontact old ones. It's never too late.

> **Trouble getting started?**
> **What would you say to the person if he or she were sitting across from you right now? Consider that as the opening of your follow-up letter.**

> **Job hunters make a mistake when they fail to *recontact* people with whom they have formed relationships earlier in their search.**
> **Keep in touch on a regular basis so you increase your chances of contacting them just at a time when they have heard of something that may interest you —or may have a new need themselves.**

*William Pilder*

*163 York Avenue - 12B*
*New York, New York 10000*
*(212) 555-2231 (day)*
*(212) 555-1674 (message)*

**Follow up with a customized note specifically acknowledging the help you received.**

June 25, 19xx

Ms. Barbara Earley
Director of Outplacement
Time-Warner Communications
8 Pine Street
New York, NY 10001

Dear Ms. Earley:

Thanks so much for seeing me. Your center is very impressive and seems very well run. But of course, that's what I had heard before I met you.

As you suggested, I sent for information on ASTD, and was pleasantly surprised to see your name in there! It sounds like a great organization, and I can't wait until they start to have meetings again in the fall.

I will definitely follow up with both Jim Kacena and Joan Strewler, and appreciate your giving me their names. I've called them each a few times, but they and I are very busy people.

After I left your place, I wished I had asked you more about your own career. It was only at the very end that you brought up the interesting way you got your job. I had wrongly assumed that you came up through the ranks at Time-Warner Communications. Perhaps some other time I can hear the rest of the story. You certainly do seem to know your stuff.

I've enclosed The Five O'Clock Club calendar for June, July and August. In addition, I'll be speaking at The New School in a few weeks, and have a lot planned for myself for the fall. I will keep you posted regarding my activities, and perhaps I'll even run into you at ASTD meetings.

Thanks again for your time and insight. Till we meet again.

Cordially,

William Pilder

## Jack Schlegel

August 24, 1989

Dear Mary Ann:

Just a quick note to thank you for taking the time to meet with me yesterday. Even though it seems I've located most of the places which could use my skill set, it's always nice to revalidate that opinion.

I was interested to learn of your new position in National Product Engineering. Although I understand your current situation, I'm always excited to discover new possibilities for becoming involved in Big Red's national campaign. I've long believed this effort is paramount to Big Red's continued dominance in the industry. In fact I expressed just that opinion to Julie Ward on Tuesday. Julie is involved in Big Red's advertising program to develop a national brand image, and I commented to her how much I liked the concept.

I am very flattered, too, that you would consider involving me in your developing organization. As I mentioned to you, I am quite good at "start-up" positions which require a great amount of vision to allow for working in an indeterminate environment. Clearly my marketing liaison and consulting activities would be a natural for for your charter as well. If I can help you in any way as you define your area, I would be happy to offer you my assistance.

I would like very much to contact you again in a few weeks to learn more about your progress. In the meantime I am going to try to contact Lou Fleming and others involved in the National Marketing effort to keep abreast of this exciting new area.

Thanks again for your time--hope to see you again soon.

Sincerely,

*Jack*

**Marilyn Williamson**

To: Tish Chamberlain

Thanks again for contacting Brendan for me, and for providing all those excellent contact names.

There's such a wealth of good ideas in that list that it will take me a while to follow up with all of them, but I'm getting hard at it and will let you know what develops.

Again, thanks for your extraordinary effort. (By the way, should you ever want to "review your career options" I would be delighted to share a few names, or more than a few, with you.)

Stay tuned!

*Marilyn*

**Joel Bramble**

To: Marion Flomenhoft

I enjoyed our conversation, which I found most helpful.

I will meet with Betsy Austin when she returns from overseas, and will talk to Jim about seeing Susan Geisenheimer. I'll also contact Bob Potvin and Clive Murray, per your suggestion.

Again, thanks for your help. I'll let you know how things develop.

*Joel*

> **Follow-up letters don't have to be long, but they *do* have to be personal. Make sure the letters you write could not be sent to anyone else on your list.**

Mr. Joseph Duffy
President
Commerce and Industry Association
Street Address
City, State

Dear Joe:

Thank you for the time from your busy schedule. I enjoyed our discussion and appreciated your suggestions towards marketing myself in the northern part of the state. Your idea on using the Big 8 firms as pivot points in networking is a excellent one. As you requested, I have enclosed copies of my résumé. I plan to call you next week, Joe, so that I can obtain the names of the firms where my résumé was sent.

I have been thinking about using Robert Dobbs (Dobbs & Firth) in my networking efforts. As a past president of Commerce and Industry I would be foolish not to tap such a source. Thanks again, Joe.

Sincerely,

Liz Branstead

# How to Handle Rejection Letters

*In nature, there are neither rewards nor punishments—there are consequences.*—Robert Green Ingersoll

Companies generally send the same rejection letter to everyone—complimenting the applicant on his or her credentials and offering regret that there are no appropriate openings at that time. A rejection letter is truly a rejection only when it follows an interview.

## Rejection Letters in Response to a Direct-Mail Campaign

If you received a respectable number of responses (meetings) from your campaign, try another campaign of the remaining companies in a few months. Direct marketers say you should then expect approximately half the response you got with your first mailing. As an alternative, network into the companies that interest you, contact someone else in the same firm, or use a targeted mailing approach.

If the response rate from your mailing was poor, you picked the wrong market for what you have to offer, or the package you sent was lacking. Chances are, you were not as knowledgeable about this market as you thought. Research or network to learn more, or network to find out what was wrong with your package.

## Rejection Letter in Response to an Ad

This is par for the course. The company probably received a thousand résumés. Or perhaps the ad was not for a legitimate opening.

If a company name was listed, network in, do a targeted mailing to someone who could be close to the hiring manager, or contact a search firm that handles the type of position mentioned. (See the chapter "What to Do When You Know There's a Job Opening.") Your résumé was probably rejected by someone other than the hiring manager, so it's worth further effort if you're interested in the position. Some companies have a policy of immediately sending out rejection letters to everyone. Then they call those people they're interested in—even though the applicants have already been "rejected." For companies that always send rejection letters, this approach saves time.

## Rejection Letter in Response to a Networking Contact You Tried to Make

The person did not understand that what you wanted was information. If many people respond to you this way, reassess your approach to networking.

## Rejection Letter Following a Job Interview

This is a true rejection letter. It used to be that it took seven job interviews to get one offer. That figure may now be higher. If you are still interested in the company, don't give up. (Read what Michael did in the chapter "Following Up When There Is No Immediate Job.")

## Lessons to Learn

When you get a rejection note in response to an interview, think about it. How interested are you in that firm? Did you hit it off with the interviewer? If you think there was some mutual interest, see if there might be other jobs with the company later—perhaps in another department. Or perhaps the person hired instead of you might not work out. Keep in touch. People rarely do, but we all like to hire people who truly want to work for us.

## Case Study: Stan
### Turning a Rejection Into an Offer

Stan was told an offer was being made to another candidate. He was crushed, but he immediately dashed off a letter to the hiring manager and hand-delivered it. A brief letter, it said, in part:

I was disappointed to hear that you have offered the position to someone else. I truly believe I am right for the position, and wish you would keep me in mind anyway. You never know—something could happen to the new person, and you may need a replacement. Please consider me no matter when this may occur, because I believe I belong at your institution.

The next day, Stan received a call with an offer. Some people may think the offer to the other candidate fell through. However, I believe Stan's letter influenced the hiring manager. When he saw the letter, he thought to himself, We're offering the position to the wrong person! and he allowed the negotiation with the other candidate to lapse.

*Do not fear death so much,*
*but rather the inadequate life.*
Bertolt Brecht

Your overall campaign can be managed with just a few important worksheets:

• Use the **Interview Record** for *every* meeting—both networking and job.

• Consider using the **Monthly Job-Hunting Calendar** to record your search activities—so it will be clear to you how much (or how little) you are doing.

• The most important worksheet for controlling your search is the **Current List of My Active Contacts by Target**. At the beginning of your search, these will simply be networking contacts with whom you want to keep in touch. At that stage, your goal is to come up with six to ten contacts you want to recontact later.

Later, the quality of your list will change. Then the names will be prospective job possibilities that you are trying to move along.

If you have six to ten job possibilities "in the works," five of them will fall away through no fault of your own (because of job freezes or the hiring manager changing his or her mind about the kind of person wanted). Then you'll need to get more things in the works. With this critical mass of ongoing possible positions, you stand a chance of landing the kind of job you want.

## Other Worksheets

The worksheets mentioned above are critical to the management of your search. Other worksheets guide specific parts of your search.

• In the beginning, the **Seven Stories Exercise** and **Your Forty-Year Plan** will help you select job targets that are appropriate for you (see our book *Targeting the Job You Want*).

• **Measuring Your Targets** will assure that you

have targets of a size that have a reasonable chance of working.

• Your **List of Companies to Contact** will help you organize who you should contact in your search—either in person or some other way.

• The **Summary of What I Have/Want to Offer** will help you "position" yourself appropriately to each of your targets.

• **People to Contact in Each Target Area** is a way to get your search off to a quick start through networking or targeted mailings.

• The **Format of a Networking Interview** is your guide to properly managing the networking-type interviews you get through networking, targeted or direct mailings, or cold calls.

• **The Follow-Up Checklist: Turing Job Interviews Into Offers** will help you assess the interview and decide what to do next. Your goal, after all, is to move the process along and see if you can create a job for yourself.

• Assessing whether you are at **Stage 1, 2 or 3** of your search will help you see where you really stand, rather than hoping for a job offer too soon.

## Four-Step Salary Negotiation

• Are you keeping all four steps in mind?

• Are you **negotiating the job** to make it appropriate for you and for the hiring manager?

• Are you **paying attention to your competition**, what they have to offer and what you must do to outshine and outlast them? Are you aware that your competitors may not be real people, but may be in the mind of the hiring manager?

• Are you trying to postpone discussion of salary until after you **get the offer**?

The Five O'Clock Club®

# Current List of My
# Active Contacts by Target

Make copies of this page for each target, and keep track of your active contacts in each target area. To see how well you are penetrating each target market, compare the total number of appropriate contacts in your market with the number you have actually contacted. Keep adding names to your list. Certain people will become inappropriate. Cross their names off. You should probably have some contact once every month or two with the people who remain on your list.

After your search is up and running, keep track of your contacts by the stage you are in for each one. This will tell you how well you are doing in your search, and will give you some idea of how likely it is for you to get an offer.

**For Target** _____:

Geographic area: _____
Industry or company size: _____
Position/Function: _____

| Name of Contact | Company | Position | Date of Last Contact | Targeted Date of Next Contact |
|---|---|---|---|---|
| 1. | | | | |
| 2. | | | | |
| 3. | | | | |
| 4. | | | | |
| 5. | | | | |
| 6. | | | | |
| 7. | | | | |
| 8. | | | | |
| 9. | | | | |
| 10. | | | | |
| 11. | | | | |
| 12. | | | | |
| 13. | | | | |
| 14. | | | | |
| 15. | | | | |
| 16. | | | | |
| 17. | | | | |
| 18. | | | | |
| 19. | | | | |
| 20. | | | | |

The
Five
O'Clock
Club®

# Current List of Active Stage-1 Contacts:

**Networking Contacts with whom you want to keep in touch**

## *the beginning of a search*

**Measure the effectiveness of your search** by listing the number of people with whom you are currently in contact on an ongoing basis, either by phone or mail, who are in a position to hire you or recommend that you be hired. The rule of thumb: if you are seriously job-hunting, **you should have six to ten active contacts going at one time. At the beginning of your search, these will simply be networking contacts with whom you want to keep in touch**. You are unlikely to get an offer at this stage. You are gathering information to find out how things work—getting your feet wet. You look like an outsider, and outsiders are rarely given a break. Keep adding names to your list because certain people will become inappropriate. Cross their names off. You should probably have some contact once a month with the people who remain on your list.

Because you have already developed targets for your search, please note below the target area for each contact, or note that it is serendipitous and does not fit in with any of your organized targets. This will help you see the progress you are making in each target area.

| | Name of Contact | Company | Position | Date of Last Contact | Targeted Date of Next Contact | Target Area or Serend. |
|---|---|---|---|---|---|---|
| 1. | | | | | | |
| 2. | | | | | | |
| 3. | | | | | | |
| 4. | | | | | | |
| 5. | | | | | | |
| 6. | | | | | | |
| 7. | | | | | | |
| 8. | | | | | | |
| 9. | | | | | | |
| 10. | | | | | | |
| 11. | | | | | | |
| 12. | | | | | | |
| 13. | | | | | | |
| 14. | | | | | | |
| 15. | | | | | | |
| 16. | | | | | | |
| 17. | | | | | | |
| 18. | | | | | | |
| 19. | | | | | | |
| 20. | | | | | | |

The
Five
O'Clock
Club®

# Current List of Active Stage-2 Contacts:

### The right people at the right levels in the right companies

## *the middle of a search*

The nature of your "six to ten things in the works" changes over time. Instead of simply finding networking contacts to get your search started, you meet people who are closer to what you want.

Getting a job offer is not the way to test the quality of your campaign. A real test is when people say they'd want you—but not now. Do some people say: **"Boy, I wish I had an opening. I'd sure like to have someone like you here."**? Then you are interviewing well with the right people. All you need now are luck and timing to help you contact (and recontact) the right people when they also have a need.

If people are *not* saying they want you, find out why not. If you think you are in the right targets, talking to people at the right level, and are not early on in your search, you need feedback. Ask : "If you had an opening, would you consider hiring someone like me?" Find out what is wrong.

Become an insider—a competent person who can prove that he or she has somehow already done what the interviewer needs. *Prove* you can do the job, and that the interviewer is *not* taking a chance on you.

You still need six to ten contacts at this level whom you will recontact later. Keep adding names to your list because certain people will become inappropriate. Cross their names off. You should probably have some contact once a month with the people who remain on your list.

| Name of Contact | Company | Position | Date of Last Contact | Targeted Date of Next Contact | Target Area or Serend. |
|---|---|---|---|---|---|
| 1. | | | | | |
| 2. | | | | | |
| 3. | | | | | |
| 4. | | | | | |
| 5. | | | | | |
| 6. | | | | | |
| 7. | | | | | |
| 8. | | | | | |
| 9. | | | | | |
| 10. | | | | | |
| 11. | | | | | |
| 12. | | | | | |
| 13. | | | | | |
| 14. | | | | | |
| 15. | | | | | |
| 16. | | | | | |
| 17. | | | | | |
| 18. | | | | | |
| 19. | | | | | |
| 20. | | | | | |

© 1996, Kate Wendleton and The Five O'Clock Club®

# Current List of Active Stage-3 Contacts:

**Moving along actual jobs or the possibility of creating a job**

### *the final stages of a search*

In this stage, you **uncover six to ten actual jobs (or the possibility of creating a job) to move along**. These job possibilities could come from *any* of your target areas or from serendipitous leads. Find a *lot* of people who would hire you if they could. If you have only one lead that could turn into an offer, you are likely to try to close too soon. Get more leads. You will be more attractive to the manager, will interview better, and will not lose momentum if your best lead falls apart. A good number of your job possibilities will fall away through no fault of your own (such as job freezes or major changes in the job requirements).

To get more leads, notice which targets are working and which are not. Make *additional* contacts in the targets that seem to be working, or develop new targets. **Recontact just about everyone you have met earlier in your search**. You want to develop more offers.

**Aim for three offers**: this is the stage of your search when you want them. When an offer comes during Stage 1 or Stage 2, you probably have not had a chance to develop momentum so you can get a number of offers. When choosing between offers, **select the job that positions you best for the long term**.

| | Name of Contact | Company | Position | Date of Last Contact | Targeted Date of Next Contact | Target Area or Serend. |
|---|---|---|---|---|---|---|
| 1. | | | | | | |
| 2. | | | | | | |
| 3. | | | | | | |
| 4. | | | | | | |
| 5. | | | | | | |
| 6. | | | | | | |
| 7. | | | | | | |
| 8. | | | | | | |
| 9. | | | | | | |
| 10. | | | | | | |
| 11. | | | | | | |
| 12. | | | | | | |
| 13. | | | | | | |
| 14. | | | | | | |
| 15. | | | | | | |
| 16. | | | | | | |
| 17. | | | | | | |
| 18. | | | | | | |
| 19. | | | | | | |
| 20. | | | | | | |

The Five O'Clock Club®

# Stuck in Your Search?
# What to Do Next

## How to Measure the
## Effectiveness of Your Search

Most job hunters say, "I'll know my search was good when I get a job." That's not a very good way to measure your search. You need to be able to tell as you go along whether you are heading in the right direction. There are a number of hints you can pick up along the way.

### What Stage Are You In?

As you go along, the basic measurement tool to use in your search is this: "Do you have six to ten things in the works?" That is, are you talking to six to ten people on an ongoing basis who are in a position to hire you or recommend that you be hired?"

The quality of your contacts varies with where you are in your search.

• In the beginning of your search, you will speak to as many people as possible in your target market—regardless of the company for which they work. At this stage, you simply want market information. If you plan to stay in touch with them on an ongoing basis, they are Stage-1 contacts. To have any momentum going in the beginning of your search, keep in touch  with six to ten people on an ongoing basis (every few months).

Over time, you will talk to more and more people who are Stage-1 contacts--perhaps 60 to 100 people during the course of your search. Some of those contacts will bubble up and become Stage-2 contacts.

• Stage-2 contacts are people who are the right people at the right level in the right jobs in the right companies in your targeted areas. They are senior to you, perhaps future hiring managers. Your goal is to have contact with six to ten of the right people on an ongoing basis. Then you have a full Stage-2 search going: you are in the middle of your search.

However, you will rarely get a good job offer at Stage 2. You aren't even talking to these people about real jobs at this point. You just want the right people to know you and remember you. And if one later happens to have a job opening, you still need to go after six to ten other job possibilities, because five will fall away through no fault of your own. If you do get an offer at Stage 2, you won't have many others with which to compare it. Keep in touch with your current Stage-1 contacts (using *networking* follow-ups), and develop additional Stage-1 contacts, so more will bubble up to Stage 2. Some of those will bubble up to Stage 3 (real job possibilities)—and then you're really cooking.

• You are in a full Stage-3 search when you are talking to six to ten people on an ongoing basis who actually have a job opening or who have the possibility of creating a job for you. Then you have a number of opportunities that you can move along (using *job* follow-ups), and are in the best possible position to get the right job for you: the one that positions you best for the long term and the one that pays you what you are worth.

If you have six to ten possibilities in Stage 3, you have the chance of getting three offers. Remember, these do not have to be ideal jobs— some may be even be disgusting. But an offer is an offer, and makes you more desirable in the market. You don't have to want to work at each of these places, but at least you will have a fallback position, and can honestly say, if appropriate, "I have a number of job offers, but there's no place I'd rather work than yours." With a number of offers in hand, you are less likely to be taken advantage of by a prospective employer who thinks you are desperate.

## How's Your Search Going?

When I ask you how your search is going, I don't want to hear that a prospective employer really likes you. That's not a good measure of how well your search is going, because that one prospect could easily fall away: they may decide to hire no one, or they may decide they want an accounting person instead of a marketing person.

A lot can happen that is beyond your control.

Instead I expect you to tell me how many things you have in the works. You would say, for example, "My search is going great. I have five Stage-1 contacts in the works. I'm just getting started."

Or you might say, "I have nine Stage-2 contacts, and three contacts in Stage 3." If you are expert at this, you may even add: "I want more Stage-3 contacts, so my goal is to get thirty more in Stage 2. Right now, I'm digging up lots of new contacts, and keeping the other ones going. With my Stage-2 contacts, I'm generally doing networking follow-ups, and with my Stage-3 contacts, I'm generally doing job follow-ups."

That kind of talk is music to my ears.

It usually takes very little effort to get a few more things "in the works." Simply recontact your network, network into someone you haven't met with yet, directly contact someone, talk to a search firm, answer an ad. You will soon have more activity in your search.

## What Job Hunters Do Wrong

In addition to looking at the *stage* of your overall search, it is also helpful to look at what can go wrong in each *phase* of your campaigns. Some job hunters err in their overall search approach or attitude. Then there are things that can go wrong in the Assessment Phase, or in the parts of your campaigns (in the Planning, Interviewing, or Follow-Up phases). We'll examine each of these to determine what you may be doing wrong, if anything.

## The Overall Search: What Can Go Wrong?

Here are some problems that are general to the entire search:

• **Not spending enough time** on your search. If you are unemployed, you should be spending 35 hours a week on your search. If you are employed, spend 15 hours a week to get some momentum going. If you spend only two or three hours a week on your job search, you may complain that you have been searching

*Procrastination is the fear of success. People procrastinate because they are afraid of the success that they know will result if they move ahead now. Because success is heavy, carries a responsibility with it, it is much easier to procrastinate and live on the "someday I'll" philosophy.*
Denis Waitley

forever, when actually you have not even begun. If you are employed, you can do most of your work in the evenings and on weekends—research, write cover letters and follow-up letters. You can even schedule your meetings in the evenings or early mornings.

- **Not having enough fun**. Some job hunters—especially those who are unemployed—say they will start having fun after they get a job. But your search may take many months, and you are more likely to come across as desperate if you are not allowing yourself to have some fun. Having fun will make you seem like a more normal person on your interviews, and you'll feel better about yourself. The Five O'Clock Club formula is that you *must* have at least three hours of fun a week.

- **Not having six to ten things in the works**. See the beginning of this chapter about Stage 1, 2, and 3 of your search.

- **Talking to people who are at the wrong level**. At the beginning of your search, talk to peers just to gather information to decide whether a prospective target is worth a full campaign. When you have selected a few good targets, then talk to those who are higher level.

- **Trying to bypass the system**. Some job hunters feel they don't have time for this, and simply want to go on job interviews (usually through search firms or answering ads). Others want to skip the assessment process (see our book *Targeting the Job You Want*), or don't even do the Seven Stories Exercise. Their campaigns are weaker because they have no foundation.

At least touch on every step in the process. You will have a quicker and more productive search.

- **Lowering your salary expectations just because you have been unemployed a while**. Even those who have been unemployed a year or two land jobs at market rates. They get what they are worth in the market because they have followed the system.

At The Five O'Clock Club, half the people who attend are employed; half are unemployed.

Many of those who are unemployed have been out of work for a year or two. Usually, they have been doing something wrong in their searches, and the counselor and their group can help them figure out what it is. When they get a job (which they almost certainly will if they stick with the system), they usually wind up getting something appropriate at an appropriate salary level.

Sometimes, if people really need money, we suggest that they take something inappropriate to earn some money, and continue to search while they are working.

- **Getting discouraged**. Half the battle is controlling your emotions. Jack had been unemployed one and a half years when he joined us. He seemed very agitated—almost angry—which happens when a person has been working at a job search for so long. I told him I was afraid that he might come across that way during interviews. He assured me (with irritation in his voice) that he was completely pleasant during the interview, but was simply letting his hair down in the group.

In career counseling, we have nothing to go on but the way the person acts in the group: the way you are in the group probably bears some resemblance to the way you are in the interview. We would recognize you as being the same person. Anyway, it's all we have to go on, so we have to point out to you what we see.

The next week, Jack still seemed angry. I asked the group what they thought, and of course they could see it too. It was easier for him to hear it from his peers, and, because he was a mature person, Jack listened to them.

The third week, Jack laughingly announced that he had had a lobotomy, and was a completely different person. He said he had changed his attitude, and that his interviews reflected this change.

The fourth week, he announced that he had had another lobotomy because he felt he still had room for improvement. He was a noticeably different person, and did not seem at all like someone who had been out of work a long time.

214

*Quit now, you'll never make it.*
*If you disregard this advice, you'll be halfway there.*
David Zucker

Jack read every day the books we use at The Five O'Clock Club, and provided very good insights to the other job hunters in our small group.

By the fifth week, Jack was almost acting like a co-counselor in the group. He had made great strides in his own search (with three Stage-3 contacts, and lots of contacts in Stage 2), and was able to astutely analyze the problems others were having. He was a wonderful contributor.

By the seventh week, Jack was close to a number of offers, and in the eighth week, Jack proudly addressed the large group and reported on his successful search. We were sorry to see him go.

By the way, Jack did not have to take a pay cut or a job that was beneath him. His prolonged search did not affect his salary negotiation.

Do what you need to do to keep your spirits up. Don't ask yourself if you feel like searching. Of course you don't. Just do it anyway. And act as if you enjoy it.

• **Not having support**. Looking for a job is a lonely business. A job hunter may "buddy" with another job hunter. They call each other every morning to talk about what they are each going to do that day and to review what they each accomplished the day before. Other job hunters join free emotional- support groups at places of worship. You may find you need that help in addition to the job-search strategy you get at The Five O'Clock Club. Or you may find you would like to see a counselor privately to help you with specifics having to do with your search, such as your résumé, a review of your search, salary negotiation, or the follow-up to a very important job interview. Get the help you need.

• **Inflating in your own mind the time you have actually been searching**. You may feel as though you've been searching forever. But if you are searching only three hours a week, you have not yet begun. If at the end of a year, you finally start to put in the required 15 to 35 hours a week, you have just really started to search. Then when people ask how long you have been searching, the correct answer is "a few weeks." It's good to

be honest with yourself about how long you have actually been searching.

### During the Assessment Phase: What Can Go Wrong?

In the Assessment Phase you use our book, *Trageting the Job You Want*, to go through the exercises (The Seven Stories, Values, Forty-Year Plan, and so on), and select job targets (industries or companies of a certain size; the position you would like in each target; and the geographic area).

If you are not sure what you should do with your life, assessment is a time to explore—perhaps with the help of a career counselor. What can go wrong in this phase?

• **Selecting one or two targets too quickly**. Rather than exploring, a job hunter may pick a target, go after it, find out it doesn't work, and then not know what to do next. Instead, brainstorm as many targets as you can at the beginning of your search, rank them, and go after them in a methodical way.

• **Not being specific in selecting a target**. Some job hunters say, "I just want a job. I don't care what it is." You may not care, but the hiring team wants someone who cares about their specific industry and organization. In the beginning of your search, you want to explore, and stay calm while you are doing your research to find out what the likely targets are for you. If you don't have targets defined (such as "being a COBOL computer programmer in a medium-sized company in the Albuquerque area"), then you are still exploring, and that's okay. But it is not an organized search. And even when your search is organized and targeted, you will still have plenty of room for serendipitous leads.

• **Not doing the right research**. Read the extensive material Wendy Alfus Rothman wrote on research, including the annotated bibliography at the back of *Targeting the Job You Want*. Research is critical throughout your search, and separates those who follow The Five O'Clock Club method from other job hunters.

*The thing always happens that you believe in; and the belief in a thing makes it happen.*
Frank Lloyd Wright

*If you want a quality, act as if you already had it. Try the "as if" technique.*
William James

---

Instead of just "doing" research, why not learn to enjoy it and make it part of your life?

The better your research, the richer your targets will become—well defined rather than superficial—and the more knowledgeable you will sound to prospective employers. In addition, you will save a lot of time as you discover where the markets are and which ones are the best fit for you.

• **Not ranking your targets**. Some job hunters go after everything at once. For a more organized search, overlap your targets, but still conduct a condensed search focusing on each target and keeping them separate in your mind.

Take a look at the chart below, which shows a campaign aimed at each target (T1, T2, and T3). Yet the targets overlap to speed up the search.

Next, let's look at what can go wrong in the various phases of the campaign aimed at each target.

**During the Preparation Phase:**
**What Can Go Wrong?**

• **Relying on only one technique for getting interviews**. Consider using all four techniques for getting interviews: networking, direct contact, search firms, and ads. Even in fields where people like to talk to people, such as sales or human resources, though networking is easier, it is not thorough. It is a scattered approach.

Make a list of all the companies in your target area—say, 120 companies.

- Perhaps network into 20 of them;
- Do a targeted mailing into 20—it's just like networking: use a letter with a follow-up phone call. Remember that you want to see this person whether or not he or she has a job opening;
- Talk to search firms (if appropriate); and
- Answer ads.
- You can also do a direct-mail campaign (no follow-up phone call) to the remaining 80 companies—just to be thorough so all the companies in your target area know that you exist and are looking.

• **Contacting the wrong person**. The human resources person is the wrong one unless you want a job in human resources. The right person is one or two levels higher than you are in the department or division in which you want to work. If you are very senior and want to work for the president, the right person for you to contact is the president or perhaps someone on the board. If you want to be the president, the right person is someone on the board, or whoever may influence the selection of the president.

• **Being positioned improperly**. If you are not positioned properly, you will not be able to get interviews. Write out your Two-Minute Pitch. In your small group, be sure to practice your pitch. Try role-playing. Tell the group who they are pretending to be, and ask them to critique you. You want to make sure you have your pitch down pat. Write it out.

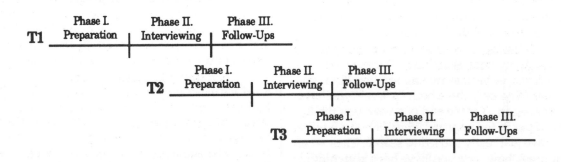

*If you are distressed by anything external, the pain is not due to the thing itself, but to your estimate of it; and this you have the power to revoke at any moment.*

Marcus Aurelius

- **Using skimpy cover letters**. We use a four-paragraph approach that is thorough. Most job hunters write paragraphs one and four, and skip the meat.
- **Having a weak or inappropriate résumé**. If your résumé doesn't speak for you in your absence, and tell them exactly who you are, your level, and what you bring to the party, develop one that helps you. We have a whole book on this topic—along with case studies of real live people. See our book *Building a Great Résumé*.
- **Skipping the research phase to develop a good list of target companies**. If you have a good list, you will get more out of every one of your networking contacts. Show your list of prospective companies to your contacts, ask them what they think of the companies on the list, who they suggest you should contact at the good companies, and ask, "May I use your name?"

### During the Interviewing Phase: What Can Go Wrong?

- **Trying to close too soon**. When a company is interested in you, you may have the tendency, like most job hunters, to focus on that one possibility and hope you get an offer. Because everything depends on that one possibility, chances are that you will do something wrong—trying to force them to decide before they are ready.

Instead, get other things going while you keep an eye on the company you are already interested in. Ease the pressure on yourself and that company. Get your six to ten things in the works and you'll have a balanced search.

- **Being seen as an outsider**. It's okay to be an outsider when it is early in your search. However, to get offers, you must be seen as an insider. When you are an insider, higher-level networking contacts say, "I really wish I had an opening because I would love to have someone like you on board." You are being well received, and this person counts as a Stage-2 contact. Keep in touch with him or her. Find lots more. It's only a matter of time until you get a job: if the target you

picked is a good one; if you contact more and more people who say the same thing; and if you keep in touch with those whom you already met.

- **Not using the worksheets**. Fill out What I Have/Want to Offer. This will help you position yourself to each targeted area. Use one for each of your targets. Make a zillion copies of the Interview Record. Fill one out every time you go on an interview. Note to whom you spoke, to whom they referred you, their important issues, and so on. Two weeks later you may not remember what you discussed.

If you are having a terrific search, you may meet with five to fifteen people each week. Keep track of them with your Interview Record. Some people keep the records in a three-ring binder, alphabetically or by industry or target. Every time they write a follow-up letter, they attach a copy of that letter to the Interview Record. They cross-reference the information, and become very methodical.

That way, when you conduct your networking follow-ups every two months, you will have the notes from your last discussion, and copies of the letters you had sent earlier.

- Other things that can go wrong in the Interviewing Phase include:
- Not thinking like a consultant.
- Not looking or acting like the level for which you are searching.
- Not seeing the interview as only the beginning of the process.
- Not getting information/giving information to move it along. "Where are you in the hiring process?" "How many other people are you talking to?" "How do I compare with them?" Be impersonal in the way you ask these questions so you can find out about your competition.
- Not preparing for the interview by having a 3X5 card or finding out with whom you will be meeting.
- Not being in sync with their timing (trying to close too soon or not moving quickly enough).
- Not listening to what is really going on.

## During the Follow-Up Phase:
## What Can Go Wrong?

In addition to targeting, follow-up is the most important reason Five O'Clock Clubbers land jobs quickly. This is the brainiest part of the process. Notice that the earlier diagram showed the three parts as equal: Preparation, Interviewing, and Follow-Ups. Spend an equal amount of time on each.

Study thoroughly those parts of this book. Some of the obvious things that go wrong include:

• **Taking the first offer**. Try to get three offers at the same time. Then select the one that positions you best for the long run.

• **Not recontacting your contacts**. If you have been in search a while, the most important action you can take to develop new momentum is to recontact those with whom you have already met—perhaps every two to three months. That way they have a better chance of thinking of you when they come across news that may help you in your search.

Tell them, "It's been a while since we've met, and I am having a very interesting time. My search has taken a slightly different direction, and I now find there is a lot of activity in the roof-repair market, which I am currently exploring. You were such a help to me before that I would like to call you again to find out what is going on at your end, and to tell you a little about what I've been doing." However you do it, recontact your contacts.

• **Not studying the books**. Follow-up is covered in great detail in this book. Study it and spend the time it takes to think through what you can do next to move along the *job* contacts you have made. While those you have networked with should be contacted every few months, job follow-up is more complicated.

• **Stating your salary requirements too soon**. The discussion of salary negotiation in this book is another thing you should read thoroughly *at the beginning of your search*. Salary negotiation starts with the way you position yourself at your very first meeting.

• **Not reassessing where you stand in your search.** Let's say you have been in search a while, and would like to know where you stand. Take all of the contacts you have in the works (people you are in touch with on a regular basis), and divide them up into Stage 1, Stage 2, or Stage 3 contacts. You will probably have a ratio of 60 Stage 1 to 20 Stage 2 to 6 Stage 3. Therefore, to increase the number of contacts you have in Stage 3, your only recourse is to increase the number of contacts you have in Stage 1. Some will bubble up to Stage 2, and others to Stage 3.

Now that we've taken a break from your search to assess how you are doing, it's time to get back to work. After you read the section "Additional Thoughts," on the next page, use the worksheets that follow that to note the companies/people you have contacted for each stage of your search.

# Additional Thoughts

## Hints for Seemingly Low-Key People

In this country, we often think that people who are openly assertive, forceful, and dynamic are more able to get work done through others than those who are thoughtful, persistent—and perhaps relentless. These seemingly low-key, quiet types may have their abilities undervalued and their working style misunderstood. The hiring team may incorrectly see them as unable to make a strong impression on a customer, sell their ideas internally, or push projects through. They may even seem less intelligent than they actually are. Sometimes these people do not get the jobs they deserve because the interviewer is not able to see the full force of their personality at the interview itself.

If you are a low-key person, you may come across as more meek in the interview than you have been in your jobs. So be sure to sit forward in your seat, use more hand gestures than may be usual for you, and constantly put active, dynamic words into your conversation. Help the hiring team to understand your true style on the job. For example:

"I aggressively promoted products."

"I inspire and motivate people to go beyond whatever goals are set."

"Despite my low-key demeanor, I'm seen as a person who is relentless in meeting goals through others."

"I'm able to sell to anyone by using a low-key approach that disarms people."

"Once I am on the job, people see me as someone to be reckoned with, and I am able to convince them to do what needs to be done."

Make sure the hiring team sees you the way you really are on the job, and also sees the benefit of having someone with your style.

---

*Darest thou, now O soul,*
*Walk out with me toward*
*the unknown region*
*Where neither ground is*
*for the feet nor any path to follow?*
Walt Whitman

## It's Not Necessarily Easier to Get a Lower-Level Job

When job hunters have problems finding a job at their current level, they often want to lower their sights. They think, I'll take a job two levels lower than the one I just had. But there is competition at that level too.

Recently, a man was forced into early retirement after having been president of a major chain of retail stores. He didn't need much money, and he simply wanted to work at an easy job. He admired The Five O'Clock Club and asked if he could do junior-level office work for a modest salary. He said he was willing to run errands, stuff envelopes, and do other mundane assignments. He assumed that we would be eager to hire him for that job, since he was such a bargain.

But many people wanted that office-administration position, and most were more qualified for the job than he was. The other candidates knew how to use computers, would be better at taking phone messages and following up than he would have been, and had actually had experience doing those tasks.

If you honestly want a lower-level job, present a logical rationale to the hiring team, and think about your competition exactly the same way you would if you were going after a job at your most recent level.

---

*One of the best ways to properly evaluate and adapt to the many environmental stresses of life is to view them as normal. The adversity and failures in our lives, if adapted to and viewed as normal corrective feedback to use to get back on target, serve to develop in us an immunity against anxiety, depression, and the adverse responses to stress.*
*Instead of tackling the most important priorities that would make us successful and effective in life, we prefer the path of least resistance and do things simply that will relieve our tension, such as shuffling papers and majoring in minors.*
Denis Waitley

---

# Summary of Search Progress

**The Five O'Clock Club**

| For Target 1: | | # of companies in this target | # contacted | # met with | Quality/Status of Contacts |
|---|---|---|---|---|---|
| Geog. area: | Chicago metro | 10 | 10 | 3 | Stage 3 - 1 job lead |
| Ind. or co. size: | Consumer goods companies | | | | Stage 2 - 2 |
| Pos./Function: | Director of direct mail | | | | Stage 1 - 2 |
| Note: Not a great target. Keep in touch with same 5 people. | | | | | |

| For Target 2: | | # of companies in this target | # contacted | # met with | Quality/Status of Contacts |
|---|---|---|---|---|---|
| Geog. area: | Chicago metro | 200 | 70 | 30 | Stage 3 - 3 - 1 close to offer |
| Ind. or co. size: | Direct marketing service cos. | | | | Stage 2 - 9 |
| Pos./Function: | Director of direct mail | | | | Stage 1 - 16 |
| Note: I'll aim to get 80 Stage-1 contacts; 30 Stage-2 contacts. | | | | | |

| For Target 3: | | # of companies in this target | # contacted | # met with | Quality/Status of Contacts |
|---|---|---|---|---|---|
| Geog. area: | Chicago metro | 120 | 11 | 4 | Stage 3 - 0 |
| Ind. or co. size: | Direct marketing-based co. | | | | Stage 2 - 0 |
| Pos./Function: | Vice Pres., Marketing | | | | Stage 1 - 4 |
| Note: I need to do a lot more work in this target. | | | | | |

| For Target 4: | | # of companies in this target | # contacted | # met with | Quality/Status of Contacts |
|---|---|---|---|---|---|
| Geog. area: | Chicago metro | 15 | 15 | 4 | Stage 3 - 0 |
| Ind. or co. size: | Advertising agencies | | | | Stage 2 - 0 |
| Pos./Function: | Director of direct mail | | | | Stage 1 - 2 |
| Note: This is the field I'm in now, but I want to get out of it. | | | | | |

Note: In the far right column, note those contacts you are keeping in touch with on an ongoing basis:

Stage 1 contacts: People with whom I want to keep in touch—regardless of level or ability to hire.

Stage 2 contacts: The right people at the right levels in the right companies (Potential hiring managers with whom I am keeping in touch. They may be telling me: I wish I had an opening. If I did, I'd like to hire someone like you.)

Stage 3 contacts: Moving along actual jobs or the possibility of creating a job.

# Summary of Search Progress

**The Five O'Clock Club**

| | # of companies in this target | # contacted | # met with | Quality/Status of Contacts |
|---|---|---|---|---|
| **For Target 1:**<br>Geog. area: ___<br>Ind. or co. size: ___<br>Pos./Function: ___<br><br>Note: | | | | Stage 3 -<br>Stage 2 -<br>Stage 1 - |
| **For Target 2:**<br>Geog. area: ___<br>Ind. or co. size: ___<br>Pos./Function: ___<br><br>Note: | # of companies in this target | # contacted | # met with | Quality/Status of Contacts<br>Stage 3 -<br>Stage 2 -<br>Stage 1 - |
| **For Target 3:**<br>Geog. area: ___<br>Ind. or co. size: ___<br>Pos./Function: ___<br><br>Note: | # of companies in this target | # contacted | # met with | Quality/Status of Contacts<br>Stage 3 -<br>Stage 2 -<br>Stage 1 - |
| **For Target 4:**<br>Geog. area: ___<br>Ind. or co. size: ___<br>Pos./Function: ___<br><br>Note: | # of companies in this target | # contacted | # met with | Quality/Status of Contacts<br>Stage 3 -<br>Stage 2 -<br>Stage 1 - |

Note: In the far right column, __note those contacts you are keeping in touch with on an ongoing basis__:

Stage 1 contacts: People with whom I want to keep in touch—regardless of level or ability to hire.

Stage 2 contacts: The right people at the right levels in the right companies (Potential hiring managers with whom I am keeping in touch.

They may be telling me: I wish I had an opening. If I did, I'd like to hire someone like you.)

Stage 3 contacts: Moving along actual jobs or the possibility of creating a job.

(I aim to have a total of six to ten when I am in stage 3 of my search.)

# Monthly Job-Hunting Calendar

The Five O'Clock Club

| SUNDAY | MONDAY | TUESDAY | WEDNESDAY | THURSDAY | FRIDAY | SATURDAY |
|---|---|---|---|---|---|---|
| ☐ | ☐ | ☐ | ☐ | ☐ | ☐ | ☐ |
| ☐ | ☐ | ☐ | ☐ | ☐ | ☐ | ☐ |
| ☐ | ☐ | ☐ | ☐ | ☐ | ☐ | ☐ |
| ☐ | ☐ | ☐ | ☐ | ☐ | ☐ | ☐ |
| ☐ | ☐ | ☐ | ☐ | ☐ | ☐ | ☐ |
| ☐ | ☐ | ☐ | ☐ | ☐ | ☐ | ☐ |

It's a good idea to have a calendar that you use only for job hunting. That way, you'll clearly see how much effort you have put in as well as the amount of follow-up you plan to do.

Note all interviews (networking/direct contact, job interviews and search firms), mailings and the number mailed, networking follow-up notes written, job follow-up notes written, follow-up calls made, and the dates when you plan to make future calls. You may also list ads answered.

The
Five
O'Clock
Club

# How to Handle Your References

by Wendy Alfus Rothman

*In an exploratory meeting, the ball ends up in the savvy manager's court, which is exactly the intent. An observant manager also gains valuable information about the political lay of the land from such a meeting. The manager should come out with a good sense of how hard a sell the idea is going to be. A great number of objections indicate a tough road but still can be used to develop strategy. Every objection or reservation shows a concern that needs to be taken into account or an agenda item of the manager who is objecting.*
Joel M. DeLuca, Ph.D., *Political Savvy*

---

References are often the last thing you think about during your job search—literally. You expect to be asked for references at the very end of the process, almost as an afterthought. It just doesn't seem that important early on. And after all, you're busy enough thinking about the hiring manager's issues, the company's problems, your own strategy, and the pluses and minuses of your competition. Those are the things that really matter. References are just meant to cement the deal, once the decision to extend an offer has been made. Right?

Wrong. References are not a casual component stuck on at the end of a carefully thought-out job search. Rather, they are another strategic tool that can significantly impact the results of your search, and all of your career management. And while you certainly don't want to give out your references too soon in the interviewing cycle, you absolutely do want to be planning them and preparing them from the very beginning in Phase 1 of your search.

There is a method of handling references—things to pay attention to and situations to watch out for. Let's go through ten basic rules of references.

## Rule #1.
*Don't give out your references too soon.*

Wait until the hiring company is absolutely ready to extend an offer to you before you allow

them to make those contacts.

The people you use as references are very busy. They are doing you a favor every time they answer one of these requests. If the request does not end up leading to a serious job offer, you have unwittingly played a game of the Boy Who Cried Wolf. When the company that is serious about making an offer calls, your references may very well not be willing to extend themselves yet another time. And when they get a lot of calls, they may begin to wonder, "What's wrong with Shirley? Why doesn't she have a job by now?"

## Rule #2.
*Make sure you understand the issues that need to be addressed.*

Often the hiring manager asks for references to check out a nagging doubt he or she may have about you. Perhaps there is an unvoiced concern or undisclosed objection. If a question does exist, it will be within a framework of three categories. The first is whether or not you have the qualifications—the skills and abilities—to get the job done. The second is whether or not you are motivated to get the job done. Do you really want the job? And the third is whether or not you fit into the culture and personality of the hiring company.

It is your responsibility to decide which of these three categories is the one in question when you are asked for a reference. Then choose a person who can address the appropriate issues. After all, your references can support your case, but they cannot create it for you.

So be sure to have your references prepared for each of the three categories. This framework can help you provide better references, and it provides something more: thinking about your skills, motivation and fit can lead to significant insights about whether the company you are considering is really a place where you will be happy and productive.

---

## Rule #3.
*Help your references to help you by providing them with a script.*

There are many reasons you want to prepare a script for your references, and even help them rehearse their lines.

One is that it takes time and skill to prepare an eloquent reference, and many people simply do not have the time or the talent. Offer to assist your references with a script of the points you would like them to cover. Provide specific supporting examples. They will appreciate your taking the time to help them help you.

A second reason to provide a script is that your references may not know what they should say to help your case unless you tell them. Even well-meaning people can actually give counter-productive kudos, if they do not know what concerns the hiring manager has about you, or what issues surround your potential new job. It won't help you land a management position if your reference gives accolades about your ability to take supervision.

Still another reason for scripts is the problem of the reference who fired you, or with whom you have had a difference of opinion. Often, these people would provide you with some sort of reference, but they really don't know what to say that would be sincere yet not too negative. A script provides a more positive response for those who would have been inclined to give you a negative reference. Otherwise, these people can wreak havoc on a potential offer.

If you provide a script, it should include several components.

It should have **a statement of your major strengths**, as well as **examples of those strengths**, tailored to the requirements for the position you want to be offered. Tell your reference the job you are going after and what the new company is looking for. Remind the person of the work you did for him or her that would be of interest to the new company. Let the person know the issues the new company may want to cover.

Your script should also have a prepared response to the question, **"Tell me about some areas for improvement—some weaknesses."** Always try to use a strength to illustrate your area of weakness. For example, you might say something like, "Sometimes I expect too much from the people who report to me—I expect them to be as dedicated as I am." Now, that's not too terrible a weakness! Be sure your reference is prepared for this question, but remind him or her to offer the response only if the question is asked.

You also want to **have a response ready regarding your reason for leaving your prior company**. Again, this needs to be framed positively, and should always be based on the truth. You can often work out an explanation that fits into your long-term plan. ("The company's goals and my career goals are moving in two different directions.") Clearly, you need to think this through and prepare it in advance with your reference.

## Rule #4.
*Select your references strategically.*

From the beginning of your search, think about who might be potential references for each of your targets. Understand what issues are important to your target, and understand what your strengths and weaknesses are in each unique situation. Select references who can support your case to overcome potential obstacles. You may well find that you have different references for each of your targets.

Stage your references so that the hiring company talks to your best ones first. If Bill Good is a better reference than Sally Rough, tell your prospective employer that Sally is tied up in meetings for two weeks, and that Bill is available immediately.

If you do this, be sure to call Sally and tell her that you would like her to be a backup reference. Explain that because you do not expect her to have to provide a primary reference, you indicated that her schedule was very tight for the next few weeks. That way, Sally doesn't feel put

*All managers establish relationships over their careers. A difference between the Savvy and the unsavvy is that the unsavvy form fewer of those relationships. They are also more likely to let relationships fade when they move on to new positions . . . . The savvy managers, on the other hand, consistently seek to build relationships and then keep them up once they move on. It doesn't take much time, just a phone call now and then to ask, How are you doing?*

Joel M. DeLuca, Ph.D., *Political Savvy*

on the spot, and there are no surprises if the new company does make a call.

### Rule #5.
*Ask your references to follow up with you.*

You need to know whether someone was called. Ask your references to let you know when they are contacted. If you have given out three names and none of them has been called within two to three weeks, you are probably not as close to an offer as you think. Call the hiring company and try to uncover any possible hidden objections.

### Rule #6.
*Be sure you follow up with your references.*

Let your references know whether you take the new job, and what you will be doing. Let them know how they helped you, even if you decided not to take the position. This is a great opportunity to keep your network alive and well.

### Rule #7.
*Reciprocate in any way that you can.*

People do not like to feel as though they have been taken advantage of. It is always appropriate to ask whether there is any way that you can be of assistance to the person who has helped you, or even has just agreed to help you. This kind of give-and-take is what networking is all about. Staying in touch with your references is exactly the way you develop long-term relationships.

### Rule #8.
*Develop references as you develop your network—over the long term.*

When you call people to ask whether they will give you references, several things happen.

• You let them know that you are looking for a new position without putting them on the spot by asking for a job.

• You can ask for their opinion about the company in which you are interested, and in so doing learn more. Your references may also have ideas about other companies that would be worth pursuing.

• You let them know that other people are interested in you. It's more likely that people will help you if they know that other professionals are interested in you as well.

• You remind them of your sterling qualities without sounding too much like a braggadocio.

• You flatter them by asking for their help—something people usually love to give.

• You also stay current regarding the whereabouts of your references. This is very important because you eliminate the problem of not being able to locate a particular person who could provide the perfect reference when you need it.

### Rule #9.
*Settle on a mutually agreeable story if you are being fired or if you have had problems with your direct manager. If this is impossible, think of a substitute reference.*

A hiring manager will absolutely want to talk to your immediate boss, or want to know why he or she can't. Scripting will certainly help in this situation (See Rule #3).

I do not recommend fabricating stories. Often what you need to do is determine what the positives really are about why you left your position. If you didn't get along with your boss, you probably had a difference in management style. Perhaps your style is more like the style of the company you are now interested in. Present this as a positive to both the hiring person and the prior boss. Point out that you have learned from your past where you fit and where you don't, and that is why you are so excited about this new opportunity. You see it as a much more appropriate match.

Sometimes it is very difficult to avoid saying something bad about a prior company or manager, yet bad-mouthing companies is viewed as quite unprofessional. If you are asked to give as a reference the name of a former boss with whom you really clashed, don't say how terrible he or she was. Try saying something like this:

"I'll be happy to give you Susan's phone

*The heights by great men reached and kept
Were not attained by sudden flight,
But they, while their companions slept,
Were toiling upward in the night.*
Henry Wadsworth Longfellow

number—I agree you should call her, since I did work for her for two years. I'm sure she will be able to share pertinent information about my management style. Let me remind you that one of the main reasons I am excited about the opportunity with your company is the motivating and enthusiastic attitude of the senior management team which, as we discussed, was not the case in my last job. I think Susan embodies their more stand-offish style, so please keep that in mind when you speak with her."

If there is no way you can risk giving your boss's name as a reference, be prepared with names of peers, subordinates, or your boss's boss as stand-in references.

## Rule #10.
### *DO NOT LIE.*

Do not make up names of people who you once worked for who have now "moved far, far away." Do not create fictitious companies that have now "gone out of business." Do not make up degrees and universities attended. Somehow, some way, it will come back to haunt you. And it is so unnecessary!

There are many stories of people who have a brilliant track record with ten or fifteen years' experience. Then they go after a new job, and lie about having a B.A. They get caught and then are rejected for a terrific job.

Usually the truth is that the degree (or whatever the issue is) was not that critical a component of the job requirements. And even if it were, you need to understand how this requirement relates to job performance. Explore the reasons behind the criteria a company establishes as prerequisites for employment and deal with your shortfalls directly.

If you keep these ten rules in mind, your references will support your job search—not sabotage it. In addition, you will have renewed valuable professional alliances that will continue to serve you throughout your career.

### Reference Case Studies

## CASE STUDY: CHARLEY
### *Don't Give Out Your References Too Soon*

Charley was having a very difficult search. He had several problems: He was working, so his time was limited. He couldn't clarify his targets, so his efforts were haphazard and unfocused. He couldn't put a pitch together, and yet he insisted on doing his search his own way. It simply wasn't working. He couldn't get any momentum going, and he was getting more and more frustrated.

Naturally he was elated when he finally managed to get an actual job interview with a small company in market research, for a sales position. He thought he liked the industry, although he had no idea why the industry might need his skills. He knew even less about the company with which he was to interview, except that they apparently had a job opening.

Nevertheless, he hoped the hiring manager would like him, that he would get an offer, and that he could short-cut the entire search process.

He and the hiring manager, Sheila, met offsite, so Charley did not have the benefit of gaining insights by seeing the company. He had no idea what the flow of traffic was in and out of the location, what the other employees looked like, whether the environment was busy or slow, clean or dirty, corporate or relaxed. He and Sheila talked for close to two hours, but their conversation was primarily about Charley, his life-style, his values, and his career objectives.

Now, to the trained participant at The Five O'Clock Club, Charley was obviously making a lot of mistakes. He hadn't picked a target, he had not developed a search campaign strategy, he had done no research into this industry or this company, he knew absolutely nothing about their issues or concerns. He surely did not know who his competition was or why the job was open in the first place, how many other people had been interviewed, and who the real decision-

*Know how to ask. There is nothing more difficult*
*for some people. Nor for others, easier.*
Baltasar Gracian, *The Art of Worldly Wisdom*

makers were. Still, after the two hours, Sheila asked Charley for his references.

Why would she do that? Charley didn't know if Sheila questioned his skills, motivation or fit. Perhaps the job was impossible to fill, and she simply needed a body. Charley would fit the bill, as long as his references were reasonable. On the other hand, perhaps she really did think he was talented. Charley had no idea. Nor did he have any idea whether he would like the job—he hadn't even seen the office building yet, let alone talked to the people inside with whom he would be spending every day! But Charley wanted the process to be over with, and so he hoped for the best and gave Sheila his references.

Charley called me the next day to express a tiny bit of concern: one of the references he had given might not support the job title Charley claimed to have had, and he wanted to know whether he should call that person, and what he might say. He realized that he would have to explain to his reference what this new opportunity was all about, and how excited he was about it. When I asked him to tell me what he would say in this regard, Charley realized that he couldn't say anything—he had no idea what this opportunity was about at all! How could he ask his reference to support his strengths, when he didn't know what would be expected from him on the job?

Charley started to panic—what could he do? He had already given out the name of his reference. He was sure he would be caught in a foolish lie. He was afraid he might lose an offer from a company he wasn't even sure he wanted to work for in the first place.

As we strategized, Charley calmed down. This wasn't the only company in the world. The job title he had used was not so different from the one he actually had. Nothing catastrophic was going to happen. But he did need to refocus his attention on what the real issues were. And there was obviously a lot more information that he needed that had nothing whatsoever to do with his references.

Rather than call those references to discuss a job he knew nothing about and appear totally foolish, Charley decided to call Sheila instead. He explained that he had been so interested in their conversation, it was only after reflection that he realized there was much they both still needed to know about each other.

"I don't think either one of us is ready yet to seriously discuss an offer, and so I think it is premature to contact my references. After all, they are busy people and so are you. Why don't we get together again in your office and talk more specifically about some of the challenges you are facing and how I might be able to fit in to the company. Then, I can be sure that my references are appropriate and that the move is the right one for both of us."

Well, Sheila saw Charley again, but it turned out that she was not at all interested in him and hadn't been from the beginning of their first meeting. She felt that a good sales person should control the conversation much more than Charley had. She felt that he should have done much more of the questioning, and tried to understand her needs and the goals of the organization. She had been very disappointed in his lack of assertive questioning, and assumed it was due to a lack of experience. Sheila had asked for his references, thinking that his prior bosses would be at the right level for the job she had in mind. She was hoping to recruit them directly, while pretending to call for a reference!

By identifying the objections Sheila had, Charley was able to clarify the strengths he needed to discuss if he were to pursue the bigger target of all market research firms in his geographic area. He began to understand how to position himself in order to be a more attractive sales candidate.

He called his references, but it was not to discuss his old job titles. It was to talk about what traits and skills they felt were important in the industry, and to solicit their views on several different companies. In other words, he used this as an opportunity to do real Phase 1 exploration

*Courage is doing what you are afraid to do.*
*There can be no courage unless you're scared.*
Eddie Rickenbacker

and research. They were happy to share their knowledge with him; Charley sent them sales leads and kept them informed of his progress.

When the time came for a good offer, Charley knew just which references to use. In fact, the job offer came from a lead generated by one of those references!

Charley ended up taking a position with a larger market research firm after a five-month, focused job search. One and a half years after he started, his company bought the firm Sheila had worked for, and they ended up at the same company after all. Except that by the time it happened, Charley had been promoted to sales manager, and Sheila was working for him!

The references that he had contacted for advice and assistance remained close professional allies, and Charley stays in touch with them to this day, sharing information and industry insights.

## CASE STUDY: MITCHELL
### Preparing Your References

Mitchell had been an independent financial planning consultant to small businesses for several years, and was now looking to get back into a corporate environment.

He had targeted several boutique investment firms. His qualifications were outstanding and his case was strong. He had several interviews and always got to the last round . . . and then came in second.

Mitch was puzzled. He knew he came on strong initially, but after that, something was happening that was making him lose the final offers. He needed to find out what it was and correct it. Together we examined what was happening during his last meetings—what he said and what the companies were saying. It turned out that in five out of six instances, he had been asked for references. Right after that, someone else was being offered the job. We decided to examine those references.

They were not the same as those of most people. Since Mitch had been in his own consult-

ing practice for several years, he did not have the typical managers and bosses available for reference. Instead, he was using the presidents and other officers of the companies that were his current and past clients. That seemed okay.

He had called and asked them if they would be willing to serve as references and explained the requirements of each position he was interested in. Each of them assured Mitch that they would provide accolades regarding his professionalism, his financial knowledge, and his skill. "My references are great," he told me. "It couldn't be that."

Nevertheless, something was happening, so I asked Mitch to double check. He reviewed his interview notes from the last company he had been interviewing with. One of the concerns he had written down was that the hiring manager was apparently nervous about bringing someone on board who had been independent for so long. He was afraid that the person might be "unmanageable, too independent, and not a team player."

Mitch thought that he had addressed this issue by verbally reassuring the manager that he was a strong participant in group efforts, but when Mitch followed up he learned that the company had gone with another candidate who was actually *less* qualified than Mitchell. Interestingly enough, the person who did land the job had worked as a project leader in a self-managing team.

Mitch knew he was onto something. He guessed that this team-orientation objection was not an isolated occurrence, and that probably it was a significant factor in all his rejections. Perhaps people were afraid that he really had been independent for too long, and would be difficult to manage.

What could Mitchell say on his own behalf when it wasn't his ability that was in question—it was his willingness to be a team player. He didn't *have* team members to call on since he worked on his own. Or did he?

Mitchell thought about what he did when he was working for his clients. He had to work with

> *Language reflects social reality, and the reality of the pre-nineteenth-century world was that people did not "have" jobs in the fixed and unitary sense; they "did" jobs in the form of a constantly changing string of tasks.*
> William Bridges, *JobShift: How to Prosper in a Workplace Without Jobs*

managers, owners, employees, their banks and loan officers, their insurance agents and accountants. All of these people had different agendas, and different strengths and weaknesses—just like members of work teams. Mitch's position as a consultant was very much like that of the team leader: he didn't make the actual decisions, but rather mobilized divergent groups into action, around a common goal.

Put that way, he had a lot more than verbal reassurance of his teamwork. He had hard evidence of his willingness to be part of a group rather than stand alone.

He called his clients and explained what he needed them to discuss about his work habits when called to provide a reference—not to discuss his financial-planning ability (which had never been in question), but to talk about his ability to cooperate as a team member, to take direction and supervision, and to be a collaborative group player. He selected one of each of the professionals he had worked with, and reminded them of specific instances that they could refer back to.

The end of this story should be that Mitch used these references, and turned his next three interviews into job offers. In fact, that is exactly what happened. The twist on this case study however, is that after contacting all those people for references, they were reminded of what a terrific guy Mitchell really was, and they all actually gave him *more* leads that turned into more consulting opportunities. Mitchell ended up staying in his own consulting firm, expanding his practice, and hiring an associate—starting his *own* team!

---

Not only can references help you overcome objections and position you for an offer, sometimes they can generate new offers themselves.

Remember that a job offer is made through *effective follow-up*. By contacting your references, you are both networking <u>and</u> following up, at the same time. Look at what happened to Phillip.

## CASE STUDY: PHILLIP
### *Following Up with References Can Lead to New Job Offers*

Phil had worked as a product manager for a pharmaceutical company in New Jersey for six months before his mother became ill. He had to return home to take care of her, and home was in Denver, Colorado. At first, his boss, Ray, granted him a leave of absence. It soon became clear that Phil's stay in Denver would be prolonged, and Raymond had no choice but to hire someone new. It was unfortunate and neither party wanted the relationship to end, but it just couldn't be helped. Ray found another project manager, and Phil found project work in Denver. The two lost touch as they went on with their lives and careers.

Thirteen months later, Phil's mother was fully recovered and he decided to return to New Jersey. He began a job search and interviewed at several pharmaceutical firms. One company was ready to extend an offer to him, and Claire (the hiring manager) asked for his references. Phil thought of Ray, since they had enjoyed an excellent professional relationship and it was also his last business contact in New Jersey.

Claire called Ray. He was delighted to hear that Phil had returned to the area. The reference he provided was outstanding, and started Ray thinking . . .

Claire called Phil the following day to arrange a time for him to come in and receive a formal offer. Phil was thrilled, but had actually changed his mind about the job! It turned out that Ray, after receiving Claire's phone call, decided to call Phil himself. Ray had been searching for a project director, and Phil was a natural choice. It seemed so obvious that Ray should think of Phil himself, but if he hadn't been called to provide a reference, the two might never have hooked up once again.

---

Both Mitch and Phil had good references. Not everyone is so fortunate. What happens if your references are somewhat less than laudatory?

## CASE STUDY: SUSAN
### Handling Negative References

Susan was going to get an offer to be a production coordinator for a company in teleconferencing technologies. She had been searching for this position for four months, after being fired from her prior company—a long-distance carrier where she had been a director of creative services.

Her prior boss had let Susan go primarily because of a "fit" issue. Susan was a creative person and preferred to work fairly autonomously. Her boss was a very structured person who checked everyone's work on an hourly basis, and ruled with an iron fist.

One day Susan and this boss had an argument; the manager berated Susan in front of her peers, and Susan retaliated by complaining to the senior vice president, who was annoyed by this petty problem, and felt it to be an inappropriate communication. He told Susan's boss that he did not want to bothered with these kinds of issues, and to "handle any insubordination appropriately." Susan was fired. These are not the circumstances under which you want to give a reference!

Susan realized this was an opportunity to find a place where she really did fit, and so she built this experience into her job search. During her interviews, when people asked her why she was looking, she told them that she wanted to work in a different environment. More specifically, she wanted to a part of a company that wanted independent but responsible people—people that were trusted to complete projects on time without requiring a great deal of supervision. She let her prospects know that her prior company was very hierarchical, and that she frankly did not fit in; that she had in fact left because of a culture fit.

When asked for references, Susan reiterated the circumstances that had prompted her to look for a new position in the first place. "My manager will feel that I was too independent and that I

didn't work well in a corporate hierarchy. As we've already discussed, I would agree with that assessment! I believe that is also the reason we get along so well. I'm sure you will find that my prior manager has no complaint whatsoever with my performance and ability."

Susan also called the person who had fired her. She informed him that he would be getting a reference phone call, and told him what she had already told her prospective employers. "When they call, I don't want you to be in an uncomfortable position, nor do I want to lose the job opportunity. Perhaps you could tell them that you are about to go into a meeting, but can talk for a few moments. I thought you could say that we did in fact have a cultural fit problem, primarily because your company is quite structured and I am not. However my work performance was always satisfactory, and given the right personality variable you would recommend me for a position. Then if they want to continue the conversation, you can always say you have to go into your meeting."

Susan was uncomfortable making that call, but her former employer was happy to receive it. He had no interest in Susan's remaining unemployed, but he never would have known what to say on such a call.

Susan received the offer, ultimately she made amends with her former employer, and she found a position with a company where she truly did fit!

---

Wendy Alfus Rothman is president of Wenroth Consulting, managing director at Advantage Staffing Services, Inc., and one of the original counselors at The Five O'Clock Club.

---

*The first principle of ethical power is Purpose. . . .
By purpose, I mean your objective or intention—
something toward which you are always striving.
Purpose is something bigger. It is the picture
you have of yourself—the kind of person you want to
be or the kind of life you want to lead.*
Kenneth Blanchard and Norman Vincent Peale,
*The Power of Ethical Management*

# PART FOUR

## GETTING WHAT YOU WANT

### THE FIVE O'CLOCK CLUB APPROACH TO INTERVIEWING AND NEGOTIATING

# Basic Interview Techniques

*Just know your lines and
don't bump into the furniture.*
Spencer Tracy's advice on acting

---

*Make yourself necessary to someone.*
Ralph Waldo Emerson

---

*I have always tried to be true to myself,
to pick those battles I felt were important.*
Arthur Ashe

An interview is not simply a conversation; it's show time, folks. You will be competing against people who are well-rehearsed and know their lines.

### Develop Your Lines

In an interview, an inability to express yourself clearly is worse than a lack of experience. Refine your sales pitch by listing on a 3 X 5 card:

- the main reason the employer would want to hire you;
- what you have to offer in the way of experience, credentials, and personality;
- two key accomplishments to support your interest in this position;
- an answer to what you think might be the employer's main objection to you, if any;
- a statement of why you would want to work for this company.

Keep this card in your pocket or purse and review it just before going in for the interview so that you will know your lines.

### Look and Act the Part

Remember, this is show biz. Even if you don't feel self-confident, act as if you do. If you come in looking defeated, like a loser, why would anyone want to hire you? *Act* as if you are successful and feel good about yourself, and you will increase your chances of actually *feeling* that way. Enthusiasm counts. Every manager is receptive to someone who is sincerely interested in the company and the position.

### During the Interview
### —Play the Part of a Consultant

Pretend for a minute that you own a small consulting company. When you first meet a prospective client, you want to probe to better understand the problems this person is facing. If the client has no problems, or if you cannot solve them, there is no place for you.

You are also there to sell your company. Therefore, as the manager talks about company problems, you reveal your own company's experience and credentials by asking questions or by telling

---

*The people you want to reach, whether they're your coworkers, your boss or an organizational president, should be viewed as distinct target audiences that require different approaches and strategies.*

Jeffrey P. Davidson, Management World, September/October, 1987

how you have handled similar situations. You want to see how your company fits in with this company.

If the conversation goes astray, lead it back to the topics on your 3 X 5 card—the work you would do for them and your abilities. That way, you can make your points in context.

It is your responsibility to reassure the hiring manager that everything will work out. The manager does not want to be embarrassed later by discovering he's made a hiring mistake. It is almost as if you are patting the manager on the arm and saying, "There, there. Everything will be just fine. You can count on me."

> ## If the interviewer has no problems, or if you cannot solve them, there is no place for you.

You must display self-confidence in your ability to handle the position. If you are not confident, why should the hiring manager take a chance on you? If you want the job, take a stand and say that you believe it will work.

If you are asked how you would handle a situation, reassure the manager that even though you do not know specifically what you would do (because, after all, you are not on the job yet), you know you can figure it out because:

• It won't be a problem. I'm good at these things.

• I'm very resourceful. Here's what I did as company controller. . .

• I've been in that situation before. I can handle your situation even though I don't know the specifics.

Let the manager air his or her doubts about you. If you are told what these reservations are, you can reassure the manager right then, or you can mull it over later and reassure the manager in writing.

Do not appear to be "shopping around." Be sincerely interested in this particular company—at least during the interview.

Follow up on your meetings. Address the important issues, stress your interest and enthusiasm for the job, and state your major selling points—especially since you now know what is of interest to the interviewer.

## Questions You Might Ask in an Interview

You are there not only to answer the interviewer's questions, but also to make sure you get the information you need. Ask questions that are appropriate. What do you really want to know? Here are a few to get you thinking in the right direction:

### QUESTIONS TO ASK PERSONNEL

• Can you tell me more about the responsibilities of the job?
• What skills do you think would be most critical for this job?
• Is there a current organization chart available for this area?
• What happened to the person who held this job before?
• What kinds of people are most successful in this area?
• What do you see as the department's strengths and weaknesses?

### QUESTIONS TO ASK MANAGERS (AND PERHAPS PEERS)

• What are the key responsibilities of the job?
• What is the most important part of the job?
• What is the first problem that would need the attention of the person you hire?
• What other problems need attention now? Over the next six months?
• How has this job been performed in the past?
• Are there other things you would like someone to do that are not a formal part of the job?
• What would you like to be able to say about the new hire one year from now?
• What significant changes do you see in the future?
• May I ask what your background is?
• What do you find most satisfying about working here? Most frustrating?
• How would you describe your management style?
• How is the department organized?
• May I meet the other people who work in the area?
• How is one's performance evaluated? By whom? How often?
• What skills are in short supply here?

---

> **Follow-up will dramatically increase the number of job offers you get. It is one of the most powerful tools you have to influence the situation.**

Follow up on your meetings. Address the important issues, stress your interest and enthusiasm for the job, and state your major selling points—especially since you now know what is of interest to the interviewer.

> **Be sure to record every networking and job interview on the Interview Record.**

### Do Your Homework

Before the interview, research the company and the industry. If you're asked why you are interested in them, you will have your answer. Do library research. Call the company's public relations department and ask for literature or an annual report. Ask others about the company. Show up early and read company literature in the reception area, talk to the receptionist, and observe the people. Get a feel for the place.

### The Rehearsal

*It may sound like a contradiction, but you achieve spontaneity on the set through preparation of the dialogue at home. As you prepare, find ways of making your responses seem newly minted, not preprogrammed.*
Michael Caine, *Acting in Film*

Even experienced job hunters need practice. Each interview smooths out your presentation and responses. As you get better, your self-confidence grows.

By now, you've had networking or information-gathering interviews. You will have practiced talking about yourself and will have information about your area of interest and the possibilities for someone like you.

When I was unemployed, I had lots of interviews, but I was not doing well in them. I was under so much stress that I kept talking about what *I* wanted to do rather than what I could do *for the company*. I knew better, but I could not think straight. An old friend, who belongs to The Five O'Clock Club, helped me develop my "lines" for my 3X5 card. Then we practiced. After that, my interviews went well.

### Get a Job Offer

*To take what there is and use it, without waiting forever in vain for the preconceived—to dig deep into the actual and get something out of that —this doubtless is the right way to live.*
Henry James

Sincerely intend to tun each interview into a solid job offer. Do your best to make the position and the pay into something acceptable. Make the most of each interview. Negotiate changes in the job itself. Suggest additional things you can do for the company—jobs often can be upgraded a level or two. Or perhaps the manager could refer you to another area of the company. You should make every effort to turn an interview into a reasonable job offer.

- This is an opportunity to practice your negotiation skills and increase the number of interviews you turn into offers. You can always turn the job down later.
- Getting job offers helps your self-esteem. You can say you received a number of offers, but they didn't seem right for you. This puts you in a stronger negotiating position.
- Even if you turn down an offer, stay friendly with the hiring manager. This may lead to another offer later that is more appropriate.
- When you get an offer you are not sure about, say that you have a few other things you must attend to, but will get back to them in a week. Then contact other companies that were of real interest to you. Tell them you have received an offer but were hoping to work something out with them.

---

They may tell you to take the other offer—or they may consider you more seriously because the other offer makes you more valuable. Sometimes knowing you got another offer is the only thing that will make a company act.

• You may be surprised: perhaps what you originally found objectionable can be changed to your liking. If you end the process too early, you lose the possibility of changing the situation to suit you. Having a job created especially for you is the best outcome.

### Coming in As a Freelancer or Consultant

Some job hunters are willing to work for a company as a freelancer or consultant and hope the company will later put them on the payroll. This rarely happens. If you are doing a great job for little money, the company has no incentive to change that arrangement. If you want to be "on salary," consult only if you are sure you have the self-discipline to continue job hunting after you start consulting.

You can parlay a consulting assignment into a full-time job at a decent salary if you do outstanding work on the assignment, and get a decent offer somewhere else. Then tell your manager that you enjoy what you are doing and would like to be a salaried employee—but have received another job offer. You would prefer working for his company, but this temporary arrangement is not what you want.

### Aiming for the Second Job Out

Sometimes the job you really want is too big a step for you right now. Instead of trying to get it in one move, go for it in two moves. Make your next job one that will qualify you for the job you really want.

### What Do You Really Want?

*I am proud of the fact that I never invented weapons to kill.*
Thomas A. Edison

*If I had known, I should have become a watchmaker.*
Albert Einstein,
on his role in making the atomic bomb possible.

To get ahead, many people compromise what they want. A lot of compromising can result in

material success but also feelings of self-betrayal and not knowing who you really are.

It can be difficult to hold on to your values and live the kind of life that is right for you. You may feel there is no hope for change. If you are really honest, you may discover that you have tried very little to make changes. Ask yourself what you have done to improve your situation.

Deciding where you want to work is a complex problem. Many unhappy professionals, managers, and executives admit they made a mistake in deciding to work for their present companies. They think they should have done more research and more thinking before they took the job.

The stress of job hunting can impair your judgment. You may make a decision without enough information simply because you want to "get a job." Ego can also be involved: you want to get an offer quickly so you can tell others and yourself that you are worth something. Or you may deceive yourself into thinking you have enough information. Even if you are normally a good decision-maker, you can short-circuit the decision-making process when it comes to your own career.

You will make better decisions when you are not deciding under pressure. Start now to see what your options are. Then you already will have thought them through in case you have to make a move quickly later.

Objectively evaluate the information you come up with, and develop contingency plans. Decide whether to leave your present position, and evaluate new opportunities. List the pros and cons of each possibility for you and those close to you.

You may decide, for example, that a certain position is higher level, higher paying, and more prestigious, but you will have less time for your family, and the job will make demands on your income because you will have to take on a more expensive lifestyle. You may even decide that you don't like the kind of work, the conditions, or the people, or that your lack of leisure time will push you farther away from the way you want to live.

Depending on your values, the job may be worth it or not. If you list the pros and cons, you are more likely to adhere to your decision and have fewer regrets. You are more likely to weigh the tradeoffs, and perhaps think of other alternatives. You will decide what is important to you. You will have fewer negative surprises later, and will be warned of areas where you may need more information. You will make better decisions and have more realistic expectations about the future.

## What If Your Interviews Are Not Turning into Job Offers?

*If one man says to thee, "Thou art a donkey," pay no heed. If two speak thus, purchase a saddle.*
The Talmud

*Listen to gather better information.* You may find that your target market is declining, or that you don't have the required background, or whatever. One of my clients kept saying that managers insulted her. If you have the same experiences again and again, find out what you are doing wrong.

*Perhaps you are unconsciously turning people down.* A job hunter may make unreasonable demands because, deep inside, he or she knows there are things dramatically wrong with a situation. The requests for more money or a better title are really to make up for the unacceptable working conditions. Then the company rejects the applicant. One job hunter thought he was turned down for the job. In reality, *he* turned down the job. He did not let an offer happen because he knew the job was not right, and he made it fall through. There is nothing wrong with this—so long as he knows he could have had a job offer if he had wanted one.

Job hunters are under tremendous pressure to answer to a lot of people who want to know "how your job hunt is going." If you say you are still looking and have not gotten any offers, you may feel bad. That's another reason why you may want to get a few offers—even though you are not interested in those particular jobs. On the other hand, if your job hunt seems to be going very quickly, you may not want to waste your time on practice offers.

*Make sure you are addressing the company's problems—not your own.* A major mistake that I have made myself is focusing on what I wanted rather than on what the company or the manager needed.

*Perhaps you are not talking to the right people.* Are you interviewing with people two levels higher than you are—those in a position to hire you? If you are spending a lot of time talking to people at your own level, you can learn about the field, but this is unlikely to result in job offers.

*If you don't know why, ask them.* If appropriate, you may want to call a few of the people with whom you interviewed to find out why you did not get the job. If you are really stuck and feel you are not interviewing well, this can be very valuable feedback for you. You may even be able to turn a negative situation around.

## Do Your Best, Then Let It Go

*. . . you ought to say, "If it is the Lord's will."*
James 4:15

You are trying to find a match between yourself and a company. You are not going to click with everyone, any more than everyone is going to click with you. Don't expect every interview to turn into a job offer. The more interviews you have, the better you will do at each one.

And don't punish yourself later. Do your best, and then do your best again.

Hang in there. Get a lot of interviews. Know your lines. And don't bump into the furniture. You will find the right job. As M. H. Anderson said: "If at first you don't succeed, you are running about average."

---

*So to avoid all that horror, prepare. Apart from anything else, preparation uses up a lot of the nervous energy that otherwise might rise up to betray you. Channel that energy; focus it into areas that you control.*

*The first step in preparation is to learn your lines until saying them becomes a predictable reflex. And don't mouth them silently; say them aloud until they become totally your property. Hear yourself say them, because the last thing you want is the sound of your own voice taking you by surprise or not striking you as completely convincing.*

Michael Caine, *Acting in Film*

# Difficult Interview Questions and Possible Answers

> Do not allow the interview to get offtrack. When the interviewer brings up something that takes you in a direction in which you don't want to go, briefly give a response that satisfies the interviewer, and then *get back ontrack*. Give your answer, and then say, for example, "But I really wanted to tell you about a special project I worked on." It is *your* responsibility to get the conversation back ontrack.

*A sudden, bold, and unexpected question doth many times surprise a man and lay him open.*
Francis Bacon, "Of Cunning"

Business is a game, and interviewing is part of the game. You are asked a question to see how well you handle it—and to see how well you play the game. This is not like a discussion with a friend. Don't take questions literally.

For example, if the interviewer asks you why you didn't go to college, should you tell the truth? such as:

- I came from a town where no one went to college, or
- My mother died and I had to help out, or
- I didn't have the money.

These answers are negative and also take you both away from what should be the main discussion: the company's needs and how you can help.

The interviewer is not interested in you and your mother. There is a job to fill. Talking about certain subjects weakens your position—regardless of who brought them up. Keep the interview positive, and do not discuss subjects that are offtrack.

A businesslike answer, however, moves the interview along. Many times hiring managers say to me, "Why did Joe (the applicant) have to tell me that? I was ready to hire him, but now I can't.

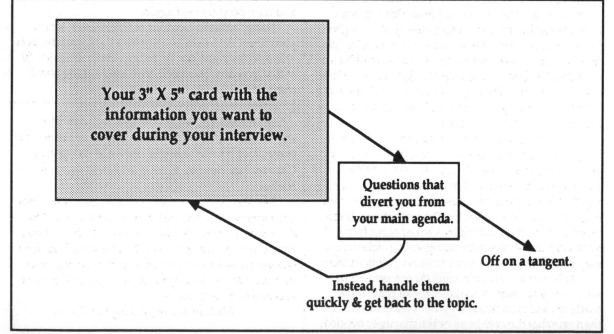

Your 3" X 5" card with the information you want to cover during your interview.

Questions that divert you from your main agenda.

Off on a tangent.

Instead, handle them quickly & get back to the topic.

*Midway in our life's journey, I went astray from the straight road
and woke to find myself alone in a dark wood.*
Dante, *The Inferno*

When my boss confronts me about Joe's lack of college, I don't have a good answer."

Some job hunters insist on being "honest." They think, I'll just tell them the way it is, and if they don't hire me, then so be it. These job hunters are putting their responsibility on the interviewer. We've all had problems. The interviewer doesn't have to hear about them.

Let's try the question again—from a responsible, businesslike point of view.

Lettice: *Let me play the interviewer for once: you be the victim.*
Peter Schaeffer, *Lettice & Vovage*

### Why didn't you go to college?

"I like to be out there doing things. I thought about college a few times (or: I took a few courses), but I wanted to get more done. And that's what my bosses have always said: I'm someone who gets things done. They've all been happy with me."

Briefly and politely handle those questions that might take you off course. Do not go into long discussions, but smoothly move the conversation back to the company's needs or your abilities—the things on your 3X5 card that you had planned to cover. Give your answer, and then say, for example, "but I really wanted to tell you about a special project I worked on." It is your responsibility to get the conversation back on track.

Let's try a few others, but remember that you must find your own answers depending on your situation.

### What would you like to be doing five years from now?

"Actually, I'd like to do the best job I can possibly do in the position we're talking about right now. I know that if I do a great job, good things will happen to me later. They always have."

### Tell me about yourself.

See Your Two-Minute Pitch.

### Tell me about the worst boss you've ever had.

No matter what your bosses have been like: "I've been really lucky. I've been blessed with good bosses. They've all been different, but I've learned from each of them."

### Why are you looking?

"My company is going through a reorganization. I had the option of taking another job internally, but I decided to look elsewhere."

Or

"X company has been great for me, but the career possibilities in the areas that interest me are extremely limited."

Or

"Perhaps you've heard that the _____ industry has been going through a major restructuring. I was caught along with three thousand others."

Or

Your own answer for this one.

### How would you handle this?

The interviewer describes a problem situation and asks how you would handle it. You can't think that quickly.

"I'm not sure. I'm the type who really likes to think things through. I've been up against problems like this before, such as when we were behind schedule at X company. I thought about the problem, and quickly decided we should do a,b,c. This reduced our processing time and everyone was happy.

"Everywhere I've worked, I've been able to assess situations and resolve them, and I'd do the same for you. I don't know how to answer your question at the moment, but I know I would handle the problem the way I have handled things in the past. I have a good track record."

### What are your greatest weaknesses?

After taking time to mull it over:
"Actually, I can't think of any work-related weakness. My bosses have always thought I was great. I'm the kind not only to do my own job, but also to

*There are no hopeless situations. There are only men
who have grown hopeless about them*
Clare Booth Luce, *Europe in the Spring*

notice what else needed to be done in other areas and pitch in to help."

Or, name a weakness and show how you have resolved it, such as:
"Sometimes I get impatient with people because I want the job to get done, but I make sure I find out what's going on and help them with whatever may be stopping them."

### What is your current salary?

See Salary Negotiation.

### How long have you been unemployed?

If you've been unemployed awhile, and you answer, "twenty-six months," how likely are you to be hired? I have run job-hunt groups of people who have been unemployed two years or more. The first thing we work on is an answer to this question.

From a moral point of view, I must help these people develop a good story so they can get back to work. It would be cruel for me to insist they tell the truth. Who will hire an applicant who says, "When I was fired, I got depressed for six months and couldn't move, and then my mother got sick and I had to help. By then, I had been unemployed eleven months, and no one would hire me. I'm hoping you will give me chance."

No one will give this person a chance, and that makes sense to me.

By "telling the truth," this job hunter is saying: "I've had all these problems, but I'm better now. Will you risk your business for me?" It's not fair to burden the interviewer. All the interviewer wants to do is fill a job—not save lives.

Develop a good answer you can live with. Think of what you have actually been doing. Have you been working on your computer? Helping at your church or synagogue? Helping friends with their businesses? Most people can think of something they've been doing—even something little— that they can build a story around.

If you really haven't been doing anything at all, then go *do something*. You are unlikely to interview

well if you haven't been out there at all. Get your adrenalin going. Walk dogs, pick strawberries, usher at church. Get active.

Better yet: learn a new skill. Try computers. Volunteer your skills, or get paid something nominal. You might even consider saying you were paid for volunteer work, if you think they would back you up. Then think up a good story:

1. "I've actually been *looking* only a month or so. After I left X company, I spent some time working on a special project for a small company."

Or

2. "I've been looking only a few weeks now. After working for more than twenty years, this was my first time off, and I took advantage of the time to (fix up my house, take care of a sick familiy member, learn tax accounting, etc.). I was glad to have the opportunity to (help out, learn something new, etc.). But now I'm ready to get back to work and put in another twenty years."

Or

3. Take the work you've done:
"I've been doing public relations work for a small firm. I thought it would be fun to try after so many years with a big corporation, but now I know I like corporate life and I want to get back."

If your answers aren't working, and seem to be causing you not to get hired, change them.

---

*Shy persons often act like they were captured
and are being interrogated.*
Garrison Keillor

*We can become anything. That is why injustice is impossible here. There may be the accident of birth, there is no accident of death. Nothing forces us to remain what we were.*
John Berger, *Pig Earth*

---

*Each handicap is like a hurdle in a steeplechase, and when you ride up to it, if you throw your heart over, the horse will go along, too.*
Lawrence Bixby, "Comeback from a Brain Operation," *Harper's*, Nov., 1952

---

*A man's accomplishments in life are the cumulative effect of his attention to detail.*
John Foster Dulles,
Quoted by Leonard Mosley, *Dulles*

---

*You can never enslave somebody who knows who he is.*
Alex Haley

---

*Here's a little number I do before a long take: take a slow deep breath in, then bend over and let your arms dangle, really relaxed. Straighten up slowly, breathing out gently and evenly. This exercise relaxes you, helps concentration and gives you control. . . . it gets the oxygen to the brain. You feel and look like a twit, panting away, but you find you get a rush to your head, your eyes begin to sparkle a bit, and you're ready to play an energetic scene, mental or physical. Just be careful not to overdo the panting or you will hyperventilate and pass out.*
Michael Caine, *Acting in Film*

---

*If they ask if you own a horse, say yes. If they ask if you are a horse, say yes. And you'll learn how to do it that night.*
Robert Parrish,
Award-winning film editor-director.
Advice he received from his mother
Quoted in *The New York Times*

---

**M**ost people think job hunting consists of lining up interviews and then being brilliant. But there's more to the process than that. And there's much more that you can do to influence the outcome.

## Consultative Sale

The interview is only the beginning of the job search. Go into it to learn—not just to sell. When job hunters go into the interview selling themselves rather than giving and getting information, they may be lucky and get the job. On the other hand, if they need to do some follow-up to keep the job prospect alive, they are usually lacking in the information needed to decide what to do next.

When preparing for the interview, remember to act like a consultant. Think about them first, and then think about yourself. Certainly you want to look the part, not ramble, present yourself clearly, understand their needs, and handle the tricky questions. But you can go a lot further.

## With Whom Will You Meet?

If you were invited to a business meeting that was going to take place next week, you would naturally want to know who else would be there, and you might want to know something about them, such as:

- their names and job titles;
- the issues important to each of them;
- what they are like;
- their ages; and
- the length of time they have been with the company.

Yet most job hunters go into interviews—which, of course, are business meetings—unprepared, knowing little about the people. As John Leonard, a Five O'Clock Club counselor, suggests, it is helpful to your self-esteem to think of interviews as meetings, and even refer to them that way.

## Ask the Person Who Arranged the Meetings

To be better prepared, ask whoever set up the meeting—whether it was personnel, the hiring manager, a search firm, or a secretary—to give you the information you need. You can say, "I'm ex-

*If you have an important point to make, don't try to be subtle or clever. Use a pile driver.*
*Hit the point once. Then come back and hit it again. Then hit it a third time—a tremendous whack.*
Winston Churchill, On public speaking, quoted by Edward, Duke of Windsor, *A King's Story*

cited about the meeting next week, and want to prepare. I'd like to know something about the people I'll be meeting and the issues that are of concern to them." You may not find out everything you would like to, but even a little bit of information will help.

## Think About Their Issues

Then try to go beyond what you have been told. Think about additional issues that are likely to be important to each person. Decide how you will address these issues. A financial person, for example, will most likely be concerned about the bottom line. An operations person, a marketing person, or someone in human resources will probably have different concerns.

You can also think about a person's concerns based on his or her position in the hierarchy. People higher up are generally more concerned about the direction of the department, division or company, while those lower down are usually more concerned about the day-to-day workings of the job. From their own perspective, each person will care about whether or not you can do the job, and perhaps whether or not you will fit in.

In addition, do library research. Find out about how the company and the position you are interviewing for may be impacted by the facts or trends you uncover. Finally, gather information from other individuals who may know about the company, or who may actually work there.

## During the Meeting

To better understand the situation, you may need to find out more about their operation, how they are organized, their visions for the department, and the problems they are facing.

---

**Be sure to ask where they are in the hiring process, how many other people they are considering, and how you compare with them. If you don't know something about your competition, you are less likely to win.**

---

## Like a Game of Chess

In chess, the idea is to think a number of moves ahead. Based on what you know about the person you are playing with, what you know about yourself, and what you know about the game, as a chess player you would form a hypothesis about what the other player's moves are likely to be. Then you would plan what to do in response to those moves.

So, too, based on the information you have gathered, you can form a hypothesis about the person with whom you will be meeting. Then you can envision various scenarios and your strategy for each in advance. Even if you are incorrect, you will do better in the meeting than if you simply went in there cold.

If you have thought all this through, you can be more observant about other things during the interviews. Afterwards, you can reflect: What was the mood of the meeting? What issues actually were important to this person? What were the pluses—the reason that he or she might want to have me on board? What were the objections—the reason that he or she might not want to have me on board? What would the next steps be to move me along in the process? The work you will do next—the follow-up—is covered in great detail later.

## Most Job Hunters Try to Close Too Soon

Job hunters are under a lot of pressure. When they are going in for their first meeting, everyone says: "I hope you get the job." As your career coach, I hope you *don't*. It is unlikely that you will get an offer for a good job after just one meeting. I would wonder what is wrong with the company: are they the type that hires easily and fires easily?

Instead of trying to land a job immediately, conduct yourself at the first interview so that they will want you back for a second one. Get enough information so that you can follow up intelligently. It is not uncommon in today's market to have twelve to fifteen meetings at one company for one job. You may have fewer, but don't count on it.

Instead, plan to be in this for the long run with this company, and with six to ten other companies.

## Hiring Someone May Not Be Their Most Important Issue

The average job hunter goes into the interview saying, "I sure hope you want somebody like me, and here are my credentials."

This may not be the issue. The issue may be whether or not they should start a new system, for example, and how they should go about it. Until they have figured this out, they won't know who would be right for the job. Address the issue that's bothering them rather than the issue that's bothering you (that is, getting a job).

If they don't know whether or not they want to start a new system, you can say: "I've been sitting here thinking about your new system and how it should be done."

If you can be as objective as possible—taking the stance of coaching them and helping them figure out their problem—you will stand a much better chance of getting the position.

## The First Two Minutes

Some say that the hiring decision is made during the first two minutes. While it is true that they will quickly decide against you if you look like a slob or tell an dumb joke, the average job hunter has many more chances than the first two minutes. In fact, by following The Five O'Clock Club approach, you can turn around a situation that normally would have ended in failure.

## CASE STUDY: DOROTHY
*Overcoming Their Objections*

Dorothy, a reserved, but highly intelligent and refined woman, was interviewing for a position as a consultant. She prepared thoroughly, dressed in a manner that she thought was appropriate, and conducted the meeting the best way she could.

She asked them if there was any reason that they might be hesitant to bring her on board compared with some of the other people they had seen. The interviewer responded that she was afraid that Dorothy would not come across as strong enough in her meetings with prospective clients: "In this business, you need to wow them."

When Dorothy did her follow-up letter, she stressed how successful she had been in the past with clients. She asked for another meeting.

This time she dressed in a "power" suit—a red one that would have been inappropriate for a first interview, and conducted herself very differently. The interviewer said she wondered why she had ever thought those negative things because they obviously were not true. Dorothy got the job and was very successful.

## CASE STUDY: BOB
*Prepared for the Meetings*

Bob, a marketing executive, had been looking for a job for a while when I met him, and he was very tired. He was now applying for a plum marketing job at a major information-services company, and was going in for his initial meeting.

Before the meeting, he researched to find out what was going on in the company. He formed a hypothesis about why they might have wanted to see him. He prepared his 3"X5" card to address the issues he thought would be important to them, and wrote out a two-minute pitch specifically for this company.

At this first meeting, he probed to find out the problems the company faced. He also tried to get a feel for the company culture.

When Bob had interviewed at other companies, they loved his ability to think up new product ideas. But he learned that this company already had plenty of new products; they wanted someone who could make their products successful.

Bob did a thorough follow-up after the first round of interviews. He addressed the issues that were important to each person with whom he met, reminded each of the positives they found in him, handled the negatives (the reasons why each person might not want to have him on board). He decided that his next step should be to meet more people.

## The Second Round of Interviews

Bob was called back to meet with five more people. Before the meetings, he asked their names and titles, and found out a little about each person, including the issues that might be important to him or her, and the number of years he or she had been

*If you don't go, you'll never know. You have to not look at it like a rejection.*
*There are so many reasons you're not picked that you can't even worry about it.*
Robert DeNiro, actor

with the company.

Bob typed up a sheet with every name and job title and a hypothesis about what each person's concerns might be, how he could address those concerns, and the questions he wanted to ask each person. His sheets included, in brief:
—the head of sales, who Bob thought might be threatened by a new marketing person;
—the head of finance, who would probably be concerned about the profitability of the new products;
—the head of operations, who might be worried about being ignored by sales and marketing;
—the head of human resources, who may be concerned about how well Bob would fit in; and
—his future boss, the head of all marketing. (Bob had prepared three pages of notes on this person!)

Rather than going into each meeting cold, Bob had hypotheses and solutions in mind. Thus he would be in a position to have the best meetings possible. In addition to the questions he designed specifically for each individual, he asked them all:
• What would you like from whomever you hire for the new job?
• What are the things you would be afraid he or she might do in the new marketing position?
• How could the new person make your life easier?
• What are your most important concerns about this job and the new hire?

He also asked questions that had to do specifically with this company, and the job, such as:
• Who are your key competitors for these new products?
• Have you targeted new growth industries?
• I've heard that your company wants to move towards greater predictive offerings. Is this true? Have you been successful?

He also asked questions having to do with organizational issues, such as:
• The job seems to be in a state of flux. What is your impression of it?
• How would the new person work with each of the department heads?
• What would you like to see this person accomplish after the first year? After three to four years?

• What support could the new person look forward to from you?
• Would the new person work only within this one division, or explore appropriate opportunities with other divisions?

In addition, Bob asked other selected people:
• Where are they in the hiring process?
• How many others are they considering?
• How do I stack up against them?

Bob treated everyone he met as an individual to be reckoned with and courted. He handled them all differently. **His goal was to have each person see him as the ideal candidate.** To do this, he probed to understand thoroughly the situation for each of them.

During all this, Bob had to resist his natural tendency to think up new product ideas, since this was not something they wanted.

---

Don't ask: "Is there anything I can do to convince you that I'm the right person?" The answer is always no. Decide for yourself what you must do to convince them.

---

### Problem Areas

There were a few problem areas:
• Bob's future boss seemed weak and might be threatened by him. Bob had to reassure the boss in his follow-up that he would be a support and not a threat.
• Bob was not happy with the way he had come across to the operations head. When he wrote his follow-up, he said he was not pleased with the way he had addressed some issues, and went into great detail explaining his position.

Bob was able to write a very tailored follow-up to each person only because he had thoroughly prepared—he also took notes during the meetings so he would accurately remember what each person said.

Bob asked to meet with his future boss again to discuss some details, and followed up in writing again after that meeting. Since this was a protracted process, Bob decided the human resources person, who was smart and also open, was the best one to

*The meeting of two personalities is like the contact of two chemical substances;*
*if there is any reaction, both are transformed.*
Carl Jung, *Modern Man in Search of a Soul*

keep in touch with for the status of the situation. In addition to all of his follow-up in writing, he wanted to have a feel for how things were going so that he could decide whether additional effort would be needed—for instance, if another candidate were to enter the race.

## Round Three

Bob was called back for another round of meetings, this time with the head of management information services, the division head, and the human resources manager. When he went back for this round of interviews, Bob made a point of stopping in to see his future boss, and also the operations head—to keep the contacts alive.

---

**Your goal is to have each person be an advocate of having you on board. If there is anyone who objects to you, make sure you handle it now.**

---

## And Then the Wait...

Human resources had already asked for six to eight references, and had checked them out. Everything was fine. The head of human resources said, "They want you. In five years, I've never seen such enthusiasm. I'm sure they're about to make you an offer. Are you interested? When do you think you could start?"

Then suddenly everything was put on hold for seven weeks while the company decided to "re-engineer" (reorganize). They assured Bob that everything was okay, and that he would be happy with the results—especially the money.

But Bob panicked. He couldn't stand the stress any more. He had been in search a long time, and his nerves were giving way. He was anxious to force their hand. If they wanted him, they could make him an offer now. What on earth could make them wait for seven more weeks?

## Don't Force It; Instead, Make Sure You Have Six to Ten Things in the Works

As his career coach, it was all I could do to get Bob to focus on the rest of his search while he stayed in touch with them. Because he had such a good relationship with the human resources manager, Bob mostly spoke with that person. For the next seven weeks, the manager continued to assure Bob that things were going well, and he should just hang in there.

Bob bravely focused on the rest of his search. He said I couldn't possibly imagine the strain he was under. He told me of his daughter's health problems at home.

I warned him that the strain he was under now would be nothing compared to what he would feel if this job fell through and he had nothing else in the works. Starting a job search from scratch would be truly a nightmare. It's much better not to let one's momentum slip. So Bob got a lot of other things in the works, though he never relaxed.

Finally, the seven weeks was up. The company asked him to wait one more week. Then they made him an offer.

---

**Do not drop your search activities when an offer seems almost certain. If it doesn't materialize, the lost momentum is difficult to recover.**
—Advice from a successful job hunter at The Five O'Clock Club

---

## Finally... the Offer

The offer was for the boss's job! Bob was not the only one who had seen the boss as weak: the rest of management did too. Still, they offered Bob the job only because he played by the rules and did not try to undermine his prospective manager or make him look bad. The pay was phenomenal, and Bob deserved it.

Look at all the planning that Bob put into wooing this one company. Make sure you plan for each person with whom you will meet and keep notes on each (use the Interview Record). Make sure everyone you meet wants to have you on board. Be in sync with their time frame, not your own. And be sure to have six to ten things in the works—just in case. That is what's required in a successful job hunt.

---

*Obviously the way you move will be affected by the character you are playing; but natural movement comes from your "center," from the same place as a natural voice. When you walk from your center, you will project a solid perspective of yourself. Walk with that certainty and ease, and your path becomes a center of gravity. Your force pulls all eyes to you. Slouch or poke your head forward, or pull your shoulders back uncomfortably, and that power seeps away.*

*Only a relaxed, centered walk creates a sense of strength. A centered walk can be very menacing, too. Even if you don't get film work on the basis of this advice, follow it and you'll never get mugged, either.*

*Mind you, if you look like I do you'll never get mugged anyway because people generally think I have just been mugged.*
Michael Caine, *Acting in Film*

---

*What convinces is conviction. Believe in the argument you're advancing. If you don't, you're as good as dead. The other person will sense that something isn't there, and no chain of reasoning, no matter how logical or brilliant, will win your case for you.*
Lyndon Baines Johnson

---

*Until you value yourself, you will not value your time. Until you value your time, you will not do anything with it.*
Dr. M. Scott Peck

On the next page is a very important worksheet: the Interview Record. Make a lot of copies of this page for your own personal search. Every time you have a meeting— **whether a networking meeting or a job interview**—fill it out. Make note of with whom you met, to whom they referred you, and what happened in the meeting. Attach to the Interview Record a copy of your notes from the meeting, the follow-up letter that you sent, perhaps the letter that led to the meeting.

Two weeks after the meeting, you may not remember what you discussed. If you are having a productive search and you are meeting with 10 to 15 people each week, you will not be able to remember what each person said, let alone how you met that person. To keep track of your meetings, maintain a record of each one.

Some job hunters use a three-ring binder, and arrange all of the Interview Records alphabetically or by industry or in some other logical order, with their letters attached.

Some job hunters methodically cross-reference the names by noting who referred whom.

At the beginning of your search, you may think you will be searching for a short time. But part of a good search is to follow up with your contacts at least every two months. You can have a more intelligent follow-up if you have an Interview Record to refer to.

The Five O'Clock Club®

# Interview Record

Name: _____

Position: _____

Company: _____

Address: _____

_____

_____

Phone: Bus: _____

      Home: _____

Referred by:

Link to referral:

People spoken to (May require separate sheets.):

Issues (advice, problems, plans, etc.):

Key points to remember:

Referrals (Write additional names on back.):

Name: _____

Position: _____

Company: _____

Address: _____

_____

_____

Phone: Bus: _____

      Home: _____

Date of initial contact:_____

Method used:_____

(If letter, copy and attach to this sheet.)

Planned date of follow-up call to set up
  appointment: _____

(Also record date on job-hunting calendar.)

Actual dates of calls to set up appointment:

_____

_____

_____

_____

Appointment:_____

Follow-up note mailed:_____

(Copy attached.)

Follow-up 2:_____

Follow-up 3:_____

Follow-up 4:_____

Follow-up 5:_____

Follow-up 6:_____

(Copies attached.)

Other comments:
- tone of the meeting
- positives about you
- objections to you
- key issues to address
- logical next steps
- influencers
- your feelings about the job

# Follow-Up After a Job Interview: Consider Your Competition

*Bullock shrugged. He'd been thinking about Bill that afternoon, trying to decide how to fit him into Deadwood Brickworks, Inc. It wasn't a question he could be useful. Anybody could be useful when you decided where they fit. That was what business was.*
Pete Dexter, *Deadwood*

So far in the interview process, we have considered you and the hiring manager. By acting like a consultant, you can negotiate a job that's right for both you and him or her. But there are other players and other complexities in this drama. First, there are all the other people you meet during the hiring process. They are influencers and, in fact, may influence the hiring decision more than the hiring manager does. These are people the hiring manager trusts and on whose opinions he relies. In addition, there are complexities such as outside influencers, the timing of the hiring decision, and salary considerations. Finally, you have competitors. They may be other people the interviewer is seeing, or your competition can be an ideal candidate in the interviewer's mind.

This chapter contains case studies of how some people considered and dealt with their competition. In the next chapter, we'll give you the guidelines they followed, which helped them decide what they could do to win the job. Remember, the job hunt really starts after the interview. What can you do to turn the interview into an offer? This is the part of the process that requires the most analysis and strategic thinking. Think *objectively* about the needs of the organization and of everyone you met, and think about what you can do to influence *each* person.

*If you're in a seller's market*, however, you may not need to follow up: You'll be brought back for more meetings before you have a chance to breathe. *If you're in a buyer's market*, you will probably have to do some thoughtful follow-up to get the job.

Because effective follow-up is a lot of work, your first decision should be: Do I want to get an offer for this job? Do I want to "go for it"? If you are ambivalent, and are in a competitive market, you will probably *not* get the job. Someone else will do

what he or she needs to do to get it.

Follow-ups will not guarantee you a specific job, but extensive follow-ups on a number of possibilities increase the number and quality of your offers. If you focus too much on one specific situation and how you can *make* them hire you, that won't work. You need both breadth and depth in your job hunt: you have both when you are in contact on a regular basis with six to ten people who are in a position to hire you or recommend that you be hired. You must have six to ten of these contacts in the works, *each* of which you are trying to move along.

Ideally, you will get to a point where you are moving them along together, slowing certain ones down and speeding others up, so you wind up with three concurrent job offers. Then you can select the one that is best for you. This will usually be the job that positions you best for the long run—the one that fits best into your Forty-Year Plan. It will rarely be sensible to make a decision based on money alone.

Therefore, if one situation is taking all of your energy, stop right now for ten minutes and think of how you can quickly contact other people in your target area (through networking, direct contact, search firms, or ads). It will take the pressure off, and prevent you from trying to close too soon on this one possibility.

## CASE STUDY: THE ARTIST
### Status Checks Rarely Work

Most people think follow-up means calling for the status of the search. This is not the case:

At Citibank, a project I managed needed an artist. I interviewed twenty and came up with two piles: one of seventeen rejects, and another of the three I would present to my boss and my boss's boss. A few people called to "follow up." Here's one:

Artist: "I'm calling to find out the procedure and the status. Do you mind?"

Me: "Not at all. I interviewed twenty people. I'll select three and present them to my boss and my boss's boss."

Artist: "Thanks a lot. Do you mind if I call back later?"

Me: "No, I don't mind."

The artist called every couple of weeks for three months, asked the same thing, and stayed in the reject pile. To move out, he could have said things like:

• Is there more information I can give you?

• I've been giving a lot of thought to your project and have some new ideas. I'd like to show them to you.

• Where do I stand? How does my work compare with the work others presented?

If all you're doing is finding out where you are in the process, that's rarely enough. *The ball is always in your court*. It is your responsibility to figure out what the next step should be. Job hunters view the whole process as if it were a tennis game where— *thwack*—the ball is in the hiring manager's court. Wrong.

Me to job hunter: "How's it going?"

Job hunter to Kate: *(Thwack!)* "The ball's in their court now. They're going to call me."

When they call, it will probably be to say, "You are not included." If you wait, not many of your interviews will turn into offers.

## CASE STUDY: RACHEL
### *Trust Me*

> *A man is not finished when he's defeated;*
> *he's finished when he quits.*
> Richard Milhous Nixon

Rachel had been unemployed for nine months. This was her first Five O'Clock Club meeting. She was disgusted. "I had an interview," she said. "I know what will happen: I'll be a finalist and they'll hire the other person."

Rachel was nice, enthusiastic, and smart: she was always a finalist. Yet the more experienced person was always hired.

Here's the story. Rachel, a lobbyist, was interviewing at a law firm. The firm liked her back-ground, but it needed some public relations help and perhaps an internal newsletter. Rachel did not have experience in either of those areas, though she knew she could do those things. She wrote a typical thank you note playing up her strengths, playing down her weaknesses, but essentially ignoring the firm's objections. She highlighted the lobbying, and said that PR and a newsletter would not be a problem. She could do it. She was asking the firm to "trust her."

## Lots of Job Hunters Take the "Trust Me" Approach

The following occurred during a group meeting at The Five O'Clock Club:

Me: "Do you want this job? Are you willing to go through a brick wall to get it?"

Rachel: "Yes. I am. I really want this job."

Me: "Let's think about overcoming their objections. If you can write a PR plan after you get hired, why not do it now? Why ask them to trust you?"

Two people in the group had old PR plans, which they lent her. Remember: the proposals or ideas you write will probably be wrong. That's okay. You're showing the company you can think the problem through and actually come up with solutions.

Rachel's lack of experience with newsletters was also an objection. We suggested Rachel call law firms in other cities and get their newsletters.

After doing research, Rachel sent a very different note. In this one she said she had been giving it more thought, and was very excited about working for the firm. She had put together a PR plan, *which she would like to review with them,* and had gotten copies of newsletters from other law firms, which gave her ideas of what she could do in a newsletter for them. Of course, she got the job.

## Uncovering Their Objections

Rachel got the job because she overcame the objections of the hiring committee. Start thinking about how you can overcome objections. This will change the way you interview, and you will become more attuned to picking up valid objections rather than quashing them. Then you can even solicit negatives. For example, you can ask:

- Who else is being considered?
- What do they have to offer?
- How do I stand in comparison with them?
- What kind of person would be considered an ideal candidate?
- What would you like to say about a new hire one year from now?

Get good at interviewing so you can solicit valid objections to hiring you.

### Act Like a Consultant

Since most jobs are created for people, find out what the manager needs. Hiring managers often decide to structure the job differently depending on who they hire. Why not influence the hiring manager to structure the job for you?

Probe—and don't expect anything to happen in the first meeting. If you were a consultant trying to sell a $30,000 or $130,000 project (your salary), you wouldn't expect someone to immediately say, "Fine. Start working." Yet job hunters often expect to get an offer during the first meeting.

Forget about job hunting. This is regular business. You're selling an expensive package. Do what a consultant or a salesperson does: Ask about the company's problems and its situation; think how you could get back to the interviewer later. Get enough information so you can follow up and give the interviewer enough information so he'll want to see you again. Move the process along: Suggest you meet with more people there. Do research. Have someone influence the interviewer on your behalf. Then get back to him again. That's what a consultant does. Remember to move the process along; outshine and outlast your competition.

### CASE STUDY: KEN
*Identifying the Issues/Timing*

Ken was the first person interviewed for a senior vice president of marketing position. When Ken asked, the interviewer said he would see five or six more people. As you will see shortly, being first is the weakest position. Get rid of your competition quickly, or find ways to maintain the interviewer's interest and meet with him or her again.

Ken identified the company's most important issue—it was not wondering what Ken would do as the head of marketing, but something more basic: it was debating the *role* marketing should play in the new organization.

Determining the real issues is critical in deciding your follow-up plan. And since the timing was against him, Ken acted fast. He wrote a handsome four-page proposal about the role marketing should play, and he sent it overnight.

When Ken was called for a second round of interviews, he found there were no other candidates. Ken had gotten rid of his competition. Ken not only identified the issues, he was in sync in terms of timing. The company was planning to decide quickly, so he acted quickly, too.

### CASE STUDY: LEON
*How Did He Get the Job?*

Leon came to The Five O'Clock Club after fifteen months of interviews. After three Club meetings, he got two job offers simply because he followed the group's advice and wrote proposals. When he told the group his good news, someone asked him how he got the two jobs. He said that one offer was from a search firm, and one was from networking. Leon had been pursuing jobs through networking and search firms for fifteen months, but it wasn't until he decided to do real follow-up on these that he was offered a job.

### CASE STUDY: JOHN
*Consider Your Likely Competitors and Go For It*

Most job hunters think *anxiously* about the competition out there. Instead, be *objective* about your likely competitors.

John thought he had been job hunting for a year. He answered ads, met with search firms, and even went on interviews, but he wasn't job hunting: *in a tight market, the job hunt starts* after *the interview.*

At our first meeting, John recounted his activity.

One ad he'd answered was for a job at the Kennedy Foundation, and he'd met three people there two weeks earlier. He was waiting for their call. Before John went on, I stopped him.

"John," I said, "do you want that job?"

"Well," he replied, "I'll see what happens next. If they call me, I'll consider it."

"The way things stand, John, you are *not* going to get that job. If they call, they'll say they found a better match. Are you willing to go through a brick wall to get that job? If you are, I can help you—and it's a *lot* of work. But if you essentially want to sit on the bench answering ads, there's not much a coach can do."

John said he was willing to go after the job. A job hunter's total commitment is absolutely necessary, or he will not be willing to do—or even notice—what needs to be done to win the job.

## Who Are John's Likely Competitors?

The Kennedy Foundation wanted a controller. John had been a controller in a major corporation for twenty years. What kind of controller would the Kennedy Foundation most likely want?

Develop a prototype of your likely competitors. You have to guess about your competition. But once you form a hypothesis about who your competitors are, you can figure out a plan to outshine and outlast them. It's better to have some hypothetical competitor in mind than nobody. Remember, your competition might not be real people, but an ideal in the mind of the hiring manager. Get rid of that competitor, too, or the hiring manager will continue looking for that ideal person.

John thought his likely competitors were people who had been controllers in not-for-profit organizations. I suggested that he spend a day at The Foundation Center (a library), and research the controllership function at other foundations. I told him to make sure he could handle the work and knew the jargon.

John came back with good news: "I know how to do that kind of accounting. It's actually what I've done all along."

## How Does John *Now* Stand in Relation to His Likely Competitors?

*Don't forget that it (your product or service) is not differentiated until the customer understands the difference.*
Tom Peters, *Thriving on Chaos*

John now has twenty years of corporate controllership experience and a day in the library. His likely competitors have real hands-on experience. At this stage, John is *not* even with them. He has to do more if he wants the job.

John and I searched his background for areas that might interest the Kennedy Foundation—experience his likely competitors would not have, such as securities accounting.

Look at all the work and thought John has put in so far—without a request from the hiring manager. The ball is *always* in your court.

John had met with three people at the Kennedy Foundation. Among the three was a financial person and someone from personnel. His first draft of the letter to the financial person was negative: "Despite the fact that I have no not-for-profit experience, I believe my credentials . . . "

Wrong. Come up with something that *beats out* your competition. You must be in a position to say, in so many words, "Unlike others who have spent a lot of time doing this work, I bring something extra to the party."

Also remember that you are interviewing with individuals—not organizations. You are *not* interviewing with the Kennedy Foundation or IBM. Each person you meet has his or her own opinions about the issues that are important, the things that person likes about you, and the reasons he or she might not want you there. Address these points with *each* person.

## The Other Decision-Makers/Influencers

*The people you want to reach . . . should be viewed as distinct target audiences that require different approaches and strategies.*
Jeffrey P. Davidson, marketing consultant
*Management World*, September/October 1987

Many job hunters assume the hiring manager is the only person who matters. Big mistake. Others are not only influencers; in some cases, they may actually be the decision-makers.

I'm a good example. I make terrible hiring decisions: Everyone I interview seems fine to me. So I have others meet with the candidates. Their opinions weigh more than mine. Any applicant who ignores them is ignoring the decision-makers—or at least the serious influencers.

Take seriously every person you meet. Don't be rude to the receptionist. She may say to the boss, "If you hire him, I'm quitting." That receptionist is definitely an influencer.

### Identifying the Issues

*You must call each thing by its proper name
or that which must get done will not.*
A. Harvey Block

When John first met with the personnel person at the Kennedy Foundation, she asked him questions such as, "So, what do you do on weekends?" and "Where do your kids go to school?" Assuming these were not idle questions, what issue was she getting at?

We decided the issue was *fit.* When John wrote his first follow-up letter to her, he said he was excited about the position and had spent a day doing research—and he addressed the issue of fit. He did this by emphasizing his qualities of loyalty and commitment. Also, he correctly sensed that they would be impressed with where he went to college and his relationship with his family.

Three months, eleven grueling interviews, and seven in-depth reference checks later, John's credentials were presented to the board of directors for approval. To make sure his important arguments were brought before the board, John prepared one more follow-up letter (see the next page). By the way, John had three more interviews after the board meeting. He got the job—and he's still there.

Many job hunters ask John how he got the job. They are asking the wrong question. They mean, "How did you get the interview?" John is forced to reply, "I got it through an ad." I hope you can see that John got the *job* through his analysis and follow-up. It was just the *interview* that he got through an ad.

### What Happens As Time Passes

*He had made a fortune in business and owed it to being
able to see the truth in any situation.*
Ethan Canin, *Emperor of the Air*

Most jobs are *created* for people: Most interviewers don't know clearly what they will want the new person to do. Yet job hunters expect the hiring manager to tell them exactly what the job will be like, and get annoyed when the manager can't tell them.

Generally the job description depends on who will be in the job. Therefore, help the hiring manager figure out what the new person should do. If you don't help him, another job hunter will. This is called "negotiating the job." You are trying to remove all of the company's objections to hiring you, as well as all of *your* objections to working for them. Try to make it work for both of you. But time is your enemy. Imagine what happens in the hiring process as time passes:

You have an interview. When I, your counselor, ask how it went, you tell me how great it was: The two of you hit it off, and you are sure you will be called back. You see this interview as something frozen in time, and you wait for the magical phone call.

But after you left, the manager met with someone else, who brought up new issues. Now his criteria for what he wants have changed somewhat, and consequently, his impression of you has also changed. He was honest when he said he liked you, but things look different to him now. Perhaps you have what he needs to meet his new criteria, or perhaps you could convince him that his new direction is wrong, but you don't know what is now on his mind.

You call to find out "how things are going." He says he is still interviewing and will call you later

July 18, 19xx

Mr. John Resier
The Kennedy Foundation
1234 13th Street, NW
Washington, D.C. 12345

Dear John:

Now that you are in the final stage of your search, I wanted to take the opportunity to summarize my feelings about the position and address what I see as some of the major issues affecting your decision.

## Long-term commitment

My almost twenty-year career at Gotham unequivocally attests to my loyalty and commitment to my employer and my job. It is only because this opportunity is so exceptional that, for the very first time, I am seriously considering leaving Gotham. You can be assured that this sense of loyalty will remain with me at the Foundation.

## Profit-making background

I feel strongly that my experience in the for-profit sector represents value added to the Foundation. I base this upon the following:

- My experience in securities accounting, clearance and custody, where virtually 100% of your assets and revenues reside, is critical to your organization.
- My review of the Marwick Report on its review of the Comptroller's Office very interestingly included recommendations identical to the initial conclusions I drew from some of the specifics we discussed Thursday.
- The cultural changes you are introducing represent concepts ingrained in me. My experience in the for-profit sector would nicely complement, support and help expedite your initiatives to become more businesslike in your operations.
- My independent research on foundation accounting, primarily at the Foundation Center, illustrated the striking similarity in the Statements on Financial Accounting Standards and the Statements on Financial Accounting Concepts between the two sectors.
- My in-depth study of the Foundation's Annual Report assured me that the differences in accounting and financial reporting between the two sectors are insignificant. My conversation with Bob Maher, Senior Manager at Ernst & Young, confirmed my conclusion.

I have a very positive feel for the Foundation, its philanthropic work, its infrastructure and its personnel practices, both in general terms and as it would affect me directly.

John, I believe that the Foundation and I are ideally suited for each other. My broad managerial and technical expertise is needed for the immediate tasks at hand but will also be of value in your other areas of responsibility. My experience in operating in a decentralized environment has honed my decision-making skills and my ability to interface with others at all levels.

I am looking forward to your favorable decision.

Very truly yours,

John H. Norton

when he has decided. Actually, then it will probably be too late for you. His thinking is constantly evolving as he meets with people. You were already out of the running. *Your call did nothing to influence his thinking*: you did not address his new concerns. You asked for a status report of where he was in the hiring process, and that's what you got. You did nothing to get back into the loop of people he might consider, or find out the new issues that are now on his mind.

> *Oh I could show my prowess,*
> *be a lion not a mou-esse,*
> *if I only had the nerve.*
> The Cowardly Lion in the movie *The Wizard of Oz*
> (from the book by L. Frank Baum)
> by E. Y. Harburg and Harold Arlen

The manager meets more people, and further defines the position. Interviewing helps him decide what he wants. You are getting further and further away from his new requirements.

You are not aware of this. You remember the great meeting you two had. You remind me that he said he really liked you. You insist on freezing that moment in time. You don't want to do anything to rock the boat or appear desperate. You hope it works out. "The ball is in his court," you say. "I gave it my best. There's nothing I can do but wait." So you decide to give it more time . . . time to go wrong.

> Annie:  . . . *you want to give it time—*
> Henry:  *Yes—*
> Annie:  . . . *time to go wrong, change, spoil. Then you'll know it wasn't the real thing.*
> Tom Stoppard, *The Real Thing*

You have to imagine what is going on as time passes. Perhaps the hiring manager is simply very busy and is not working on this at all. Or perhaps things are moving along without you. Statistics prove that the person who is interviewed last has the best chance of being hired. That's because the last person benefits from all the thinking the manager has done. The manager is able to discuss all of the issues of concern with this final applicant.

## What You Can Do During the Interview

If you go into an interview with the goal of getting a job, you are putting too much pressure on yourself to come to closure. When you walk away without an offer, you feel discouraged. When you walk away without even knowing what the job is, you feel confused and lost.

> *Boone smiled and nodded. The muscles in his jaw hurt. "What I meant was did you ever shoot anybody but your own self. Not that that don't count."*
> Pete Dexter, *Deadwood*

Instead of criticizing managers who do not know what they want, try to understand them: "I can understand that there are a number of ways you can structure this position. Let's talk about your problems and your needs. Perhaps I can help."

Your goal in the interview is not to get an offer, but to build a relationship with the manager. This means you are on the manager's side—assessing the situation, and figuring out how to move the process along so you can continue to help define the job.

## Pay Attention to Your Competition

Most job hunters think only about themselves and the hiring manager. They don't think about the others being considered for the position. But you are different. You are acutely aware at all times that you have competition. Your goal is to get rid of them.

As you move the process along, you can see your competitors dropping away because you are doing a better job of addressing the hiring manager's needs, coming up with solutions to his problems, and showing more interest and more competence than they are.

You are in a problem-solving mode. Here's the way you think: "My goal isn't to get a job immediately, but to build a relationship. How can I build a relationship so that someday when this person decides what he or she wants, it'll be me?" You have hung in there. You have eliminated your competition. You have helped define the job in a way that suits both you and the hiring manager. You have the option of saying, "Do I want this job or don't I?"

The Five O'Clock Club®

# Follow-Up Checklist: Turning Job Interviews into Offers

Do you want a job? Follow-up is the only technique that influences the person who interviewed you. You may *think* you can get a job through a search firm, answering an ad, networking, or directly contacting a company. But what you are getting is *interviews* in your target area. You are not job hunting yet. You prove your mettle by seeing how—over the long run—you can turn each interview into a job. *Now* you're job hunting. And that's where follow-up comes in.

Remember, you generally don't want a job offer at that first meeting. An easy hire decision may mean an easy fire decision later. Instead, establish a long-term relationship. It is not unusual to be brought in for anywhere from three to nine or more interviews.

---

*Biblical waiting,*
*the kind of waiting Abram and Sarai did,*
*and which you and I must learn to do,*
*is a very active kind of waiting.*
*It's a faith-journey; the waiting of a pilgrimage.*
*We can only wait for God to give us what we cannot do*
*ourselves; but, paradoxically, we must move toward it*
*in faith as we wait, asking, seeking and knocking . . . .*
Ben Patterson, *Waiting*

---

*Waiting is not just the thing we have to*
*do until we get what we hoped for.*
*Waiting is part of the process of*
*becoming what we hope for.*
Ben Patterson, *Waiting*

---

*The key to being a strategic player is to*
*be in play, working on a significant level.*
Thomas Krens, Director,
The Guggenheim Museum,
*The New York Times*, May 29, 1988

---

*We are what we repeatedly do. Excellence, then,*
*is not an act, but a habit.*
Aristotle

In the last chapter, you read a few examples of job hunters turning job interviews into offers. They had to think hard about what to do next. They objectively and methodically analyzed *all* the interviews they had and developed strategies for addressing every issue for *each* person with whom they met. They thought about who their likely competitors were, and what the hiring managers probably preferred. Who are your likely competitors? How do you stack up against them? Prove you're better than they are, or you won't get the job.

*The heights by great men reached and kept*
*Were not attained by sudden flight,*
*But they, while their companions slept,*
*Were toiling upward in the night.*
Henry Wadsworth Longfellow

> **Follow-up will dramatically increase the number of job offers you get. It is one of the most powerful tools you have to influence the situation.**

### Why Bother with Follow-Up?
- to influence both the decision-makers and the influencers
- to move things along
- to show interest and competence
- to knock out your competition
- to reassure the hiring manager
- to turn a losing situation into a winning one
- to make it difficult for them to reject you
- to set the right tone/buy yourself time after you are hired.

In a tight market, follow-up helps. But still *strive to have six to ten contacts in the works at all times*. The job you are interviewing for may vanish: the manager may decide not to hire at all, or hire a finance instead of a marketing person. There may be a hiring freeze, or a major reorganization. Follow-up techniques will generally not help in these situations. If you are in a competitive market, put extra effort into those job possibilities that are still alive.

*Nothing is more dangerous than an idea*
*when it is the only one you have.*
Emile Chartier

And if you have lots of other contacts in the works, you will be less likely to allow yourself to be abused by hiring managers trying to take advantage of "desperate" job hunters. You can assess ridiculous requests and be more willing to walk away.

The Interview Record is a checklist of items to consider in assessing your interviews and planning your follow-up. Try to remember everything that happened at each of your meetings. Many job hunters take notes during the interviews so they will do a better follow-up. After all, wouldn't a consultant take notes during a meeting? How else can you remember all the important issues that come up? At the very least, take notes immediately after the meeting. Some job hunters keep track of every person with whom they met by using the Interview Record. Make plenty of copies of the form for your job search. Keep them in a folder or a three-ring binder, in alphabetical order within target area.

### Assess the Interview(s)

*Anyone who fears effort, anyone who backs off from frustration and possibly even pain will never get anywhere.*
Erich Fromm

*Anyone who listens well takes notes.*
Dante

Effective follow-up depends on knowing what happened in the interview. In fact, you will begin to interview very differently now. You now know you are there to gather enough information so you can follow up, and to give enough information back so the interviewer will be willing to meet with you again. As your counselor, I'd want the following background information:

- How did it go? What did they say? What did you say?
- How many people did you see?
- How much time did you spend with each?
- What role does each of them play?
- Who is important?
- Who is the hiring manager?

- Who is the decision-maker?
- Who most *influences* the decision?
- Who else did you meet (secretaries, receptionists, bosses from other areas)? How influential might they be? (Do not dismiss them too readily. They may be more influential than you think. A trusted secretary, for example, has a lot of influence. She had better want you there.)
- How quickly do they want to decide? A year? Months? Next week?
- What do you have to offer that your competition doesn't?
- What problems did the interviewer have? Do you have any solutions to those problems?
- How badly do you want this job? (If you want it a lot, you will be more likely to do what you need to do to get it. Or perhaps someone wants it more than you. *That* person will do the things he or she needs to do to get the job.)

*He said, however, that the real secret of his fortune was that none of his mules worked as hard and with so much determination as he did himself.*
Gabriel García Márquez
*Love in the Time of Cholera*

### Follow Up with *Each* Person

*There is a tide in the affairs of men, Which, taken at the flood, leads on to fortune; Omitted, all the voyage of their life Is bound in shallows and in miseries.*
William Shakespeare
*Julius Caesar*, IV, iii

For *each* person with whom you interviewed, analyze and craft a follow-up note which takes into account:

- **the tone of the conversation**. Was it friendly? Formal? Family-like? Follow up with a similar tone.

- **the positives about you.** Why would this

*Whoever loves discipline loves knowledge,*
*but he who hates correction is stupid.*
Proverbs 12:1

person want you there? If you interviewed with peers, why would they want you on the team? In the interview, it is *your* job to make sure each person you meet can see the benefit of having you on board.

- **the objections to you**—for *each* person you met, whether or not these objections were expressed. For example, you may know that the company typically hires someone with a background that is different from yours, or you may not have certain experience it is looking for, or your past salary may be too high, or it may see you as overqualified. A future peer may see you as a threat (let that peer know you are not) or think you will not fit in. You may be seen as too old or too young or too something else. If you think the company is worried about having you on board for some reason, address that reason. For example, if someone sees you as too old, think of the benefits that come with age. Then you might say, "I hope you are interested in hiring someone with maturity and a broad base of experience."

*Even in a highly controlled meeting, there is a lot . . .*
*going on. The real process of making decisions,*
*of gathering support, of developing opinions, happens*
*before the meeting—or after.*
Terrence E. Deal and Allan A. Kennedy,
*Corporate Cultures*

Many job hunters want to ignore or gloss over the objections; instead, pay attention to why *each* person may not want you there. Joel DeLuca, Ph.D., author of *Political Savvy,* noted that if you are observant, you should come out of a meeting with a good sense of how hard a sell this is going to be, as well as some idea of the political lay of the land.

*If [a man] is brusque in his manner,*
*others will not cooperate. If he is agitated in his words,*
*they will awaken no echo in others. If he asks for*
*something without having first established a proper*
*relationship, it will not be given to him.*
I Ching

- **the key issues**. Was the interviewer concerned about interdepartmental relationships?

Work overload? The political situation with a key vendor? How you will support people in other areas? How you can make his or her job easier? What makes you different from your competition? Identify those issues that are key to the interviewer(s).

- **your feelings about the job**. If this is the one place you really want to work, say so. If you would enjoy working with your prospective manager and peers, say so. **At the executive level, most decisions are based on fit.** In addition to competence, people want someone they'd *like* to work with and someone who *wants* to work with them. Write with enthusiasm. Let your personality come through.

- **the next steps**. Regardless of *who* should take the next steps, what exactly are the next logical steps? What will move the process along?

*The average sale is made after the prospect*
*has said "no" six times.*
Jeffrey P. Davidson, marketing consultant
*The Washington Post,* May 20, 1985

For example, the next step could be:
- another meeting to discuss something in greater detail
- meeting(s) with other people
- another meeting after the other candidates have been interviewed
- an in-depth review of documents
- discussing a few of your ideas with them
- drafting a proposal about how you would handle a certain area.

*Let him who wants to move and convince*
*others be first moved and convinced himself.*
Thomas Carlyle

State the "next steps" in your follow-up note. For example, "I'd like to get together with you to discuss my ideas on . . . " or "If I don't hear from George in a week or so, I'll give you a call."

If you were the first person interviewed, try to be interviewed again. "As you interview others, you may more clearly define what you want. I would appreciate the opportunity to address the new issues that may arise."

## Influence the Influencers

*Progress always involves risk.*
*You can't steal second base and keep your foot on first.*
Frederick B. Wilcox

*Success seems to be largely a matter of*
*hanging on after others have let go.*
William Feather

Most job hunters pay attention to the hiring manager and ignore everyone else. However, most hiring managers want the input of others. You may be rejected if a future peer or subordinate says that you seem difficult to work with, or the receptionist complains that you were rude to her. Remember that everyone is an influencer. *Follow up with everyone you met formally.* Cultivate as many advocates as you can. Have people inside rooting for you. It's better if your future peers, for example, say that you would be great to have on the team. You can influence the influencers with a letter or phone call.

Who might *influence* the hiring decision? **If they are future coworkers, follow the analysis in "Follow Up With *Each* Person" above.** Tell outside influencers the position in which you are interested and why, and how they can help you.

Joe, a well-known top-level executive, felt one of his interviews went very well, but he was afraid the interviewer would tap into the corporate pipeline and hear untrue negative rumors about him. Joe has two choices: he can hope the interviewer doesn't hear the rumors, or he can fight for the job he deserves.

Joe has to try to control the pipeline—the key influencers in this situation. First, Joe called some influential people who thought well of him and who the hiring manager would respect. He stated why he wanted this job, and asked them to put in a good word for him. Second, Joe thought of the people the hiring manager was most likely to run into or call for information. Joe called them first and did his best to influence them to support him. Joe successfully fended off bad reports and landed the job he wanted.

## Be in Sync with Their Timing

*Even if you're on the right track,*
*you'll get run over if you just sit there.*
Will Rogers

Move the process along to the next step, but at *the interviewer's pace,* not yours. The timing depends on the personality of the interviewer and his or her sense of urgency.

If the situation is urgent, write your letter overnight, and hand-deliver it in the morning. If the manager is laid back, an urgent delivery is inappropriate.

**Use your judgment.** If things are going along at a good clip, and you are being brought in every other day, you may want to let it ride *if* you think you have no competition.

Also be aware that if things are *not* moving along quickly, it may have nothing to do with you. It may well be that the interviewer is not doing *anything* about filling the position—he or she may be busy with other business. If you were the hiring manager, you would find that you can't work on the hire every minute, because you have your regular job to do, and emergencies come up as well.

If you have no idea what is going on, it would help if you've formed a good relationship with the hiring manager's secretary. Then you could call and say, "Hi, Jane. This is Joe. I was wondering if you could help me with something. I haven't heard from Ellis [her boss] for two weeks and I had expected to hear something by now. I was going to drop him a note, but I didn't want to bother him if he's really busy. I was wondering if he's still interviewing other people or if he's just been tied up, or what." Who knows what she'll say? But if she says he had a death in the family and has been out of town, that gives you some idea of what is happening. He is not sitting around talking about you all day long. He is doing other things, and the hiring process often moves more slowly than you think.

*Understanding is a wellspring of life*
*to him that hath it.*
Proverbs 16:22

*Sometimes I go off on a tangent, but I follow my intuitions and if it doesn't work, it doesn't matter.*
*There's no such thing as failure; you just learn from it and go on.*
David Hockney (from the audiocassette: David Hockney: A Retrospective,
Metropolitan Museum of Art, July 1988

## How Can You Tell If a Follow-Up Letter Is a Good One?

*There is no such thing as "soft sell" or hard sell."*
*There is only "smart sell" and stupid sell."*
Charles Bower, President, BBD&O
*Editor & Publisher*, December 7, 1957

A good letter is *tailored* to the situation. It would be impossible to send it to someone other than the addressee. *It sells you, separates you from your competition, addresses all issues and objections, and states a next step*. Finally, its tone *replicates* the tone of the interview (or creates a good tone if the interview wasn't so good). For example, John's various follow-up notes to those he met at the Kennedy Foundation addressed each manager's issues.

Your letters to some people will be very detailed and meticulous. These may take you half a day to write. For others, you will write a simple letter saying that you thought they would be great to work with, and addressing the issues they brought up.

Most job hunters err, however, when they assume someone who is lower-level has no influence. Be careful about whom you dismiss. During the interview, try to pick up on the relationships between people. In brief, remember to influence the influencers. Write notes to prospective peers you have met. They have some say in the hiring decision—maybe a lot of say. If they don't want you, you might not get hired. For each person you met, think of why he or she would want you there. What do you bring to the party? Make sure you are not a threat. Overcome his or her objections. Address any issues raised. Use the tone set in the interview.

A job hunter, Philip, put a lot of thought into his follow-up with *a prospective peer*, Jonathan. Philip considered Jonathan an important influencer, and had noted the following from their meeting:

• Philip sensed that Jonathan was worried about losing his standing as the second-in-command to George, the hiring manager, when the new person came in.

• He was also concerned that the new person might not be a team player or a hard worker, or might not be willing to help out with his special projects, which involved computer simulations.

• He was concerned about losing the camaraderie in the department, and hoped the new person would have a good sense of humor to offset the stress of working under deadline.

• He was obviously trying to conduct a very professional interview, and asked Philip a number of times what he thought of the questions.

• He was relieved when Philip said he would enjoy developing materials for the department, although it was not central to the job. This is a project none of the other competitors would be able to handle.

• He wondered about the department's reputation outside the company.

The conversation had been light and friendly. Philip considered Jonathan to be the key influencer, and thought George, the hiring manager, would be making the decision with Jonathan. Philip wrote to each of his prospective peers and also to George. This is the letter he wrote to Jonathan:

---

Dear Jonathan:

I was glad finally to have a chance to meet you. George had spoken of you so proudly, I knew you had earned everything you've gotten at Bluekill and have worked very hard. I, too, am a hard worker, and I know we would complement each other.

I liked your professional approach to the interview, and found your questions and direction quite interesting. I hope I "did okay." I believe I could work out a schedule to accommodate your many projects—and one thing you can count on is that I'm good at developing computer simulations. In my last position, I was considered the best, and would enjoy doing the same for you. I work very hard at it, and it pays off.

My impression is that George depends on you a lot, and perhaps I could help out also. I think I could develop materials that could be used both inside and with customers, and I will be glad to hear your ideas on the matter. I've developed a great deal of material in the past that I will be happy to show you.

All things considered, I think I would make a good addition to the group, and I believe you and I would enjoy working together. As I said to you when we met, I've worked in a few companies, and I do my best to make every place I work as enjoyable as it can be. Your sense of humor surely helps, and I'm sure mine will also.

Cordially,
Philip Johnson

Time passed. Philip met again with George and with other peers. But he was concerned about whether Jonathan would still be in favor of him in light of the number of additional applicants Jonathan had met by then. Philip decided to contact Jonathan again, this time more informally. In reviewing his notes, he fixed on what Jonathan had said about the reputation of the department. Philip then arranged a networking meeting with an important person in the industry so he would have something to contact Jonathan about. The information would also help him make up his mind in case he received a job offer. Then he wrote on informal stationery:

Dear Jonathan,
In our meeting, you wondered about the reputation of your department. I'm sure you will be happy to hear, as I was, that your department is thought of as the best in the industry. I met with Cheryl Jenkins yesterday and she raved about each person in your group—including you. You should be proud of her commendation, and I admit that I was proud as well because I sincerely hope I wind up working with you.

I mentioned to you that I would be happy to show you the computer simulation materials I have developed in the past. I have finally put them together, and will call you to see if you still want to look at them. It shouldn't take more than fifteen minutes of your time.

Hope all is well.

Best regards,
Philip

Sometimes an important influencer is the best way to sway the hiring manager. Philip got the job, but he got much more: he started the job with a very good relationship with each of the people with whom he would he working. When you analyze what is important to each person, you not only increase your chances of getting the job, you increase your chances of having the new job go smoothly.

Discuss your follow-up problems at Five O'Clock Club meetings. Make the effort required to develop strategies for your follow-up moves. It's worth the trouble.

As one Five O'Clock Clubber advised, "Make sure the follow-up letter you write is absolutely the best the company will see—or don't write it." Be sure to read the follow-up case studies in this book.

# Job Interview Follow-Up: Sample Letters

*Influence belongs to men of action, and for purposes of action nothing is more useful than narrowness of thought combined with energy of will.*
Henri Frédéric Amiel, *Journal intime*

---

*Motivation will almost always beat mere talent.*
Norman R. Augustine, *Augustine's Laws*

---

*Method is much, technique is much, but inspiration is even more.*
Benjamin Nathan Cardoza,
U.S. Supreme Court Justice, *Law and Literature*

---

*The fearful Unbelief is unbelief in yourself.*
Thomas Carlyle, *Sartor Resartus*

---

*We are perplexed but not in despair.*
New Testament, II Corinthians 4:8

---

*It is better to wear out than to rust out.*
Richard Cumberland, 1632 - 1718
Bishop of Peterborough, Attributed

---

*To him that will, ways are not wanting.*
George Herbert, *Jacula Prudentum*

---

*It is fatal to enter any war without the will to win it.*
Douglas MacArthur, Speech to the Republican National Convention, July 7, 1952

---

> **Job follow-ups are not merely "thank-you" notes. Your primary goal is not to *thank* the interviewer, but to *influence* him or her.**

**How can you tell whether a follow-up letter is a good one?**

A good letter is **tailored** to the situation. It would be impossible to send it to someone other than the addressee. It **sells the writer, separates the writer from the competition, addresses all issues and objections, and states a next step**. Finally, its **tone replicates the tone of the interview** (or creates a good tone if the interview wasn't so good).

**For example . . .**
Look at the follow-up letter on the next page.

Paragraph 1:
- talks about the next steps.
- separates me from the competition: they're talking about counseling, but I'm trying to offer something additional—the development of program materials.

Paragraph 2:
- handles an objection: would I enjoy working with this kind of client?

Paragraphs 3 & 4:
- another objection: would I be too independent in the job, (or would I listen to my boss)?

Paragraph 5:
- another objection: why hire a strong, older person when someone with less experience would do?

Paragraph 6:
- recalls the camaraderie of the interview.

Note: Most objections are unstated. You have to notice them for yourself based on the questions at the interview or your assessment of who your competition is likely to be. Also be aware of tone, facial expression, and body language.

M. Catherine Wendleton

163 York Avenue - 12B
New York, New York 10000
(212) 555-2231 (day)
(212) 555-1674 (message)

July 18, 19xx

Ms. Sandra Bandler
Director of Outplacement
RightBank
100 Madison Avenue
New York, NY 10000

Dear Sandra:

Now I've met everyone in your group, and I'll be glad to get together with you again. I can see how carefully you have parcelled out your assignments to each person. I can also see where I would fit in—something we can discuss in more detail when we get together. I certainly am expert in developing program materials, and will be happy to show you things I have done in that area.

In general, I enjoy the type of client you get at RightBank because a good deal of my approach is business-oriented and based on business systems and logic. That is essentially the way I operate with people from other banks as well as from the Big 8 accounting firms. These people tend to be self-motivated and direct, and I like that. They tend to not want to be psychoanalzed too much, and that's fine with me. I'm all for getting on with it.

On the other hand, I believe I can learn a lot from you, and am looking forward to the opportunity to do so. I am even planning to join the Jung Foundation, and visited there for the first time today.

I know you are in a delicate position dealing with the RightBank corporate problems, and I do understand the difficulties of your job. For most of my career, I have worked for Senior Management. All of my bosses have been able to count on me to see what needs to be done, to do it, and to work smoothly with the rest of the organization. I have a lot of ideas, but I also follow through on them, and know how to get the willing cooperation of others.

I hope you are looking to hire a strong person—one you can depend on to carry out your vision as well as add to it—a person with maturity and strong corporate experience as well as one who is a solid counselor and good at running a small business—which is what you are trying to do. I look forward to helping you and will do more than my share to support you.

I hope you have a wonderful vacation, and I can't tell you how jealous I am. I've never had two weeks together in my life.

I'll see you when you get back. Don't think about all of this.

Cheers,

---

### Influence the Influencers.
These are <u>notes to prospective peers</u> for the job on the preceeding page. They have some say in the hiring decision. Maybe a *lot* of say. Make sure your follow-up letters influence them. If they don't want you, you might not get hired. Write to *each* person with whom you interviewed. For each, think of <u>why they would want you there</u>. What's in it for them? What do you bring to the party? Make sure you are not a threat to them. Overcome their objections. Address any issues raised. Use the tone set in the interview.

---

*M. Catherine Wendleton*

Dear Carolyn:

I was glad to finally have a chance to meet you. Sandy had spoken of you so proudly, she made me proud too. I can see that you've earned everything you've gotten at RightBank and have worked very hard. I too am a hard worker, and I know we would complement each other.

I liked your professional approach to the interview, and your questions and direction were quite interesting to me as a professional. I hope I "did OK." I believe I could work out a schedule to accommodate your needs in the group training area—and one thing you can count on is that I'm <u>good</u> at it. I believe I was the favorite counselor at JC Penney—which was essentially all group work. I put a lot of effort into it, and I got rave reviews.

My impression is that Sandy depends on you a lot, and perhaps I could help out also. I could develop materials that could be used in the group as well as in the individual program, and I will be glad to hear your ideas on the matter. I've developed a great deal of material in the past that I will be happy to show you.

All things considered, I think I would make a happy addition to the group, and I believe you and I would enjoy working together. As I said to you when we met, I've been around, and I certainly do my best to make every place I work as enjoyable as it can be. Your sense of humor surely helps, and I'm sure mine will also.

Cordially,
*Kate Wendleton*

---

*M. Catherine Wendleton*

July 18, 19xx

Dear Peter:

It certainly was a pleasure meeting you. You add a lot of humor and a lot of ability to the place. All things considered, I think I would make a happy addition to the group, and I believe you and I would enjoy working together. I believe you are a person I would turn to to broaden my expertise in the area of evaluation. I would also help you out with the reception area, as I can see that is one of your major duties. (Just kidding.)

Sandy said she would like me to concentrate on the area of materials development—something I have some experience in and would enjoy doing.

I hope you and I will have the opportunity to work together.

Cordially,
*Kate*

---

*M. Catherine Wendleton*

Dear Alan:

I'm glad to have met you. Your smile seems to soften things in the office, and I'm sure we would enjoy working together. I believe I could learn from each person in the group, and I also think I bring a lot to the party. My special assignment from Sandy would be in developing program materials—something that is right up my alley.

All things considered, I think I would make a happy addition to the group. As I said to you when we met, I certainly do my best to make every place I work as enjoyable as possible. Your attitude surely helps in that area, and I'm sure mine will also.

Cordially,
*Kate Wendleton*

The
Five
O'Clock
Club®

## Psalm 23

*The Lord is my shepherd, I shall not want.*

*He makes me lie down in green pastures;*
*He leads me beside quiet waters.*
*He restores my soul;*
*He guides me in the paths of righteousness*
*For His name's sake.*

*Even though I walk through the valley of the*
*shadow of death, I fear no evil; for Thou art with me;*
*Thy rod and Thy staff, they comfort me.*

*Thou dost prepare a table before me*
*in the presence of my enemies;*
*Thou hast anointed my head with oil;*
*My cup overflows.*

*Surely goodness and lovingkindness will follow me*
*all the days of my life,*
*And I will dwell in the house of the Lord forever.*

**Although this note is short, it still contains a strategy for moving this process along to the next step.**

The most overlooked part of job follow-up is the statement of next steps. It is *your* responsibility to make sure the process is moved along to the next step.

For example, if they say they'll call you in a week, you can say: If I don't hear from you in a week or so, I'll give you a call."

Don't be surprised if they don't call: everyone is very busy, and you are probably not at the top of their list. Gently move them along—within *their* time frame—in your follow-up note.

---

**Charles Cates**

To: Wally Dobbs

I enjoyed our conversation last week. Your need to modernize and integrate existing systems, and to make them flexible enough to accommodate future opportunities such as the repeal of Glass-Steagall, certainly sounds like an intriguing challenge.

I appreciate your suggestion that I meet with some of the people in your group, and would like very much to talk with you further. I'll call you in a few days to set something up.

Best regards,
*Charles*

## Frederika Balzano

Street Address
City, State, Zip
(555) 555-2231

July 18, 19xx

Mr. James Gallagher
General Counsel and Senior Vice President
Valentino
100 Madison Avenue
New York, NY 10000

> **Applying to be Assistant General Counsel.
> The hiring manager
> considers the "family environment" crucial.**

Dear Jim:

The opportunity to meet and speak with you last week was a real pleasure. It is clear to me that Valentino offers the close, family environment and real team feeling that I so much enjoyed at Campeau. Since we were great friends there, we were very supportive of each other as colleagues and the experience was one of the most rewarding I have had. I know that I would feel equally at home at Valentino, as the chemistry seems right for me.

It also seems that my 20 years experience with Fortune 20 companies in the fashion / retail industry, both as a merchant and as a legal executive, could not be more ideally suited for heading up your new leather division.

In addition, after talking with you, I can't imagine a legal background that's a better fit:
  • Extensive marketing law experience (and Valentino is a "marketing-driven" company);
  • Litigation (both actual practice and complex management);
  • Environmental compliance (set up a $40 million program);
  • Commercial contracts (UCC Article 2);
  • Antitrust compliance;
  • Responsibility for a worldwide trademark program
    (with 200 domestic and 70 foreign registrations in 35 countries);
  • Licensing arrangements; and,
  • Legislative matters (we do need to do something about grey market matters).

> **During the interview,
> she convinced him to
> hire a legal generalist.
> But just in case he
> wants a specialist,
> she's covered.**

> **Can you handle
> these young,
> unmanageable
> clients? Yes, I can.
> And I also work
> well with the top
> brass.**

Finally, I enjoy working with the type of client you have: young, innovative, creative people who have an enthusiasm and eagerness to get the job done quickly. I appreciate their creativity because I am a creative person myself. Since I have a business background (which most attorneys do not have), I also empathize with their desire to get on with things—but in their eagerness important issues may be overlooked. I'm able to bring to bear on those issues (business as well as legal), yet encourage their initiative and still protect the company from any unwarranted liability or exposure.

Of course, I'm also experienced in working with Senior Management. At Campeau I advised them on a daily basis and understand the type of advice appropriate at that level.

I'm very excited about being part of the team you are building. I just know that it would prove to be a mutually rewarding experience. I look forward to getting together with you again. As you meet other candidates, other issues may arise, and I would appreciate the opportunity to address them. In the meantime I will keep you apprised of any new developments in my search.

Cordially,

*In the realm of ideas, everything depends on
enthusiasm; in the real world,
all rests on perseverance.*
Goethe

*All right, I hated the job. You're right:
I admit it. I'm glad to be done with it—all right!*
Peter Schaeffer, *Lettice & Lovage*

*The mode by which the inevitable
is reached is effort.*
Felix Frankfurter

## A Few Hints

1. This note and the one on the following page
were written after a job interview. This one is to
personnel, while the other is to the hiring manager.

The strategy is to keep personnel informed (and
perhaps have them as an advocate), but to **"do the
deal" with the hiring manager**.

2. It's rare that a job offer is made after the first
interview. In fact, you don't want an offer that early
in the process. Therefore, think of what would be
required next to move the process along so it *could*
turn into a job offer.

What logically do you think should happen

### Nancy Geffner

March 24, 19xx

Dear Kim:

I enjoyed the chance to meet with you and discuss American
Express. I also found John to be a very dynamic and
stimulating individual.

The position we discussed requires a combination of creative, strategic thinking and hard-nosed, practical, get-it-
done skills. I think it would be a very good fit for my abilities
and experience, and, further, would be the most stimulating
and exciting thing that I have ever done.

Thus I would like to meet with John again. I suggested to
him that we discuss one region's business in depth, to better
understand the key business issues and opportunities, and
give him a clearer sense of how I would approach them.

I look forward to hearing from you.

Sincerely,

*Nancy*

## Carl Gimber

March 24, 19xx

Dear Bob:

I greatly enjoyed the chance to meet with you and learn about the structure and needs of your business.

It became increasingly clear to me that the position we discussed would be a good fit for my skills and interests. You are confronted with a complex mosaic of regional businesses, with very different profit dynamics, competitive situations and broker/customer relationships. Major variations in regional economic trends and industry structures make this situation even more complex.

Thus you clearly need someone who can quickly develop an understanding of each regional business, and of the needs and goals of the profit centers, and then <u>visualize</u> opportunities that this creates. These could take the form of improved marketing or product development programs against current businesses, or innovative plans for the new industries and market segments that will emerge as the regional economies develop.

I think that this is consistent with my strongest skills. I am a quick study and a good strategic thinker who can digest a lot of complex information and build a coherent, actionable structure from it. I am also very good at sensing marketing opportunities and creating unique ways to capitalize on them. My broad-based marketing background provides a wide range of ideas and experience to draw from. At the same time, line management assignments in the branches have tempered my "visionary" thinking with a hard-nosed practical approach and an appreciation for the day-to-day realities of running a business.

For these reasons, I think the assignment we discussed would be more exciting and intellectually stimulating than anything I have ever done. Thus I would like very much to talk more about it.

As a next step, it might be valuable to discuss one region in some depth, reviewing American Express's current business, broker and customer relations, competitive factors and economic trends in the market. This would allow me to give you a clearer sense of how I would actually identify opportunities and develop programs against them, and would give me a more detailed understanding of the key opportunities and problems faced by your business.

I think this discussion could be of value to both of us, and I look forward to meeting with you again.

Sincerely,

*Carl*

## Edward Witherell

Street Address
City, State, Zip
(212) 555-2231

March 10, 1986

Mr. William Stanley
Golden Casino
Seaside Avenue
Atlantic City, NJ 08401

Dear Bill:

Thanks for the time and insight you provided on the Gaming Industry and Golden's. The Industry is extremely interesting to me and, since its early years in Atlantic City, opportunity and growth lie ahead. Golden's, as the premier operator, is in the best position to benefit from this growth.

I can bring both a conceptual and statistical approach to the evaluation of promotional programs in your department. My financial and marketing experience in the evaluation of merchandising programs can be transferred to the Gaming Industry. I believe the cross-industry perspective and approach is a positive addition.

The position you are starting up is a most challenging and exciting spot. The future structure, design, implementation and evaluation of merchandising/promotional offers will be significantly influenced by this position. It will provide a very logical look at the true impact promotions have on the business.

I think that as competition becomes greater and profit margins are closely watched, it will be very important to know what promotional button to push to get the best results. I know I can provide that input based on analytical studies.

I look forward to hearing from you in a week.

Sincerely,

Ed Witherell

The

Five

O'Clock

Club

# Follow-Up After a Job Interview

## Nancy Mercante

Street Address
City, State
(212) 555-2231

May 10, 19xx

Mr. John Leonard
Senior Vice President
United Way of Tristate
Street Address
City, State, Zip

Dear John:

First of all, thank you for giving me the opportunity to speak with you last week. It was really a pleasure for me to meet you, and I appreciated learning about the goals and needs of the Unted Way of Tristate from your perspective and experience.

Because of our discussion I am even more eager to pursue finding a place for myself in the planning, management, and support of human-care services. I am encouraged that there might be such an opportunity for me within the United Way of Tristate.

I spent some time reading the materials you gave me and am especially impressed with the Strategic Plan. I believe that I have skills, experience, and motivations that would be instrumental in the successful implementation of the Plan, for example:

- strong quantitative skills: conducting research, financial, and technical information analyses.
- experience in developing and assessing marketing plans and strategies for diverse target markets.
- problem-solving ability that is challenged by new and continually varied situations.
- excellent oral and written communication skills, with experience in delivering presentations to top-level corporate executives.
- enthusiasm for the mission of United Way.

I welcome and appreciate the effort you are making to explore the possibilities for me within your organization. I would like to stay in touch with you during this time, and would be pleased to meet again for additional discussions.

Thank you for your support. I'm looking forward to hearing from you when you have more information about your situation and its potential for me.

Sincerely,

Nancy Mercante

The
Five
O'Clock
Club

# Follow-Up After a
# Job Interview

Robert Riscica
Glen Ridge Cove
San Francisco, CA 66666

April 15, 199x

Mr. Victor Colon-Rivera
Technology Planning Division
Bank of America
One Pickalilly Square-40th Floor
San Francisco, CA 66620

> **This is a logical format to follow. Each issue identified in the interview process becomes a paragraph heading.**

Dear Victor,

Your department is an impressive one. I remain very interested in the position we discussed, and think that the following elements of my skills and relevant experience would serve me well in accomplishing your objectives:

## Project Management

My responsibilities as <u>Project Director</u> at General Dynamics included collecting data from a project team comprised of accounting and technology professionals and <u>writing comprehensive functional specifications</u> for a new front-end interface to the General Ledger System. I also prepared and gave periodic progress presentations to a steering committee comprised of senior bank executives.

## Computer Systems/Technology Exposure

Throughout my career, I have had close involvement with technology professionals, most significantly:

- at <u>Bank of America,</u> particularly in my most recent position as Project Manager where I was involved in the conversion of the community banks to B of A's "Utility" systems;
- at <u>General Dynamics,</u> as mentioned above and as an <u>Accounting Systems Liaison</u> where I was responsible for ensuring adherence to bankwide accounting standards in the development of new application systems;
- at <u>Wells Fargo,</u> where I was directly involved in the detailed evaluation of new General Ledger software vs Wells' older, in-house developed package;
- at <u>Walt Disney Co.,</u> where I reviewed and approved new application systems for inclusion of effective audit controls.

## Finance

My experience as Regional Financial Controller for B of A's West Region corporate business units and that as a Business Manager within the former National Corporate Division required a thorough understanding of global finance products and services.

## Training

In my most recent position at Bank of America (Project Manager), I provided extensive training via "Hands-on" workshops in the use of automated Proof Collection/Clearance to employees in retail business units nationally. I also prepared training materials and developed test procedures for use in connection with training exercises.

## PC Skills/Lotus Notes

I have extensive PC skills and experience at developing PC based applications for general use:

- As Controller for B of A in San Francisco, I developed a <u>PFS database application</u> which tracked premises receivable and billed all tenants for rent and other costs.
- As Business Manager for Corporate Finance Analysis, I developed comprehensive <u>Paradox databases</u> to control Personnel/Staffing as well as Accounts Payable.

I have a high level of technical proficiency in Lotus Notes based on my intensive self-training efforts over the last few months and, as I mentioned, have a Notes Server and two workstations set-up on the computer network which I maintain in my home.

As we discussed, should you select another candidate for the position, I would greatly appreciate consideration for a temporary position involved with Lotus Notes. The benefit of such an arrangement, besides the obvious one of extending my severance period, is that it would provide me the opportunity to contribute to B of A's Notes environment and thereby establish myself as a viable candidate for future Notes related positions within the bank.

Again, thank you for your interest. I look forward to hearing from you.

Sincerely,

Robert Riscica

**Stacy Feldman**
444 Pound Ridge Road
Dallas, Texas 44444

April 4, 199x

Roy Cohen
Kendall Guaranty Trust Company
666 Brick Wall West
Dallas, Texas 44444-0060

> Here's another approach to organizing your
> follow-up around the important issues.
> Of course, Stacy wrote a customized follow-up
> to every person with whom she met.

Dear Roy,

It was an exciting and eventful day. Thank you for giving me the opportunity. I learned even more about Kendall and training's mission there.

In my view, three issues about me came up during the day's meeting. I wanted to tell you about them.

- There was some concern about my lack of experience with Fortune 500 clients. But I think my experience with a wide range of underwriting and advisory work is more to the point. I know firsthand what it takes to develop a corporate finance opportunity, compete for a mandate and take an issuer to market. I can bring that practical perspective to my work in training, even if I've had relatively few Fortune 500 clients in my recent banking career.

- My job changes understandably drew comments. I realize Kendall is a company where long service is the norm. As you know, I've put a lot of time, thought and effort into this career change, and I'm committed to it and to Kendall as well. You have the kind of challenging standards and defining principles that I found compelling in the Navy and have missed in my work life ever since.

- There may have been some concern about whether I bring to the job a larger vision of training's strategic role. I know from the Navy how crucial corporate values can be to success and how training at all levels can be used to reinforce values. In business, I've been very interested in how General Electric is using values to improve its competitiveness and performance. Aside from that, I've been more focused on corporate finance practice than strategic issues in training.

I hope you had a good time in New Orleans and Natchez. If you have any questions or other concerns I can address, please don't hesitate to call.

Sincerely,

Stacy Feldman

**JEANNETTE MOBLEY**
10 Park Terrace East
Chicago, IL 00007

December 1, 199x

Ms. Linda Davidson
Vice President - Manager Asset Securitization
Bank of Germany
1211 Bird-in-Cage Way
Chicago, IL 00007

Dear Linda:

I admired greatly your thoroughness and enthusiasm, and I came away with a good understanding of Bank of Germany's strategies for growing the business in North America. I believe that given Bank of Germany's size and reach worldwide, you could become a major bank in the U.S., and I would like to help you to do that. I have given it a great deal of thought and I have decided that I'd love to work for you and for Bank of Germany.

I believe I could add value to Bank of Germany's asset securitization business in the following ways:

### Ability to immediately close deals and also address critical tax accounting issues

Because of my in-depth knowledge of the market, I am able to immediately contribute to closing existing transactions and make necessary marketing calls jointly and separately to build a profile of active deals for 1995 1st quarter closure. I have structured and closed asset securitization deals in the past and I am willing to do the detailed, unexciting, plodding work that it takes to execute the transactions.

Moreover, I am intimately aware of the complicated tax issues facing Bank of Germany as a U.S. branch of a foreign bank.

### Superb Contacts

Having worked with Fortune 500 companies and foreign banks for over 16 years in project finance, tax leasing, debt and equity placement, lending and structuring corporate finance solutions for multinationals, I am confident that Bank of Germany could become a niche player in several product lines including lead manager for asset secured deals for a select number of corporations. In the past 6 months I have had numerous discussions with several companies and institutional investors, and I have already done the target marketing. These companies place high value on competence, debt rating and execution skills. They would relish working with us and Bank of Germany.

*It may be that the race is not always to the swift,
nor the battle to the strong, but that's the way to bet.*
Damon Runyon

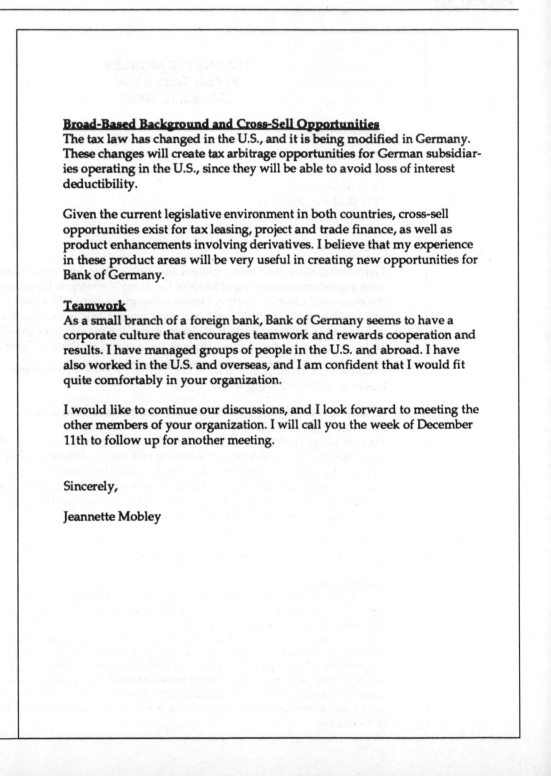

**Broad-Based Background and Cross-Sell Opportunities**
The tax law has changed in the U.S., and it is being modified in Germany.
These changes will create tax arbitrage opportunities for German subsidiaries operating in the U.S., since they will be able to avoid loss of interest
deductibility.

Given the current legislative environment in both countries, cross-sell
opportunities exist for tax leasing, project and trade finance, as well as
product enhancements involving derivatives. I believe that my experience
in these product areas will be very useful in creating new opportunities for
Bank of Germany.

**Teamwork**
As a small branch of a foreign bank, Bank of Germany seems to have a
corporate culture that encourages teamwork and rewards cooperation and
results. I have managed groups of people in the U.S. and abroad. I have
also worked in the U.S. and overseas, and I am confident that I would fit
quite comfortably in your organization.

I would like to continue our discussions, and I look forward to meeting the
other members of your organization. I will call you the week of December
11th to follow up for another meeting.


Sincerely,

Jeannette Mobley

The
Five
O'Clock
Club

# Four-Step Salary Negotiation Strategy

*I've got all the money I'll ever*
*need if I die by four o'clock.*
Henny Youngman

---

*There arises from the hearts of busy [people] a love of*
*variety, a yearning for relaxation of thought as well as of*
*body, and a craving for a generous and*
*spontaneous fraternity.*
J. Hampton Moore
*History of The Five O'Clock Club*, 1891

Now you know you not only have to impress the hiring manager, but also other influencers so they will want to have you on board. In addition, you have to think about your likely competitors, and how you can convince everyone you meet that you are the best choice. During the interview, a job hunter may also think about salary.

When job hunters ask about salary negotiation, they usually want to know how to answer the questions What are you making now? and What are you looking for? We'll cover these issues in detail a little later, but it is more important to first look at salary negotiation from a strategic point of view. From the very first meeting, you can set the stage for compensation discussions later.

Most job hunters think about salary—unconsciously and anxiously—during their first meeting. They think, I'm making $50,000 now (or $150,000), but I know this person won't pay more than $35,000 (or $135,000). Most job hunters try to get rid of the anxiety. They don't want to waste their time if this person isn't going to pay them fairly. So when the hiring manager mentions money, the job hunter is relieved to talk about it.

> Hiring manager: How much are you making now?
> Job hunter: I'm making $50,000.
> Hiring manager: That's a little rich for us. We were thinking about $35,000.
> Job hunter: I couldn't possibly take $35,000.

End of discussion. Another wasted interview. But there is a better way. Intend to turn every job interview into an appropriate offer. Overcome the company's objections to hiring you, and overcome your own objections to working there. If the salary or something else bothers you about the job, think about how you can change it.

Think more consciously and more strategically. Intend to negotiate. Most job hunters don't negotiate at all.

- They don't negotiate the job. They listen passively to what the job is, and try to fit themselves into it—or reject it.

- They certainly don't negotiate the salary. They listen to the offer, and then decide whether they want to take it.

## Don't accept or reject a job until it is offered to you.

Job hunters decide whether or not they want the job without negotiating to make it more appropriate—and without even getting an offer! Career counselors have a maxim: Don't accept or reject a job until it is offered to you.

We'll see how you can be more proactive rather than passive. The following guidelines will allow you to take more control and more responsibility for what happens to you. Following these steps will not guarantee you the compensation you want, but you will certainly do much better than if you do not follow them. Remember the four steps you will learn here—and pay attention to where you are in those steps.

## If you can remember these four steps with regard to a particular company, you will do better in your salary negotiation —*and in your entire search as well.*

### Step 1: Negotiate the Job

By now, you have already negotiated the job. You have created a job that suits both you and the hiring manager. Make sure it is at an appropriate level for you. If the job is too low-level, don't ask about the salary—*upgrade the job.* Add responsibilities until the job is worth your while. Make sure the hiring manager agrees that this new job is what he or she wants. Don't negotiate the salary yet.

### Step 2: Outshine and Outlast Your Competition

By now, you have already killed off your competition. You have kept in the running by offering to do more than your competitors. You have paid more attention to the progress made in your meetings, and you have moved the process along. You have satisfied every need, and responded to every objection. For some jobs, it can take five interviews before the subject of salary is discussed. All the while, your competitors have been dropping out. It is best to postpone the discussion of salary until they are all gone.

### Step 3: Get the Offer

Once a manager has decided that you are the right person, you are in a better position to negotiate a package that is appropriate for you. Until you actually get the offer, postpone the discussion of salary.

### Step 4: Negotiate Your Compensation Package

Most job hunters hear the offer and then either accept or reject it. This is not negotiating. If you have never negotiated a package for yourself, you need to practice. Why not try to get some offers that don't even interest you, just so you can practice negotiating the salary? Here are some hints to get you started:

- Know the company's, and the industry's pay scales.

- Know what you want in a negotiation session, and know what you are willing to do without. Negotiate one point at a time. Negotiate base pay first and then the points the employer would easily agree to. Save for last the issues of conflict. Be prepared to back off, or not even bring up, issues that are not important to you.

- You are both on the same side. Each of you should want a deal that works now and works later—not one that will make either of you resentful.

- Care—but not too much. If you desperately want the job—at any cost—you will not do a good job of negotiating. You must convince yourself, at least for the time you are interviewing, that you have alternatives.

- Try to get them to state the first bid. If they say: "How much do you want?" You say: "How much are you offering?" If pressed about your

*The moment you feel foolish, you look foolish. Concentrate, block it out, and relax. Of course, that's not always easy.*
Michael Caine, *Acting in Film*

prior salary, either say instead what you are looking for, or be sure to include bonus and perks. Some include an expected bonus or increase in salary.

• If the manager makes you an unacceptable offer, *talk about the job*. Look disappointed and say how enthusiastic you are about the position, the company, and the possibility of doing great things for this manager. Say everything is great, and you can't wait to start—but your only reservation is the compensation. Ask what can be done about this.

Be reasonable. As the saying goes: bulls win, and bears win, but pigs never win.

### It Works at All Levels

Once I did a salary negotiation seminar for low-level corporate people. One person had been a paper-burster for twenty-five years: He tore the sheets of paper as they came off the computer. But because he had been at the company for twenty-five years, his salary was at the top of the range of paper bursters. He had the same kind of salary problem a lot of us have.

The four steps worked for him, too. He told the hiring managers, "Not only can I burst the paper, But I can fix the machines. This will save you on machine downtime and machine repair costs. And I can train people, which will also save you money."

He was:

**1. Negotiating the job**

And:

**2. Killing off his competition**

And after he:

**3. Gets the offer**

He'll have no trouble:

**4. Negotiating the salary.**

Know where you are in the four steps. If you have not yet done steps one, two and three, try to postpone step four.

### CASE STUDY: BESSIE
*It Can Even Work Against Me*

Once when I was a CFO for a small firm, I wanted to hire an accounting manager who would supervise a staff of four.

I told an excellent search firm exactly what I wanted and the salary range I was looking for: "someone in the $50,000 range."

I received lots of résumés—all of which the search firm had marked at the top: "Asking for $50,000." I interviewed a lot of people, but Bessie stood out from the crowd. I had Bessie meet with a peer of mine and also with the president. Everyone loved her.

Finally, I told Bessie that we were pleased to offer her the $50,000 she wanted. Bessie said, "I would love to work here, but I would not be happy with $50,000. I didn't put that there."

I was stunned, but I was also stuck. We had made an investment in Bessie. Everyone had met her and loved her, and she wisely stayed mum about the money until she received the offer. A more anxious job hunter might have said early on, "I see that it says $50,000 at the top of my résumé, but I just want you to know that I am already making more than that." That would have been admirable honesty but the person would have been out of the running.

Bessie wound up with $55,000, which is what she was worth—and we wound up with an excellent employee. Bessie had followed the four steps exactly.

---

1. **Negotiate the job.**
2. **Outshine and outlast your competition.**
3. **Get the offer.**
4. **Negotiate your package.**

---

### CASE STUDY: KATE, 1980
*All Four Steps in Action*

I was earning, let's say, around $60,000 in 1980. A search firm called me about a job that paid $40,000. Remember, search firms are a means for getting *interviews—not* for getting jobs. Don't negotiate salary with the search firm. Simply decide whether you want the *interview*.

I asked the recruiter what the job was. "It's with

an advertising agency," she said. "They're looking for a woman to supervise the secretarial staff."

I had an MBA, was making $60,000, and specialized in turning around troubled firms. The average recruiter cannot negotiate job content but *can* give information. When she described the situation, it seemed to me that the company was in trouble and was using the wrong solutions to solve their problems. I told her I would like to meet with the president. She said, "You *would*?"

I like situations in which I know who my competition is: people who want to supervise secretaries for $40,000. I asked the president:

- How is your company organized?
- What are your biggest accounts?
- What is the profit margin on each?
- Do you have a cost-accounting system?
- May I see your computer system?
- Did you know that certain reports would give you better profit control?

His eyes lit up. I was headed in the right direction—and was killing off my competition while I created a job more appropriate for myself. I kept

talking to him about his business and what we could do to turn it around. I was trying to move it along, move it along, move it along—and kill off my competition.

After the offer, we got into the formal discussion of salary. At this point, I wanted:

- the title "VP of Operations"
- to chair the executive committee so we could turn the company around
- easy access to the CPA firm. They would be my partners in this.

The actual salary was not a problem. But you can see that it would have been if I had discussed it too early, when the president was thinking about a much lower-level job. After we defined a new job and he definitely wanted me, we were in a better position to discuss a salary that was right for the new position.

"Salary negotiation" involves more than salary. It can involve negotiating for anything you need to do the job well, in addition to your compensation package.

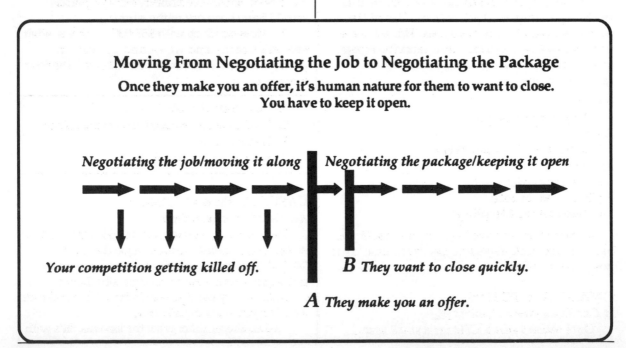

## Moving From Negotiating the Job to Negotiating the Package

Once they make you an offer, it's human nature for them to want to close.
You have to keep it open.

*Negotiating the job/moving it along*

*Negotiating the package/keeping it open*

*Your competition getting killed off.*

*B They want to close quickly.*

*A They make you an offer.*

## Do the Deal Yourself

If possible, negotiate directly with the hiring manager—yourself. You can see from the last example that I did all of my negotiation with the president of the firm and not through the recruiter. The recruiter was not in a position to do the kind of negotiation that I was able to do on my own. Yet the recruiter still received a fee based on the larger amount that I was offered.

By the time you receive an offer, the hiring manager has already decided that he or she wants you, and is the only one who can see your true worth. He or she has an emotional stake in the outcome, and is therefore usually an easier person with whom to negotiate. In addition, the negotiation is not simply about compensation, but about the work you will do in return for that compensation. All of these issues are difficult to negotiate through a middleman.

If you are scared, you may actually prefer to negotiate your compensation through a search firm or through human resources. But it sometimes happens that the message you were trying to send through the middleman winds up very different from what you intended.

The recruiter feels that he or she has a stake in the outcome because, after all, it could mean the loss of a fee if you mess up. But the recruiter does not understand that you know a lot about negotiating. On the other hand, there are recruiters who do an excellent job in handling the negotiation. Simply make sure you are aware of everything they are doing so you can interject yourself back into the process if need be.

## How to Interject Yourself Back into the Process

This is tricky. Sometimes you find yourself dealing with a middleman when you really want to speak directly to the hiring manager. Simply tell the middle man that you have come up with a few more issues related to the job that you would like to discuss with the hiring manger. Once you have gained access to the manager, discuss those job-related issues, develop a rapport, and then bring up the compensation issues you would like to discuss.

Certain issues, such as benefits, are usually discussed with personnel—so don't burden the hiring manager with those. Meet directly with personnel to review the benefits package.

If you are in a complex situation, you may want to work with your career coach on this. It's very helpful to have the point of view of a trusted advisor.

> **Be sure the person with whom you are negotiating is at the right level. If you find yourself constantly bumping up against the salary level of the people with whom you are negotiating, the problem is not your salary negotiation technique. The problem is that you are talking to people who are at the wrong level.**

## CASE STUDY: GEORGIA
### *Using All Four Steps*

I had been coaching Georgia throughout her job search. She had interviewed to head a small profit center at a hospital. She would be involved with eleven radiologists who gave cancer tests in a mobile unit, and two administrators. She also had competition.

Georgia had met with six doctors. One particularly unpleasant one asked for a proposal on how she would handle the job. This was Wednesday—the day before Thanksgiving. He wanted it back the Monday after Thanksgiving!

Georgia and I worked at my dining room table over Thanksgiving. "You can be sure no one else is putting in this much effort," I told her.

Georgia hand-delivered not one proposal, but *six,* and on time. She did not want her fate in the hands of one nasty doctor. Her cover notes were different, but essentially said, "Dr. So-and-So asked for this proposal. I felt duty-bound to give you a copy as well, since the things we discussed are reflected here."

Within an hour of the delivery, Georgia got a call from her future boss (not the nasty doctor). She told me that he was elated: "We want to offer you

*You can get more with a kind word and a gun*
*than you can get with a kind word alone.*
Johnny Carson

the job. If you don't take it, we're stuck. We don't want any of the other people who interviewed, and we'll be forced to start our search over." This was music to my ears, because in effect he was telling her that she *no longer had competitors*.

Now we were in a different phase of the search. It's human nature that the person making the offer simply wants to come to closure. However, you need time to discuss things.

I said to Georgia, "You've spent plenty of time defining the job. You need an equal amount of time to define the compensation."

She went back to the doctors and repeated my words verbatim: "We've spent plenty of time defining..."

They immediately backed off. "You're right. We'll spend whatever time it takes to resolve these issues."

They didn't want to lose Georgia. She had paid her dues, and now she was in a strong position to negotiate. They made her a written offer. Then we worked up a counteroffer.

- She wanted a certain base pay.
- She would need entertainment expenses to sell this program.
- The bonus was important to her.

### Calculating the Bonus

We wanted a bonus based on the volume the high-tech $250,000 trucks could handle. We decided that each truck would probably need one day of maintenance a month, and that each radiologist would be able to do $x$ number of tests.

With the bonus based on truck volume, we figured what Georgia's maximum salary would be. To allow for year two, we asked the hospital to buy another truck if the volume reached a certain amount.

When Georgia delivered the counteroffer, the doctors couldn't believe it; they now had a truck operating at almost no volume, and Georgia was talking about buying another truck! It showed that she planned on making this a successful venture.

Georgia got the compensation she wanted, and something else...

### Georgia Got to Keep Her Job

Because she followed up with every person with whom she met, and because she wrote such a detailed proposal, they were committed to her. Georgia had bought six months of safety in the job: she could do no wrong. The very first day, Georgia realized she'd had a misunderstanding during the interview process and needed to change something about the way the job was done. It was no problem. A job hunter who is thorough in the search process has laid the foundation for keeping her job. Unlike other new hires, the jury is *not* out on her. Georgia had proved herself. The doctors knew that no one knew more about this business than she did. She knew even more than *they* did!

That's why you want to follow up with *everyone*—including future peers and subordinates—during your search. You may be working with them later. And if any of them has an objection to hiring you, try to settle it during the search, rather than handling it after you are hired. Build strong relationships during the interview phase.

Know where you are in the process. Take the steps in sequence. You will not get the offer until after you have negotiated the job and also killed off your competition.

If a job pays $20,000 less than you want, that's fine for now. Postpone the salary discussion. Remember that you are there not for this specific job, but for a position that has not yet been completely defined—and in which you have some say.

A skilled negotiator has a different approach—and much more power—than someone who does not know these techniques. A skilled negotiator chases companies, not jobs. A certain position may not be right, but the job hunter wants to make a good impression anyway because there may be other places in the organization that are right for him or her.

---

**Have you already received an offer? If they are *thinking* about making you an offer, that's not the same as actually *making* you an offer. It's not time to negotiate your compensation until you actually receive an offer.**

**Where is your competition, by the way? You cannot assess your negotiating leverage until you know how the hiring team sees you compared with your competition. You may have already received the offer, but could the company easily consider someone else? If so, you are not in a strong negotiating position. If the hiring team wants nobody but you, you are in a stronger negotiating position.**

## CASE STUDY: STANLEY
### Using All Four Steps

Stanley, an executive who had been in the fashion industry his entire life, heard about a job opening that was being handled by a search firm. He met with the recruiter who could not put him in for the job because Stanley's salary was a great deal more than what the company was willing to pay.

This is not the search firm's fault. They represent the company. They were hired by the company to fill a certain job at a certain salary level. They cannot go back to the company and say, "I know you wanted me to find someone at $100,000. I have found someone who is at $200,000, but I think you should see him."

After it was clear that the search firm would not put Stanley in for the job, he approached the firm directly.

He first wrote to the chairman (this is a targeted mailing) and followed up with a phone call. The chairman refused to see him. Then he wrote to the president, followed up with a phone call, and got a meeting.

The president said, "Not only is your base too high by $50,000, your total package would be so high that it would be out of the question." Stanley said, "I assure you that salary will not be a problem." (You will see this technique in the next chapter.) "I have always done well every place I have ever worked, and I am sure the same would happen here. May I keep in touch with you?" (He intended to "follow up" as every good Five

O'Clock Clubber does.)

Stanley kept in touch by meeting with others in his industry and coming up with ideas for the president. They met a number of times. Stanley started to look better and better compared with the other candidates. This was understandable, since they were all much lower-level than he was.

Eventually, Stanley got the job—at the salary that was appropriate for him. After Stanley had met with the president—and the chairman—a number of times, they tried to figure out some way to get Stanley on board.

As it happened, the chairman was planning to retire in two years, and the president was going to become chairman. Stanley was brought in to be the heir apparent to the president.

For more on this topic, read "What To Do When You Know There's a Job Opening."

In summary, think about where you are in the four steps. It will help you concentrate on what you should be doing. If you still have competitors, for example, it is too early to negotiate salary. And practice. Salary negotiation takes a lot of skill, but by doing it right you are more likely to wind up getting paid what you are worth.

*They're only puttin' in a nickel,
but they want a dollar song.*
Song title

*To do this job right is an all-encompassing proposition. I felt I wasn't doing as good a job with the kids as I wanted, and I wasn't doing as well with the business as I wanted. I needed to have a better balance between work and my family,
and have some time left over for me.*
Jeffrey A. Stiefler, resigning as
president of American Express Co.
Quoted by G. Bruce Knecht,
*Wall Street Journal*, November 22, 1995

> **Are you presently at market rates?**
> **Below market?**
> **Above market?**
> **Knowing where you stand will help you answer the questions:**
> **"What are you making now?"**
> **and**
> **"What are you looking for?"**

B y now, you know where you are in the four steps. In fact, for each company with whom you are meeting, you know exactly where you are in the process. If you are conscious of where you are, you will do much better than if you simply do what seems reasonable without regard to where you are in the process.

In addition, the more experienced you become in negotiating your compensation, the more you can assess what is appropriate for a given situation and deviate from the rules. However, until you are an experienced negotiator, it is best to play by the rules.

## What Are You Making Now?
## What Are You Looking For?

Now we'll look at the questions you've been waiting for. But we'll look at them strategically-so you can *plan* an appropriate answer depending on your situation. First, you need to develop some background information before you can plan your strategy for answering the questions. The strategy will also give you hints for postponing the discussion of salary until you have an offer.

### Background Information: Figure out what you really make.

Start with your base salary, but also include your bonus and any perks, such as a company car, a savings plan, deferred compensation, company lunches, company contribution to insurance plans, and so on. That's what you really make—but that may not be what you will tell the prospective employer.

### Background Information: Figure out what you are worth in the market.

Talk to search firms, ask people at association meetings, look at ads in the paper, and—most of all—network. At networking meetings, ask, "What kind of salary could someone like me expect at your company?" A few networking meetings will give you a good idea of the market rates for someone like you.

*We're all in this alone.*
Lily Tomlin

However, you must remember that you are worth different amount in different markets. You may be worth a certain amount in one industry, field or geographic area, and a different amount in other industries, fields or geographic areas.

What's more, you may be worth more to one company than you would be to another.

Research what you are worth in each of your target markets. And when you are interviewing at a specific company, find out as much as you can about the way they pay.

### Background Information: Compare what you are making (total compensation) with what the market is paying.

You need to know if you are presently at market rates, below market, or above market. *This is the key* to how you will answer a hiring manager or search firm that asks you, "What are you making?" or, ""What are you looking for?"

### How to Answer:
### If You Are Within the Market Range

Most companies want to know what you are making and, if you are within the market range, they will pay you 10 to 15 percent above what you are currently making. Therefore, if you are making $40,000 and you know the market is paying $43,000 to $45,000, then you could say, "Right now I'm at $40,000, but I'm looking to move a little away from that." The only time you can safely state your current compensation is when you are at market rates.

### How to Answer:
### If You Are Above Market Rates

A counselor asked me to have a meeting with his client Sam, who was having problems finding a job because of his high salary. I did an interview role play with Sam. At one point I said, "So, Sam, what are you making now?" Sam replied, "Two hundred thousand dollars plus-plus-plus." I said, "I know you're a very competent person, but we simply cannot afford someone at your high level."

Sam's salary was not hurting him, but his way of talking about it was. Even if your salary isn't $200,000-plus-plus-plus, you can easily put off the hiring manager if she thinks your salary will be a problem. You have to give her a chance to find out about you, and you have to think about how you can create a job that is appropriate for your salary. You must tell her, "Salary will not be a problem"—*especially if you know it is a problem*. You have to think to yourself that it won't be a problem when she gets to know you better and understands what you will do for her. Otherwise, you will not get anywhere.

---

**Your position has to be that "salary won't be a problem." It is your job to reassure the hiring manager that you are both on the same team and can work this out. When they get to know you better—and what you have to offer—salary *won't* be a problem.**

---

If you are making more than the market rate, do your best to create a job that warrants the salary you want and defer the discussion of salary until you have the offer. When you're asked, "What are you making now?" use a response from the list below to reassure the hiring manager that you are both on the same team and can work this out. These responses are listed in sequence from easiest to most difficult. Try the easy response first. If the hiring manager persists you may have to move on to one of the other responses. You are simply trying to postpone the discussion of salary until she knows you better and you have an offer.

The manager asks, "What are you making now?" You respond:

• "I'd prefer to postpone talking about the salary until I'm more clear about the job I'll be doing. When we come to some agreement on the job, I know that salary won't be a problem."
• "Salary won't be a problem. But I'm not exactly sure what the job is, so maybe we can talk more about that. I'm very flexible, and I'm sure that when we come to some agreement on the job, we can work out the salary."
• "Salary won't be a problem. I know that you

© 1996, Kate Wendleton and The Five O'Clock Club®　　283

> *Are you not ashamed of heaping up the greatest amount money and honor and reputation, and caring so little about wisdom and truth and the greatest improvement of the soul, which you never regard or heed at all?* Socrates

do not want to bring someone in at a salary that makes you resentful, and I'm sure you do not want me to be resentful either. I know that we'll come to a happy agreement."

• "I'm making very good money right now, and I deserve it. But I'd hate to tell you what it is because I'm afraid it will put you off. I know that salary will not be a problem. I'm a fair person and I'm sure you are, too I know we'll come to an agreement."

• "I'm being paid very well, and I'm worth it. But I'm very interested in your company and I'm willing to make an investment in this if you are. As far as I'm concerned, salary won't be a problem."

Marie successfully postponed the discussion of salary for two years. When she came to The Five O'Clock Club, she had been unemployed for a long while. It took six months before she was on the verge of a job offer at a major fashion house, the company of her dreams. On the day she was to receive the offer, the company went "into play." That is, another company was trying to take this one over, so all hiring was put on hold. Marie was more desperate than ever. Within a month or two, she received an offer from a major entertainment company, went to work there, and continued to keep in touch with the fashion house.

Over the next year and a half, she had meetings with the president and most of the senior executives at the fashion house. Each one asked her about her salary, and to each one she replied with one of the statements listed above. She eventually got a tremendous offer—after having postponed the discussion of salary for two years. By the way, Marie's boss at the entertainment company told her that lie hired her because she was so persistent in her follow-up. He thought she acted a little desperate, which she was after having been unemployed for so long, but he gave her the job because it seemed to mean so much to her. And, of course, she later got the job at the fashion house because she followed up with them for *two years!* If this desperate job hunter could postpone the discussion of salary, so can you. But you need to practice with someone. It does not come naturally.

## How to Answer:
### If You are Making Below Market Rates

Again, you have a few options. For example, if a manager asks what you are making, you could answer instead with what you are looking for:

Manager: "What are you making right now?"
You: "I understand the market is paying in the $65,000 to $75,000 range."
Manager: "That's outrageous. We can't pay that."
You: "What range are you thinking of for this position?"

Note: You haven't revealed either what you are making or what you want—but you've still tested the hiring manager's expectations. The person who states a number first is at a negotiation disadvantage.

Or you could say, "My current salary is $32,000. I know the marketplace today is closer to $45,000. I have been willing to trade off the salary in order to build my skills [or whatever]. But now I am in a position where I don't need to trade off money, and I'm ready to take a position at market rates."

### If You Are Pushed to Name Your Salary

Don't simply state your salary—develop a line of patter to soften it. Simply stating a number can be very confrontational, as with the $200,000-plus-plus-plus job hunter. If you have exhausted all the responses, and the hiring manager throws you up against the wall and shouts, "I want to know what you are making!" you can still soften your answer by saying, for example:

• "I'm earning very good money right now-in the $90,000 to $120,000 range, depending on bonus. And I'm certainly worth it. But I'm very interested in your company, and I know we can work something out."

• "My salary is very low-only $20,000, and I know that's dramatically below market rates. But I was willing to do that as an investment in my future. Now, however, I expect to make market rates."

You should name your salary only as a last resort. Managers want to know your last salary as a way of determining your worth to them, but it is certainly not the most reasonable way to decide

*I was taught that the way of progress
is neither swift nor easy.*
Marie Curie

what you are worth. For example, you would want to be paid more if the job requires seventy hours a week and lots of travel, versus one that requires only thirty-five hours a week. How do you know how much you want unless you know what the job entails? You are being sensible to talk about the job first and the salary later.

Some managers cannot deal that way, so you have to be prepared in case you are forced to discuss salary prematurely. And even if you do name your salary, there are different ways you can couch it. For example:

- "My current salary is $32,500."
- "I make in the high sixties."
- "My base is around $25,000 and my bonus [commissions] is usually around $15,000, which brings my total package to $40,000."
- "I make in the range of $100,000 to $200,000, depending on my bonus." (This, of course, tells them very little.)

Remember to soften your mention of your salary with a line of patter or your response will sound too confrontational and too much like a demand: "I make . . . but salary won't be a problem because . . ."

### More Complex Compensation Situations

Most people are in the position of negotiating salary, perhaps a bonus or commission, and perhaps a training program, association membership, or the timing of the first salary review.

Others have a more complex situation. For example, a senior executive may say (at the appropriate time), "You'd like to know how much I'm now making? Let me write it out for you." (Or perhaps he or she would go into the meeting with the information already filled out.) The table below contains the current year's compensation, the next year's compensation (if it is relevant) to account for bonuses, pay increases, and so on. The third column would contain a skeleton of what you are looking for, or would be left blank and used as a worksheet. Be sure to write footnotes as commentary on those lines requiring it. For example, you may want to document that if you leave before April you will lose your year-end bonus. Therefore,

you could not start work until after April, or the hiring company would have to make up for your loss:

| | 19xx | 19xx | Looking For |
|---|---|---|---|
| Base salary | $89,000 | $95,000 | $95,000 |
| Bonus | 26,000 | 35,000 | |
| Deferred Comp. | 20,000 | 30,000 | |
| Car Allowance | 8,000 | 8,000 | |
| Stock Options | 40,000 | 40,000 | |
| Addtl Medical | 4,000 | 4,000 | |
| TOTAL COMP. | 187,000 | 212,000 | 250,000 |

You may leave the third column completely blank and fill it in as you are speaking. For example, you could say, "This is an exciting opportunity you are presenting, and I want to be part of it. To make it easier for you, I could imagine staying at my present base compensation level for next year, $95,000. To make the move worth my while, I could imagine a total package of $250,000, for example, and we could figure out the numbers in between."

In stating your "requirements" in a collaborative way, there is plenty of room for flexibility as well as for their comments and input. You do not run the risk of having the offer fall apart before you have actually gotten one. As you will see later, you want to hear their best offer, and *then* you can accept it or reject it.

### CASE STUDY: BETSY
*Simplifying the Request*

Betsy went to Europe on a consulting assignment, and was later offered a full-time position. She had a list of 20 or so expenses that she thought the company should cover: moving expenses, household purchases, trips home, phone calls home, gym, and so on. When we added up the entire package it exceeded $200,000, but it would have been too clumsy and too unprofessional to itemize all the things or her list.

Instead, we came up with a very neat package that included having the company pay completely for her apartments in both Prague and Duseldorf, where housing was very expensive. Those items alone more than made up for the extra expense of phone calls and other miscellany. The resulting

*Armies of worried men in suits stormed off the Lexington Avenue subway line and
marched down the crooked pavements. For rich people, they didn't look very happy.*
Michael Lewis, *Liars Poker*

package was well in excess of what she had originally wanted, and gave her the comfort of knowing
that unexpected expenses would not cause her
great loss.

---

**You are trying to postpone the discussion of
salary until after you have an offer, but in
real life that is not always possible. Therefore, postpone it if you can. And if you can't,
be sure you *know* how you want to
answer the questions:**
- **"What are you making now?" and**
  - **"What are you looking for?"**

---

## No Absolute One Way

Salary negotiation is the most nervewracking
part of the job hunting process. At the beginning of
your job hunt you are at loose ends-not knowing
where you are going, and feeling like you will
never get there. But salary negotiation is the part
people fear the most. It is a surprise monster at the
end of your search.

---

**You're in a great negotiating position if you
can walk away from the deal. Therefore,
make sure you have 6 to 10 things in the
works. If this deal is the only thing you
have going, see how quickly you can get
something else going.**

---

## Search Firms

Search firms must know the *range* of salary you
are making or the amount you are looking for. They
do not need an exact amount.

## Ads

In answering ads, you will rarely give your
salary requirements. The trend at the moment is for
many ads to read, "Please state salary requirements." Most job hunters do not, and the hiring
company does *not* exclude them. Stating your
salary or requirements not only puts you at a
negotiating disadvantage, it also allows you to be
eliminated from consideration because you are too
high or too low.

On the other hand, some ads state, "You will
absolutely not be considered unless you state your
salary requirements." Then, you should state them.

## What Is Negotiable?

Everything's negotiable. That doesn't mean
you'll *get* it, but it is negotiable. First, think of what
is important to you. Make a personal list of what
you must have versus what you want. Decide
where you can be flexible, but also know the issues
that are deal breakers for you.

Think of your musts versus your wants. If you
get everything you "must" have, then perhaps you
won't even mention items on your "want" list. Go in
knowing your bottom-line requirements, what you
would be willing to trade off, and what benefits/
perks could compensate you if you hit a salary
snag. Have your own goals in the negotiation
clearly in mind.

Salary is not the only form of compensation that
might be negotiated. Other items might include:

- the timing of the first review
- closing costs on a new home or a relocation
  package
- use of a company car
- association or club memberships
- reimbursements for education
- bonus

Which is the most meaningful or valuable to you?

## Forms of Compensation

**Basic Compensation:**
- the timing of the first review
- base salary
- deferred compensation
- incentive compensation (short and long term)
  - performance bonus
  - sales commission
  - sales incentive plans
  - stock options
- sign-on bonus
- matching investment programs
- profit sharing.

*The pay is good and I can walk to work.*
John F. Kennedy, on becoming president,
quoted by Ralph G. Martin, *A Hero for Our Time*

## Vacations:

- extra vacation: vacation length is becoming tied to level or length of work experience rather than time spent with one company.

## Perquisites:

- expense accounts
- company car or gas allowance
- memberships
  - country club
  - luncheon club
  - athletic club
  - professional associations
- executive dining room privileges
- extra insurance
- first-class hotels or air travel
- personal use of frequent-flyer awards
- paid travel for spouse
- executive office
- private secretary
- employee discounts
- financial-planning assistance
- C.P.A. and tax assistance
- tuition assistance
- continuing professional education
- conventions
- furlough trips for overseas assignments.

## Relocation Expenses:

- moving expenses
- mortgage-rate differential/housing allowance
- mortgage prepayment penalty
- real estate brokerage fees
- closing costs, bridge loan
- home-buying trips
- lodging while between homes
- company purchase of your home
- mortgage funds/short-term loans
- discounted loans/mortgages
- temporary dual housing
- trips home during dual housing
- outplacement assistance for spouse.

## Related to Severance:

- severance pay and outplacement
- consulting fees after termination
- insurance benefits after termination.

## GLOSSARY

Deferred Compensation: Ability to make deposits to a deferred salary plan from your pay on a before-tax basis so that amount of income is subject to taxation in the year you make the deposit.

Employment contract: A formal written agreement between yourself and the employer guaranteeing certain benefits such as severance pay should you lose the job through no fault of your own. At high levels sometimes known as a "golden parachute."

Letter of Intent: A written confirmation of a job offer summarizing the items agreed upon (salary, benefits, perks, etc.). Not a formal contract but hard for a company to rescind. If you write it, it's called a reverse letter of intent.

Matching investment programs: Savings incentive plan in which company matches employee basic award or personal contribution toward investment.

Performance bonus: An amount of money to be paid you contingent on your performance on the job. May be a specific amount or a percentage. Can be tied to individual, group, or corporate performance.

"Perks" or perquisites: Extra benefits that come with the position such as executive dining room privileges, company car, etc. May be negotiable or standard company policy.

Profit sharing: Cash award based on corporate earnings. Unusual outside of banks.

Sales commissions: Compensation directly related to sales at a predetermined percentage.

Sales incentive plans: Additional compensation based on sales volume.

Signing bonus: A one-time amount of money paid as an inducement for you to join the company. Also known as a signing or "up-front" bonus.

Stock options: A grant to purchase stock at a fixed price.

**The most important negotiating leverage you have is being in demand elsewhere. Develop other options. Be able to walk away from the deal. You can create this situation without much difficulty.**

Most job hunters say to themselves, "I'm so far along with this one possibility, I'll just ride it out and see what happens. If I don't get an offer from them, then I'll think of what else I should do."

Bad move. Have at least a tentative answer to the question of what you would do if this doesn't work. Having an alternative:

- helps you to be more relaxed in your discussions
- increases your chances of having this possibility work out
- puts you in a better position to negotiate this position wisely
- helps you to tolerate the months that may go by before it comes to closure
- gives you something with which to compare this offer to so you can make a more objective decision.

As one Five O'Clock Clubber said during her "graduation speech" after accepting a new position, "When you are going after only one job, you think that, fi it falls through, you will lose a few weeks in your search. Instead of losing a few weeks, you lose a few months. First, you have to recover from the disappointment. Then you have to gear yourself up and decide where to look next. Then you have to get your entire search going again. Take it from me, it's better to never lose that momentum at all."

## CASE STUDY: GREGORY
### Skipping a Step

When I met Gregory, he had three job possibilities in the works, and wanted to bring them to closure. After all, he said, he had a family to support.

It seemed to me that Gregory's prospects were not a good match for him. After much discussion, Gregory agreed to contact additional prospective employers: this would not slow down his current negotiations, and may even make things move faster.

To develop more appropriate targets, Gregory had to complete the assessment process (The Seven Stories and other exercises), which he had skipped. Perhaps Gregory could find work that he would enjoy doing and also meet his family responsibilities.

Gregory received six job offers. The three new companies offered him appropriate positions *before* the first three companies made him any offers at all.

Do not skip the assessment part of your search. The results help you to target correctly from the start, give you something against which to compare your offers, and help you to be more objective about which job you should take next.

## CASE STUDY: CAROLINA
### Self-Discipline to Do The Right Thing

Carolina had only one job prospect, and was anxious about whether she would get an offer. Her most important meeting with the company was scheduled for the following week, and she wanted to land that job. "Believe it or not," I told her, "you will do better in your upcoming round of interviews if we could first develop a strategy for getting more possibilities in the works."

That day, after Carolina prepared for the interview, she went to the library, researched 150 other companies in her target area, wrote a great cover letter and sent it with a résumé to all of them.

By the time her important meeting came around, Carolina was so relaxed that she had almost forgotten about it. When the small things inevitably went wrong, she could say to herself, "At least I've got 150 letters in the mail working for me."

Three weeks later, Carolina got the offer she wanted. In addition, she received calls because of her mail campaign. She accepted the job with the

*No one can possibly achieve any real and lasting success
or "get rich" in business by being a conformist.*
J. Paul Getty, *International Herald Tribune*

company with whom she had been meeting, but continued to speak with the other companies just to be sure she had made the right choice. For a few weeks after starting the new job, she still kept in touch with the other companies—until she was com-pletely sure that she had made the correct decision.

## CASE STUDY: SERGIO
### Acting Like a Consultant

In search only two weeks, Sergio had no trouble getting interviews. However, he was having an important first interview the day after our Five O'Clock Club meeting. He was hyped up, stressed out, and breathlessly told the group, "This job pays a lot of money. I want to go in tomorrow and get them to hire me. I think they want someone who is more technical than I am, so I have to sell myself really hard. I've prepared a handout to give them at the end of the meeting. Take a look at it and see if she is likely to give me the job."

At first, the group was mildly confused. No one looked at the handout. They knew that was not the problem. Then people in the group com-mented:

"Do you really want this job, Sergio?"

"What other companies are you talking to? It's so easy for you to get interviews."

"You've got to slow down."

"If this job pays as much as you say it does, they're not going to make you an offer at the first meeting."

I built on the group's good comments: "Sergio, become this woman's friend. To help her, you need more information. Find out why she wants a person with strong technical experience. Find out more about her vision for the depart-ment. Help her decide what is really best for her—even if it seems, from time to time, as though you are putting yourself out of the run-ning. Tell her that you will think about her situa-tion, and get back to her later. Then do some research. What you want from this first meeting is another meeting."

Sergio immediately calmed down. The group could hear it in his voice. In his panicky state, Sergio could not have done well in that inter-view. He was very grateful for the group's guid-ance.

Sergio met a few times with that company, kept his search going, and received four excellent offers from other companies. The one he had been so eager about faded from his interest.

### If You Are Presently Working

Employed people have the same leverage as those who have other possibilities in the works. If a hiring manager says to you, "Why are you leaving?" You can say, "I don't know that I am. I may stay right here." You don't know that for sure *what* you are going to do. To be in a strong negotiating position—and an appealing candi-date—you need options.

### Pretending to Have Other Offers

Why not say that you have other possibilities when, if fact, you have nothing else? That rarely works. It's not that lying is a bad thing to do. The danger is that the company may say, "You should take the other offer," and three months later you still have no other alternatives, and you have also closed off this possibility. It's so easy to get other job possibilities in the works, focus on doing that.

---

*Human . . . life is a succession of choices, which every
conscious human being has to make every moment.
At times these choices are of decisive importance;
and the very quality of these choices will often reveal
that person's character and decide his fate.
But that fate is by no means prescribed:
for he may go beyond his inclinations,
inherited as well as acquired ones.
The decision and the responsibility is his:
for he is a free moral agent,
responsible for his actions.*
John Lukacs, *A History of the Cold War*

# Communications Skills for Negotiating

## Most Job Hunters Try to Close Too Soon

If you were a consultant trying to land a contract, you would not expect to land that contract after just one meeting. You would not leave the meeting and say, "I think they liked me," expecting to get the contract based on that alone. You would know that the purpose of that meeting was to get information so you could better understand their issues and needs and who the players are, go back and think things through, and figure out how you could help the company. Then you would figure out what else you would need to know. Perhaps you would have to do some outside research, meet with additional people inside or outside the company, find out what other consulting firms they are considering so you would know how you stack up, or call a friend who could put in a good word for you.

Yet many job hunters come out of their very first meeting hoping they will get the job; they actually expect to get that job based on just that one meeting. There's a lot more work to be done. Be sure to read the chapter "Follow Up After a Job Interview: Consider Your Competition." Otherwise, you may try to close too soon.

*There can be no greater reward than goodness to your fellow man.*
Charles Dickens
*A Christmas Carol*

**It's time to negotiate. You have an offer. You and the hiring manager are no longer, figuratively speaking, on opposite sides of the table; you are now side-by-side. In this part of the process, it's up to *you* to set the tone of the conversation.**

Obstacles and disagreements may arise, but your intentions are in agreement: You want to work together, pending the outcome of the negotiations.

Ideally, you will both use a collaborative, problem-solving approach—perhaps with some compliments thrown in because you value each other. You will each resolve the details calmly, and try to understand the ideas and the situations faced by the other person. The goal of any negotiation is to reach an agreement.

It may take some time to hear the various aspects of the offer, respond to them, and discuss a compromise that will be acceptable to both of you. After all is said and done, you may decide to accept or reject the offer, once you hear all of the details.

However, you bear the larger part of the burden in the compensation discussion. After the hiring manager has spent so much time interviewing prospects and has made a decision about whom to hire, he or she wants to come to closure. It is your job to keep the conversation open until all of the items you want to discuss have been discussed. It is your responsibility to manage the conversation, keep it flowing, and thank the hiring manager for discussing these details when all he or she wants to do is get someone into the job and get on with it.

### Express Enthusiasm

Some job hunters think that showing enthusiasm for the job will negatively impact their negotiating position. Quite the contrary. I have seen many an offer retracted because the job hunter did not seem enthusiastic about the position during the negotiating stage. I cannot

*A man is great not because he hasn't failed;*
*a man is great because failure hasn't stopped him.*
Confucius

imagine a consultant or freelancer feigning disinterest, thinking it would help to negotiate a higher rate. Instead, be sure to show enthusiasm for the position throughout the negotiation process. You can always turn the offer down later—after you have heard the entire package.

## A Few Hints

Here are a few things to remember:
- Aim for a win-win situation.
- Go in knowing what you want, and what you would settle for.
- Keep the business discussion going.
- Do not be rigid or demanding.
- When the hiring manager says that he or she is faced with a problem, such as other employees who would make less than you, acknowledge the problem, and try to show why it is not relevant in your case. Perhaps, for example, the job you will be doing is somewhat different from what the others are doing.
- Do not get ruffled, upset, confrontational, or sarcastic.
- Maintain a tone of speech that is business-like, positive, and calm.

If the hiring manager will not budge on the offer, you may still decide to ask for the offer in writing so you can think about it—and to make sure you have at least one offer in your pocket. You would also still say that you want to work there. You are "Playing the End Game" (see that chapter).

## Preparing Your Response to the Offer

To keep things simple, let's assume you are negotiating salary alone, although your compensation discussion may have many more elements. Some experts say that you should listen to the offer, and say that you'll get back to the manager in a few days. In real life, that often does not work.

For example, if you are currently making $80,000, and you are offered $40,000, you can't say, "Thank you for the offer. I'll think it over and get back to you in a few days." Whatever you say

in a few days will seem idiotic. With an offer so out-of-line, it seems that you could have had *some* response, such as: "I just want to be sure we're talking about the same job. As I understand it, you would like me to [describe the job]." This lets the manager know that you are disappointed with the offer.

## Low Offers

One time I received an extremely low offer. I was making $80,000. The manager offered me $40,000—obviously trying to see what he could get away with.

I said: "I was thinking more like $160,000."
He said: "$160,000?!?!"
I said: "I was just kidding. I thought you were too."

And then he became more realistic. You should probably not try this, but I don't like to get too serious when I know someone is playing with me.

I actually wound up with a very good offer and went to work for that company. The position fit perfectly with my Forty-Year Plan. I stayed there three years while I continued to build The Five O'Clock Club.

If the offer is $60,000 and you want $80,000, perhaps you could express a little disappointment, such as: "Well, I'm thrilled to receive an offer. I really want to work here and I especially want to work for you. That salary is a bit low compared to what I had been thinking. Let's keep talking about it."

If you have the manager put the offer in writing, then you can hustle around to the other companies with whom you have been meeting, and see how much better you can do (see "Playing the End Game"). At the very least, it will give you time to think. Then you could say to them, for example, "I've been giving it a lot of thought . . ." (or "My wife and I have been talking about this . . ." or "I've talked this over with my accountant and we can't figure out how I could manage on the amount you've offered me. I was wondering how far you could move away from this amount. What are the possibilities of [name something for the manager to consider]?"

## High Offers

Let's say, for example, that you would like an offer of $90,000, and you think that is an appropriate amount.

What if you are offered $120,000? (Remember, you don't want to be greedy. Can you live up to that amount?) If you decide it is a fair figure, then you can say, "I'm very pleased with your offer, and I'm not one to quibble, so let's call it a deal."

If you are offered $110,000, $100,000 or even $90,000, your response may well be exactly the same.

Once, when I had decided to take a straight career-counseling position—after having worked for many years as a CFO—I went through the entire negotiation process, but postponed discussing salary for four months while I met a dozen or so people. I went in for the offer meeting, and the manager asked me what I had been making before. She was astonished to find out that we had not already discussed salary. After some consultation with her boss, she said that she was happy to offer me what I had been paid previously. It was a salary that was way out-of-line (too high) for the responsibilities we were talking about. After all, I was not going to have a staff or any of the other responsibilities I had previously had. I wanted this job so I could have virtually *no* responsibilities and simply concentrate on growing The Five O'Clock Club.

I told her that the amount she offered was very generous, but seemed too high for what I expected I would be doing there. I named a number that was fair—but much lower. She said, "Okay. How about if we split the difference?" And I was still paid handsomely.

It doesn't pay to be greedy. If I had come in at a salary level that was too high, I might have lost my job the first time they needed to cut expenses, or my boss might have given me assignments to justify my high salary, such as a lot of overseas travel, coaching foreign executives. I wanted to coach executives only in the city where I lived because I had to run The Five O'Clock Club at night. You are always aiming for a fair compensation.

## The Middle Ground

In the middle ground, that is, an offer that is just below or just above your goal, you may want to think it over, develop your lines, and then get back to the manager.

It is usually best to do all compensation negotiations in person so you can get a feel for the manager's response. Work with him or her to come up with something that is acceptable to both of you.

## Other Negotiation Communications Hints

**Ask open-ended questions** such as, "Can you think of anything else we can do to bring our positions closer together?"

**Offer ideas or information.** One Five O'Clock Clubber was thrilled to get an offer to work for a certain major company, but their hands were tied. She wanted $90,000. They wanted to give it to her, but could only manage $80,000. Then she realized that two association memberships would have cost her $500 each. Would they pay for them? And what if she went to two conferences a year? Those conferences usually cost around $3000 each, including room and transportation and conference fees.

The company was very happy with this suggestion. It was much easier for them to give her the conferences and memberships than it would have been to give her extra pay. (Managers have to be conscious of keeping the salaries equitable among employees, but may have more flexibility in other budget categories.)

**Build on what you have already agreed upon.** "Your suggestion that you pay for my trips back home once a month helps a lot. I was wondering if you would also pay if my husband were to visit me some of those times instead of my going home."

*The more a man lays stress on possessions, and the less sensitivity*
*he has for what is essential, the less satisfying is his life.*
Carl Jung

**When you are negotiating,
use a collaborative tone.
You are both on the same
side of the table now.**

## Negotiating Items that are "Nonnegotiable"

Peter received a written offer from a major corporation. He liked it, all except the job title: He'd been offered the title of vice president, but he wanted senior vice president. The company policy was that no one could be hired from outside with a title higher than vice president.

I said to Peter, "Are you willing to walk away from the job if you don't get the title you want?" I needed to know that so I could help him plan his strategy. Peter said he would walk away from it. Then I needed to know why. Peter said he had had the title of vice president fifteen years ago, and it was too much of a blow to his ego to go back to that title. Furthermore, he felt he would not be able to do a good job if he had the lower-level title, because everyone would know his title and therefore would not respond to his requests. He felt he would fail in the job if he had the title of vice president.

The rule here may surprise you. If you are at an impasse because the hiring manager wants to give you one thing and you want another, you have only one recourse: *Talk about the job!* If Peter had directly addressed the title issue, they probably would not have come to an agreement. He would have quoted company policy. In fact when job hunters are negotiating, hiring managers sometimes get the impression that the job hunter does not care about the job, but only about the salary and the benefits. Therefore, be different. Talk about the job to reassure him that that is what is most important to you. Below is a shortened, paraphrased version of the letter Peter sent to the hiring manager. Please note the italicized part, which is an important strategy for you to use:

Dear Mr. Williams:

I was thrilled to receive your offer to head up the Rickety Division, and am eager to get in there and work with you to move it in a new direction. I know we will hit all of the targets you and I spoke about.

I was pleased with the compensation package you offered, and am also glad about the car situation. However, I *find it difficult to accept the offer* with the title of vice president. I had that title fifteen years ago, so I feel I'd be going backward in my career. But I am also concerned that the lower title will affect my credibility and effectiveness.

I am sure we can come to some agreement. I am very eager to dig in and am looking forward to hearing from you.

Peter did not reject the offer; he said he really wanted to work there, but would find it difficult to accept. It took three weeks for the company to get back to him and give Peter the title he wanted. But that was not necessarily the only result that would have been positive. For example, the company could have said, "Come in and get started, Peter. We can give you the title after three months." Or it could have said, "Peter, I'm sorry, our hands are tied on this one. But I assure you that you will not experience the problems you are dreading. Our employees will know you are division head, and that will matter to them more than the vice president title. Beth Segal came in as vice president only two years ago, and look at her now."

Peter kept the process open until he heard their best offer. That allowed him to either accept that offer if they gave him the higher title, or to change his mind and take the job with the lower title and the reassurances from the company that it would be okay.

**If you are at an impasse because the hiring
manager wants to give you one thing and you
want another, you have only one recourse:
*Talk about the job!***

That's what you want to do also. Hear the entire offer before you decide. *Do not accept or reject any job until it is offered to you.* Before their first interview with a company, some job hunters say, "I really

*You must establish your dreams*
*and quietly move in the direction of attaining them.*
Dr. Hugh Gloster, past president, Morehouse College

want this job" or "I don't want this job." They don't even know what the job is, and they have already made up their minds. This is the wrong attitude. Go into each interview intending to make it into the best job for you and for the company. This means you will probably have to negotiate—both the job and the compensation.

## How to Talk About the Items You Want

Here's the rule to follow when you want to ask for something:

- Talk about the job (if you haven't been doing so already).
- Describe the situation as you see it.
- Venture a solution.

You can imagine what it feels like when you are making an offer to someone who talks incessantly about all the things he or she wants. In the back of your mind, you say to yourself, "I don't believe this person cares about the job at all. All they care about is the benefits." Sometimes job hunters even find that the offer is retracted for this reason. So make sure you mention how excited you are about the job.

---

**Talk first about the job.
Then explain why you want something.**

---

Let's say that you want a company car. Don't say, "I want a car." Instead, say, for example, "I appreciate your offer, and cannot wait to get started. I know we will really turn that place around. I am looking forward to starting on the twenty-third, and am pleased with the package you have offered. However, I was wondering what we might do about a car. I was thinking that I would have to do a lot of traveling between these three cities, and wonder what we might do about that. I have no car at present, and I think that renting a car might be a big expense. Is there any possibility that we could lease a car? It would be much cheaper."

Compensation negotiation is a problem-solving session. Don't be rigid. Hear them out and see what they come up with, but also come up with suggestions yourself.

## How to Negotiate Severance

After you have negotiated everything else, you may bring up the issue of severance. Here is one scenario:

You have settled on everything, including the start date. The deal is in the bag—but perhaps not in writing.

Set the stage by telling them how happy you are to be joining their firm. Then further set the stage by expressing your concern that you may be at risk through no fault of your own. For example:

You: "I am thrilled to be joining your firm. I know this is a good match, and I believe in what you are trying to accomplish."

Hiring manager: "We're glad you will be joining us."

You: "My only hesitation is that I am leaving a firm where I felt very secure. I'm afraid that there is the chance that your company may be taken over, or that you may wind up leaving the firm, and I wonder what would happen to me. I was wondering if there was any way you could give me some comfort about that."

Hiring manager: "Well, that's always the chance you take in today's market."

You: "Yes, you're right. But I was wondering if I could receive, for example, six months' notice if my job [or assignment] were to go away for any reason."

Notice that you are asking for payment if your are dismissed for *any* reason, but when you set the stage, you named situations that have nothing to do with you. This way, you will not appear worried about whether or not you can do a good job.

Asking for six months' notice is the same as asking for six months' severance. When your offer letter gets written up, it will usually be written up as severance. That will give you the cushion you could need for your next search.

These days, six months is common. One executive had to move across the country to take a job. He got three years' severance during the first two years, and then two years' severance if something

*Things which matter most must never be at the mercy of things which matter least.*
Goethe

happened during years two to four, and eighteen months' severance after that. That severance would alleviate the trauma of losing his job shortly after a major move.

## Overcome Their Objections— And Also Your Own

Throughout this chapter, we have focused on the company, what their objections might be, and how you can overcome those objections. You also need to be aware of your own objections and handle those during the negotiations. Many job hunters think that the negotiation is strictly about salary, but it is also about whatever else worries you, and whatever else you may need to have to do well in your job. You may want to discuss some of those things before you come on board, and other things after you are in the saddle.

What if, for example, the company expects you to travel 60 percent of the time? You could negotiate for 40 percent travel. People have negotiated to work out of their homes two days a week, have a budget for a special project, and so on. Think these things over, and be sure they are included.

## Win-Win

You want a win-win situation—one with which you can both live. After you have received a job offer, the situation is no longer adversarial. You and the company are both on the same side of the table, trying to make this deal work.

Actually, it is up to you to control this part of the process. You have the most at stake. The fact is, once a hiring manager has made an offer, he or she usually wants to close quickly. His or her job is done. Now your job begins.

Therefore, you must make sure you bring up everything you want in a way that is collaborative. Set a tone that reassures the hiring manager that you are thrilled to have the job, cannot wait to get started but have just a few details to work out. You can say, for example, "I really appreciate your spending this time. Some of these things may not mean much to you, but they mean a lot to me."

## Look at the Entire Package

Look at the entire compensation package. Do your homework so that you know the typical compensation for a similar position in the industry, and make allowances—especially in the area of benefits—as you move from one industry to another. The benefits may differ, but they should be on a par. Find out which items are automatic benefits and which are negotiable; every company's plan is different.

Be reasonable. In the past, it has almost been a given that job seekers would move only for a salary increase of 20 percent or more. In these economic times, lateral moves are much more common. Know your market worth.

> Do not be swayed by the possibility of making $2,000 or $10,000 more.
> Select the job or assignment that positions you best for the long term.
> That is the most important criterion.

### Job Seekers Are Too Eager to Take Pay Cuts

An estimated 40 percent of all job seekers may start new jobs for less money than they should be getting because they do not know how to handle salary negotiations.

When people call to attend The Five O'Clock Club, we need to know their salary range and field so we can assign them to the right counselor. No matter what their salary is, they often say, "Right now I'm making x dollars, but I'm willing to take a pay cut." I usually say back to them, "Isn't is a little early to negotiate?" They haven't even started their searches, and they are willing to settle for less.

Many job hunters think that a willingness to take a pay cut will make them more marketable, but this may not be true. For one thing, there are plenty of job hunters at that lower salary, and so there will be plenty of competition at that level too. What's more, employers may be reluctant to hire someone who they think may leave when a more appropriate offer comes along.

*History records the successes of men with objectives and a sense of direction.*
*Oblivion is the position of small men overwhelmed by obstacles.*
William H. Danforth

Instead, learn to play the game, and find out what you are worth on the market. Use that as your gauge. If you were overpaid before, then you may have to take a pay cut. But if you were underpaid, you are likely to get what you are worth.

### The Length of Unemployment Has No Effect on a Person's Future Pay

The Five O'Clock Club is a research-based organization. Therefore, we study such things as the length of a person's unemployment in relation to the pay at which they are hired. Most of those Five O'Clock Clubbers who had been unemployed a year and a half to two years were able to get jobs at their old pay or more.

Most of these participants had had trouble landing a new job because of the techniques they had been using—not because of a lack of competence or because of their pay rates. When they started using the right search techniques, they quickly got jobs at the level they were worth in the market. For most people, this was at—or greater than—their old salaries.

Many noticed that their searches took a turn for the better after only two or three sessions at The Five O'Clock Club. Here, they were encouraged to:

• Develop a positive attitude and refresh themselves after a period of discouragement.

• Consider this a new search, and be willing to use our methodology in their search from this day forward.

• Make sure they were positioned properly for the areas they were targeting.

• Recontact those with whom they had already met *who were in an appropriate target area.*

• **Get six to ten things in the works.** Then the issue became "Who else are you talking to?" rather than "How long have you been looking?" (See "Playing the End Game.")

• Most of the searchers found appropriate positions with appropriate salaries within ten sessions.

## CASE STUDY: ELLEN
### *Abused in Her Present Position*

Ellen had earned good money in the financial-services industry. She lost her job, and took something with a major retailer out of desperation. She earned only one-third of her former salary.

By the time we met her at The Five O'Clock Club, she had been working there for over two years, and spending eighty hours a week with no end in sight and no hope.

After only six weeks at The Five O'Clock Club, she landed a terrific position in an industry related to the financial-services industry at more than she had previously been making. Her present compensation never came up. It was not an issue.

---

### Job-Hunting Hint

It's a good idea to have a calendar that you use only for job hunting. That way, you will clearly see how much effort you have (or have not) put in, as well as the amount of follow-up you plan to do.

Note the following:

• all interviews (networking, job, and search firm)

• mailings

• networking notes written

• follow-up notes written

• follow-up calls made, and

• the dates when you plan to make future calls.

You can also list ads answered.

A Monthly Job-Hunting Calendar is included in this book.

# Negotiating a Consulting or Freelance Assignment

CYRUS (trying to be friendly): *I'll tell you what. You want to work, I'll give you a job. Nothing permanent, mind you, but that upstairs room over there—the one above the office—is a hell of a mess. It looks like they've been throwing junk in there for twenty years, and it's time it got cleaned up.*

RASHID (Playing it cool): *What's your offer?*

CYRUS: *Five bucks an hour. That's the going rate, isn't it? ... If you can't finish today, you can do the rest tomorrow.*

RASHID (Getting to his feet): *Is there a benefits package, or are you hiring me on a freelance basis?*

CYRUS: *Benefits?*

RASHID: *You know, health insurance, dental plan, paid vacation. It's not fun being exploited. Workers have to stand up for their rights.*

CYRUS: *I'm afraid we'll be working on a strictly freelance basis.*

RASHID (Long pause. Pretending to think it over): *I'll take it.*

Paul Auster, *Smoke*

---

*Here comes the future, rolling towards us like a meteorite, a satellite, a giant iron snowball, a two-ton truck in the wrong lane, careering downhill with broken brakes, and whose fault is it? No time to think about that. Blink and it's here.*
Margaret Atwood,
*Good Bones and Simple Murders*

---

*Hey, no matter what—it's better than working at the post office.*
Jerry Sterner, *Other People's Money*

## Being a Consultant or Freelancer

All positions are temporary. You may receive a W-2 form at year-end, or you may receive a 1099—but no work you do is permanent. However you are paid, make sure you are paid fairly. And make sure you are gaining experience that will help you get your next assignment—inside or outside your present company. Have a backup plan. What would you do if your current assignment or situation ends?

If you happen to be looking for full-time work on-payroll, you still may be offered consulting assignments. So you should learn how to negotiate them.

Today, more and more companies are bringing in workers on a contract, consulting, or freelance basis. Such workers usually get no benefits (health insurance, paid time off, training, memberships, company-paid contribution to Social Security, etc.). Other contract or temp workers are hired through an intermediary company that may or may not put the workers on payroll, and pay for their benefits.

Even very senior managers find themselves serving as full-time consultants. Some companies are actually doing this illegally. If you are working full-time for a company which decides your hours and the content of your work, you are not a consultant but an employee. This means that the company must put you on payroll and pay the extra costs associated with that.

At one very large company where I was consulting, there was a relatively low-level person who worked on computers, kept the same hours as everyone else on staff, but who was paid a flat $15 an hour as a "consultant"—no benefits, no insurance, no paid time off. Large companies are sometimes even more likely than smaller companies to get away with this because they have so many employees. A manager may hire "consultants" because the company has a "freeze on head-counts"—he or she is not allowed to put more people on payroll because that would count as a "head." Yet the manager is allowed to hire consultants, temps, and freelancers.

The worker is stuck. The company has all of the power. If the worker wants to work, he or she is not going to complain about unfair treatment.

To counteract this trend, workers are sometimes opting to have "a job and a dream"—a job that pays them regular wages, and other work done on the side to build a future that may be more secure than working for one company. Some workers are able to grow what was once a sideline into a stable source of income. That work may include consulting or selling part-time, trying to build a business, and so on.

Regardless of how you are paid, develop your skills and your marketability to the point where you are less likely to be taken advantage of.

## The Search for Consulting or Freelance Work

The search for consulting or freelance assignments is exactly the same as the search for full-time work "on payroll." Target the areas in which you are interested—following the system we use at The Five O'Clock Club. At your meeting with your prospective employer—or perhaps even in your cover letter—you can mention that you would be open to either full- or part-time work. Sometimes a consulting assignment turns into an on-payroll assignment. Sometimes the reverse is true.

Those who have successfully made the transition to consulting or freelance work often say they would never go back to working for someone full-time. Some feel and indeed may be much more secure having a number of sources of income rather than just one.

The downside to consulting is that you must both market and deliver your services. Some consultants get so involved in delivery that they don't allow time to market. They suffer having intense periods of work, with periods of no work in between. Consultants don't get unemployment benefits during those down times. Some consultants may tend to take no time off: If you don't work, you don't get paid.

Therefore, you must set your consulting rates high enough to allow for time off. You also need

time for marketing. A rule of thumb is to allow half of your time for marketing and administration, and half for the actual delivery of your services. "Marketing" includes everything you do to make yourself known, such as writing articles and then reprinting them as handouts to build your credibility, delivering speeches, building a database of possible targets and mailing to them regularly, and calling on companies.

Decide if you want to start a consulting business, or if you would simply like to take a few consulting assignments while you are searching for full-time employment. This will influence what you decide to do in marketing yourself. At some point—but not now—you may need a brochure, business cards, and even an office. If you are truly trying to build a consulting business, think through how big you would like your practice to be, how many others you would eventually like to work with you, and everything else you need to develop a rudimentary business plan.

In any case, you must be positioned properly (see Two-Minute Pitch). Decide what your target market is, what you have that would be of interest to this market, the services you want to offer, and how you can position yourself to seem worthwhile. Whether you are looking for on-payroll or consulting work, you must learn how to differentiate yourself from your likely competitors. Then you must call on prospects.

Follow the Stages of the Search and pay attention to the stage you are in (Stage 1, 2, or 3). Be sure to have six to ten things in the works at all times. Next, figure out how to price your services.

### Pricing Your Services

There are two numbers you need to start with to determine your consulting fee. One is what you are now making—or have been making most recently, or what others are making—in the field you are targeting.

We are assuming your consulting will be in the field where your are now considered an expert. If you want to consult in a new field

*Maury had enormous admiration for Bennett's grandfather, a self-made man who had opened the store by himself in 1934, a man who always believed things would turn out in his favor and who made things turn out in his favor.*

Alan Lightman, *Good Benito*

(perhaps as a way to learn that field), instead of your present base plus bonus, use the rate of those at your level in the new field.

The second number to consider is what the market will bear.

### Calculating Your "Cost Rate"

Take your present base plus bonus. Let's say it's $50,000 a year. Add a factor for benefits, such as health insurance. Let's say 20 percent (this includes health insurance, company-paid Social Security, and so on, but does not include paid time off).

So that's $50,000 X 1.20 = $60,000

Divide that number by the number of hours the average person is available to work in a year. We'll use 2000 hours, just to keep the calculation simple.

(You may want to use 1600 hours, which allows for 10 holidays and 4 weeks of vacation and sick time.)

$60,000 / 2000 = $30 per hour.

Your cost is $30 per hour—which is very different from what you will bill your customer. If you were to be able to bill 2000 hours a year at $30 per hour, you would stay even with what you are now making.

## A Model for Estimating Your Billing Rate

| Base Salary & Bonus | Adj. Base = Base x 1.20 for benefits | COST (Adj. Base/ 2000) | Low Billing Rate[1] (cost x 1.2) | Aver. Billing Rate[2] (cost x 2) | High Billing Rate[3] (cost x 3) | Aver. per diem rate (aver. billing x 7) | MARKET RATES | My Tentative Rate |
|---|---|---|---|---|---|---|---|---|
| $20,000 | $24,000 | $12/hr | $14.40/hr | $24/hr | $36/hr | $168/day | | |
| $30,000 | $36,000 | $18/hr | $21.60 | $36 | $54 | $252 | | |
| $40,000 | $48,000 | $24/hr | $28.80 | $48 | $72 | $336 | | |
| $50,000 | $60,000 | $30/hr | $36.00 | $60 | $90 | $420 | | |
| $75,000 | $90,000 | $45/hr | $54.00 | $90 | $135 | $630 | | |
| $100,000 | $120,000 | $60/hr | $72 | $120 | $180 | $840 | | |
| $125,000 | $150,000 | $75/hr | $90 | $150 | $225 | $1050 | | |
| $150,000 | $180,000 | $90/hr | $108 | $180 | $270 | $1260 | | |
| $200,000 | $240,000 | $120/hr | $144 | $240 | $360 | $1680 | | |
| $250,000 | $300,000 | $150/hr | $180 | $300 | $450 | $2100 | | |
| $300,000 | $360,000 | $180/hr | $216 | $360 | $540 | $2520 | | |
| $500,000 | $600,000 | $300/hr | $360 | $600 | $900 | $4200 | | |

[1] Low Billing Rate. Use this rate if you are just starting out, or if you are on a long-term consulting assignment with a guaranteed significant number of hours per week.

[2] Average Billing Rate. Use this rate if you are in a specialized field and in demand. You may also use this rate if you are a serious independent consultant and want to sell your consulting services long-term. You will need to make up for the time you spend marketing and so on.

[3] High Billing Rate. If you have or are setting up a consulting firm, the rule of thumb is to bill out at three times labor cost to cover the cost of overhead, which includes support staff who are not billable, rent, marketing, and so on.

*You work Saturdays? Well, you must make good money. Well, so you hate it, I'm
sorry, I can't help that. What are your aspirations, in that case?*
Craig Lucas, *Prelude to a Kiss*

However, not only are you unlikely to bill 2000 hours a year, you still have to buy your own health insurance, put money aside for your vacations, pay your own Social Security, arrange for your own training, sub-scriptions, memberships, and so on.

## Calculating Your Low Billing Rate

To account for some of that expense, increase your cost rate by 20 percent—just so you will come out a little higher than your adjusted cost rate. This allows for benefits and also for paid time off. (See chart: Low Billing Rate)

$30 x 1.20 = $36.00 per hour (Low Billing Rate)

You would try to bill at your Low Billing Rate if you are just starting out, or if you are on a long-term consulting assignment with a guaranteed significant number of hours per week.

---

**A rule of thumb for
short-term consulting fees is
twice your cost.**

---

## Calculating Your Average Billing Rate

If you need to have more than one customer, you probably won't be able to bill 2000 hours a year because you will have to spend time marketing your services. Earlier you saw that a rule of thumb is to spend half your time marketing. So to keep even with what you made before, you would have to bill twice your cost rate.

That's $30 X 2 = $60 per hour.
(See chart: Average Billing Rate)

You would try to charge the Average Billing Rate for your salary level if you are in a specialized field and in demand. You would also try this rate if you are a serious independent consultant and want to sell your consulting services long-term. You will need to make up for the time you spend marketing.

## Calculating Your High Billing Rate

If you are well-established as a consulting firm with lots of overhead, such as office space and administrative support, two-times cost will probably not be enough to cover your overhead. The standard factor for this situation is three times cost. In addition, if you are seriously starting a consulting firm (rather than being an independent consultant representing only yourself), you would most likely charge the three-times rate for every billable member of your staff, or for each person you bring in to work on a project.

Finally, if you are well-known in your field, you may also insist on three times your cost rate—or, lucky you, whatever the market will bear.

$30 X 3 = $90 per hour.
(See chart: High Billing Rate)

Charge this rate if you are well-known in your field, or to cover your overhead if you have or are setting up a consulting firm. Overhead includes support staff who are not billable, rent, marketing, and so on.

## Your "Market Worth" Is
## Whatever the Market Will Bear

When I'm hiring someone as a consultant, I ask them their hourly rate, multiply it in my head by 2000, and decide if the person would be worth that much on-staff. For example, if someone wants to charge me $25 per hour, I estimate whether that person would be worth $50,000 on staff including benefits. That way, I can quickly assess whether the person is worth it to me.

If there are plenty of people who can do the same job for less, I can simply find someone else. If, however, this person is a known expert, my friends tell me that he or she is reliable, or if there is some other reason for me to think that this person is special, I may be willing to pay more than the typical going rate.

When you think about the rates you will charge as a consultant, remember that someone will be deciding whether or not you are worth it. So decide whether you are someone who can be easily replaced, or are unique and in demand. "What the market will bear" will be the most important determinant of what you can charge.

What you charge will probably change over time. At first, you simply want to get a few jobs

*In playing baseball, or in life, a person occasionally gets the opportunity to do something great. When that time comes, only two things matter: being prepared to seize the moment and having the courage to take your best swing.*
Hank Aaron, former baseball player,
commencement address to Emory University School of Law, May, 1995

and a few clients. Later, as you become better-known in your field, the amount and the way you charge will change.

You must test the waters. Talk to others in your field and find out what they are charging, network in to see prospective hiring managers and see what they would pay. When all else fails, start negotiating with the hiring manager and observe his or her reaction. Follow exactly the rules in the "Four-Step Salary Negotiation Strategy."

After you are well-established—and have a name in the market, there is a lot of flexibility. I have counseled clients who have ended up working two days a week for one company, and two days a week for another company—getting a flat $100,000 a year from each company! These clients had paid their dues in their respective fields, and deserved what they got. They each worked only four days a week, and if they lost an assignment at one company, they still had the other one to keep them going while they looked for a replacement. Not a bad way to earn a living.

### Corporate Rates

Although the three-times rate is standard for organizations with overhead, companies use different numbers of hours as the base. That is, instead of using 2000, they may use 1600 or even as low as 1300 to 1400 hours. This increases the hourly rate. Or they may hike up the direct labor rates by including not only base plus bonus, but also all benefits, payroll taxes, estimated raises, car allowances, and so on.

Then they come up with a rate card, which may contain inflated rates. When it comes time to negotiate, they may come down quite a bit from their rate card.

For example, one company's "Rates to Use in Pricing Projects" are as follows:

Use a billing rate of $225/hr. or $1800/day for:
- Employees with salaries in the $65,000 to $80,000 range.
- Outside consultants who cost us more than $500 per day.

Use a billing rate of $190/hr. or $1500/day for:

- Employees with salaries in the $50,000 to $64,000 range.
- Anyone not on staff who costs us $300 to $500 per day.

Use a billing rate of $150/hr. or $1200/day for:
- Professional staff with salaries less than $50,000.
- Anyone not on staff who costs us $150 to $275 per day.

Use a billing rate of $50/hr. or $400/day for:
- Administrative support staff.
- All temps assigned to this project.

You too may want to create a rate card for your consulting firm. But be sure to be realistic about your worth in the market.

### Setting Your Rates

When you are starting out, you will probably use just one system for charging your clients, such as an hourly rate.

When you are experienced, you may still wind up charging every client the same rate, or each client a different rate. For example, you may have one or two clients who form a stable core for you, and you may have gotten far enough in your career that you are able to be on a monthly retainer with them. You may charge other clients an hourly fee. You may charge one client per project, one a low hourly fee, and another a high hourly fee. You may charge a large corporation a higher rate than a small company, a for-profit organization more than you charge a not-for-profit (although not necessarily).

Your rates may differ by geographic area. You may charge a certain rate in the big urban areas, and a lower rate in the countryside; or one rate for one part of the country, and another rate for a different part.

If you are offering your services to individuals, you may use a sliding scale depending on the person's ability to pay, the way that many therapists do.

Finally, you may charge different rates for different kinds of work. When I am hiring a

*We are what we repeatedly do.*
*Excellence, then, is not an act, but a habit.*
Aristotle

public relations person, to name one example, I may hire someone who is already working full-time for someone else and wants to earn extra money on the side. That person may charge me a certain hourly fee for the brainy work, such as developing strategy, writing press releases, and so on, and a lower hourly rate for the "mindless" work, such as stuffing envelopes.

---

**Find out the standard fee arrangements for the industries or fields that you are targeting. The variety is endless.**

---

## Fee Structures

Therapists and attorneys charge per hour. Workshop leaders usually charge per diem. Determine how people in your field charge, and do the same—at least when you are starting out.

The two basic structures are per time (such as per hour, per diem, etc.) and per project. There are almost infinite variations on charging structures going, from a per-head rate for running a seminar, to a percent of gross billing (as in the old days of advertising). There are certain fields in which a success fee rules (that is, if the project works, you make lots of money; if it doesn't, you don't). And then there are lots of combination fee structures, such as a success fee for completion with a guaranteed nominal base amount. If you are working with a start-up company, and already have a full range of consulting assignments, you may be paid in stock. Other common arrangements are retainer, commission, percent of sales, bonus, or a combination of the above. Find out the standard fee structures for the industries or fields you are targeting. The variety is endless.

For now, we will cover the "per time" and "per project" structures. The thought processes behind these form the core of most other billing methods.

When considering the fee structure you want to use for a certain situation, remember that some structures are low-risk with a predictable reward. Others are high-risk (that is, you may wind up losing money or making no money), but high-reward (big bucks if things work out). All fee structures can be analyzed using this criterion.

### Project pricing vs. time-based pricing

The benefit of pricing per project, rather than charging a time-based rate, is that you could make much more money that way. You could also lose money if you price incorrectly or if you do not control your costs while delivering the service.

With time-based pricing, on the other hand, you can be sure of getting paid for every hour you work. As long as you get paid, there is no risk on your part. However, you cannot make a great deal of money.

If you simply want to pick up some consulting work while you search for a full-time job, you may want to stick to time-based pricing so you are not at risk. If you want to have a consulting business, you may want to become very good at project pricing (although actually many consulting businesses charge solely by time-based pricing).

### Out-of-Pocket or Pass-Along Expenses

Depending on the kind of work you are doing, certain expenses may be passed along directly to your client. Out-of-pocket expenses include items such as telephone, postage, and overnight mail expenses. Travel could also be considered an out-of-pocket expense—depending on the situation. Even entertainment sometimes falls into this category. If I hire a public relations consultant, I expect that person to keep track of out-of-pocket expenses and bill me monthly.

This is standard operating practice. However, check with others in your field or industry to be sure that this practice applies.

Pass-along expenses could include the cost of hiring an outside photographer, for example. Established consulting firms often "mark up" the cost of these pass-along expenses, say by 15 percent, to make a profit on them. In many cases, this is acceptable.

Pass-along expenses are not to be confused with the cost of outside consultants you may use as if they were part of your staff. These outside consultants would be billed the same as if they were on your staff, but you would have to think through the multiplier to use: perhaps two or three times the rate they charge you. Of course, you have to do what seems reasonable.

## Time-Based Pricing

If you are in a field that normally charges an hourly rate, as is the case with a therapist or attorney, you need to find out what you are worth in the field, and then develop yourself to the point where you have no trouble saying with confidence, "My rate is fifty dollars per hour."

But if you are doing project work for which you want to be paid hourly, that is another matter. As the hiring manager, I will be afraid of how much time you will spend on the project. If you tell me that your rate is $30 per hour, I will still want an estimate of how much a particular job will cost me. I cannot afford to pay you $30 an hour to do graphic design work, for example, if there is no limit. You may decide to fiddle with a design for 40 hours "just to make it perfect" when all I wanted was something that was "good enough." You may stay up all night working at home on your slow computer. Why should I pay you $30 an hour for that work, when you could have gotten it done in half that time if you had worked on my faster computer? You may have decided to make four different sketches for me, but if you were working out of my office instead of yours, I might have told you exactly what I wanted and saved all that extra time.

Therefore, if I am paying you per hour for a project, I want to know the limit on this project. Perhaps you will do 15 hours of work at your regular rate, and then come back to me to see if everything is on track before you rack up 50 hours for which you expect me to pay.

If you are willing to do the job on-site, there is less risk that you will go off in a direction I don't want. The on-site work is safer for both of us.

You will get paid for every hour you work, and I will know what you are doing for the time you are billing me.

If you are working for an hourly rate, you will charge less for per-diem work, and even less for a monthly rate. Of course, you must spell out the number of hours you will work for a per-diem rate. If you charge $200 per day and don't specify the number of hours in a day, your employer may expect 10- or 12-hour days. If you charge per month, you must specify that it is an 8.0-hour day (or 7.5-hour day), 20-day month (there are 4.3 weeks in an average month; 21.5 work days in an average month—not allowing for holidays or other time off). If you don't specify the number of days you will work per month, your employer will expect you to be there every day for the agreed-upon monthly rate. You will never have a day off.

If you are charging an hourly rate for on-site presentations, or for other work for which you have preparation time, make sure your hourly rate includes your preparation time.

If you are required to be on-site, bear in mind that most consultants charge a 4-hour minimum to make the unbillable travel worthwhile. However, if you are doing a lot of work for a certain client, you may come in for an important meeting and charge only for the time the meeting takes, even if it is only two hours. That's called establishing good will.

If you are straight hourly, you do not charge, of course, when you and your prospective client are discussing a possible assignment, or when you both are reviewing the work you did.

### How long will the assignment last?

Another consideration is the length of the assignment. If you should normally get $86 per hour, but the company wants to pay you per diem, you would not normally charge the company $86 X 8.0 hours = $688. If it's likely to be an 8-hour day, you would then charge them, say, $600 per diem ($86 X 7.0 hours). And if the company wants to pay you monthly, you probably would not charge them $600 X 21.5 = $12,900

*Man is born with his hands clenched, but his hands are open in death,*
*because on entering the world he desires to grasp everything, but on leaving,*
*he takes nothing away.*
The Talmud

(because the average month has 21.5 work days). Instead, you would say that your fee is normally about $15,000 ($688 X 21.5), but you will charge them only $10,000 per month for a 20-day month with, for example, a six-month minimum with 60-days, (or 30-days), notice to terminate. That's still $60,000 for six months, with time to search if the contract is not extended.

Your rates are reduced for longer amounts of time because you will have to do less marketing than if you sold your services by the hour.

### Billable vs. Unbillable time

Sometimes every hour you spend is billable, and sometimes it isn't. This can be tricky, and you should think about it with regard to the situation you are in. For many of your assignments, you may bill a straight hourly, per diem, or other kind of rate. But if you wind up at a company on a regular basis, you may attend weekly staff meetings, travel on company business, and so on. May you charge for this time at your normal rate? It depends. If you are at a large company, and being paid on a monthly basis, there is no discussion. They are paying you monthly, so that includes everything.

If, however, you are being paid hourly, you may or may not be paid for extraordinary travel time. Large companies may sometimes pay you for travel at half your normal rate—depending on the circumstances, while smaller companies may pay you nothing for travel. This is something you may want to negotiate if you think it could get out of hand.

If you are attending staff or other meetings—where you aren't really "working"—may you charge for that time? Again, it depends. If you are on an hourly basis, you may be able to charge half-time for regular (such as weekly) staff meetings. If the staff meeting is an unusual event, you may be able to charge at your regular rate. If you are attending a training seminar just to learn a new skill, for example, it is unlikely that you will be able to charge anything. However, if you are delivering a seminar, you would, of course, charge at your full billing rate. After all, you are working to your full capacity.

To keep a good relationship, make sure you do not nickel-and-dime your client to death. Throw in extra time for free sometimes (and let them know that). Perhaps call in with an idea on days when you are not there—gratis. Give a little to an important client just to keep a good relationship going.

### What will your market bear?

After all of that, consider what is reasonable and customary in the market and for the company to which you are selling yourself. Would they pay someone like you $86 an hour? Or is that unlikely? If the market tends to pay only $50 an hour, that is what you are likely to get. If you get that amount, just be sure you understand that you are not making what you used to make— unless you manage to work 2000 hours a year (or 1600 hours, which allows for four weeks' vacation and 10 paid holidays).

## Project-Based Pricing

Before you can possibly know what you want to charge a customer, you must figure out how much it will cost you to deliver the project. Go through the following steps:

### Step 1.

List in detail the services you will provide, and who will provide them.

### Step 2.

Price out these services using the billing rate for each person. This means you must be able to estimate accurately how much time you and/or every other person will spend on the project. Then you will apply your billing rate (perhaps two times cost).

### Step 3.

Get it in writing.

### Step 4.

Control your costs.

Now let's examine each step in detail.

*You have no idea what a poor opinion I have of myself*
*—and how little I deserve it.*
W.S. Gilbert

## Step 1: List in detail the service you will provide.

List everything you will provide—both labor and out-of-pocket expenses. Be sure to include all planning and project-management time, as well as all clerical and other support time. It is not enough to include just the time you actually spend with your client. For out-of-pocket expenses, be sure to include items such as travel and printing costs.

Then estimate how much of each service will be provided. For example, how many hours do you think this project will take overall, for each component of it, and for each person working on it? How much travel will be involved (apart from routine travel to and from their office)?

## Step 2: Figure out the price of each of those services.

Note the actual person or the level of the person who will be delivering each piece. Then use the billing rate for each person to determine the price of each service.

After you have priced each piece of the project, add up all the prices. This will tell you the total amount of revenue you will need on this project. It will also give you a feel for what goes into your project.

## Step 3: Get it in writing.

Make sure the client understands what is included in the project and what is not. In Step 1, you detailed everything that would be included in the project. Make sure the client understands this. Put it in writing. As you get into the project, both you and the client will probably think of lots more you could do. Or the client will change the specifications. All of that is fine as long as the client understands what is included in the project fee, and what they must pay extra for (perhaps at your hourly billing rate) because it is outside the scope of what you originally agreed upon.

## Step 4: Control your costs.

You must keep track of the number of hours you and everyone working for you spends on the project—or you most likely will lose money, perhaps a lot of money.

Many consultants are so happy to get the projects that they overdeliver to the extent that they lose money. You must track the number of hours you spend on the project. In Step 1, you detailed all of the services you would deliver. Now you must see how you did against those projections of what you thought the project would include.

I have seen everyone from fine artists to senior executives bid on jobs expecting to spend a certain amount of time on them, and wind up spending twice or three times what they had originally projected. Then they are disappointed that they cannot make money.

### Starting out

When you are starting out, it may be that you have to "give away the store" to get experience.

You have to figure out what the market will bear, perhaps take what you can get, build up your credentials, and market yourself to other companies. You may even decide to do a small assignment for free—perhaps for a not-for-profit or for a friend—just so you can say you are doing that kind of work.

On the other hand, you may think you are in a weak negotiating position when in fact you are not. I have worked with many an executive whose initial thought was to undercharge dramatically for his or her services.

Follow the rules for basic salary negotiation. If there are lots of people who can do what you do, and if you have no way to separate yourself from your competition, then you are in a weaker negotiating position. On the other hand, if you are offering a service that is somewhat unique and you cannot be easily replaced, you are in a solid negotiating position.

*Life is to be lived. If you have to support yourself, you had bloody well better find some way that is going to be interesting. And you don't do that by sitting around wondering about yourself.*
Katherine Hepburn

# Salary Negotiation: Power and Positioning

*The amount of money you receive will always be in direct proportion to the demand for what you do, your ability to do it, and the difficulty of replacing you.*
Napoleon Hill
paraphrased by Dennis Kimbro,
*Think and Grow Rich: A Black Choice*

---

*Occasionally I would start thinking how such dull people could make money.*
*I should have known that money-making has more to do with emotional stability than with intellect.*
J.P.Marquand, *Women and Thomas Harrow*

---

*. . . now does he feel his title hang loose upon him, like a giant's robe upon a dwarfish thief.*
Shakespeare, *Macbeth, V, ii*

*Well, march we on, to give obedience where 'tis truly owed . . .*
Shakespeare, *Macbeth, V, ii*

---

*Son, I am sorry that I am not able to bankroll you to a very large start, but not having any potatoes to give you I am now going to stake you to some very valuable advice. One of these days in your travels a guy is going to come up to you and show you a nice, brand-new deck of cards on which the seal is not yet broken, and this guy is going to offer to bet you that he can make the jack of spades jump out of the deck and squirt cider in your ear. But son, do not bet this man. For as sure as you stand there you are going to wind up with an earful of cider.*
Advice from Sky Masterson's father
to his son on a bet that sounds
too good to be true,
from Damon Runyon's *Guys and Dolls*

L et's assume a company is about to make you an offer, and you want to prepare for the salary negotiation. What are your chances of getting the compensation you think you deserve? How can you tell whether you are in a strong negotiating position or a weak one?

Salary negotiation is about power. The more you are in demand, the better your chances of getting what you are worth. You need to know what you are worth in the market, but you also need to know how easily they could they be satisfied with someone else. If it's easy for them to replace you, you have little room to negotiate. On the other hand, if you have convinced the hiring team that you and only you are the right person for the job, you are in a better position to get the offer and also to be paid fairly.

The earlier in the process that you differentiate yourself from your competition, the better. Establishing your worth takes time, and rarely happens during one interview. However, it can happen over a series of meetings where they get to know you better and appreciate you more.

## Starting Out:
### Little Room for Negotiation

A recent graduate may resemble the ten other people applying for the same job. Each has very little room for salary negotiation. Usually the best a person can hope for is to land the job by proving that he or she is superior to the other applicants, the same way as experienced people do. Just landing the job may be a major accomplishment. When people are starting out, they usually have to pay their dues. They have little power.

After you gain some experience, you have more negotiating power—providing you can differentiate yourself from others.

### Don't Accept or Reject a Job
### Until It Is Offered to You

Sandy Bowers, Director of Career Services at Citibank, observed that job hunters often go into the interview thinking, "I want that job," or "I

*When God loves a creature he wants the creature to know the highest happiness and the deepest misery . . .*
*He wants him to know all that being alive can bring.*
*That is his best gift . . . There is no happiness save in understanding the whole.*
Thornton Wilder, *The Eighth Day*

don't want that job." But the job hasn't even been offered to them yet. It would be better if they had a more open mind, trying to assess the situation, and doing what they can to get an offer. As Sandy says, "*After* you have heard their best possible offer, *then* you decide to accept or reject it. Not before."

## Position Yourself with Your Résumé

As you have seen in a previous chapter, "Four-Step Salary Negotiation Strategy," you are positioning yourself for the salary discussion in the first interview. But you are doing it even before that—when you are preparing your résumé. Examine the summary statement in your résumé—especially the first three lines. Make sure that people get the right impression of your level and what you have to offer them. If your description could work for someone who is lower level than you are, rewrite it.

Take a look at all the résumé samples in the *Building a Great Résumé*. A lot of work went into the first three lines to make sure that people understand—within a few seconds—what each person has to offer and his or her level.

## Position Yourself with Your Appearance and Demeanor

Do you look and act the level you say you are? You've heard people say, "Jane just looks like an executive." Be more conscious of how people look and act at the level at which you think you should be.

## Position Yourself by Being in Demand

An important way to gain power is by having six to ten things in the works. Your increased self-esteem will cause you to come across differently, and you will be better positioned to play the game.

## The Game: Unspoken Salary Negotiation While You Position Yourself

Much of the "salary negotiation" process is unspoken. Beginning with the very first meeting,

you are thinking about the needs of the hiring team, and measuring yourself against your competition. You are assessing how well you are doing without overtly discussing salary. If you think that the job is too low level to warrant the salary you want, or that the hiring team likes your competition more than they like you, there is no sense in discussing salary. First redefine the job, if you can, to make it worth more. And then "kill off" your competitors.

## Position Yourself versus Your Competition

You kill off your competitors by doing follow-up that is better than the hiring team could ever possibly get from anyone else. To do this well, you need to know where you stand regarding your competition.

## After You Get the Offer, Is Your Competition Still Close Behind?

Even after you hear their best possible offer, you need to assess how far ahead of your competition you are.

There's a very big difference between "Let's offer it to John. If it doesn't work out, we can offer it to Jane" and "If John doesn't take it, we're dead. There's no one else who even comes close to what he has to offer." Certainly, you want to get the offer, but you also want to be a clear choice—far ahead of your other competitors. Be sure to ask:

- "Where are you in the hiring process?"
- "How many others are you considering?"
- "How do I compare with them?"

Remember, you need to uncover any objections they may have to hiring you. It is wise to ask, "Is there any reason why you might be reluctant about bringing me on board?"

When you get the offer, don't think you can necessarily start playing hardball. Is your competition waiting in the wings, or have you left your competition in the dust? As you become a more experienced job hunter, you will get better at finding out how you stand versus your competition.

*Storybook happiness involves every form of pleasant thumb-twiddling;
true happiness involves the full use of one's powers and talents.*
John W. Gardner, *Self-Renewal: The Individual and the Innovative Society*

## Aim to Be Paid Fairly

Sometimes job hunters focus on getting a higher and higher salary, and lose perspective on what they are worth. Your goal is to get what you are worth. If you convince them to pay you more than that, they will expect more, and you may not be able to live up to their expectations. That's why it is so important to know what you are worth in the market, and then do your best to get it.

## CASE STUDY: JUDY
### *In the Best Negotiations, You May Never Have to Say a Word*

Judy, a retail manager earning $50,000, uncovered three job possibilities. One company in particular, Apex—a large retail chain—interested her. Apex had two openings—one higher level and one lower level.

Her first goal was to get the hiring team at Apex to see her as appropriate for the higher-level position. She spent some time doing library research about the company, and she talked to people she already knew who were Apex customers. She learned a lot about what the company could be doing better.

The next time she had a meeting with the prospective employer, she mentioned her findings and proposed changes that Apex could make to remedy these problems. The hiring team was very interested in her advice, and also admired her initiative. They knew she would be just as proactive on the job. Her future employer began to imagine her in the higher-level job, and told her that. They also told her that she had a number of competitors for that higher-level job.

## Judy Positions Herself for the Higher-Level Salary

Judy did *more* work—to position herself against her competitors. She visited various store locations, and assessed what the store personnel seemed to be doing right or wrong. She asked more people what they thought of Apex, and came up with more ideas about what the company could do.

At her next meeting, she told them what she had done, and they were amazed. They wanted her for the higher-level job, and told her that. They also told her the salary range for that job, and it was very broad—anywhere from $50,000 to $75,000.

But remember, other companies were interested in Judy, and some spoke of offering her more money than Apex would pay her. She told the hiring manager that while she was talking to other companies, she wanted to work for Apex.

When they made her the offer, they did not want to risk losing her to *their* competitors—the other companies with whom Judy was talking. The hiring manager said, "We don't want to quibble, so we're going to offer you the very top salary to start, as well as a few other perks. We really want you here."

Judy never had to formally negotiate her salary. She positioned herself so well that their best offer came first.

Does this always work? No. But it is important for you to follow the same strategy that Judy did. You increase your chances of getting the best the company can offer when you:

- think about and outshine your competition;
- have other potential offers; and
- show the company what it would be like to have you in the job you want.

However, be sure you are qualified for that higher-level position, or your tenure in the job may be short lived.

## CASE STUDY: RICK
### *Bargaining for What He Wants*

This is an advanced technique that you may skip if you like. Sometimes a company may want you very much, but may be afraid to bring you in at the appropriate level. It may be too big a decision for them. You can help make that decision easier.

Rick, an architect, saw himself at the partnership level of a prestigious architectural firm. Although the company wanted to hire him, they were afraid to bring him in as a partner. Job hunters think they are the only ones who are scared. But often companies are scared too—afraid of doing the wrong thing.

Rick said to them: "I believe this is the right place for me, and I believe that partnership is the right level for me. I'm so convinced of that, I'm willing to make an investment in this if you are. Bring me in at the level just below partner. But starting with my first day on the job, give me assignments at the partner level. At the end of three months, I'd like a salary and level review, and you decide."

The company felt very comfortable with this approach. If Rick could not perform at the level of partner, he would still be a good hire at the next-lower level.

At the *two*-month mark, Rick became a partner.

## It's a Career-Management Issue

Job hunters say that they are often promised something in a new job, but it never materializes. And they are correct. Companies soon forget what they thought of you during the hiring process, and you are stereotyped by the new job. Everyone is soon back to business as usual.

The trick is to make sure they agree to do something *starting with your first day on the job* that reminds them of their promise to you. In Rick's case, for example, he asked for assignments at the partner level—starting with his very first day on the job. The following is another example.

## CASE STUDY: CHARLIE
### *Negotiating a Career Change*

Charlie is a great administrator. Department heads always succeed with him at their side. But he wanted to move into product management.

He interviewed for a product- management position, but the hiring manager realized what an asset Charlie would be as an administrative manager, and wanted him in that job instead.

Charlie said: "As your chief administrator, I would be able to help you greatly. But I want to move into product management. Perhaps we can negotiate something that will satisfy us both.

"Your department will take a while to straighten out. I'm afraid that if I come in and kill myself working as your administrator, you will soon forget what I had really wanted.

"So let's make a deal. I'll come in as your administrator providing that, day one, you put me on a product-management task force or do something that gets me involved in product management. In the beginning, I'll spend 90 percent of my time on administration, and 10 percent on product management. At the end of the first year, I want to be spending 90 percent of my time on product management and 10 percent of my time on administration. I'll even find and train my successor."

The boss liked that idea. To prove his commitment, he allowed Charlie to spend the first week on the job working as part of a product-management team. That way, he got to know everyone in that group. When Charlie started working in the administrative area, he continued to go to the product-management staff meetings. It was clear to everyone what Charlie was promised, and he was able to make the transition.

It is unreasonable to expect people to remember the career promises they make to you during the interview. Even getting those promises in writing is not much help. With the press of everyday business—and because you are good at what you do—there is never a good time to make the transition, and you find yourself negotiating all over again while you are doing work you do not want to do. Over time, your resentment will build, and your only conclusion will be that people don't keep their promises.

Instead, your conclusion should be that you gave away too much. You should have negotiated something that reminded them on a daily basis what they had promised you. When a company wants what you have to offer, you are in a very strong position to negotiate a career change.

The
Five
O'Clock
Club®

# Playing the End Game

*Of all the traps and pitfalls in life, self-disesteem
is the deadliest, and the hardest to overcome,
for it is a pit designed and dug by our own hands,
summed up in the phrase,
"It's no use—I can't do it."*
Maxwell Maltz,
"You Can Do the Impossible," *This Week*

---

*Success is a process,
a quality of mind and way of being,
an outgoing affirmation of life.*
Alex Noble, "In Touch with the Present,"
*Christian Science Monitor*, March 6, 1979

---

*You just got to be very levelheaded
and keep moving forward.*
Robert DeNiro, actor

---

*No passion so effectively robs the mind of
all its power of acting and reasoning as fear.*
Edmund Burke,
*On the Sublime and Beautiful*

---

*It'll be a game! Imagine you are looking
for employment and I'm the woman at the agency.
In front of me is an enormous desk, covered with
details of jobs—for none of which you are suitable.
That's what they always imply anyway. (Stern voice)
"Sit down, please, Miss—er, Schoen, isn't it?"*
Peter Schaeffer,
*Lettice & Lovage*

This is the fun part—the part you've worked so hard to get to. You have had successful interviews, done thorough follow-ups. Now the offers are about to come in. Let's suppose you have a number of job possibilities. The game is to have them all come to closure within the same general time frame. It is not as effective to get an offer, turn it down, and a few months later, get another offer. Instead, try to have them happen at the same time. Then you'll seem more valuable in the marketplace, increase your chances of getting fair offers, and you'll be able to select the one that positions you best for the long run.

To do that, first get a lot of Stage 1 and Stage 2 contacts going all at once. When a company is interested in you, don't wait to see what they offer you. Instead, rush out and get more things going.

## CASE STUDY: PAUL
### *No Longer Saw Himself As "Unemployed"*

That's what Paul learned to do. He was unemployed, and felt that his situation was a major handicap. He had created a self-fulfilling prophesy.

When Paul got his first offer, from Englander, Inc., it was not a good one. The job was too low-level for him, and the pay was inadequate. He felt that the company was taking advantage of him because he was unemployed—and he was right.

They wanted him to drop everything and help out in an emergency by going on a sales call in another city—before putting him on payroll. They were acting as if "He's unemployed and desperate." Actually, Paul was feeling the same way about himself.

Despite his feelings of desperation, Paul declined to go on the trip. It would have made him feel worse. He told the company he was tied up with other things and simply could not make it.

310

© 1996, Kate Wendleton and The Five O'Clock Club®

*A great deal of fat has been cut, and perhaps a little bone as well . . . . Downsizing was becoming a fad.*
*Because everyone is doing it, a manager who isn't wonders why he's not and*
*looks around at his staff to see who he can do without.*
Eric Rolfe Greenberg, American Management Association
*The New York Times*, August 23, 1987

## Paul Decides to Play the Game

Instead of deciding whether to accept or reject the offer, Paul decided to play the game. Hiding his hurt and anger, he said, "I truly believe that yours is the company I want to work for. The problem is that I'm talking to a number of other companies right now, and I think it may take me a few weeks to wrap things up. I feel I owe it to myself to see these other possibilities through. Would it be okay if I got back to you in two weeks?" They agreed.

Paul then spent all of his energy making new contacts, getting new things in the works—and getting other offers.

The two weeks came and went as he continued to stay in touch with Englander, Inc., letting them know that he was still interested in them. He said that he would probably wind up working there, but that a few additional companies had expressed interest in him, and it would take a few weeks longer. Was that okay with them?

Paul wound up with 18 job possibilities and 8 job offers! He had written extensive follow-ups to every person in all 18 companies. That's how he turned his interviews into offers.

Many of the offers were excellent, and some were jobs he would consider taking only reluctantly. The other offers greatly enhanced his value in the eyes of every company with whom he was speaking—including Englander, Inc.

Paul continued to report back to them on the way he was being received in the marketplace. They started to see other roles for him in their company. His "unemployed" status was no longer relevant to them because it was no longer relevant to Paul. As he spoke to more and more hiring teams, he started feeling better about himself. The companies also sensed the difference. The issue was no longer Paul's status, but the fact that so many companies valued what he had to offer.

In the end, Paul's main decision had to do with the direction he wanted his career to take: he needed to decide which job would position him best for the long run. It was not easy.

As he continued his talks with all 18 companies, a number of them increased the responsibilities of the jobs they were talking to him about. Paul was having a lot of fun, and his self-esteem was greatly improved.

## Increasing His Desirability

Paul ended up taking a position with Englander, Inc., after all—but not the position about which they were originally speaking to him. They offered him a job that was two levels higher than the original one, with greatly increased pay. What's more, they were proud to have him on board, and even issued a press release telling the world that he had joined their company.

By the way, you don't need eight offers to play the game. Three is a good number.

## Slowing Down a Company That Is Ahead of the Others

What can you do to slow down an offer while waiting for others to come through? If you are paying attention, you will most likely see an offer edging towards the finish line way ahead of the others. The time to slow it down is earlier on. When a company asks you back for another interview, and you feel it is getting too far ahead of the others, say, "I'm really eager to come back and meet with you again, but my schedule is pretty full next week. Could we schedule it for the week after that?" Use your judgment, of course. It may be that putting them off for a week would be inappropriate. If you feel you would just irritate them by postponing a meeting, then don't do it.

But what if Paul was not able to get so many other possibilities going? What if he had been made a terrible offer, and felt he was forced to accept or reject it with no assurance that others would come his way? This could well have been the case because, after all, offers are more likely to come your way when you have momentum—a lot of things going all at once. If Paul had really been in need of money, he might have decided to take that first offer and do well at it while he was there, but continue to search for a job that was more appropriate for his experience.

Some people may consider it unethical to take a job knowing that they will continue to search for another one. But if you were a career counselor, you would see many cases in which a company hired someone—perhaps even moving his or her family—and then fired that person after a very short while for reasons having nothing to do with the employee. "Oh, I'm sorry we moved you here to Chicago. The project you were assigned to has been canceled. We'll give you some severance, but you are out of a job."

Companies are no longer dependable. Job hunters must fend for themselves and protect themselves. They didn't start this. Company executives did when they decided to cut people rather than retrain them or find another place for them inside the same company. In self-defense, employees must learn how to play the game—the new game of having a job in the nineties.

You will give the company a full day's work for a full day's pay. What you are not giving them is your loyalty—until companies decide to be loyal back.

## CASE STUDY: CHARLIE AND BRAD
### The Numbers You Need

The company Charlie and Brad worked for decided they no longer wanted to be in the insurance business. They closed that business down.

Charlie and Brad had always wanted their own business and—with some severance pay in hand—they saw this as an opportunity to explore their dream. Perhaps they could sell their original business idea to a financial-services company— yet keep part of the equity. That way they could essentially have their own business but with the backing of a large organization.

The search Charlie and Brad conducted is exactly like a job search, and the numbers are the same. So see what you can learn from their experience.

## Initial Contacts from Networking

At the time I met Charlie and Brad, they had already spoken to twenty large companies. They had actually known for some time that the business they were in would close, so as soon as they learned this, they had gotten to work. Four of the companies were somewhat interested in their idea. Charlie and Brad wanted me to help them make those four companies more interested.

Although they did not want to hear it, I told Brad that the problem was not with the four companies. Their numbers were too small, and they needed to drum up more interest in their idea. That would make their reluctant suitors more interested in doing a deal with them. When a company sees that others are pursuing you, they feel more secure about considering you for themselves. That's the way the game is played.

Here are the numbers that Charlie and Brad were working with:

| Companies Contacted | Companies Interested | Offers To Date |
|---|---|---|
| 20 | 4 | 0 |

After all Charlie and Brad had done, it would be difficult to get offers by working and reworkng their contacts with those same four companies. The number that first had to change is the number of companies contacted. Then the other numbers would also be likely to increase.

But human nature being what it is, Charlie and Brad did not feel like taking their eyes off the companies that were already interested. It took a number of weeks before they agreed to think about how to contact additional companies.

## Networking, by Definition, is Serendipitous; Direct Mail Can Fill in the Gaps

Charlie and Brad had networked into those twenty companies. They both agreed that there were hundreds of companies that could possibly be excited about their idea, but most of those companies did not even know that there was an idea to be had.

*Formerly when great fortunes were only made in war, war was a business;*
*but now when great fortunes are only made by business, business is war.*
Christian N. Bovee, 1820 - 1904

Charlie and Brad had no certain way to network into any companies besides the ones with which they had already met. And even if they could network in, that method would take too much time to uncover even one additional interested company.

They were willing to do a direct-mail campaign to sixty more companies. After all, they already knew how to express their idea in an appealing way.

Charlie and Brad quickly did research to find the names and addresses of the sixty companies, as well as the appropriate people to contact. They sent out a well-written one-page letter to each of them. In the letter, they asked the companies to call them if they were interested. (If they had decided to follow up each letter with a phone call, that would have been a targeted mailing rather than a direct-mail campaign.)

Within one day, an important company called. Within the next two weeks, three more called—including two highly prestigious companies they were very excited about. They met with those companies. Now they had a good reason to recontact the companies with which they had originally met. Within a short time, they received three offers. The numbers in their campaign were now as follows:

| Companies Contacted | Companies Interested | Offers To Date |
|---|---|---|
| 80 | 8 | 3 |

This was a lot of work, but it increased their chances of having something happen. Of the three offers they finally recieved, they accepted one that offered them the best of both worlds. They got 51 percent equity, a base pay higher than what either of them had been making in their previous jobs, plus full benefits.

---

**The next time you want a company to make you an offer, instead of focusing on that, contact additional companies and try to get them interested in you. It actually shortens your search.**

---

You can get a job at any point in the process. You may not have to go to the lengths that Charlie and Brad and Paul went to. Luck can always be a factor. It is something you should allow for, but it is certainly not something you want to count on—and even if you're lucky once, it probably won't happen again in your next search.

The approach these job hunters used is the most dependable way to get a number of genuinely good offers in the shortest period of time.

---

*In fact, I tried to conduct my whole career the way the big studios used to handle their actors. I did as many films a year as I could, to get the experience. If you sit around waiting for "the big one," when that opportunity finally comes along, you won't be ready for it. You won't have all that small time experience that adds up to big time ability. Success, it may surprise some to hear comes from doing, not negotiating, not counting lines, not weighing credits. Do it, do it, don't wait for it. Some very good actors sit out their entire lives while waiting for the right part. Make every part the one you've been waiting for. Learn the confidence you can only gain under fire. The confidence lends relaxation. Relaxation opens all your resources for the demands of your role. And when the big role does come along you'll need all 100 percent of what you've got to give. Don't be caught 25 percent short; don't be caught one percent short. Be completely available to whatever challenge comes your way, by being totally in charge of your craft, your material, yourself.*

Michael Caine, *Acting in Film*

The Five O'Clock Club®

# PART FIVE

# KEEPING IT GOING

### AFTER YOU'VE GOTTEN
### THE JOB YOU WANT

The Five O'Clock Club

# Starting Out on the Right Foot in Your New Job

*It is not the critic who counts;*
*not the man who points out how the strong man*
*stumbled or where the doer of deeds*
*could have done better.*
*The credit belongs to the man who is actually in the*
*arena, whose face is marred by dust and sweat and*
*blood; who strives valiently; who errs and comes*
*short again and again; who knows the*
*great enthusiasms, the great devotions;*
*who spends himself in a worthy cause;*
*who, at best, knows in the end*
*the triumph of achievement,*
*and who, at worst, if he fails,*
*at least fails while daring greatly,*
*so that his place shall never be with those timid souls*
*who knew neither victory nor defeat.*
Theodore Roosevelt

---

*Destiny is not a matter of chance,*
*it is a matter of choice;*
*it is not a thing to be waited for,*
*it is a thing to be achieved.*
William Jennings Bryan

---

*. . . be patient toward all that is unsolved in your*
*heart and try to love the questions themselves like*
*locked rooms and like books that are*
*written in a foreign tongue.*
Rainer Maria Rilke

Starting out can be tricky: you are "on board" but "the jury is still out" on you. It is a time of trial. You are often being watched to see if you will work out. Here are some things you need to do to start out on the right foot and keep moving in the right direction:

**Before You Start**
• Say thank you. Contact all the people who helped you get the new position. Often people don't make this effort because they feel they'll be in the new job for a long time. But today, when the average American changes jobs every four years, the odds say you're going to change jobs again soon. You need to keep up those contacts.

Then think about ways to keep in touch with these contacts—if you read something that someone on your list would appreciate, clip it and send it.

**Right Away**
• Don't fix things or do anything "big" for the first three months. That is one of the biggest mistakes people make. Take time to learn the system, the people, and the culture.

You cannot possibly understand, in those first months, the implications of certain decisions you may make. You may be criticizing a project that was done by someone really important. Or you could be changing something that will affect someone on the staff in ways of which you aren't aware.

• Make yourself productive immediately. This does not contradict the point I just made. Do things that are safe. For example, install a new system where there has been none. This is "safe" because you aren't getting rid of some other system. What isn't safe? Firing half your staff the first week!

• Introduce yourself to everybody. Be visible—walk around and meet people as soon as possible, including those who work for you. Meet everybody. Too many managers meet only the "important" people while ignoring those who will actually do the day-to-day work.

• Don't make friends too fast. Someone who befriends you right away could also be on the way

*Know how to ask. There is nothing more difficult for some people.*
*Nor for others, easier.*
Baltasar Gracian, *The Art of Worldly Wisdom*

out. That doesn't mean you shouldn't be friendly, however. Go to lunch with several people rather than becoming known as someone who associates only with so-and-so. Get to know everybody, and then decide with whom to get closer.

• Take over compensation of your subordinates immediately. Look at review and raise dates, and make sure no one is overlooked. You can't afford to wait three months to get settled while one of your people is stewing about an overdue salary review.

• Get your budget—quickly. If it isn't good, build a better one. If you spend some time at the beginning trying to understand the budget, the things you hear over the next few weeks will mean more to you.

---

## Try not to do anything too daring for the first 3 months.
## Take time to learn the system.

---

### In the First Three Months
• Learn the corporate culture. People new to jobs lose those jobs often because of personality conflicts rather than a lack of competence.

Keep your head low until you learn how the company operates. Some companies have certain writing styles. Some expect you to speak a certain way. In certain companies, it's the way they hold parties. Do people work with their doors open or their doors shut?

All those things are part of the culture, and they are unwritten. To learn them, you have to pay attention.

I had a client, for example, who lost his job because his management style rubbed everyone the wrong way. He is a "touchy feely" manager who, when he wants his employees to do things, schmoozes with them, saying things such as, "You know, I was kind of thinking about this and . . ." But the corporate culture was such that the employ-

ees liked and expected to be asked straight out. His style made them feel patronized and manipulated. And his own staff did him in.

Pay your dues before doing things at a variance with the corporate culture. After you build up some credits, you have more leeway. Let your personality emerge when you understand the company and after you have made some contribution.

• Learn the organizational structure—the real structure, not the one that is drawn on the charts. Ask your secretary to tell you who relates how with whom, who knows what, who thought of this project, who is important. You could be surprised.

• As far as subordinates are concerned, find out other people's opinions and then form your own. Consider that you may have a different perception because you have different values.

• Find out what is important in your job. For example, when I counsel people for a corporation, counseling is not the only important thing in my job. The people who come to me are sent by personnel, and I must manage my relationship with the personnel people. It doesn't matter how good a counselor I am if I don't maintain a good relationship with personnel.

• Pay attention to your peers. Your peers can prove as valuable to you as your boss and subordinates. Do not try to impress them with your brilliance. That would be the kiss of death because you'd cause envy and have a very large reputation to live up to. Instead, encourage them to talk to you. They know more than you do. They also know your boss. Look to them to teach you and, in some cases, protect you.

I know one executive who found out that her last three predecessors had been fired. She knew from talking to people that her boss was the type whose ego was bruised when someone had ideas. He had a talent for getting rid of these people.

---

**Pay attention to your peers.**
**Look to them to teach you**
**and, in some cases, protect you.**

---

To protect herself, she built relationships with her peers, the heads of offices around the country. After a year and a half, her boss's brother took her to breakfast and told her that, unlike her predecessors, she could not be fired: it would have been such an unpopular decision that it would have backfired on her boss.

• Don't set up competition. Everyone brings something to the party and should be respected for his or her talent, no matter what their level. Find ways to show your respect by asking for their input on projects that require their expertise.

• Set precedents you want to keep. If you start out working twelve-hour days, people come to expect it of you—even if no one else is doing it. When you stop, people wonder what's wrong.

• Set modest goals for your own personal achievement and high goals for your department. Make your people look good and you will too.

## Three Months and Beyond ...

• Continue to develop contacts outside the company. If you need information for your job, sometimes the worst people to ask are your boss and people around you. A network is also a tremendous resource to fall back on when your boss is busy—and you will seem resourceful, smart and connected.

---

**You'll be busy in your new job, and may not keep up your outside contacts. In today's economy, that's a big mistake.**

---

• Keep a hero file for yourself, a hanging file where you place written descriptions of all your successes. If you have to job-hunt in a hurry, you'll be able to recall what you've done.

You will also use it if you stay. If you want anything, whether it be a raise or a promotion, or the responsibility for a particular project, you can use the file to build a case for yourself.

• Keep managing your career. Don't think, "I'll just take this job and do what they tell me," because you might get off on some tangent. Remember where you were heading and make sure your career keeps going that way.

Be proactive in moving towards your goal. Take on lots of assignments. If a project comes up that fits into your long-term plan, do it. If one doesn't fit into your plan, you can do it or you can say, "Oh, I'd love to do that, but I'm really busy." Make those kinds of choices all the time.

---

*To act with confidence, one must be willing to look ahead and consider uncertainties: "What challenges could the world present me? How might others respond to my actions?" Rather than asking such questions, too many people react to uncertainty with denial.*
Peter Schwartz, *The Art of the Long View*

Someday soon you'll be able
to write one of these too.

Sandra Wybel
400 First Avenue
Dayton, Ohio 22090

May 8, 19xx

Mr. Trevor Hicks
3450 Garden Place
Des Moines, Iowa 44466

Dear Trevor:

The happy news is that I have accepted a position at Ohio State
Trust as Controller for their Ohio branches. I'll be responsible for
financial reporting and analysis, loans administration, budgeting
and planning. I think it's a great match and will make good use of
both my management skills and banking experience and the
environment is congenial and professional.

I really appreciated your interest in my job search. I very much
enjoyed speaking with people like you about your career and I
appreciated your advice and encouragement. The fact that you so
willingly gave of your time meant a great deal to me, and certainly
was beneficial.

If I can reciprocate in some way, please feel free to be in touch with
me. I will also probably be in contact with you in the months
ahead. My new office is at 75 Rockfast Corner, Dayton 22091.
You can reach me at 200-555-1212.

Sincerely,

Sandra Wybel

*. . . the country demands bold, persistent experimentation. It is common sense to take a method and try it. If it fails, admit it frankly and try another. But above all, try something.*
Franklin Delano Roosevelt
Speech, Atlanta, 1932

There is no one way to job hunt; one neat solution to job hunting cannot answer it all. There are many ways.

The results of what you do in a job hunt are neither good nor bad; they are simply results to be observed and thought about. They are indicators of the correctness of the direction you are pursuing; they are not indictments. They are not personal; they are the world's feedback to what we are doing. These results can keep us on track, and if we look at them objectively, then they should not throw us offtrack.

Information is not good or bad, it is simply information. Things are changing so fast that we each need all the relevant information we can get. We may tend to block out information we find threatening—but that is precisely the information we need to get. Knowing the truth of what is happening around us may help us decide how to take care of ourselves. The information is not out to harm us—it is simply there.

*To view your life as blessed does not require you to deny your pain. It simply demands a more complicated vision, one in which a condition or event is not either good or bad but is, rather, both good and bad, not sequentially but simultaneously.*
Nancy Mairs (who has multiple sclerosis)
*Carnal Acts*

*To be what we are, and to become what we are capable of becoming is the only end of life.*
Robert Louis Stevenson

There is a place for you, and you must look for it. Do not be stopped when others seem as though they are moving ahead. You, too, have a lot to offer if you would only think about yourself and not

them. You are on your own track. Put your energy into discovering what is special about you, and then hold on to it.

You will be knocked down enough during your job hunting. Don't knock yourself; push back. Push past the people who offer you discouragement. Find those nurturing souls who recognize your worth and encourage you.

*. . . there are days when the result is so bad that no fewer than five revisions are required. In contrast, when I'm greatly inspired, only four revisions are needed.*
John Kenneth Galbraith

Don't tell me the facts about yourself; tell me who you really are. When you are writing to someone, ask yourself, What am I really trying to say to this person? What would I say if this person were right here? You are writing to a real person, and when your personality comes through and you say what you mean to say, then your note is unique.

Read your work out loud. It will give you a sense of the timing, the flow. You will find out if it is readable. You will notice where it stumbles. Have someone else read it, too. Most people need an editor.

Take a few risks, but do it with some restraint. Don't be self-indulgent, but do let your personality seep through. You are not simply a "banker with twenty years major banking experience." You are "mature, with worldwide contacts, and a sense of stability."

Pare down your writing. Get rid of the lines that have no energy. Think about getting rid of your first paragraph completely. Perhaps you wrote it just to warm up.

Write to make an impact, to influence the reader.

*It is impossible to enjoy idling thoroughly unless one has plenty of work to do.*
Jerome K. Jerome

Continue to job hunt, but be easy on yourself. I worked on this book whenever I could, but some days I didn't feel like thinking, so I researched quotes, or made a chart, or organized my material. All of these things later made my writing easier—so I was always making progress.

The same can be applied to your job hunt. Some days you may research an industry or a number of companies, or you may write a proposal or a follow-up note. But you have to spend most of your time interviewing—just as I had to spend most of my time writing.

Job hunting takes practice, just as writing takes practice. I am not a professional writer, and you are not a professional job hunter. Neither of us, you or I, is perfect. But we are each trying to understand the process. This understanding will make us each less anxious, and more patient, about what we are doing.

Develop tricks to nudge yourself along. Find someone to report your progress to. If you cannot join a job hunt group, then meet with a friend. Talking gives you perspective and gives you the energy to keep on going.

Set goals for yourself. For example, aim at all times to be in contact, either in person or in writing, with six people who are in a position to hire you or recommend that you be hired. Keep in touch with these six people. Strive to add more people to your list, because others will drop off. Plan to continue to network even after you find a job. Make networking a part of your life.

Keep pushing even when you get afraid—especially when you get afraid. On the other hand, if you have been pushing nonstop for a while, take a break completely, relax, and then push again.

Get together with a friend and talk about your dreams. In talking about them, they seem possible. And in hearing yourself say them out loud, you can test how you really feel about them. Then you can discover the central dream—the one that will drive you.

*Where I was born and how I have lived is unimportant. It is what I have done with where I have been that should be of interest.*
Georgia O'Keefe

You will find endless resources inside yourself. Get inside yourself and find out what the dream is, and then do it. Stir yourself up. Go for it.

The fact is, if you don't try, no one will care anyway. The only reason to do it is for yourself—so you can take your rightful place in the universe. The only reason to do it is because we each have our place, and it seems a shame to be born and then to die without doing our part.

*We are all controlled by the world in which we live . . . The question is this: are we to be controlled by accidents, by tyrants, or by ourselves?*
B. F. Skinner

The world is big. There are many options; some job hunters try to investigate them all. Instead begin with yourself. Understand that part. Then look at some options and test them against what you are. You can hold on to that as a sure thing. You can depend on what you are for stability.

*I am larger, better than I thought, I did not know I held so much goodness.*
Walt Whitman

A former client called me today. When I first met him, he had been out of work for a year. Now he was calling to say that he had been made vice president of his company. He has found his niche and has never been happier. Everyone notices it. And he keeps on networking—keeps on enjoying the process.

The world keeps changing. It won't stop. We must change, too. We are the dreamers of dreams.

*We are the music-makers, And we are the dreamers of dreams . . . Yet we are the movers and shakers of the world for ever, it seems.*
Arthur O'Shaughnessy
"Music and Moonlight"

The Five O'Clock Club®

# PART SIX

# JOIN THE
# FIVE O'CLOCK CLUB

## *"FOR BUSY, CAREER-MINDED PEOPLE"*

## The Five O'Clock Club:

- **Job-Search Strategy Groups**
- **Private Coaching**
- **Membership Information**

The Five O'Clock Club was founded by Kate Wendleton in 1978 to provide thoughtful career-development help for busy people of all levels. The programs and materials have helped thousands take control of their careers and find good jobs fast.

*The original Five O'Clock Club was formed in Philadelphia in 1886. It was made up of the leaders of the day, who shared their experiences "in a spirit of fellowship and good humor."*

**For a listing of local Affiliates, or more information on becoming a member, please fill out the Membership Application Form in this book, or call: 1-800-538-6645, ext. 600**

Note: The following pages are taken from brochures and handouts of The Five O'Clock Club.

## The Five O'Clock Club Search Process

The Five O'Clock Club process, as outlined in Kate Wendleton's three books, is a targeted, strategic approach to career development and job search. Five O'Clock Club members become proficient at skills which prove invaluable during their *entire working lives*.

We train our members to *manage their careers*, and always look ahead to their *next* job search. Research shows that an average worker spends only four years in a job—and will have 12 jobs, in as many as 5 career fields—during his or her working life.

Five O'Clock Club members find *better jobs, faster*. The average job search for a managerial position is now estimated at 8.1 months. The average Five O'Clock Club member who regularly attends weekly sessions finds a job by his or her tenth session. Even the discouraged, long-term job searcher can find immediate help.

The keystone to The Five O'Clock Club process is in teaching our members an understanding of the entire hiring process. A first interview is only a time for exchanging critical information. The real work starts after the interview. We teach our members *how to turn job interviews into offers*, and to negotiate the best possible employment package.

The Five O'Clock Club is *action-oriented*. **We'll help you decide what you should do this very next week to move your search along**. By their third session, our members have set definite job targets by industry or company size, position, and geographic location, and are out in the field, gathering information and making the contacts which will lead to interviews with hiring managers.

*Our approach evolves* with the changing job market. We're able to synthesize information from hundreds of Five O'Clock Club members, and come up with new approaches for our members. For example, we now discuss temporary placement for executives, how to handle voice mail, and how to network when doors are slamming shut all over town.

> *Let us consider how we may spur one another on toward love and good deeds.*
> *Let us not give up meeting together, as some are in the habit of doing, but let us encourage one another.*
> Hebrews 10:24-25

## The Job-Search Strategy Group

The Five O'Clock Club meeting is a carefully planned *job-search strategy session*. We provide members with the tools and tricks necessary to get a good job fast—even in a tight market. Networking and emotional support are also included in the meeting.

The first part of the meeting is devoted to a forty-minute *main group presentation* on a particular aspect of job search; another part, to *small group strategy sessions* led by trained career consultants.

The *main group presentations* are given on a rotating schedule, so a job searcher can join The Five O'Clock Club at any time. Members are encouraged to attend ten sessions in a row, after which they are free to stay with the main group or switch to the *advanced discussion group*, if one is offered.

Your *small group strategy session* is your chance to get feedback and advice on your own search, listen to and learn from others, and build your business network. All groups are led by trained career consultants, who bring years of experience to your search. The small group is generally no more than eight to ten people, so everyone gets the chance to speak up.

The first fifteen minutes of every meeting are given over to *informal networking*; the fifteen minutes between the main lecture and the small group strategy sessions are set aside for members to report on new jobs. The meetings are information-packed and action-oriented, move rapidly, and give you the tools and incentive to keep your search going.

## Private Coaching

Your local Affiliate can give you a list of career consultants available between group meetings for *private coaching*. Individual sessions help you answer specific questions, solve current job problems, prepare your résumé, or take an in-depth look at your career path. Please pay the consultant directly, as *private coaching is **not** included in The Five O'Clock Club seminar or membership fee.*

## From the Club history, written in the 1890's

*At The Five O'Clock Club, [people] of all shades of political belief—as might be said of all trades and creeds—have met together. . . The variety continues almost to a monotony. . . [The Club's] good fellowship and geniality—not to say hospitality—has reached them all.*

*It has been remarked of clubs that they serve to level rank. If that were possible in this country, it would probably be true, if leveling rank means the appreciation of people of equal abilities as equals; but in The Five O'Clock Club it has been a most gratifying and noteworthy fact that no lines have ever been drawn save those which are essential to the honor and good name of any association. Strangers are invited by the club or by any members, [as gentlepeople], irrespective of aristocracy, plutocracy or occupation, and are so treated always. Nor does the thought of a [person's] social position ever enter into the meetings. People of wealth and people of moderate means sit side by side, finding in each other much to praise and admire and little to justify snarlishness or adverse criticism. People meet as people—not as the representatives of a set—and having so met, dwell not in worlds of envy or distrust, but in union and collegiality, forming kindly thoughts of each other in their heart of hearts.*

*In its methods, The Five O'Clock Club is plain, easy-going and unconventional. It has its "isms" and some peculiarities of procedure, but simplicity characterizes them all. The sense of propriety, rather than rules of order, governs its meetings, and that informality which carries with it sincerity of motive and spontaneity of effort, prevails within it. Its very name indicates informality, and, indeed, one of the reasons said to have induced its adoption was the fact that members or guests need not don their dress suits to attend the meetings, if they so desired. This informality, however, must be distinguished from the informality of Bohemianism. For The Five O'Clock Club, informality, above convenience, means sobriety, refinement of thought and speech, good breeding and good order. To this sort of informality much of its success is due.*

---

# Questions You May Have About the Weekly Job-Search Strategy Group

## The Weekly Job-Search Strategy Group

is a Professional Career-Counseling Program presented by Affiliates of The Five O'Clock Club "For busy, career-minded people"

Job hunters are not always the best judges of what they need during a search. For example, most are interested in lectures on answering ads or working with search firms. We will cover those topics, but, strategically, they are relatively unimportant in an effective job search.

At The Five O'Clock Club, you get the information you really need in your search—such as how to target more effectively, how to get more interviews, and how to turn job interviews into offers.

What's more, you will work in a small group with some of the best counselors around. In these strategy sessions, your group will help you decide what to do, this week and every week, to move your search along. And you will learn by coaching and being coached by others in your group.

Here are a few other points:

• For best results, attend on a regular basis. Your group gets to know you and will coach you to eliminate whatever you may be doing wrong—or refine what you are doing right.

• Those who think they need to come to a session only to ask a quick question are usually wrong. Often the problem started weeks before the job hunter realized it. Or the problem may be more complex than the job hunter realizes and require a few sessions to straighten out.

• You must be a member to attend the strategy group sessions. Some Affiliates will allow you to have a sample session, after which you must become a member before continuing in the group.

• Most Affiliates charge for multiple sessions at a time to make administration easier. If you miss a session, you may make it up at any time. You may even transfer unused time to a friend.

• Although many people find jobs quickly (even people who have been unemployed a long time), others have more difficult searches. Plan to be in it for the long haul and you'll do better.

• Carefully read all of the material in the Beginner's Kit that you got with your membership in The Five O'Clock Club. It will help you decide whether or not to attend.

The first week, pay attention to the strategies used by the others in your group. Soak up all the information you can.

• Read the books before you come in the second week. They will help you move your search along.

### To register

1. Call 1-800-538-6645 ext. 600 for the current list of Affiliates.

2. After you become a member and get your Beginner's Kit, call your local Affiliate to reserve a space for the first time you attend. If there is a waiting list, preference is given to current members of The Five O'Clock Club.

3. Read the books ahead of time, or purchase them at your first meeting.

To assign you to a counselor, your Affiliate liaison needs to know:

• your current (or last) field or industry,

• the kind of job you would like next (if you know),

• your desired salary range in general terms.

If you would rather see a private counselor before starting, call for suggested names.

### What Happens at the Meetings?

Each week, job searchers from various industries and professions attend. Some Affiliates specialize in professionals, managers and executives; others in recent college graduates, specific minority groups, or those over fifty years of age.. Usually, half are employed; half unemployed.

The two-hour weekly program is in two parts. First, there is a lecture on a job-hunting topic appropriate to those in the audience. In the second hour, job hunters meet in small groups headed by senior full-time, professional counselors.

*We find ourselves not independently of other people and institutions but through them.*
*We never get to the bottom of our selves on our own. We discover who we are face to face*
*and side by side with others in work, love, and learning.*
Robert N. Bellah, et al, *Habits of the Heart*

The first week, you get the text books, hear the lecture, are assigned to your small group, and listen to the others in your group. You learn a lot by listening to how your peers are strategizing their searches.

By the second week, you will have read the materials. Now we can start to work on your search strategy and help you decide what to do next to move your search along. For example, we'll help you figure out how to get more interviews in your target area, or how to turn an interview into a job offer.

In the third week, you will see major progress in the other members of your group, and you may notice major progress in your own search as well.

By the third or fourth week, most members are conducting a full and effective search. Over the remaining weeks, you will tend to keep up a full search rather than go after only one possibility. You will regularly aim to have six to ten things "in the works" at all times. These will generally be in specific target areas that you have identified, will keep your search on target, and increase your chances of getting multiple job offers to choose from.

Those who stick with the process find that it works.

Some people prefer to just observe for a few weeks before they start their job search, and that's okay, too.

## How Much Does it Cost?

The fees vary by location. Although each Affiliate may charge what they want, an average fee is 5 sessions for $200: 10 for $350. For administrative reasons, most Affiliates charge for 5 sessions at a time. This avoids having a large number of people paying each week.

You must have the materials so you can look at them before the second session. That's why it is important for you to buy the books provided at the seminar. Otherwise, you will tend to waste the time of the others in the group by asking questions that are covered in the texts.

## Is The Club right for me?

The Five O'Clock Club process is for you if:
• You are looking for a job or consulting work.

• You have some idea of the kind of work you want.
• You fit the salary profile of the Affiliate.
• You want to participate in a group process on a regular basis.
• You realize that finding or changing jobs and careers is hard work . . . which you are absolutely willing and able to do.

If you have no idea about the kind of job you want next, you could see a counselor privately for one or two sessions, develop tentative job targets, and then join the group. On the other hand, some job hunters prefer to start the group program and see a counselor individually later if they still haven't come up with some-thing. The choice is yours. Your Affiliate liaison will be happy to provide you with the names of counselors you can see privately.

## How long will it take me to get a job?

Although our members tend to be from difficult fields or industries, the average person who attends regularly finds a new position within ten sessions. Some take less time, and others take more. One thing we know for sure: *those who get regular coaching during their searches get jobs faster and at higher rates of pay than those who search on their own or simply take a course.* This makes sense. If a person comes only when they think they have a problem, they are usually wrong. They probably had a problem a few weeks ago, but didn't realize it. Or the problem may be different from what they thought. Those who come regularly benefit from the observations others make about their searches. Problems are solved before they become severe, or are prevented altogether.

Those who attend regularly also learn a lot by paying attention and helping others in the group. This "vicarious" learning can cut weeks from your search. When you hear the problems of others who are ahead of you in the search, you can avoid those problems completely. People in your group will come to know you, and will point out sub-tleties you may not have noticed and interviewers will never tell you.

*The Five O'Clock Club is plain, easy-going and unconventional. . . .*
*Members or guests need not don their dress suits to attend the meetings.*
(From the Club History, written in the 1890's)

## Will I be with others from my same field/industry?

Probably, but it's not that important. If you were a salesperson, for example, would you want to be with seven other salespeople?

Probably not. The search techniques are the same for the level handled by your Affiliate. You will learn a lot and have a much more creative search if you are in a group with people who are in your general salary range but not exactly like you. Our clients are from virtually every field and industry. The process is what will help you.

We've been doing this since 1978, and understand your needs. That's why the mix we provide is the best you can get.

## How can you charge such a small session fee?

1. We have no advertising costs because 90% of those who attend have been referred by other members.

We need a certain number of people to cover expenses. When lots of people get jobs quickly and leave us, we could go into the red. But so long as members refer others, we will continue to provide this service at a fair price.

2. We focus strictly on job search strategy, and encourage our clients to attend free support groups if they need emotional support. We focus on getting jobs, which reduces the time clients spend with us and the amount they pay.

3. We attract the best counselors, and our clients make more progress per session than they would elsewhere, which also reduces their costs.

4. We have expert administrators and a sophisticated computer system that reduces our overhead and increases our ability to track your progress.

## May I change counselors at my local Affiliate?

Yes. Some care is taken in assigning you to your initial counselor. However, if you want to change once for any reason, you may do it. We don't encourage group hopping: it is better for you to stick with a group so that everyone gets to know you. On the other hand, we want you to feel comfortable. So if you tell your Affiliate liaison you prefer a different group, you will be transferred immediately.

## What if I have questions outside of the group?

Some people prefer to see their group counselor privately. Others prefer to meet with a different counselor to get another point-of-view. Whatever you decide, remember that the group fee does not cover counselor time outside of the group session. Therefore, if you want to be able to ask a counselor a "quick question" in between sessions, you would normally meet with the counselor first for a private session so he or she gets to know you better. "Easy, quick questions" are often more complicated than they appear on the surface. After your first private session, some counselors will allow you to establish an account by paying in advance for one hour of counseling time, which you can then use for quick questions (usually a 15-minute minimum is charged). Since each counselor has an individual way of operating, find out how the counselor arranges these things.

## What if I want to start my own business?

The process of becoming a consultant is essentially the same as job hunting, and lots of consultants attend regular Five O'Clock Club meetings. However, if you want to buy a franchise or an existing business or start a growth business, you should see a private counselor, or attend the entrepreneurial program that is offered by a few of our Affiliates.

## What if I'm still not sure what to do.

Some Affiliates allow you to take a sample session before you become a member, for a modest fee. Then you can experience for yourself how we operate.

Whatever you decide, just remember that it has been proven that those who receive regular help during their searches get a job faster and at higher rates of pay than those who search on their own or simply attend a course. If you get a job just one or two weeks faster because of this program, it will more than have paid for itself. And you may transfer unused sessions to anyone you choose. However, the person that you choose must attend the Affiliate from which you purchased your sessions.

# The Way We Are

*The Five O'Clock Club means sobriety, refinement of thought and speech,
good breeding and good order. To this, much of its success is due.
The Five O'Clock Club is easy-going and unconventional.
A sense of propriety, rather than rules of order, governs its meetings.*

J. Hampton Moore, *History of The Five O'Clock Club*
(written in the 1890's)

Just like the members of the original Five O'Clock Club, today's members want an ongoing relationship. George Vaillant, in his seminal work on successful people, found that "what makes or breaks our luck seems to be . . . our sustained relationships with other people." (George E. Vaillant, *Adaptation to Life*)

Five O'Clock Club members know that much of the program's benefit comes from simply showing up. Showing up will encourage you to do what you need to do when you are not here. And over the course of several weeks, certain things will become evident that are not evident now.

Five O'Clock Club members learn from each other: the group leader is not the only one with answers. The leader brings factual information to the meetings, and keeps the discussion in line. But the answers to some problems may lie within you, or with others in the group.

Five O'Clock Club members encourage each other. They listen, see similarities with their own situations, and learn from that. And they listen to see how they may help others. You may come across information or a contact that will help someone else in the group. Passing on that information is what we're all about.

If you are a new member here, listen to others to learn the process. And read the books so you will know the basics that others already know. When everyone understands the basics, this keeps the meetings on a high level, interesting, and helpful to everyone.

Five O'Clock Club members are in this together, but they know that ultimately they are each responsible for solving their own problems with God's help. Take the time to learn the process, and you will become better at analyzing your own situation, as well as the situations of others. You will be learning a method that will serve you the rest of your life, and in areas of your life apart from your career.

Five O'Clock Club members are kind to each other. They control their frustrations—because venting helps no one. Because many may be stressed, be kind and go the extra length to keep this place calm and happy. It is your respite from the world outside and a place for you to find comfort and FUN. Relax and enjoy yourself, learn what you can, and help where you can. And have a ball doing it.

*There arises from the hearts of busy [people] a love of variety,
a yearning for relaxation of thought as well as of body,
and a craving for a generous and spontaneous fraternity.*

J. Hampton Moore
*History of The Five O'Clock Club*

*The original Five O'Clock Club was formed in Philadelphia in 1886. It was made up of the leaders
of the day, who shared their experiences "in a spirit of fellowship and good humor."*

The Five
O'Clock
Club®

# Lexicon Used at
# The Five O'Clock Club

Use The Five O'Clock Club lexicon as a shorthand to express where you are in your job search. It will focus you and those in your group.

## I. Overview and Assessment

**How many hours a week are you spending on your search?** Spend 35 hours on a full-time search; 15 hours on a part-time search.

**What are your job targets?**
Tell the group. A target includes industry or company size, position, and geographic area.
The group can help assess how good your targets are. Take a look at "Measuring Your Targets."

**How does your résumé position you?**
The summary and body should make you look appropriate to your target.

**What are your back-up targets?**
Decide at the beginning of the search before the first campaign. Then you won't get stuck.

**Have you done the Assessment?** If your targets are wrong, everything is wrong. (Do the Assessment in *Targeting the Job You Want.*) Or a counselor can help you privately to determine possible job targets.

## II. Getting Interviews

**How large is your target (e.g., thirty companies)? How many of them have you contacted?** Contact them all.

**How can you get (more) leads?**
You will not get a job through search firms, ads, networking or direct contact. Those are techniques for getting interviews—job leads. Use the right terminology, especially after a person gets a job. Do not say, "How did you get the job?" if you really want to know, "Where did you get the lead for that job?"

**Do you have six to ten things in the works?**
You may want the group to help you land one job. After they help you with your strategy, they should ask, "How many other things do you have in the works?" If "none," the group can brainstorm how you can get more things going: through search firms, ads, networking, or direct contact. Then you are more likely to turn the job you want into an offer because you will seem more valuable. What's

more, five will fall away through no fault of your own. Don't go after only one job.

**How's your Two-Minute Pitch?**
Practice a *tailored* Two-Minute Pitch. Tell the group the job title and industry of the hiring manager they should pretend they are for a role-playing exercise.
You will be surprised how good the group is at critiquing pitches. (Practice a few weeks in a row.) Use your pitch to separate you from your competition.

**You seem to be in Stage One (or Stage Two or Stage Three) of your search.** Know where you are. This is the key measure of your search.

**Are you seen as insider or outsider?**
See "How to Change Careers" for becoming an insider. If people are saying, "I wish I had an opening for someone like you," you are doing well in meetings. If the industry is strong, then it's only a matter of time before you get a job.

## III. Turning Interviews into Offers

**Do you want this job?**
If you do not want the job, perhaps you want an offer, if only for practice. If you are not willing to go for it, the group's suggestions will not work.

**Who are your likely competitors and how can you outshine and outlast them?** You will not get a job simply because "they liked me." The issues are deeper. Ask the interviewer: "Where are you in the hiring process? What kind of person would be your ideal candidate? How do I stack up?"

**What are your next steps?** What are *you* planning to do if the hiring manager doesn't call by a certain date, or what are you planning to do to assure that the hiring manager *does* call you?

**Can you prove you can do the job?** Don't just take the "Trust me" approach. Consider your competition.

**Which job positions you best for the long run? Which job is the best fit?** Don't decide only on the basis of salary. You will most likely have another job after this. See which job looks best on your résumé, and will make you stronger for the next time.
In addition, find a fit for your personality. If you don't "fit," it is unlikely you will do well there. The group can help you turn interviews into offers, and give you feedback on which job is best for you.

330                                    © 1996, Kate Wendleton and The Five O'Clock Club®

**The Five O'Clock Club®**

Dear Prospective Five O'Clock Clubber:

The Five O'Clock Club has helped thousands find jobs, change, or manage their careers!

At The Five O'Clock Club, we focus your search with real-world information that tells you exactly what you need to get more interviews . . . **and turn those interviews into offers.**

As a member, you also get—

❑ An attractive **membership card** and a **Beginner's Kit** containing information based on 12 years of research regarding who gets jobs and why, that will enable you to improve your job-search technqiues . . . immediately.

❑ A **subscription to** *The Five O'Clock News*, ten issues filled with information on career development and job-search techniques— information to help you thrive in your career.

❑ **Access to reasonably priced weekly seminars** featuring individualized attention to your specific needs in small groups supervised by our senior counselors.

❑ Access to **one-on-one counseling**.

❑ The opportunity to exchange ideas, experiences, and even role-play with other job searchers and career changers.

**All that access, all that information, for the nominal membership fee of only $35.**

**The sooner you become a member, the sooner you can begin working on having a career that truly meets your financial, emotional, creative and intellectual needs.**

Believe me, with self-examination and a lot of hard work with our counselors, you **can** find the job . . . you **can** have the career . . . you **can** live the life you always wanted!

The best of luck, whatever you may decide.

Sincerely,
Kate Wendleton, President

---

❑ Yes!  I want access to the most effective methods for developing and managing my career, as well as for finding jobs.

. . . . . . . . . . . . . . . . . . . . . . . . . . . . . . . . . . . . . . . . . . .

I enclose ❑ $35.00 for one year  ❑ $60.00 for two years. I will receive a Beginner's Kit, a membership card, a subscription to *The Five O'Clock News*, a listing of current Affiliates of The Five O'Clock Club, access to a network of career counselors and to reasonably priced seminars at Affiliates of The Five O'Clock Club in the U.S. and Canada.

Name _____

Address _____

City _____ State/Prov. _____ Zip/Postal _____

Work Phone _____

Home Phone _____

Today's Date: _____

Referred by: _____

*Job Search Secrets*

. . . . . . . . . . . . . . . . . . . . . . . . . . . . . . . . . . . . . . . . . . .

**Method of payment:**

❑ I enclose my check for $35.00 U.S., made out to The Five O'Clock Club, 300 E. 40th St., Suite 6L, NY, NY 10016.

❑ MasterCard or VISA:

  (This form can be faxed to 212-286-9571)

Account Number:_____

Exp. Date:_____Signature: _____

. . . . . . . . . . . . . . . . . . . . . . . . . . . . . . . . . . . . . . . . . . .

The following information is for statistical purposes. Thanks for your help.

Age: ❑ 20-29  ❑ 30-39  ❑ 40-49  ❑ 50+

Sex: ❑ Male  ❑ Female

Salary range:

❑ under $30,000  ❑ $30-$49,999  ❑ $50-$74,999

❑ $75-$99,999  ❑ $100-$125,000  ❑ over $125,000

Current or most recent position/title: _____

_____

. . . . . . . . . . . . . . . . . . . . . . . . . . . . . . . . . . . . . . . . . . .

The original Five O'Clock Club® was formed in Philadelphia in 1886. It was made up of the leaders of the day, who shared their experiences "in a spirit of fellowship and good humor."

---

# Index

---

## About the Author

Kate Wendleton is a nationally recognized authority on career development. She has been a career coach since 1978, when she founded The Five O'Clock Club® and developed its methodology to help job hunters and career changers of all levels in job-search-strategy groups. This methodology is now used by Affiliates of The Five O'Clock Club, which meet weekly in the United States and Canada.

Kate also founded Workforce America®, a not-for-profit Affiliate of The Five O'Clock Club, serving adults in Harlem who are not yet in the professional or managerial ranks. Workforce America helps each person move into better-paying, higher-level positions as each improves in educational level and work experience.

Kate founded, and directed for seven years, The Career Center at The New School for Social Research in New York. She also advises major corporations about employee career-development programs, and coaches senior executives. A former CFO of two small companies, she has twenty years of business-management experience in both manufacturing and service businesses.

Kate attended Chestnut Hill College in Philadelphia and received her MBA from Drexel University. She is a popular speaker with groups that include The Wharton Business School Club, the Yale Club, The Columbia Business School Club, and Workforce America in Harlem.

While living in Philadelphia, Kate did long-term volunteer work for The Philadelphia Museum of Art, The Walnut Street Theatre Art Gallery, United Way, and the YMCA. Kate currently lives in Manhattan.

Kate Wendleton is the author of *Through the Brick Wall: How to Job-Hunt in a Tight Market*, the *What Color Is Your Parachute?* of the nineties, and The Five O'Clock Club's three-part career-development and job-hunting series: *Targeting the Job You Want, Job-Search Secrets (that have helped thousands of members)*, and *Building a Great Résumé*.

*The original Five O'Clock Club was formed in Philadelphia in 1886.*
*It was made up of the leaders of the day, who shared their experiences*
*"in a spirit of fellowship and good humor."*

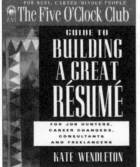